EIGHTEENTH-CENTURY MANNERS
OF READING

The market for print steadily expanded throughout the eighteenth-century Atlantic world thanks to printers' efforts to ensure that ordinary people knew how to read and use printed matter. Reading is and was a collection of practices, performed in diverse, but always very specific ways. These practices were spread down the social hierarchy through printed guides. Eve Tavor Bannet explores guides to six manners or methods of reading, each with its own social, economic, commercial, intellectual and pedagogical functions, and each promoting a variety of fragmentary and discontinuous reading practices. The increasingly widespread production of periodicals, pamphlets, prefaces, conduct books, conversation-pieces and fictions, together with schoolbooks designed for adults and children, disseminated all that people of all ages and ranks might need or wish to know about reading, and prepared them for new jobs and roles both in Britain and America.

EVE TAVOR BANNET is the George Lynn Cross Professor Emeritus of English at the University of Oklahoma. Her publications include: *The Domestic Revolution* (2000); *Empire of Letters: Letter Manuals and Transatlantic Correspondence 1688–1820* (Cambridge, 2005); *Transatlantic Stories and the History of Reading, 1720–1810* (Cambridge, 2011); and with Susan Manning (ed.), *Transatlantic Literary Studies, 1640–1830* (Cambridge, 2012). Professor Bannet also edited *British and American Letter Manuals 1680–1810* 4 vols. (2008), and *Emma Corbett* (2011) and is currently Editor of *Studies in Eighteenth-Century Culture.*

T0371254

EIGHTEENTH-CENTURY MANNERS OF READING

Print Culture and Popular Instruction in the Anglophone Atlantic World

EVE TAVOR BANNET

CAMBRIDGE
UNIVERSITY PRESS

CAMBRIDGE
UNIVERSITY PRESS

University Printing House, Cambridge CB2 8BS, United Kingdom

One Liberty Plaza, 20th Floor, New York, NY 10006, USA

477 Williamstown Road, Port Melbourne, VIC 3207, Australia

314-321, 3rd Floor, Plot 3, Splendor Forum, Jasola District Centre, New Delhi - 110025, India

79 Anson Road, #06-04/06, Singapore 079906

Cambridge University Press is part of the University of Cambridge.

It furthers the University's mission by disseminating knowledge in the pursuit of education, learning and research at the highest international levels of excellence.

www.cambridge.org
Information on this title: www.cambridge.org/9781108409490
DOI: 10.1017/9781108296915

First published 2017
First paperback edition 2019

A catalogue record for this publication is available from the British Library

ISBN 978-1-108-41910-9 Hardback
ISBN 978-1-108-40949-0 Paperback

Contents

Figures

Acknowledgments

I don't have the words to adequately acknowledge all the students and audience members who heard bits of this material in one form or another, and raised smart, thought-provoking, questions or objections. Jennie Batchelor, David Brewer, Rebecca Bullard, Rachel Carney, Patsy Fowler, Amanda Hiner, Kathryn King, the late Susan Manning, Alasdair Pettinger, Manuschag Powell, Peter Sabor, Betty Schellenburg, Theresa Strouth Gaul and Tim Youngs invited me to speak or write on topics which, productively and often unexpectedly, fed into this book. David Allan, Betty Schellenberg and Roxann Wheeler gave the manuscript that rare kind of careful and intelligent close reading for which one always hopes, and contributed immeasurably to the clarity, consistency and scope of the book. As always, I am indebted to Linda Bree for her support, encouragement and invariably sound advice. An earlier version of part of Chapter 5 appears in Rachel Carney and Rebecca Bullard (ed.) *The Age of Revelation: Reconsidering Secret History* (Cambridge, 2017).

This volume is dedicated to baby Daniel, who is irresistibly drawn to books and screens even before learning to read, and to his parents, Jonathan and Merav Bannet.

Introduction
The Schoolroom in the Marketplace

Not surprisingly, perhaps, in this age of conduct books and "how-to" books, the printing trade disseminated all that people of all ages and ranks might need or wish to know about reading books and periodicals. Eighteenth-century people could go to printed texts to learn for themselves how to decipher scripts and fonts and how to understand printers' English. Print taught readers how to absorb, remember and reflect upon their reading; how to recognize genres and interpret texts; how to decode the seditious ideas frequently secreted in popular writings; how to teach reading; and how to write themselves. Pamphlets, books and periodicals also taught readers the rudiments of reading aloud and conversing about books, and showed them what kinds of things they ought to know, how to learn subjects, how to figure as polite readers, and how to think for themselves. During the eighteenth century, printers, booksellers and the authors they patronized were energetically using print to transmit the skills, practices, apperceptions, motives, and tastes that could – and in the course of the century did –transform an unevenly and spottily educated populace into staunch readers, buyers and borrowers of newspapers, periodicals and books. What James Raven aptly calls "the complex penetration of print through eighteenth-century society" and William St. Clair, "The Reading Nation," was not achieved without ensuring that a broad range of new, non-traditional customers could learn from print how to use the printing trade's printed commodities.[1]

This is a study of printed guides to six eighteenth-century manners of reading, and an account of what they taught readers about reading. Some guides have not been noticed before, or have not been identified as such, because they took a variety of generic forms or because their contents are divided up under different modern disciplines. Some manners of reading have been overlooked for the same reasons, or because we have assumed that one kind of text tells us all that we can or need to know about how people read. Guides took many forms. Some manners of reading were transmitted primarily through schoolbooks;[2] some primarily through popular genres such as periodicals, pamphlets, miscellanies, conduct books, and fictions; many were transmitted through some combination of the two. Manners of reading were not all of a piece either. Some sharply conflicted with others – indeed, battle raged over how, as well as what, the generality of people ought to read. And while all manners of reading were conjoined to manners of writing and speaking, some favored aurality, speech and conversation more. But for most of the century, all the guides to be considered here were directed at adults outside school settings, not just at children, and either geared to, or re-presented in forms adapted to, the abilities of men and women at all ranks. This is particularly noteworthy in the case of genres that are now associated exclusively with children and middle-class schooling, such as English spellers and grammars (Chapter 1), guides to study (Chapter 3) and fables (Chapter 5). During the eighteenth century, these did double duty to the point where, by the century's end, educators were complaining that in their current forms, they were "fitter for Men than for Children."

Reading is and was a collection of practices, performed in diverse, but always very specific ways. The eighteenth century said as much by classifying reading among the "arts" – an art being a skill or craft based on special knowledge but consisting of material practices and acquired hands on. By "methodizing" reading as an art and embracing different forms of reading, eighteenth-century print culture speaks directly to those historically specific, interdisciplinary patterns and practices which Roger Chartier calls "manners of reading." I use his term because it usefully includes manners or methods of reading – the means, media, skills and mental processes that contemporaries employed to put books to specific uses – and manners or mores of reading – those proprieties, practices, rituals, and modes of judgment and expression which performed "the task of showing distinctions, of making manifest differences in the social hierarchy." The plural form, "manners," reminds us that multiple manners of reading might be in circulation at any given time, and that readers might have more than one at their disposal. Clearly, too, everyone did not acquire all manners of reading, attain the same proficiency in each, or inevitably apply them in the prescribed ways; and it was always possible to mix and match. But some familiarity with historical manners of reading in all these senses is, as Chartier points out, "indispensable to any approach that aims to reconstruct how texts could be apprehended, understood and handled by interpretative communities in the past."[3] Manners of reading can serve as a base-line of sorts, whether one's principal interests lie in history, literature, philosophy, education, grammar, rhetoric, hermeneutics, aesthetics, reader-reception, literary criticism, children's literature or women's writing, in the commonplace books of particular readers or the practices of book-related institutions, in the interactions of voice, script and print, in the history of books or the history of reading itself.

Chartier's call for study of manners of reading countered other prominent scholars who urged historians of reading to concentrate on empirical case studies. In what relates to eighteenth-century Britain, the latter has been most widely heeded. Here much of the ground-breaking recent work consists of case studies of the reading practices of individual readers as far as these can be determined from their marginalia, diaries, and commonplace books, and of studies of reader-behavior (borrowing habits, the conduct of coteries or reading clubs, the disposition of library furniture).[4] This has produced invaluable information, some of which will be incorporated below. But studies of reader behavior do not directly address what readers did, or thought they were doing, while they were reading. And scholars very properly preface their case studies with warnings that what can be discovered from an individual reader is incomplete, and possibly atypical. As John Brewer notes, "the reader's reader is a fragile, imaginative construction that grows out of an elaborate negotiation between prevailing prescriptions on how to read and the desires of the reader." Mark Towsey found, likewise, that while some rural readers of Scottish Enlightenment texts did read "compliantly," many farmers, artisans, professionals, gentlemen and merchants "trawled" books instead, to "create meanings that were informed by their professional interests, political loyalties, existing commitments, worries and deeply held beliefs."[5] What "prevailing prescriptions" eighteenth-century readers were negotiating and, indeed, whether "non-compliant" readings were demanded or encouraged by any contemporary prescriptions for reading, remains largely unexplored. To assume we know what the prevailing prescriptions were from the belletristic-formalist critics and aesthetic theorists admired by the New Critics and canonized by twentieth-century histories of criticism, is to mistake a faction of imperious but embattled – and by their own account, still largely ineffectual – "men of taste," for the whole.

Expanding our understanding of the prevailing prescriptions for reading does not replace, much less invalidate, empirical case studies; it contextualizes and supplements them. For instance, the many and varied recommendations in guides to study can help us understand the transition to "note-taking" that David Allan discovered in eighteenth-century commonplace books. They can help us see what John Money's provincial excise officer was doing, or thought he was doing, when he filled hundreds of pages with writing about his reading; why Chesterfield's early letters to his son consisted of his own summaries of Roman history; and why Ryder and his friends at Middle Temple met to exchange verbal accounts of different books each had read.[6] Studying manners of reading through printed guides sheds light on prevailing protocols and practices, and on the social, economic, political and pedagogical functions that contemporaries designed them to serve.

One of the unexpected things that emerges from this study is the extent to which the period was dominated by "discontinuous" reading practices that contradicted the now more familiar manner of reading proposed by "men of taste." "Discontinuous reading" is Peter Stallybrass' term for the kind of reading instituted and made possible by early Christianity's adoption of the codex (or "book"). Unlike the scroll preferred by the Romans, he explains, the codex was a "technology" that enabled readers to easily "navigate" compendia of miscellaneous fragments (as in the Book of Common Prayer); it therefore facilitated the reading of segments from different devotional books on the same religious occasions.[7] Inculcated and deployed at all levels of eighteenth-century culture, discontinuous reading practices were required both by the learned and unlearned, for secular as well as religious purposes. Printers and authors catered to discontinuous readers through the piecemeal and miscellaneous construction of most print publications, including books, in the conviction that like high society, the "generality of readers" who were growing the market for print, had limited attention spans, little time for sustained reading, and no patience, desire or ability to follow long convoluted arguments. Discontinuous reading was fueled and sustained in the popular marketplace by a widely disseminated curiosity- and variety-based aesthetic and by what Shaftesbury called the public's preference for "the miscellaneous manner of writing," which came to include the novel, the periodical, and the magazine.[8] Discontinuous reading was also frequently practiced spontaneously by readers – for instance, by those who read extracts from a favorite novel aloud to friends of an evening, by those who borrowed odd volumes of multi-volume novels from libraries, and by those who got through several books simultaneously, alone or *en famille*, by reading a portion of each intermittently or at set times each day.[9] Other discontinuous reading practices were shaped by the learned, from a revivification and adaptation of humanist techniques for fragmenting and recombining texts, and from new rational ways of "methodizing" information for ease of recollection and "enlargement of the mind." The "men of learning" and "men of taste" – who disparaged miscellaneous, discontinuous texts and the reading practices associated with them in an attempt to give the public a taste for "Unity, Uniformity and Probability "[10] and themselves an important public role – themselves produced fragmentary, miscellaneous texts in the form of spellers, grammars, books of elocution, anthologies of "beauties," dictionaries, encyclopedias, and collections of lectures. It is not irrelevant, either, that the first printed matter a reader encountered – the hornbook, the primer or speller, the grammar – were, like the Book of Common Prayer and the Catechism, composed of fragments. While familiarizing would-be readers with the distinctive characteristics of printed writing and the discontinuous character of texts, these instructional books provided them with strategies for negotiating a print world filled with miscellaneous discontinuous writing. Overall, this is perhaps the richest and most neglected dimension both of the history of reading and of what John Barry called eighteenth-century "literacy and literature," and will receive considerable attention below.[11]

The "New Critics" of the last century, who were in many respects their heirs, familiarized us with the principles of those eighteenth-century academic belletristic-formalist critics who were among the foremost "men of taste." But these principles were more contentious, and less widely accepted, then, than they later became. As we will see in Chapter 3, men of taste propagated, idealized and methodized neo-classical " 'laws' or 'rules' " for reading and writing perspicuously in clearly distinguished literary and oratorical genres with beginnings, middles and ends. Interpreting Aristotelian *mimesis* to mean imitation of the enduring traits of human nature, they privileged the universal over the particular or local, and excluded the marvelous or supernatural in favor of the probable and familiar. They judged that unity, continuity and connection among a work's parts was essential to its beauty as well as to its moral and emotional effect, and equated the beauty of formal unity with that of pure morality and universal truth. Equally annoying to contemporaries who favored discontinuous, hybrid forms, they insisted that the "trained taste" of classically educated men of learning like themselves, "who had experience and knowledge" of the literature of all times and places, constituted "the standard" of correct aesthetic judgment to which everyone must adhere.[12]

In the wake of deconstruction which dismantled pure and proper genres, and of hypertexts and randomized computer games, hybrid, fragmentary forms have become visible and interesting to us again. But in the absence of any history of discontinuous writing, much less of the diverse reading practices associated with it, scholars have been claiming it as new in almost every historical period: in the Renaissance; among the Romantics; in Postmodernism. Some have identified it exclusively with certain historical genres: the commonplace book, the anthology, sonnet sequences.[13] Others have studied its prevalence in the literature of Puritans or of the early Republic, without relinquishing the politically inspired hope that discontinuous elements were, or can be, unified into some virtual whole.[14]

Eighteenth-century writers, by contrast, thought more like Peter Stallybrass, who looks back to early Christianity, and Malcolm Heath, who shows that the basis of Greek poetics lay not in Aristotelian "unity" as neo-classicists and New Critics pretended, but in an idea of "completeness" and "appropriateness" that made diversity (*poikilia*) "an indispensable virtue," and digression the key to holding readers' interest through long narratives.[15] As we will see in Chapter 4, the eighteenth-century writers and scholars I call "miscellarian" (following Shaftesbury) or "miscellanists" (following Isaac Disraeli) traced discontinuous, miscellaneous writing back, through a long and learned tradition, to the ancient Greeks and Romans, or sometimes to the Bible, viewed as a compilation of diverse, generically miscellaneous and often unconnected texts. They characterized the demands of "men of taste" for pure genres and formally unified works as an artificial imposition on customary practices, and mocked the "philosophical," merely "conjectural" and usually academic, proponents of this manner of reading and writing, for marginalizing themselves.

Grounded in long-standing readerly and writerly practices, discontinuous reading was also naturalized by Lockean epistemology. Locke and his eighteenth-century followers imagined that we receive from the senses only disconnected impressions which the mind's eye initially perceives as a stream of independent and unrelated ideas. Time too is experienced as a linear succession of discrete instants. Experience (or what we might call information) thus first presents itself empirically to the mind as a succession of separate and discontinuous perceptions, like points on a line, characters in an alphabet, successive words on a printed page, or the cavalcade of unrelated units in a miscellany. Everything begins from discontinuity and disconnection. It is up to the understanding to connect and combine isolated singular impressions into more comprehensive and meaningful constructs. To understand anything at all, one has to attach separate perceptions, letters, words, or passages, by connecting them into (or through) higher-order ideas. Manners of reading might therefore be viewed as so many strategies for connecting and associating discontinuous letters, words or texts. Beginning from discontinuity did not preclude the construction of meaningful coherences; but it did make the reader's construction of meaning a partly personal, and always potentially eccentric and unpredictable, psychological act. This was a matter of some concern to conservatives who feared, and throughout the century bemoaned, the dangerously destabilizing effects of permitting literacy to spread to "the multitude" and to women.

Before turning to the method and structure of this book, it will be helpful to supply two key contexts for the chapters and the manners of reading they contain: what contemporaries said each was for; and who was engaged in disseminating which.

Uses of Reading

Conservatives could not halt the spread of literacy because reading was not just a recreation for those with leisure to enjoy it – a pleasant diversion for dull or solitary hours, a source of social entertainments for literary coteries – though it was this too. Printers, booksellers and their authors marketed reading in utilitarian terms. Some manners of reading (including those described in guides to taste) were partly or wholly conceived as training for various kinds of work. Others showed readers how to use their "idle" hours to "improve" themselves by acquiring knowledge that would enhance their working skills, or better fit them to discharge their public offices and perform their relative duties, and thus enable them to sustain their character, grace their station, or rise in the world. Printed texts tirelessly explained how reading to acquire "useful Learning" would make people at all ranks more "serviceable to themselves and others," and more "beneficial both to themselves and their country."[16] Useful reading – learning to read and reading to learn useful things– made useful citizens.

Promising to supply everything requisite in future editions of what would become a best-selling grammar, printer John Brightland pointed out in 1711 that such knowledge of grammar, rhetoric, poetry and logic as was required to read, write and speak English "Sensibly" and "without Absurdity" was "certainly commendable in Persons of all Stations, but in some indisputably necessary."[17] Literacy was indisputably necessary for what I will call "Writers by Trade" – people using reading and writing *by hand* to perform their jobs – because commerce and political institutions depended increasingly on competent readers and writers to function. If, as Adam Fox argued, during the sixteenth and most of the seventeenth century "being unable to read and write in no way restricted people's capacity to perform skillfully and dexterously in most aspects of their daily lives,"[18] the turn of the eighteenth century saw vigorous promotion of the idea that, because all the nation's commercial and government business was conducted in the vernacular, it was necessary for people even in the lower ranks to be competent readers and writers of English. Literacy had become not only *"useful* in Business" but "Essential in furnishing out a Man of Business."[19] As Malachy Postlewayt noted in 1755, merchants and tradesmen who lacked the necessary vernacular skills, were hiring clerks and factors who had them, not coincidentally making "the compting house" one target audience for grammars.[20] Reading and writing literacy were also prerequisites for "ciphering" (arithmetic) and thus for new numerate jobs such as book-keeping, surveying, land management, and navigation. Government too needed growing numbers of readers and writers to forge a paper nation and a paper empire that depended for their functioning on the literacy of coast guards, customs officers, army officers, ships' captains, justices of the peace, spies, and local councils, on the copying of clerks, the record-keeping of secretaries to committees, and the written orders sent by civil servants.

Urban, rural, commercial, government and maritime jobs requiring reading and writing were available to individuals issuing from the unpropertied ranks, including from the lower orders, provided they had the necessary skills. Consequently, one reason that was given for teaching poor children reading, writing and some arithmetic in charity schools, and for passing laws requiring masters to teach the apprentices and domestic servants indentured to them by the parish to read and write, was that this would "in useful Way" fit the poor, who did not have "any other way of Living, than by turning Vagabonds, Beggars and Thieves," with "some honest worldly Calling or Employment."[21] Reading and writing were becoming necessary for all kinds of work. As contemporaries claimed and modern studies have confirmed, servants, apprentices, minor government officials, shopkeepers, artisans and clerks, became increasingly important sectors of the new public for print.

Extending vernacular literacy was also the impetus behind the new "English School" movement, which rejected the "liberal education" in Latin and Greek provided by grammar schools and English universities as "prejudicial to the commonwealth" and "contrary to the Frame and Profit of a Trading People,"[22] in favor of instruction in the vernacular and in practically useful arts and sciences. But in practice, even at the end of our period, Britain, like the United States, contained only "a highly unregulated, disorganized, private and largely unprofessional patchwork of educational institutions," as Alan Richardson has pointed out.[23] In Britain, before the Education Act of 1870 made schooling mandatory, many more boys and girls were apprenticed, set to work after minimal schooling, or home-schooled to a point by a parent, governess or tutor, than were subject to any regular, continuous and complete course of institutionalized education. In America, outside the major cities, the situation was often complicated by vast distances and a perennial shortage of teachers and of working hands. After some instruction in the ABCs of reading at home or at a petty school, many eighteenth-century people (including those who had to teach others) were therefore, if at all, largely self-taught from books. This is certainly one reason why, for most of the century, elementary schoolbooks were designed as much for adults and youth outside school settings as for children in school, as much for women as for men, and as much to aid "ignorant teachers" and maternal instructors, as to serve as "silent teachers" for the self-taught. Nor were schoolbooks the only kind of book aimed at "a dual audience." What Matthew Grenby calls "cross-reading" – adults reading what we classify as children's books, and children reading what we classify as adult books – was common for works of all kinds.[24]

The grammar was the most important of the elementary schoolbooks. Grammarians and historical linguists today concentrate on the two parts of eighteenth-century grammar which modern grammar has retained, leaving the first part, "spelling," to historians of early childhood education and the fourth part, "prosody," to literary critics. The pioneering work done on the "mental operations" that reading taught, was extrapolated from spelling alone, and generalized from there to all reading and writing. However, as we will see in Chapter 1, taking all four parts of eighteenth-century grammar together and including *all* the miscellaneous fragments that recur in eighteenth-century books, shows that – in addition to whatever else they did – ABCs, spellers and grammars were brilliantly designed to provide would-be readers with a complex of strategies for comprehending printed writing. One overlooked function of spellers was to introduce speakers with different local and regional dialects to an already homogenized form of printed English that still differed significantly from script and speech, in order to cultivate instantaneous word recognition of print orthography and conventions. Except in copybooks, printers did little or nothing for script, with the result that, by mid-century, some were arguing that speakers and writers by hand should imitate print's artificial homogenized forms. The other three parts of grammars combined fragments of etymology, syntax, rhetoric, logic, poetics and stylistics to give beginning readers techniques for deciphering the "hard words," figurative language, elisions and convoluted structures of complex sentences in printed discursive and literary works. Separately and together, the four parts of grammars taught readers methods of analogical thinking on which reasoning and higher-order reading depended. This compound of skills, strategies and mental operations explains why contemporaries celebrated grammar as "the Foundation or Groundwork of Polite Learning," and said that grammars were designed "for all those who desire to understand what they read."[25] Though modern disciplines were in the process of formation as several modern scholars have shown,[26] they were often, as here, deployed in combination where reading was concerned.

Readers were urged to move beyond grammars by other uses of reading. If, as Adam Fox has argued, during the seventeenth century "in the small communities in which people lived, what was important was the seasonal cycle of work, the operation of local custom, the love and tradition of the neighbourhood, and the gossip about its inhabitants...none [of which] were written down,"[27] by the turn of the eighteenth century, what was important was the ability to use reading to acquire such general knowledge of the wider world and of the new scientific and geographical discoveries as would "enlarge" the "narrow" minds of people living (as most of the population did) in small, isolated localities, and fit them for an expanding commercial empire. A "Trading People," which needed literate workers to connect small communities in the British Isles, and link them to markets all over Europe and the New World, and which sent armies, governors, customs officers and other civil servants in the wake of trade, needed people with some knowledge of the larger world in which trade and government operated. But, as Isaac Watts observed in 1741 in one of his transatlantic best-sellers, men who had traveled little beyond their native town or village "know not how to believe anything wise or proper besides what they have been taught to practice." "Confin[ing] themselves within the circle of their own hereditary ideas and opinions," they refused to believe that the sun did not rotate around the earth, that the telescope and microscope did not "delude the eye with false images," or that peoples in distant places had customs, manners and beliefs different from their own. Widespread general reading was needed to cure widespread ignorance. Reading was a necessary nostrum for men who "stand amaz'd like a meer Stranger at the mention of common subjects," at once too credulous of prodigies and wonders, and too disbelieving of demonstrated fact and evident truth. After the discoveries of the new sciences and the new world, the heavens and the earth were full of things that were "new and strange" but also "true," and Britons needed to know and accept them.[28] The relevant knowledge and information was conveyed to different target audiences in different ways.

Men in the highest tiers of the "learned professions" (divinity, law, medicine) and in the higher, more prestigious, government offices had traditionally been expected to possess a "gentleman's" liberal education in Latin and Greek; indeed, they became gentlemen, whatever their birth, by virtue of this education. But efforts were now made to supplement traditional, classical humanist learning ("liberal education") in light of new knowledge and new needs, and to use printed texts to supply the gentry – as well as men of lowly birth and those younger sons and scions of declining genteel families whom Anthony Blackwall tactfully called "Gentlemen who have for some Years neglected the Advantages of their Education"[29] – with what they had failed to learn at school or university, and needed to know. As we will see in Chapter 3, guides to study insisted that men in a commercial empire should have some knowledge in "the Circle of the Sciences," especially of English history, world history, geography, and natural philosophy, and showed them how to acquire this on their own. Guides to study proposed a "regular" course of reading for men's *idle* hours, and tackled issues of concentration, attention, selection, extraction, storage, retention, and reflection, while providing their users with a variety of oral and written techniques both for processing individual books and for mastering subjects. Incorporated here was the idea that reading was "improving" – by "enlarging the Capacity of his Mind," leisure-time study would improve a man's performance in every department of his life, even if he did not seek, or ever attain, the in-depth knowledge of the man of learning who was expert in a field. Though there was nothing to prevent "youths" from pursuing the suggested course of reading with a tutor (as guides pointed out), guides to study assumed users who would employ reading to acquire general knowledge in a variety of subjects on their own, and spoke directly (in the vocative "you" or in epistolary form) to those who would be doing the reading, rather than to parents or teachers. This made them relatively easy to adapt for the use of women and girls. Female-authored guides more frequently presented the course of study they prescribed as a substitute for schooling, and as the means of acquiring the kind of education that girls failed to get from girls' schools, while these were principally engaged in teaching "accomplishments," such as dancing, sewing, drawing, music, and French.

Though we tend to attribute upward mobility only to men who gained wealth, status and estates through commerce, Britain was also an exceptionally upwardly mobile society for Writers by Trade, especially in the professions or in government service. The literate son of an artisan or farm laborer might become a clerk, factor, surveyor or land agent. But like the "new men" of the Elizabethan period, those who proceeded beyond their grammar to acquire the reading, writing and learning needed in Britain and her empire, could leave their class of origin far behind. Some were able to rise as high as the nation's top offices from quite lowly ranks. For instance, Chief Justice Ryder was the son of a Cheapside linen draper; Lord Chancellor Hardwicke, of a Dover attorney; Bishop Warburton, of a town clerk in Newark; under-secretary of state, Joseph Addison, of a Wiltshire vicar; colonial governor, Thomas Pownall, of an army officer; William Pitt, Prime Minister and first Earl of Chatham, was a merchant's grandson. The man who improved himself by reading, in or outside school, could realistically hope to substantially improve both his economic standing and his standing in the world, whatever his birth.

Unlike guides to study, belletristic guides to taste often began life as schoolbooks or university lectures before being disseminated to the public at large. As we will see in the second part of Chapter 3, they generally covered the principles of oratory and delivery, as well as those governing classical genres, because many were originally designed for young men destined for the Church, the bar, or the Senate, for the medical or military professions, for secretarial positions and for higher government employments who would have to write and speak "in consequence of their profession."[30] Such men would have to indite a sermon, speech or letter; give their superiors a narrative of some person or series of events; make their case before a judge, a parliamentary assembly or a crowd; perhaps write a coterie poem, play or novel. As Hugh Blair observed, knowledge of the rules of composition and standards of taste also had the advantage of enabling such men to "support a proper rank in social life" by demonstrating their superior judgment and refined tastes in social situations when conversation turned to literary topics. In some circles, this was a means of making oneself agreeable to a patron and his/her friends and thus of persuading them that one was precisely the kind of sociable and conversable companion whose interests and professional fortunes they wished to advance. One might say that one function of the discourse of taste promoted by academic critics was to create a distinction between unpropertied professional men who acquired the title of "gentleman" by virtue of their profession, and the general run of "Writers by Trade." Here particular manners of reading, writing and speaking functioned as signifiers of status and "gentility" which (like money) could be acquired and displayed whatever one's birth.

The discourse of politeness attached to reading in guides to study and guides to taste smacked of the performative – it was designed to produce what it described. Polite manners could feasibly be marketed as elite conduct, and presented as a passport into genteel society, because – though "easier" and more "informal" than the "oppressive gentility" of the past – the forms and rituals of eighteenth-century British and American gentility descended from the manners of courtiers, most notably in the French court. But there was nothing intrinsically polite about preferring Cowley to Marvell and the *Iliad* to the *Odyssey*, or knowing that the sun did not rotate around the earth. Here, the discourse of politeness also played other roles. As Paul Langford observed: "the downward transmission of manners" to "successive layers of society" – extension to innkeepers and boots, shopkeepers, ferrymen and servants of the demand for civility and complaisance – had a "civilizing" and "equalizing" effect.[31] This may also be said of "polite learning." Like uniform orthography, pronunciation and grammar, the downward transmission of "learning" "civilized" and "equalized." It thus facilitated commerce among ranks and among the patchwork of linguistically and culturally diverse settlements all over Britain and the Anglophone Atlantic world.[32] Lord Kames promoted belletrism to the King by claiming that sharing the same polite tastes would "unite" the whole people in "the same elegant pleasures."

Except at the beginning of the way, when reading was taught before writing and separately from it, reading was conceived and taught as the other face of writing. Blair was being perfectly conventional during the 1760s – and following a tradition that went back to Philip Melanchthon (1532) and beyond that to ancient Roman schools[33] – when he told students at the University of Edinburgh who had the means to live without working, that "the same instructions which assist others in composing, will assist them in discerning and relishing, the beauties of composition."[34] In 1704, for instance, Thomas Hearne introduced and concluded a chapter he entitled "Rules to be observed in Writing History" by stating that his instructions about how to *write* history were "intended only for Youth that shall read what is already written. Their Judgments must be elevated, and placed as it were above the Authors they peruse, that they may not servilely rely upon them, and believe whatever they have written to be unquestionable."[35] Readers and writers were often addressed simultaneously, even undecidably, in instructional materials, including those designed for popular readerships, incidentally providing us with unexpected insights into how various kinds of texts were written to be read. Though print sought to usurp many functions earlier performed by scribes or by readers in their own hand, there was no "epistemic shift" in this period from "production to consumption, invention to reception, writing to reading."[36] Interactive reading practices originating in scribal culture, in which readers and writers normatively switched places, persisted both in coteries and in the public domain well into the Romantic period, and were increasingly appropriated by non-elite groups both in Britain and America. If anything, such practices were extended and given a new lease of life in print culture, where consumers were invited to become producers of texts in their turn by printers, periodical editors and booksellers who still relied heavily on voluntary contributions from the reading public for their copy. Consequently, "it was commonly remarked that that anybody in eighteenth-century England could be an author."[37] There was no hard and fast line between readers and writers yet.

There was no hard and fast line between reading and speaking either. Writing was still conceived as "silent speech," because this equivalence still reflected social practices, where "reading" often meant "reading aloud." Britain and British-America shared a culture in which people frequently read letters, papers, sermons or books aloud to literate as well as illiterate people. They read aloud in public institutions such as churches, courts, committees, assemblies or Parliament, as well as in social and domestic settings, in coffee houses and book shops, and in workplaces, where listening to someone read displaced singing or chanting as an accompaniment to routine labor. Readers also found opportunities to display their insight, judgment and skill in "pronunciation" or reading aloud through the private theatricals that became popular during this period. Reading handwritten or printed texts aloud brought reading into the world – domestic, social, workaday, and public – in a material way that linked reading not only to orality and aurality, but also to sociality and conversation. Even silent and solitary reading was supposed to be re-presented and recycled as informed, instructive and entertaining conversation, making comprehension, interpretation, judgment, selection, citation, paraphrase and retention of the materials one had read, social as well as intellectual or professional skills. Competence in reading aloud was much prized, and useful in many circumstances, to women as well as men. Consequently, as we will see in Chapter 2, techniques for reading aloud were widely disseminated in periodicals and magazines, as well as in schoolbooks and professional aids. Guides in the form of what I call "conversation-pieces" modeled conversations demonstrating how reading aloud might be used in conjunction with "familiar conversation," especially by women, to improve young or inexperienced readers' comprehension, interpretation, and pronunciation of texts, as well as their knowledge of the subject or subjects involved. "Conversation-pieces" also showed readers how to "make Application" of their reading to their everyday lives, and how to participate in literary coteries or polite social entertainments where oral delivery of a text was followed by conversation.

The printing trade catered to the generality of readers, who were "unlearned" in the contemporary sense of lacking a Latin grammar school and/or University education, and who lacked the funds, leisure or skills to embark on an extensive course of study in or out of school, by selling "learning" to them in shorter, simpler, cheaper and more easily comprehensible forms. There were simplifying abridgements of Locke on *Human Understanding*, of Johnson's *Dictionary* and of Lowth's *Grammar* as well as of *Clarissa* and *Robinson Crusoe*; digests of Milton and Homer as well as of Newton's *Principia*; translations of Virgil and *Telemaque* as well as of Kotzebue and Rousseau. Some educators advised readers that popular travel narratives and adventure stories were easy and entertaining ways of acquiring geography and knowledge of foreign peoples. Increasingly, there were also printed shortcuts to study: simple, catechismic, introductions to subjects in the circle of the sciences, popular digests and "Preceptors," dramatized conversations and dialogues, dictionaries of the arts and sciences, and how-to books such as *Every Man his own Lawyer* (1736), *Every Man his own Physician* (1764), and *Every Man his own Letter-Writer* (1782). Abridgements, translations, serials and pamphlets abounded. So did compilations. Periodicals and magazines, olios and miscellanies, were compilations of snippets of classical learning, moral philosophy, social commentary, theology, political theory, natural philosophy, genre theory and other subjects, delivered through essays, historical anecdotes, satires, short fictions, translations, extracts, letters and conversations. Indeed, there is a sense in which these miscellarian, periodical, "Repositories of Instruction and Entertainment" epitomized in small the principal characteristics of the popular printing trade: this too offered a profusion of slivers from a variety of subjects and a variety of fictional and non-fictional genres, in short and accessible, portable and affordable, discontinuous and ever-novel forms.

Among the rest, periodicals, magazines and miscellanies included the aesthetic preferences and manner of reading promoted by "men of taste"; but these appeared jumbled together with other things, like Pope's mixed catalogue of "Puffs, Powders, Patches, Bibles, Billets doux."[38] The theories, genres and manners of reading of "conjectural critics" and "men of taste" were thus leveled to an equivalency with popular genres which such critics proscribed and despised (such as the marvelous, the exotic, the allegorical) and with essays explaining how the latter worked. Unlike belletrists, miscellarians offered readers what Bacon in *Novum Organum* called "Knowledge broken"– "short and scattered [units], not linked together by

an artificial method," which "do invite men to inquire further." As we
will see in Chapter 4, using "broken" forms which played to the curiosity,
and love of variety and novelty that many said were "natural" to readers,
miscellarians invited readers to read miscellaneous, discontinuous texts in
ways that permitted them to appropriate whatever they wished to their
own use, and prompted them to "inquire further" according to their own,
particular, interests and tastes. Miscellarians contested belletrists and men
of learning, who wished to regulate reading and "tell the Blanks of Society
what to think," in formal as well as substantive terms. For the learned often
favored works replete with "method" and "divisions" which (as Bacon
put it) "seem to embrace and comprise everything which can belong to
the subject" and discourage readers from looking further because "things
[are] delivered to them as long since perfect and complete."[39] As that word
"delivered" intimates, dividing subjects into categories and propounding
standards, rules, and tastes for each as "accepted ideas," long-established
and universally true, authorized belletrists and men of learning to dictate
to others as teachers, censors, judges and critics. Miscellarians, by contrast,
often identified their own miscellaneous and "broken" manners of writing
and reading with the subject's political liberty and the reader's freedom of
thought. The tension between "open" reading practices and those "closed"
by the conscientious application of categories, rules, standards and preor-
dained "Tastes" was a central issue in the eighteenth-century's "Politics of
Reading."[40] But this was not a simple binary. There were also what Oscar
Kenshur called "teleological discontinuous forms" where scattered discontinuous units pointed to, or could be reassembled into, a "higher" unity,[41]
just as there were methodical texts, guides to study primary among them,
which taught readers how to dismember texts, select fragments and recom-
bine them, in the process of thinking and judging for themselves. What
Kevin Sharpe and Steven Zwicker say of "the practices of humanism" in
early modern England remained true of their eighteenth-century offshoots
and variants: they "opened the book to alternative interpretations" and
"enabled readers to perform their own readings, and construct their own,
often dissenting, values and politics."[42]

Everyone agreed that one of the great uses of reading was to make readers
"serviceable to themselves and others," and "beneficial both to themselves
and their country" through the moral and religious instruction it contained. This was because contemporaries conceived of reading neither as a
purely mental activity nor as a pastime separate from living. They saw it,
rather, as a process which collapsed all distance and difference between the
reader and the book, to make the matter read an intrinsic part of a person's

physical being and being-in-the-world. This was often evoked through the shorthand of metaphor. Metaphors of reading as nourishment or food portrayed the consumption of texts as a process of absorption into the body, where the matter read was transmuted into elements tending to health and growth, or to poison and disease. Metaphors of inscription, impression or imprinting portrayed the act of reading as a copying or transcription of the words seen on a handwritten or printed sheet onto the "white page" of the mind, soul, heart, conscience, imagination (imaging-faculty) or memory. In a culture that privileged sight and used visualization for mnemonics, this correlation of mental and material pages, and of the mind's eye with the physical eye, must have resonated with felt experience – especially for those who, as children, had been required to memorize every evening the printed page they had read and explicated during the day, in order to be able to recite it "by heart" the following morning, and to those who had whole books – the Bible, the *Aeneid, Paradise Lost* – inscribed in their memory and could turn to chapter and verse at will. Once reconfigured and reordered first by mnemonic, and later by readerly and writerly techniques, such mental inscriptions or impressions were said to fill, stock and shape a person's mind and/or heart, and to determine, for good or ill, how he or she thought, felt and acted.[43] As inscription was added to inscription, and page to page, the psyche became a book that was open and legible to God, if not (on some views) to man.

Both metaphors represented reading as having real and far-reaching, beneficial or detrimental, effects on the reader's body, mind and heart, and thus on his or her conduct in society. This raised social and political concerns and required that readers install (or be given) a guardian or censor, in the form of judgment or taste, to determine what might safely enter at the mouth or be admitted to the brain. One might say that vernacular belletristic criticism and reviewing were born in the late seventeenth and early eighteenth centuries to supply readers with a guardian against manners of reading that made diversity in readers' readings inevitable. Eighteenth-century belletristic-moral criticism may be seen as an attempt to contain the destabilizing proliferation of texts and meanings by "censoring" ideas, fixing morals, regulating judgment, and forming taste.[44] Bacon famously said, "Some books are to be tasted, others to be swallowed, and some few are to be chewed and digested."[45] Eighteenth-century belletrists and reviewers added: "many are to be spat out."

Metaphors of food and inscription were not new with the eighteenth century, or even with Bacon or Locke, as G. H. Bantock, Alberto Mangel, Paul Griffiths and Eric Jager have shown. The image of "eating" a book appears in the biblical book of Revelations, was deployed by "Roman Christians" such as Cyprian and Augustine, and became commonplace during the Renaissance. Images of impressing, imprinting or engraving knowledge on the mind or heart go back to classical antiquity, when the psyche was represented as a "wax tablet" rather than as a *tabula rasa* or blank page, and when the reference was to the engraving action upon a malleable and retentive surface of a stylex or signet ring.[46] Seventeenth- and eighteenth-century writers modified, adapted and extended such metaphors to include allusions to the new technology of print, and to describe or discredit physical and mental processes which their forbears had not known they possessed. But many of the period's most discussed concerns about the mental and physical dangers of reading seem to stem from these traditional metaphors rather than from the scientific obser- vation and empiricism supposedly characterizing the age. Indeed, when empiricists described our knowledge of the world as deriving from sense impressions, they figured perception through the old inscription meta- phor of reading. They argued that we read the world (or the "Book of Nature") as we read of things through the letters in scribal or printed books – by means of "secondary" signs that are adapted to human organs but are incommensurable with the thing itself. Richard Kroll's study of eighteenth-century Epicureanism suggests that reading also became the implicit figure or model for the workings of invisible natural and cultural processes. Building on Epicurus' analogies between letters and atoms, and on contemporary methods of teaching reading which "ascended atomi- cally from letters to words to sentences to entire discourses," he argues, empiricists conceived of nature, society and the mind as combining atomic constituents into ever larger and more encompassing constructs, which could be analyzed back into their elements.[47] One might say that during the eighteenth century, the mind and the world were understood through analogies borrowed from reading, even as reading was credited with fash- ioning the mind, manners and morals of social beings, and thus of society itself.

But morals – which different manners of reading approached differently– were not the uncontroversial, apolitical things that Enlightenment phi- losophers and belletristic critics pretended when they presented virtues and vices as abstract universals, expounded them in general terms, or equated aesthetic beauty with incontrovertible moral truth. As James Noggle showed, for all its aestheticism, "taste" before Kant did not "pre- tend to be a realm of disinterested contemplation."[48] Reviewers for *The Critical Review*, for instance, who "looked upon themselves to be in some measure responsible for the morals as well as the taste of their readers,"[49] attached the virtues and vices comprising morals to everything from choice of friends and private reading to political conduct and religious beliefs. Virtues and vices had social and political import, because they shaped character and conduct; but they were controversial because different kinds of polity entailed different social norms and different systems of morality. Most obviously, Jacobites demanded the cheerful passive obedience of children to fathers, wives to husbands, servants to masters, and subjects to monarchs, and Levelers, the right of every adult to independent moral self-governance; but Britain's "mixed government" was said to rest on a system of "mutual good offices" and on the relative duties of parents and children, of husbands and wives, of masters and servants and of governor and governed.[50] It was not a matter of indifference which morals a writer advanced. Morality could be seditious. It was not a matter of indifference either, whether writers advocated reforming the manners and morals of girls, women, laborers and libertines, or those of monarchs, ministers and the great. Reform could be seditious too.

In Britain and early national America, successive ministries passed and implemented laws to prohibit, prosecute and viciously punish the expression of "seditious" views and of "libels" on the great. But this did not have the desired silencing and uniting effect. Despite efforts to unite the nation and suppress dissent, eighteenth-century Britain remained a politically and religiously factionalized kingdom; a hierarchical society in which there were, as Mingay pointed out, at least forty finely graduated ranks;[51] the seat of a diverse and composite empire both in the British Isles and abroad; and a polity whose authority and legitimacy were constantly put in question by riots, Jacobite invasions, insurrections, revolutions, and the "Celtic fringe." The early United States was in similar case: federal administrations were attempting to unite separate states with different histories and characters, each composed of a variety of self-contained religious and ethnic communities which remained linked to their points of origin in Europe, while confronting riots, insurrections and incursions on their frontiers.[52] Neither Britons nor Americans were "docile bodies" yet.

Government measures to suppress destabilizing dissent drove printers and disaffected writers to publish proscribed views in covert, indirect, ambiguous and double-voiced forms, as a growing body of recent scholarship on censorship has shown. But, to effect its purpose, covert communication – which we call "secret writing" and the eighteenth-century knew by other names – had to be recognized and decoded by readers. Chapter 5 demonstrates how printed texts throughout the century taught readers at

all ranks how to recognize different genres of seditious writings and how
to recover their clandestine messages. As we will see too, belletrists and
disaffected secret writers often wrestled over the same texts and the same
genres, in ways which suggest that the aestheticism of men of taste was the
safe and "surface reading" of its day.

The Commerce in Reading

The printing trade was a key context for guides to reading, as well as for
reading itself, because "the Booksellers [were] Masters of all the Avenues
to every Market," as ex-pat American James Ralph pointed out.[53] Printers
and booksellers held the power of technology and the power of the purse.
What got printed and sold was controlled by booksellers – who commissioned, funded, distributed and sold books, and paid others to print them
as necessary – and by printers in the British and American provinces who
continued for most of the century to combine printing and bookselling
functions. Even a disgruntled Ralph had to admit that they "feel the Pulse
of the Times," "know best what Assortment of Wares will best suit the
Market," and "give [their] Orders accordingly."[54]

With an eye to what 'suited the market,' London printers and booksellers acted as powerful impresarios, distinguishing, developing, com-
missioning, advancing, promoting, and sometimes themselves creating,
whole genres of printed matter. Karen O'Brien found, for instance, that
the London trade was responsible for the genesis, evolution, and remarkable rise to prominence of history during this period; in England, where
historians were not yet based in educational institutions, "it was the booksellers who took the initiative and made successive attempts to find or
commission polished, modern and encompassing [historical] work."[55]
"Fictional histories" or novels were likewise solicited, funded, multiplied,
distributed, lent, and sometimes written, by members of the trade. The
same held for children's literature: "it was the publishers and printers who
were primarily responsible for creating and shaping the majority of the
literature that children were consuming, not authors, illustrators or edu-
cationalists."[56] London printers John Dunton and Edward Cave invented
and launched the periodical and the magazine. And the canonization of
Shakespeare, Spenser and Milton was inseparable from the determination
of the Tonsons, who owned the copyright on their works, to make their
properties in these antiquated authors profitable. According to Marcus
Walsh, three generations of Tonsons paid successive editors to present
Spenser, Milton and Shakespeare with the full editorial apparatus of

ancient classics to make them intelligible to eighteenth-century readers and mark them, visually, *as* (English) classics, in advance of critical consensus about this.[57]

Whether they were feeling "the Pulse of the Times," shared the traditional association of books with "learning," or only sought ways of making their commodities "useful," printers and booksellers ensured that "learning" drove reading as much as entertainment did. One might say that they took full commercial advantage of the Lockean doctrine that empowered all eighteenth-century education: since everyone was born *tabula rasa*, everyone had to learn everything from something or someone. There was hardly any genre of publication – not excluding the newspapers, periodicals, reviews, sermons, voyages, memoirs, lives, conduct books, how-to books, and novels which dominated popular reading – that did not claim to inform, instruct, or "improve" their readers in some way. When we speak of the rapid growth of "consumerism" in this period, we must remember that learning – commodified, sugar-coated and "made easie" – was one of the things that the public voluntarily consumed.

Printing and bookselling were commercial enterprises run by printers and booksellers for profit. As we now realize therefore, "writing for money provide[d] the ongoing dynamic for literary production of all kinds, both at the "quality" and the "popular" ends of the market."[58] Our concomitant recognition that writing for money "professionalized" "imaginative writing" has deconstructed the false binary that the New Critics created between the "great" (and supposedly gentlemanly) eighteenth-century poets, dramatists and novelists they canonized and "Grub Street hacks." But imaginative writing cannot yet be cordoned off from other forms of professional writing: those who wrote poems, plays and/or novels for money frequently wrote all kinds of other things for money too – periodicals, pamphlets, tracts, histories, lives, dictionaries, reviews, sermons and travelogues, conduct books and translations. "Writers by Profession" – a term used here to encompass all those who published in print – wrote whatever they could sell to printers or booksellers. *All* writers who published in print operated within the book trade's economic nexus and were affected by it –regardless of what or how much they wrote, or how well or poorly they wrote it; regardless of whether they sold their manuscript to a printer, paid him to publish it, or sought subscribers who would; regardless of whether they used an intermediary to negotiate the sale, or figured openly as employees in a printer's stable of writers; and regardless of whether printers and publishers were their sole source of livelihood or not. "Writers by Profession" were no more what Marx dismissed as "unproductive workers" operating outside the economic nexus, than were "Writers by Trade."

From what I can discover, the professional writers in Britain who used print culture – or were used by it – to instruct the public in reading and to extend the market for print, formed diverse, often fluid, socio-economic groups which sometimes interconnected or overlapped. An important dividing line among male writers fell between groups in which men combined institutional work with professional writing, and groups in which they did not.

Among those who combined professional writing with institutional work, an extraordinary number of schoolmasters found their way into print, whether to publicize their own schools, to supply their pupils with suitable textbooks, or to supplement meager incomes by providing instruction for other teachers and for the self-taught. Men who authored spellers and ABCs or contributed to copybooks generally differed in education, location, quotidian jobs, and rank from those who authored and published grammars and dictionaries. Though both groups were usually teachers, the former were not considered gentlemen, generally had more limited education, and often set up their own, sometimes short-lived, venture schools. In 1763, William Massey memorialized the lives and works of fifty-seven schoolmasters who kept schools in London or the provinces and published copybooks and elementary math books between 1690 and 1761. Of these, six were sons of clerks or schoolmasters, one was the son of a sea captain, one issued from an impoverished genteel family, and three had "lowly beginnings" as orphans raised at Christ-Church hospital. Massey said of the others: "few of them ever claim the title of *Gent*."[59] On the other hand, as Ian Michael discovered, most authors of grammars and dictionaries were teachers in grammar schools, masters in "English" schools, ushers in dissenting academies, or tutors in domestic situations: Greenwood, for instance, was second master at St. Paul's, Mattaire, second master at Westminster school.[60] More dependent on extant institutions, and possibly less entrepreneurial than reading and writing masters, male grammarians and dictionary-makers were generally beneficiaries of a classical or "liberal" university education. In England and Scotland, the practice was still current of licensing schoolmasters through annual clerical visitations, which examined master, students and curriculum for their Christian orthodoxy; many schoolmaster-grammarians highlighted the Christian orientation of their grammars as a result. Many masters were also clergymen themselves.

Another group of university-trained men, characterized by contemporaries as "men of learning," "men of liberal education," or "men of taste," produced many, if not most, of the period's belletristic critics, literary theorists, classical scholars, linguists, historians, antiquarians, philosophers and male conduct book writers. This group of university-trained men overlapped in education and training with schoolmasters and domestic tutors, and sometimes in experience too, since many had acted as tutors or schoolmasters at some time in their careers. Though we like to think of them as "gentlemen-amateurs," relatively few were independently wealthy, leisured gentlemen. The majority were situated in universities and dissenter academies, in Church livings, in legal or medical practices, in government's administrative posts or in government oppositions, and wrote for the press to supplement their incomes or to advance their careers. Some evidently wrote as "hacks": printer William Bowyer II employed learned hacks to edit and translate for him who were resident fellows at the English universities; Ralph complained that when ministers "imploy the Pen," they "have recourse to the Colleges"; and collectives like the "Society of Gentlemen" which produced a Supplement to a popular Dictionary of the Arts and Sciences were surely also located there.[61]

The prominence of clergy in these last two groups also had a pervasive, shaping influence on British print culture, so it is worth considering them separately. In England and Scotland, where patronage was required to obtain a Church living, it was customary for newly ordained clergy to begin their careers, if they could, as tutors to the children of great men who were capable of rewarding them with Church livings or other employments: (Bishop) Lowth's *Grammar*, (Revd.) Isaac Watts' *Logick*, and other best-selling "schoolbooks," were first drafted for the use of pupils whom their clerical authors were tutoring as domestics in great men's households. Ordained ministers in livings were frequently schoolmasters too. Ian Green discovered in his recent trilogy on the teaching of Christianity in England, not only that "a clear majority of grammar school teachers was in holy orders," but that "beneficed Episcopalian clergy" were increasingly "combining a cure of souls with school teaching."[62] In Scotland too, as Alexander Carlyle observed in 1767, clergymen had "become the chief depositories of general learning, now that the attention and efforts of almost all other men are devoted to commerce alone" because theirs was a particularly "ungainful profession."[63] To supplement "ungainful" clerical incomes, beneficed clergymen throughout Britain were opening schools, taking in pupils as boarders, or teaching local youth on the side. By mid-century, Henry Fielding's Parson Adams, with his Aeschylus in one hand and his Bible in the other, performing his pastoral duties in the provinces while supplementing his income by keeping a school and trying to publish his sermons in London, was a widely recognizable type.

Clergy occupying livings or educational posts were in the unique position of being men outside the "idle" propertied classes who had the leisure as well as the education to pursue scholarship, and who were driven to publish both by financial need and by their perennial quest for preferment. Large numbers of clergymen published as a result, and not only on religious topics.[64] Clergymen also published as grammarians, classical scholars, historians of language, philosophers, rhetoricians, university professors, antiquarians, natural philosophers, novelists, periodical essayists, and reviewers – to the point, indeed, where lay-schoolmaster, John Clarke, protested that they had become a positive impediment to other men. "Tickled with the vain Affectation of being Thought a prodigious Philosopher or Mathematician, a monstrous Critick in the Learned Languages," or an authoritative "comment[ator] upon old Heathen Authors," Clarke complained, clergymen were pursuing "an Employment in Life, that does not belong to [them]." He wished they would confine themselves instead to "the business of [their] proper Calling" and leave other employments to "Men hired by the Publick to the Profession of them."[65] There was no effort to make them do so however. Whether they were younger sons of the gentry or hailed from "poor backgrounds," as "recruits to the elite chosen by the established elite,"[66] the clergy were dependent for work and advancement on the approval of their social and ecclesiastical superiors. This tended to make those with posts or livings a safe and conservative group that was securely attached to King and Country, and/or to local ruling elites, and aligned by its interests with the *status quo*. As government perfectly understood, the most effective way of taming bellicose writers was to get them a "place."

"Men of learning" who held vocational posts and wrote professionally part-time, are to be distinguished as a group from men who relied on the book trade for all their income, the traditional "Grub Street hacks" – but not necessarily by virtue of their qualifications, by the quality of their writing, or even invariably by the kinds of things they wrote. For it turns out that significant numbers of university- and academy-trained men were writing for the trade as "hacks." As Oliver Goldsmith explained, "the Author, when unpatronized by the Great, has naturally recourse to the bookseller."[67] Without patronage, it was impossible to obtain a Church living, a university fellowship, a government job, or employment as a secretary, much less to build a successful medical practice or gain traction in the learned professions. In England, educated dissenters, Catholics, and foreign refugees faced the further impediment of being ineligible for vocational establishment posts; known republicans, "atheists," Jacobites, and Jacobins were likely to be in the same situation. Consequently, as *The Connoisseur* noted in 1756, "The mart of literature is one of the chief resorts of unbeneficed Divines, and Lawyers and Physicians without practice."[68] Pat Rogers too found that "a surprising number" of the writers whom Pope and Swift dismissed as hacks were "members of the legal profession."[69] "Grub Street" was full of "men of learning." Like their more fortunate peers, professional writers who depended on the book trade often capitalized on their learning by adapting and disseminating what they knew for the "unlearned" reading public. But they more often channeled their learning into the briefer and more widely accessible, miscellaneous and discontinuous print genres favored by the public, and embraced the accompanying curiosity-, novelty- and variety-based aesthetic. And while both camps of learned men might agree with Horace that reading is a source of "instruction and delight," those with institutional affiliations tended to emphasize the "instruction," those entirely dependent on the marketplace, the entertainment and delight.

There was some mobility between professional writers who held a post within some established ecclesiastical, government, professional or educational hierarchy, and those who did not. The latter sometimes managed to find a patron willing to get them a "place" in government (Addison, Oldmixon, Prior, Hume), in one of the professions (Swift, Fielding), in a great man's service (Thomas Birch, William Oldys, James Ralph)[70] or, failing that, to offer them an asylum from want in their households (Watts, Johnson). But literacy's path led down as well as up. Aside from political changes, which displaced some of them, there also appears to have been an over-production of men of learning, and thus of sometimes desperate men who worked for the booksellers when their hopes of placement and advancement had been disappointed, checked or wrecked. Some never managed to use their literacy to rise (Goldsmith, Johnson). Some had checkered careers – one thinks of Richard Steele or John Wilkes, who reached their highpoint as Members of Parliament, and then fell. The careers of others, less fortunate, followed the pattern of the "unlearned" professional writers, to whom we now turn.

There appears to have been greatest mobility in and out of writing for booksellers for men and women who were "unlearned," again in the contemporary sense of lacking a liberal, classical university or grammar-school education. Many writers in this group had been or would again be engaged in other temporary work: acting, teaching, tutoring, governessing, sewing, housekeeping, spying, delivering public readings or orations, soldiering, sailing, keeping a stall, tavern or shop. It is not clear how many writers were permanently attached to printers or (given the number of printers) could have been at any one time; but the practice of paying them by the job suggests that most did "piece work." Writing for printers and booksellers was perilous and poorly remunerated; and unlike other poorly remunerated work – the diverse forms of domestic service, fellowships in colleges – it rarely supplied free board and lodging. Printers and women were the most salient groups among the unlearned writers who transmitted manners of reading.

Though most had little formal schooling, printers and their journeymen often acted as compilers, editors, abridgers, translators and authors themselves, as had been traditional in the trade since Caxton and Wynkyn de Worde. Printers were 'object[s] of considerable condescension:'[71] they were considered "mere mechanicks" (lowly artisans) because they worked with their hands, engaged in trade, and issued from the lower orders. Jacob Tonson I, for instance, was the son of a barber-surgeon; William Lane, the enormously successful publisher of the Minerva Press, was the son of a London poulterer; Samuel Richardson was the son of a Derbyshire joiner; Joseph Johnson, John Newbery and William Duane were farmers' boys; Isaiah Thomas' father was a drifter; Edward Cave was the son of a shoemaker, Benjamin Franklin of a soap-boiler. They were not gentlemen, or even descended from gentlemen. One might say that it was precisely because "meer mechanics" were successful commercial writers, editors and compilers, that "learned" authors in their employ – who sought social acceptance at a nobleman's table or in the genteel circles composed of successful professionals, wealthy merchants and lesser gentry forming in provincial towns – tried to distinguish themselves from low-born printers and other "hacks" by resorting to satire and denigration or pretending not to write for money.

Though more women than we used to think learned Latin and Greek, women writers also figured large within this group. Indeed, the number of female professional writers increased exponentially from decade to decade.[72] This is less surprising now that we know that the situation of women in most ranks was not as different from that of men as we once supposed. As Paula McDowell showed and others confirm, women in the lower and middling ranks "[went] about their business little hampered by crystallizing ideologies of femininity."[73] They participated as wives, as independent single women, and as employees in the production and sale of books and periodicals, as they did in other forms of artisanal production, trade and commerce.[74] Encouraged to acquire reading, writing and numeracy to fit themselves for "business," for domestic economy and later, for the education of their children, women were a standard target readership for grammars, periodicals, conversation-pieces, conduct books and novels. Women's education was also a prime issue for all those who espoused "the cause of women" from Bathsua Makin and Mary Astell to Mary Wollstonecraft and Hannah More, as well as for those whose target-audiences included women readers. And one might argue that, though they bitterly disparaged their options, education began to give educated women some career paths outside marriage. It qualified "ladies" descended from declining noble or genteel families, or from the mercantile, clerical or professional ranks, to seek their livelihood as governesses, teachers, and increasingly, as mistresses of their own schools. Like their male counterparts, some schoolmistresses began to publicize their school or supplement their income by writing instructional books for the press – there was a flurry of woman-authored grammars and conversation-pieces on subjects in the circle of the sciences during the 1780s and 1790s. Some women wrote professionally while acting as companions to great ladies. Others resorted to professional writing when obliged to fend for themselves by a parent's remarriage, by the death of a parent or spouse, by inadequate inherited income, or by a husband's disappearance, improvidence or bad luck.[75] Earning money from professional writing was an option for women because printers and booksellers were not hampered by upper-class "ideologies of femininity" either. They published women writers as well as men, and sponsored genres such as the novel that were dominated by female pens.

One might expect secret writing and instruction in how to read it to have issued exclusively from the disappointed, displaced, penurious, and out of place, or from writers in the pay of opposition parties. However, this does not appear to have been the case. As far as one can tell (it was often anonymous), instruction in secret writing also issued from the gentry or nobility and, even more cautiously, from authors in institutional jobs. As we will see in Chapter 5, Shaftesbury attributed the fact that secret writing was used and disseminated at one time or another by people of all political persuasions, to the period's rapid changes in ministries and forms of government, each of which used censorship to proscribe different views.

In fact, *all* manners of reading were promoted by writers of diverse party-political persuasions, because any manner of writing and reading could be used for different party-political ends. Party-political positions (Whig, Tory, Old Whig, Jacobite, Jacobin) must be distinguished from the "commercial politics" of printers, publishers and/or professional writers who were promoting their product and maneuvering to advance their own interests *as* writers, publishers or teachers. The strategies the latter adopted were not unaffected by party or government politics. But practices such as puffing the utility of a manner of reading in advancing a desirable national political goal, producing false imprints, or writing and printing for one or both sides of a political controversy, must be distinguished from politics proper. These were as much commercial strategies designed to boost sales and protect or enhance the standing and influence of the writer, as were the identification and targeting of potential readerships or competition for ascendancy over "Grub Street" rivals. Despite sometimes confusing interactions with party or government politics, strategies for promoting and disseminating manners of reading belong to print culture's "commercial politics."

Professional writers in Britain were a motley crew, whose concerns and interests did not necessarily align with those in other ranks. Rather than constituting a rank or class which fits into the usual horizontal stratifications, "Writers by Profession" traversed all ranks – as did Writers by Trade. I say "traversed" because both kinds of writer seem to have issued from a variety of different ranks and, depending on their good or ill fortune, to have moved up and down into different ranks in the course of their careers. This may be why professional writers took such pains to distinguish themselves from other ranks. Though virtually all eighteenth-century manners of reading borrowed and adapted elements from seventeenth-century courtly or learned culture, they made it clear that the manners of reading they were disseminating did not reflect the language, culture or reading habits of the aristocracy or gentry, much less of the "middle class." Teachers, tutors and professional writers complained throughout the century that most members of the propertied classes believed that possessing a handsome estate exempted them from reading and study as things "proper only for them, who must get a livelihood by their Learning." They criticized the gentry and aristocracy for writing and speaking the faulty, ungrammatical English of their forbears; for being ignorant, narrow-minded, superstitious and lazy; and for failing to adequately patronize writers, pay tutors and teachers, or value books. While marketing their products to the public as "polite reading" or "polite learning," and thus by snob appeal, men of taste reproached "persons of Estate and Standing" for wasting their time in "idleness and Vanity," and tried (they said in vain) to persuade them that pursuing "useful Learning" in order to be "good and useful...both in a private and public Capacity" were "the true Accomplishments of a Gentleman."[76] Professional writers, including the most penurious writing full-time for the market, also presented themselves as instructors to, rather than as members of, the middling sort. Professional writers distinguished themselves from tradesmen and merchants, from men of property, and from men of birth, by their "literacy and literature."

The dynamics were somewhat different in North America, where printing appeared later and more unevenly. Beginning in late seventeenth-century Cambridge and Boston, printing only gradually spread north, west and south. Population was sparse in many regions; and reading for secular purposes may have become "a Necessity of Life" later for farmers and rural inhabitants in areas where, for want of specie, the economy depended on exchanges of goods, than for city dwellers, tradesmen and merchants, practitioners of the learned professions, and participants in colonial or early republican administrations. Because printing remained local or regional throughout our period, booksellers in America often found it more profitable to sell imported books than locally printed ones. Thus while Britain and British-America shared the same manners of reading, they were inflected differently, given different cultural valences, and applied to new uses in the New World, due in part to this double economy of the American book trade.

On the one hand, both before and after Independence, the transatlantic trade flooded American booksellers' shops and subscription libraries with imported British schoolbooks, learned books and fashionable novels and journals, or with Irish reprints of them. American elites appropriated Britain's "polite" studious or belletristic manners of reading, and British manners of conversing about them, as marks of gentility, in what has been described as 'the refinement of America.'[77] In coastal cities, writing masters and schoolmasters taught young men designed for the transatlantic trade the various scripts in use from British books and often followed the practical mercantile "English-school" model for the rest. Latin grammar schools added English-school subjects, as did Harvard, whose library, like most early American libraries, was built of British books. Other universities revised their curriculae on British lines by importing English or Scottish heads, and new immigrants from Britain such as William Milns, Susanna Rowson or Eliza Fenwick opened fashionable schools. By the 1780s, prosperous and ambitious small traders and farmers in New England were sending their teenage daughters to elite boarding schools for a year to acquire polite British norms of reading, writing, conduct and taste. Imported British books, journals and manners of reading them thus helped to define the American elite, while catering to what Leonard Tennenhouse calls the ongoing 'importance of feeling English.'[78]

On the other hand, from the inception of American printing, local American printers, many of them British- or Irish-trained, fashioned distinctively American print cultures, which differed somewhat with local cultures from city to city and state to state. While "job printing" for assemblies or clergy to eke out a living, printers fashioned local and regional printscapes by compiling and writing their own newspapers or periodicals, by adapting whichever British or European books they selected for reprinting to the needs and tastes of their local readerships, and by publishing American authors as and when they could. Until the Revolution, the preponderance in America of clerical authors and lack of an equivalent to "Grub Street" led to a preponderance of American-authored sectarian religious and devotional publications. This left American printers and booksellers a key role as compilers, adapters, and disseminators of select secular, foreign (mostly British) copy texts, and, after Independence, as patriotic promoters of American-authored schoolbooks. Unlike British printers who also published learned treatises and expensive folios, American printers wrote, commissioned, reprinted and published almost exclusively in the brief and discontinuous, miscellarian forms that were accessible to, and popular among, the unlearned – newspapers, periodicals, anthologies, miscellanies, how-to books, almanacs, letter-manuals, abridgments, novels, criminal biographies and schoolbooks – to the point, indeed, where one modern scholar has described American print culture before the middle of the nineteenth century as "a factory of fragments."[79] This made practical sense in America, where markets for print were still both local and small, for such texts excluded no potential readers. Occasional attempts to publish longer, more continuous or learned works, showed that these rarely sold as well.[80] However, since early-national printers published, and themselves used, covert methods of writing during the "nativist" years leading to the Alien and Sedition Acts (1798), it might also be fair to say that they privileged discontinuous texts, which fostered a broad variety of interpretations and judgments of what one had read, because these asserted and safeguarded the liberty of each reader to think for him/herself when that liberty was under threat.

About this Book

The focus of this study is on six manners of reading that Anglophone Britons and Americans shared. A chapter is devoted to each, except for Chapter 3 which contains two. Each manner of reading is composed of several practices and techniques. Where individual guides are discussed in some detail, they are works that were imported and/or reprinted in America, usually multiple times.

Chapter 1 describes reading practices based on grammar and analogical thinking that were used primarily for purposes of comprehension and elucidation, and served as the basis for higher order reading.

Chapter 2 details oral practices centered on issues of character – reading aloud and conversing about books. Consonant with contemporary injunctions to supplement book learning with knowledge of the world, discussion of how these were modeled in printed guides is followed by some contemporary descriptions of social events in which reading and conversation occurred.

Chapter 3 turns to two manners of reading associated with more advanced schooling: study-methods for acquiring, organizing and retaining book learning that were dependent on the kind of book from which one learned; and neo-classical, belletristic (or "aesthetic") methods of judging and formulating writing in diverse genres. The former are illustrated from guides to the study of history, which also figured in altered guise among belletristic techniques.

Chapter 4 describes older, selective, discontinuous reading practices that were disseminated in the popular marketplace primarily by and for periodicals, magazines, miscellanies, collections, and novels. The last section considers belletrist attempts to supplant discontinuous reading practices in the popular marketplace by providing politically "safer" and more constraining versions of miscellanists' key methods and ideas.

Chapter 5 adds to the long history of secret writing an account of the ways in which the eighteenth-century public was instructed in diverse methods of concealing "seditious" meanings, both in expository and in fictional texts. This will also take us back to grammars.

The chapters' contents have been more fully discussed earlier in this introduction. An overview of each chapter's contents will be provided again in its opening section. This permits the book to be read continuously or discontinuously – skipping from opening section to opening section to decide which chapter/s or section/s to read in full, or to construct a sequential "survey" of the whole; returning to an opening section to recollect material already read.

The goal is to delineate common, once familiar, ideas and practices that individuals, as well as ethnic, national and gendered groups, might use or alter for their own ends. The changes gradually made by Anglophone Americans emerged and distinguished themselves from a matrix in Britain that needs to be better understood. One cannot see American difference clearly unless one knows from what, or fully understand what a particular provincial British reader was doing unless one knows what prescriptions s/he was adopting or adjusting and what his/her options and lacunae were. This book's approach to eighteenth-century materials derives from its goal.

Prior to the era of mass media and mass printings, efforts to disseminate manners of reading depended on repetition to succeed. Only when manners of reading, and information, sentiments or critical judgments, were repeated by writer after writer in innumerable books, papers, periodicals and schoolrooms, and in innumerable conversations around the country and across the English-speaking world, until they came to seem commonplace truths, did such efforts take practical effect. Eighteenth-century writers who decanted ideas or information from one text to another and repeated what others had said, were belittled during the last third of the century when "originality" began to mean inventing something new instead of going back to an origin in the past. But unoriginal decanting writers, and their living conversational echoes, played an irreplaceable disseminating and consensus-building role. Indeed, repeating as truth the idea that it was more admirable to write something entirely new, than to imitate what had been written in the past, was precisely how "originality" came to be prized by all polite and right-thinking people.

Consequently, what matters most for the communication and dissemination of manners of reading is what was repeated. Repetition did not preclude changes – there were significant changes, for instance, with changes in target readerships, when some grammars were simplified for young children or when spellers were altered in the new republic during the century's last decades. But looking at what was repeated and retained through and despite changes can prove more illuminating where reading practices are concerned than following a developmental model. As Robert Hume has shown, "evolutionary history" has problems of its own.[81] The chapters below therefore foreground what was retained and repeated. They also approach eighteenth-century manners of reading through those who instructed and wrote for the unlearned, rather than exclusively through the pronouncements of now canonical authors such as Robert Lowth, Alexander Pope, Lord Kames or Edmund Burke. Those who instructed the unlearned repeated. Better yet, they had to explain things that others thought so obvious as not to be worth mentioning, and thereby reveal a great deal that we no longer know. This also permits us to see the great canonical figures nestled among them, and the now familiar positions they took, in an unfamiliar light.

Among the things that repeated throughout the century were the composition and structure of the material books and printed matter which carried fundamentals of reading to the public. This is most obvious in instructional books (spellers, primers, copybooks, grammars, dictionaries, encyclopedias) and in periodicals. The kinds of miscellaneous fragments of which they were composed remained more or less constant throughout the period. Some of the methods in different manners of reading, as well as many key reading habits, were inculcated and transmitted silently through the lay-out and structuring of printed pages. Consistency in the composition and structuring of books and periodicals registered areas of fundamental agreement, and assumptions that debating authors shared. It also helped to contain ongoing debates, whether ideological or subject-related, and the differences in specific content they entailed. Adrian Johns disputed Roger Chartier's assertion that "the very structure of books was governed by the ways that book publishers thought their clientele read," by arguing that we are in danger of assuming that our modern responses to a book or printed page "accurately reproduce" those of contemporary readers.[82] Working from contemporary explanations in books and periodicals that were engaged in showing the unlearned how to read and use them helps to obviate this sensible objection.

Where "arts" and empirical practices are concerned, "knowing is seeing," as Locke said:[83] what "terms of art" actually alluded to in readerly practices does not necessarily leap to the intelligence of those of us who have not been directly exposed to the practices in question. Without "seeing" for oneself, it is easy to assume that eighteenth-century manners of reading were more like ours than they were, or that their objectives were much the same, especially under the influence of modern disciplinary concerns; in the wake of histories of criticism which mash together two or three manners of reading that were still distinct; or in light of modern divisions of the subject into rubrics such as literacy, grammar, rhetoric, composition, hermeneutics, theory, criticism, poetics and reader-reception. The following chapters therefore describe recommended reading practices in some detail. They work step-by-step through the concrete, practical methods of decoding writing and texts that were presented to the wider public, and through contemporaries' accounts of the protocols, goals and reading philosophies associated with them. Though I have learned from outstanding modern scholarship in multiple fields, and am profoundly grateful for it, the chapters use eighteenth-century "terms of art" and follow eighteenth-century "divisions" of the subject, rather than modern ones; and when the two disagree, they report contemporary explanations, criticisms and perceptions, rather than modern ones. Except at the beginning of Chapter 1, they follow the same policy with regard to socio-historical contexts, privileging those supplied by contemporaries, whose often unexpected characterizations of contemporary readerships, and of the impact of particular manners of reading, describe what *they* thought was going on. I have, however, used contemporary terms to cobble together names, such as "guides to study," "guides to taste," and "conversation-pieces," for "how-to-read" texts, which appeared in a variety of genres and at diverse levels of culture, and remain nameless as a result.

I am painfully conscious of how much it has been necessary to leave out to keep this book within bounds, while permitting diverse manners of reading to be viewed side by side. As chapters threatened to turn into volumes, issues, sources and debates had to be cut out; and in sections where close analysis is necessary, a few exceptionally influential texts had to stand in for the rest. It proved impossible to do as much as I intended with the ways in which early Americans, the Scots, the Irish, the Welsh, women and individual readers appropriated or altered manners of reading. Because the influence of Latin and the Ancients on English grammar and belletristic literature is well understood, they appear here only as they were invoked by miscellanists in Chapter 4 and by secret writers in Chapter 5. The religion appearing here generally takes the characteristically uncontroversial, apparently unproblematic, non-denominational forms described by Ian Green. Affect appears in the same way: guides assumed that readers needed to understand how rhetoric and literature work on the passions in order to become what we now call "resistant readers," but did not need to be taught what love, grief, anger or sympathy look and feel like, or where to locate them in their psyches, in order to produce them, for instance when reading aloud.

Among lacunae, it is important to stress that the six manners of reading delineated here were not the only options available to eighteenth-century readers. There were other, spiritual, religiously sectarian and poetic manners of reading, some of which we know more about than others. There were also those – for instance, from the various Celtic fringes or German communities of Pennsylvania – who did not share Lowland Scots' enthusiasm for the English language and Anglophone manners of reading, and prized their own traditions more. In all respects, this is very much a first pass in an area where there is a superabundance of primary material. It leaves a great deal to be done by others better qualified than myself.

The manners of reading encompassed here appear in successive chapters as unexpectedly coherent systems, each composed of a variety of practices or techniques. Despite some overlaps and points of connection, they are distinct, and sometimes contradictory. Some manners of reading participated in government efforts to "forge a nation" of "Britons" from the variety of dispersed and largely isolated settlements in England, Scotland and Ireland, which in 1707 still spoke a variety of mutually incomprehensible dialects, and elicited only local identities and loyalties in all but the elite.[84] Printers, grammarians, belletristic critics and elocutionists in Britain – and after Independence, in America – sought to create, disseminate and impose a single, undisputed and mutually intelligible, set of norms for spelling, grammar, pronunciation, reading, writing, conduct and taste. Some tried to impose unity of opinion, morality and/or religion as well. But contrary to those who now conceive of eighteenth-century grammar, criticism or elocution in exclusively prescriptive or regulatory Foucaldian terms, the evidence suggests that, in the event, grammarians and belletristic critics fell victim to the same multiplicity of texts, latitude of interpretations, and diversity of judgments that they sought to master or preclude. What one contemporary said of critics held for grammarians and other scholars too: they "often differ so very materially from one another, that although we can pretty nearly guess some one may be right, yet it is beyond all conjecture to find out who that one is."[85]

Above all, the plurality of possible manners of reading – each encompassing a variety of techniques, and several wittingly or unwittingly fostering wide diversity in interpretations, judgments and uses of what one read – made it difficult for any single manner of reading to prevail. Like Standard English, standard reading practices and standard moral-aesthetic literary criticism had to wait for the Victorians. During this period, as we will have occasion to see again and again in different domains, perfectly brilliant systematic efforts to order, "methodize," and regularize manners of reading struggled against what their framers perceived to be the real diversity, irregularity and disorder of English alphabets; of the English language; of the reading, tastes, morals, and convictions of Anglophone people; and of manners of reading themselves.

NOTES

1 Raven, "Book Trades": 1; St. Clair, *Reading Nation*.
2 For useful bibliographies, Michael, *Teaching of English*; Heal, *English Writing Masters*; Alston, *Bibliography of the English Language*.
3 Chartier, "Text, Printing, Readings": 166, 174.
4 For a survey of the field, Bannet, "History of Reading."
5 Brewer, "Reconstructing the Reader": 227; Towsey, *Reading the Scottish Enlightenment*: 231.

6 Allan, *Commonplace Books*; Money, "Teaching in the Marketplace"; Colclough, *Consuming Texts*: 69 ff.

7 Stallybrass, "Books and Scrolls": 47.

8 Shaftesbury, *Characteristics*: 339.

9 Fergus, *Provincial Readers*; Tadmor, "In the Even My Wife Read to Me"; Larpent in Pearson, *Women's Reading*: 7 ff.

10 Philip Skelton, *Candid Reader* (London, 1744): 2.

11 Barry, "Literacy and Literature in Popular Culture."

12 Wellek, *History of Modern Criticism*: 1: 19, 12, 14.

13 For instance: Colie, *Resources of Kind*; Lewalski (ed.), *Renaissance Genres*; Duff, *Romanticism and the Use of Genre*; Regier, *Fracture and Fragmentation*; Rawes (ed.) *Romanticism and Form*; Levinson, *The Romantic Fragment Poem*; Harries, *The Unfinished Manner*; Budor and Geertz, *Le Texte Hybride*; Cope, *In and After the Beginning*; Jung, *The Fragmentary Poetic*; Jung (ed.), *Experiments in Genre*; Crane, *Framing Authority*; Moss, *Printed Commonplace Books*; Benedict, *Making the Modern Reader*; Price, *Anthology and the Rise of the Novel*; Cohen, "History and Genre"; Fowler, *Kinds of Literature*.

14 Brown, *Pilgrim*; Garrett, *Episodic Poetics*.

15 Heath, *Unity in Greek Poetics*: 89.

16 Thomas Tryon, *The Merchant, Citizen and Country-man's Instructor* (London, 1701): 58; Erasmus Saunders, *A Domestick Charge or The Duty of Household Governours* (Oxford, 1701): 142.

17 John Brightland, *Reasons for an English Education* (London, 1711): 2, note 2.

18 Fox, *Oral and Literate Culture*: 22.

19 Thomas Watts, *An Essay on the Proper Method of Forming a Man of Business* (London, 1716): 16.

20 Malachy Postlethwayt, *Universal Dictionary of Trade and Commerce* (London, 1755): II: 221 ff.

21 Sir William Dawes, *The Excellency of the Charity of Charity Schools* (London, 1713): 3; Edward Nicholson, *A Method of Charity-Schools Recommended* (Dublin, 1712): 26. For the contrary view, John Trenchard, *Cato's Letters*, 4 vols. (London, 1723): 4: 243 ff.

22 Lewis Maidwell, *An Essay upon the Necessity and Excellence of Education* (London,1705): 4.

23 Richardson, *Literature, Education*: 119.

24 Grenby, *Child Reader*: 49, 50. Also, St. Clair, *Reading Nation*.

25 John Newbery, *An Easy Introduction to the English Language, or a Compendious Grammar...* (London, 1745): i.

26 For instance, Valenza, *Intellectual Disciplines*; Klancher, *Transfiguring the Arts and Sciences*.

27 Fox, *Oral and Literate Culture*: 20.

28 Isaac Watts, *The Improvement of the Mind* (2nd edn., London, 1743): 227, 231, 326.

29 Blackwall, *An Introduction to the Classics* (London, 1737): Preface.

30 Hugh Blair, *Lectures on Rhetoric and Belles Lettres*, 2 vols. (London, 1783): I: 29, 5, 8; II: 240, 234.

31 Langford, "Politeness": 313, 320.
32 Samuel Johnson, *Lives of the Most Eminent English Poets*, 4 vols. (London, 1779): 2: 16; Colley, *Britons*: 17.
33 Eden, *Hermeneutics*.
34 Blair, *Lectures*: 6–7.
35 Thomas Hearne, *Ductor Historicus* (2nd edn., London: 1704): 119.
36 Ross, *English Literary Canon*: 15, 5.
37 Griffin, "Rise of the Professional Author": 142.
38 Alexander Pope, *The Rape of the Lock* (London, 1718): 8.
39 Quoted in Kenshur, *Open Form*: 40–1.
40 Sharpe, *Reading Revolutions*.
41 Kenshur, *Open Form*: 120.
42 Sharpe and Zwicker, *Reading, Society and Politics*: 4.
43 For these metaphors in Locke, see Walker, *Locke, Literary Criticism and Philosophy*.
44 Schoenfelds, "Reading Bodies," in Sharpe and Zwicker, *Reading, Society and Politics*; Morrissey, *Constitution of Literature*; Gardiner, *Regulating Readers*.
45 Sir Francis Bacon, (1625) *Essays, moral, economical and political* (London, 1798): 232.
46 Bantock, *Educational Theory*: 1: 193–7; Mangel, *History of Reading*: 171–3; Griffiths, *Religious Reading*; Jager, *Book of the Heart*: Chap. 1.
47 Kroll, *Material Word*.
48 Noggle, *Temporality of Taste*: 3–4.
49 *The Critical Review* 18 (1764): 314.
50 Montesquieu highlighted the relation of systems of government to systems of morality in his widely influential *The Spirit of Laws* (tr. London, 1750).
51 Mingay, *English Landed Society*.
52 Greene, *Creating the British Atlantic*.
53 [James Ralph] *The Case of Authors by Profession or Trade Stated* (London, 1758): 60. Also Raven, *The Business of Books*; Feather, *The Provincial Book Trade*.
54 Ralph, *Case of Authors*: 21.
55 O'Brien, "The History Market," in Rivers, *Books and Their Readers*: 111, 108.
56 Briggs et al., *Popular Children's Literature*: 24.
57 Walsh, "Literary Scholarship and the Life of Editing," in Rivers, *Books and Their Readers*: 205. Also Raven, *Judging New Wealth*; and Raven, *Business of Books*.
58 Hammond, *Professional Imaginative Writing*: 11. Also Justice, *Manufacturers of Literature*; and Schellenberg, *Professionalization of Women Writers*.
59 William Massey, *The Origin and Progress of Letters* (London, 1763): Part II: 83.
60 Michael, *English Grammatical Categories*: 3; "Dictionary" Johnson was once a teacher in Litchfield.
61 Nichols, *Anecdotes Biographical and Literary of the Late William Bowyer, Printer* (London, 1778); Ralph, *Case*: 20.
62 Green, *Humanism and Protestantism*: 88.
63 Quoted in Sher, *Church and University*: 157, 158.
64 For their religious publications, Green, *Print and Protestantism*.

65 John Clarke, *An Essay Upon Study* (London, 1731): 41–2.

66 Axtell, *School upon a Hill*: 207.

67 Oliver Goldsmith, *Enquiry into the Present State of Polite Learning* (2nd edn. revised, London, 1774): 109.

68 *The Connoisseur* 4 (1756): 92.

69 Rogers, *Grub Street*: 286.

70 Griffin, *Authorship in the Long Eighteenth Century*: Chap. 9.

71 Chard, "Bookseller to Publisher": 152; for America, Pasley, *Tyranny of Printers*.

72 Grundy, "Women and Print": 146–60.

73 McDowell, *Women of Grub Street*: 17–18.

74 Froide, *Never Married*; Sanderson, *Women and Work*; Wulf, *Not All Wives*.

75 Turner, *Living by the Pen*; Copeland, *Women Writing about Money*; Batchelor, *Women's Work*.

76 Francis Brokesby, *Of Education with Respect to Grammar Schools and the Universities* (London, 1701): 191, 189, 186–7.

77 Bushman, *Refinement of America*; Shields, *Civil Tongues*.

78 Tennenhouse, *Importance of Feeling English*.

79 McGill, *Culture of Reprinting*: 7.

80 For the American trade see esp. Amory and Hall (eds.), *The Colonial Book in the Atlantic World*; Gross and Kelley (eds.), *An Extensive Republic*; Remer, *Printers and Men of Capital*; Sher, *Enlightenment and the Book*; Loughran, *Republic in Print*; and Durey, *Transatlantic Radicals*.

81 David Hume, "Construction and Legitimation in Literary History."

82 Chartier, *Order of Books*: 13; John, *Nature of the Book*: 46.

83 John Locke, "The Conduct of the Understanding," in *Posthumous Works* (London, 1706): 77.

84 Colley, *Britons*.

85 *Walker's Hibernian Magazine* (August 1790); also Pearson, *Women's Reading*.

CHAPTER I

The ABCs of Reading

The difficulty for would-be readers began with the multitude of widely different "hands" or manuscript alphabets, old and new, that were being used in different domains of culture, and with the way print was replacing the old black letter or "English Gothic" typeface with a *copia* of different roman and italic fonts, often on the same page. These difficulties were compounded by the fact that printed English did not resemble the local and regional dialects that most people spoke. "Standard English" and "Received Pronunciation" came after printers' English, not before, and by several hundred years. We need a sense of these difficulties, and of the variously limited and extended literacies they produced, to see how ABCs, spellers, grammars and dictionaries were designed to enable readers to read and comprehend what appeared in print. This chapter therefore begins with these issues. It goes on to describe the methods these instructional books gave readers for ordering and managing the plurality of alphabets and for overcoming the many obstacles to reading and comprehension generated by printed writing. Locke's assumption in *Essay Concerning Human Understanding* that reasoning consists of "perceiv[ing] the connection and agreement or disagreement and repugnancy of ideas" found expression, and perhaps its origin, here.[1] The reading strategies that spellers and grammars developed assumed that characters and words are analogical: resembling each other in some ways, differing in others, and capable of purely instrumental connections where some resemblance pertains.

Analogy was important from the beginning because during the eighteenth century, one did not learn "the alphabet." One learned to read one's letters in two or more of the many alphabets in use (see Figure 1.1). The number of script alphabets in use varies from ten to seventeen, depending on which writing-master one consults. In 1726, Defoe conveyed the bewildering profusion thus:

> In the present in England we divide our Manner of writing into several Hands...such as Text-Hand, Court-Hand, Italian-Hand, Round-Hand, running Hand, and the like: Mixt with Text-Italian-Hand, and Lawyers

Figure 1.1 George Bickham, *Alphabets in all the Hands Now Practis'd in Great Britain, with Sentences in Prose and Verse*, London, 1747. By Permission of the British Library.

Hand; add the Ingrossing Hand, which is indeed but a kind of Text, and that, in general, is a kind of Gothick, which had its Original from the German or High Dutch way of writing, who, to this Day, print all their Books in that Character.[2]

The ability to read script alphabets impacted people's ability to negotiate the society as much or more than the ability to read print-fonts, because the everyday written communication and record-keeping of life – administrative, diplomatic, military, institutional, commercial, legal, social, familial and personal – took handwritten form. In print culture, script alphabets could only be learned from copybooks; and writing was learned after reading, often in separate schools, as well as from separate books.

Notwithstanding the plurality of print-fonts, hornbooks, ABCs, spellers, primers and grammars presented three basic print alphabets: roman, italic and usually, black letter (Gothic). Because eighteenth-century printers favored roman and italic for everyday purposes, we mistakenly consider black letter defunct or as lingering on for a decade or two only in chapbooks designed for the vulgar and uneducated. But British proclamations and Acts of Parliament ceased to be printed in black letter only in 1794; and "gothic hands lived on in English and other courts of law until the end of the nineteenth century."[3] As one contemporary dictionary stressed, Gothic alphabets were still required for reading "our ancient Statutes, Charters, Writs, Old Records, and Processes at Law."[4] In a culture, moreover, where books were handed down in families and old libraries were sold at auction, black letter family Bibles, black letter scholarly books with annotations in roman fonts, and black letter catechisms did not disappear because new exemplars were printed in roman and italic – owner signatures in surviving books demonstrate that volumes of all kinds often remained in use for a century or more after their publication date.

Understanding printed writing also presented difficulties deriving from the fact that even at the end of the eighteenth century, people in neighboring counties often had difficulty in understanding one another's speech. William Stukeley, who lived alternately in Lincolnshire and London, said of Newcastle at mid-century, that "as one walks the streets, one can scarce understand the common person, but is apt to fancy oneself in a foreign country."[5] Others made similar remarks about other parts of England, Scotland and Wales throughout the period, and after Independence, about American communities originating from different parts of Britain, which had retained their original British pronunciation in all its native purity. Like scribes before them, printers had addressed this problem by fixing English orthography to ensure that the word-image remained the same from printed text to printed text, regardless of how the word was actually pronounced in different ranks and different regions of the English-speaking world.[6] This permitted printed writing to function like Chinese ideograms, which Joseph Priestley praised for making communication possible between regions speaking different Chinese dialects because ideograms could be pronounced differently in different speech communities while remaining legible to all. In principle, everyone would be able to read the same printed words regardless of how they pronounced them. Printers stood firm against contemporary schemes for changing characters and spellings to more accurately reflect spoken English: in time, fixed habitual spellings in print would discredit those who continued to spell words phonetically in handwritten texts and promote standardization. Orthography would help create a united kingdom by giving everyone at least the written language in common. After Independence, Americans took the same line, only ensuring that American spellings distinguished the United States from Britain.

But as contemporaries immediately understood, fixing spellings meant that there were "two very different Languages in common Use; one that is spoke...and another which is writ and printed."[7] Smollett illustrates this discrepancy, as late as 1771, in his representation of Tabitha Bramble and her maid, who wrote as they spoke: "The gardnir and the hind [hound] may lie below in the landry, to partake the house."[8] Since printed spellings did not reflect pronunciation, a reader could sound out a printed word without recognizing it. The syllabic spellings and syntax of printed writing – to say nothing of its long periodic sentences, its rhetorically informed figures and tropes, and the uses it made of the massive influx of foreign words and new "terms of art"– made reading printed writing seem like reading a foreign language. Except in the scriptoria that printers were displacing, even "the marks commonly found in books" were not yet commonly found in the manuscripts of professional writers, much less in handwritten letters. Efforts were made in the course of the century to mitigate these difficulties, for instance by simplifying sentences to make them more "perspicuous" to readers or by trying to promote a single uniform pronunciation; but the difficulties did not disappear. That is why, together with their other functions, English spellers, grammars and dictionaries were designed "for all those that desire to understand what they read," as well as to "assist Persons of Common Sense and no Learning to understand the best English Authors."[9]

For linguists and grammarians, the difficulty derived from language's loss of moorings in the real world. In the wake of Bacon and Comenius, seventeenth-century linguists had endeavored to show that characters and words represented things. Some eighteenth-century primers and spellers retained the fruits of these labors by presenting each letter of the alphabet as the first letter of the common name for some everyday object and/

or memorable event, and by juxtaposing it, emblem-like, with a picture of that object or event. As *The New England Primer* famously had it: A is for Apple–and not just any apple, for "In Adam's Fall/We sinned All." The accompanying picture was of a large apple on a small tree, with a naked, and curiously sexless, human figure standing beside it. But comparison of Latin alphabets with Egyptian hieroglyphics, Asian ideographs and Hebrew script showed eighteenth-century linguists that characters representing sounds made by the human voice bore no necessary resemblance to things. If some characters had once resembled things – the letter A descending from the graphic representation of an ox, for instance – the simplification and changing stylizations of the character over the centuries had long since obscured or broken the link. Invention of the telescope and microscope further undermined seventeenth-century linguists' efforts to attach characters and words to things by revealing, quite shockingly, that the world as humans saw it was a function of the limited optics of the human eye rather than a faithful reflection of things as they really were. If things appeared quite different when regarded through the new optical instruments, if the unaided human eye only saw those dimensions and qualities of things which it was capable of perceiving, then, as Addison put it, rather than seeing reality as it really is, "we are everywhere entertained with pleasing shows and apparitions" and only "discover imaginary glories in the Heavens, and in the earth."[10] Instead of corresponding to things, words corresponded to the appearance of things as human senses perceived them.

This problem was compounded by the troubling realization that – unlike the reassuring permanence of that international *lingua franca* of the learned, Latin – the English language was in flux. Philip Allwood was repeating a century's worth of commonplaces when he observed in 1800 that "there is scarcely anything in the whole compass of human acquisitions, more variable than [language]. The same language, in the same country, at different times, scarcely appears the same, even when there are the means of transmitting it literally by writing…Let anyone compare, if he pleases, the English of Caxton with that of Johnson or Melmoth, or that of Chaucer with that of Pope; and he will immediately perceive the alterations which this language has undergone, (independently of the introduction of foreign words into it) even when we have had opportunities of writing it."[11] As anyone realized who looked back at old documents or tried to read Spenser or Shakespeare, English had changed enormously even in a hundred years, creating barriers to understanding that detached Anglophone readers from the texts and events of their past.

Once characters and words had become detached from things as they really were or had been; once the English language itself was perceived to be in flux; and while the material dimensions of the language – its graphic images, the sounds they produced – remained various, variable and unstable across different domains of culture and different parts of the English-speaking world; grammarians and philosophers had little choice but to follow Locke in attaching words' semantic content (meaning) to what seemed marginally more constant: ideas in the mind.[12] Ideas were discontinuous and in flux in any particular mind; and there was the question of how far the ideas in different minds resembled one another. But attaching words to the mind's impressions and thought processes at least offered a starting point for organizing, ordering, and stabilizing the rest. Eighteenth-century linguists, philosophers and pedagogues therefore treated "language as thought," and produced "grammar[s] of thought expressed in the logic of linguistic functions," as Murray Cohen observed."[13] Like King Canute trying to hold back the sea, they sought to stem the chaos of geographical and social variability and of historical flux by subjecting reading, speaking, and writing to thought and rule.

The question, of course, is how many readers they were actually addressing. Contemporaries thought it was a lot. By the beginning of the eighteenth century, the perception was widespread that: "The English are so much given to Literature, that all Sorts are generally the most knowing People in the World. Men and Women, Children and Servants cannot only read, but write Letters, to the great Increase of Commerce."[14] Modern scholars agree that significant increases in writing as well as reading literacy occurred during this period throughout the Atlantic world. But numerical guestimates of the extent of literacy vary widely, especially now that the ability to sign one's name on a will or marriage register is no longer regarded as an accurate measure of how widespread reading ability was. Since reading was learned separately from writing, and reading without writing leaves no traces, we assume that many more people could read than write. But writing leaves no traces either unless it happens to be preserved in family papers, public records offices, or in what contemporaries considered the more "durable" form of print. And this was an era when people recycled manuscript and printed pages as tapers, pie cases and toilet paper, and burned their private papers to prevent them from being read. Shoemaker's son James Lackington learned his letters from his mother, forgot them, and relearned them as a journeyman shoemaker in the north of England from his master's son. We would not know this had he not published as a successful second-hand bookseller later in life. More remarkable than his rise to wealth and prominence through reading, is that Lackington found nothing remarkable about families of shoemakers being able to read, and ensuring their sons could too.

As we will see in the first section below, thinking in terms of variously limited and extended literacies may prove more illuminating than numerical estimates and assumptions about class that treat reading as one homogeneous thing. This will also introduce the cultural uses to which various scripts and fonts were put, before proceeding to considering how they were "methodized" in instructional books.

Limited and Extended Literacies

The plurality of alphabets and printers' focus on printed writing led Keith Thomas to speculate in 1986, that someone who could read print might not have been able to decipher a handwritten document, and someone who could read one script alphabet might not have been able to read others.[15] Brian Street concluded that, instead of asking whether people were literate or not, we should think in terms of a spectrum of reading and writing competencies, and of readers as having variously limited literacies.[16] Unfortunately, this line of inquiry has not been pursued for our period. But a preliminary picture of who could read what can be pieced together from a combination of contemporary evidence and modern research.

It seems clear that we can no longer assume that the same correlation obtained in the eighteenth century as in the nineteenth or twentieth between literacy and age or class. Illiteracy and limited literacies cannot yet be attributed, blanket-fashion, either to children or to "the common people."

The way both instructional and "children's" books defined their readerships suggests that limited literacy – in the sense of inadequate reading and comprehension skills and/or poor understanding of how language worked – was to be found in all ages, genders and ranks. John Brightland was fairly typical of reading masters, writing masters and grammarians throughout the century in making it clear in his preface that his grammar was designed for "Children, Women and the Ignorant of both Sexes" as well as for "ignorant Teachers." There were children and ignorant adults of both sexes at all ranks, including among ladies and gentlemen, who are more tactfully mentioned on the title page. At century's end – when mothers were dignified as pedagogues, and increasing numbers of single ladies had opened girls' schools – female schoolteacher-grammarians continued to address their grammars simultaneously to children, to mothers "to facilitate the work of teaching to those who may not have much attended to the subject themselves," and to "ladies who are engaged in tuition."[17] Printer John Newbery, who invented "children's literature" at mid-century and wrote much of it himself, designated his "little books for children six feet tall" for good reason. In a recent study, M. O. Grenby found not only that while "many deemed books notionally for children as perfectly suitable for continued use in adulthood," children as young as nine or ten were reading what we consider adult books (including sermons, tracts and adult novels). Chapbooks in particular, with their "small format, often copious illustrations, and simple and engaging texts," were bought and read by adults and children at all ranks well into the nineteenth century, as William St. Clair confirms.[18] Benjamin Franklin did not study Brightland's *Grammar* until he was a working apprentice; and James Lackington learned to read as a journeyman shoemaker. Before the institution of compulsory universal schooling advanced (almost) everyone lockstep through "age-appropriate" levels of education, reading skills were no more ineluctably tied to age than they were to rank.

Because writing, like printing, was considered an artisanal craft, writing masters – who could read and write all the different scripts, who designed typefaces for printers, and who learned their craft by apprenticeship – almost invariably issued from the common people, just as printers did. These "common people" were among the most literate in the land. As we saw, the same held for reading and elementary English-school masters – "few of them ever claim the title of *Gent.*"[19] *The Guardian* observed that even "men of letters" were "rarely Gentlemen" – complaining at the same time that, having been too "idle" to take advantage of their schooling, "those of the first quality" were "unlettered coxcombs" who showed their contempt for letters by "pay[ing] their tutors but little above half so much as they do their footmen."[20] Copyists and clerks in attorneys' offices, compting houses and government departments were not "gentlemen" either. One might say that those who traded on reading and writing possessed more extended literacy than most, even when they issued from, or remained within, the lower ranks.

Modern scholarship confirms contemporary perceptions that "all Sorts" could now read and use books. Margaret Spufford discovered that by the end of the seventeenth century, children of the poor in Cambridgeshire, Leicestershire and Kent were regularly being taught to read by their mothers or by the laborers' and artisans' wives who acted as village school-dames, and that many poor children had acquired the skill by the age of five or six. Susan Whyman found that in rural Yorkshire at the turn of the eighteenth century, the lowliest people (small farmers, cottagers, gardeners) were cognizant of the importance of literacy, and not only took great pains to acquire it for themselves and their children, but used it to advance themselves and their families to wealth and local prominence. Deborah Simonton calculated that in Staffordshire and Essex, "throughout the century and for both boys and girls, those who attended charity schools were attending long enough to acquire an ability to read and to have reinforced that skill." Jan Fergus found that provincial servants and shopkeepers' wives were reading well enough by the 1770s to borrow reviews, books of self-improvement and novels from the cheap lending-libraries in booksellers' shops.[21] In Scotland and in Puritan New England – where reading instruction was mandated by law in all settlements from the early seventeenth-century – scholars have long agreed that reading literacy was consistently high even in the lower orders. But recent work has shown that missionary schools also brought reading literacy to American Indians and slaves; and that some slaves and free blacks were able to circumvent prohibitions against learning to write well enough to forge their own travel passes.[22]

It also seems clear that while limited literacy was the norm for the majority of readers, it took different forms.

The multiplicity of print-fonts, alphabets and scripts meant that the legibility of signs might also sometimes teeter on the brink of illegibility for the learned. In November 1719, for instance, an SPCK correspondent complained that the nonpareil font in which cheap bibles were printed "needs to be decipher'd even to some of the Learned, except Printers or Scholars that have been conversant with the press."[23] When William Massey, a Hebrew as well as classical scholar, complained that "there are still wanting good engraved specimens of the Spanish and German Jews' rabbinical characters, in which the Targums or interpretations of the old Hebrew Scriptures are usually written,"[24] he too was articulating this difficulty: he and other scholars could now read the Hebrew characters of the Hebrew Bible with comparative ease, but the differently shaped characters in which the rabbinical commentaries had been written, not so much. In 1759, historian William Robertson informed novelist and translator Charlotte Lennox that Lord Royston, who had "a very large Collection of papers" from Elizabeth's reign, had had "all of them transcribed from the originals in a fair modern hand, which is a circumstance of no small advantage."[25] The point here is less that this was helpful to a mere woman, than that Royston thought that Elizabethan Gothic scripts would be difficult for the usual, learned male users of his Collection. Exploiting this as

a commercial opportunity, printers had begun in the late seventeenth century to make State papers, old letters and government documents accessible in modern print alphabets.[26]

Script alphabets produced other limited literacies. We know that otherwise competent readers among "the better sort" found it difficult or
impossible to decipher the hands of government departments and the legal
hands of the various English law courts, because this induced Parliament
in 1731 to reduce the number of obscure legal and administrative scripts.[27]
Exchequer hand, Pipe Office hand, set and running Chancery hands,
engrossing secretary hand and square text hand, court and running court
hand, were antiquated Gothic scripts, often elaborately embellished, which
a contemporary described as "ambiguous" because their embellishments
"tend to cause one Letter to be mistaken for another."[28] (See Figure 1.2.)
According to one modern scholar, obscure legal and administrative scripts
were designed to make forgery hard or impossible. But if it took a highly
trained clerical hand to write them, it also took a highly trained eye to read
them, with the result that they also played other real and symbolic social
roles. Like the "spectacular politics" of monarchs who awed their subjects
with displays of their magnificence, they impressed the viewer with the
majesty and arcane mysteries of government and law; and like Parliament's
closed-door policy on reporting its debates, they kept people at a salutary
distance from the sinews of the State.[29]

It is interesting, therefore, to find Jennifer Monaghan noting that
(like English Commonwealth-men during the Interregnum who
demanded that their records be "written in an ordinary, usual and
legible hand and character") colonists in New England kept their
town records in the plainer and more basic "round hand," that she
says was widely used in America for domestic and business purposes.
When Americans demanded that their local schoolmasters teach, and
that their local public record-keepers be able to write, "a legible hand,"
they meant not only that the writing must be neat and well formed,
but that it must be done in a script that ordinary readers could read.[30]
However, writing masters in American port cities taught other hands
besides round hand, to equip young men who expected to engage in
transatlantic communication with the range of alphabets they might
require, as well as to supply the burgeoning colonial elite with hands
that would distinguish them from more common folk. Some scholars
argue that colonial elites also sought to withhold literacy from slaves,
non-whites and poor whites, in order to attach it to social status and to
"the right to rule" in America.[31]

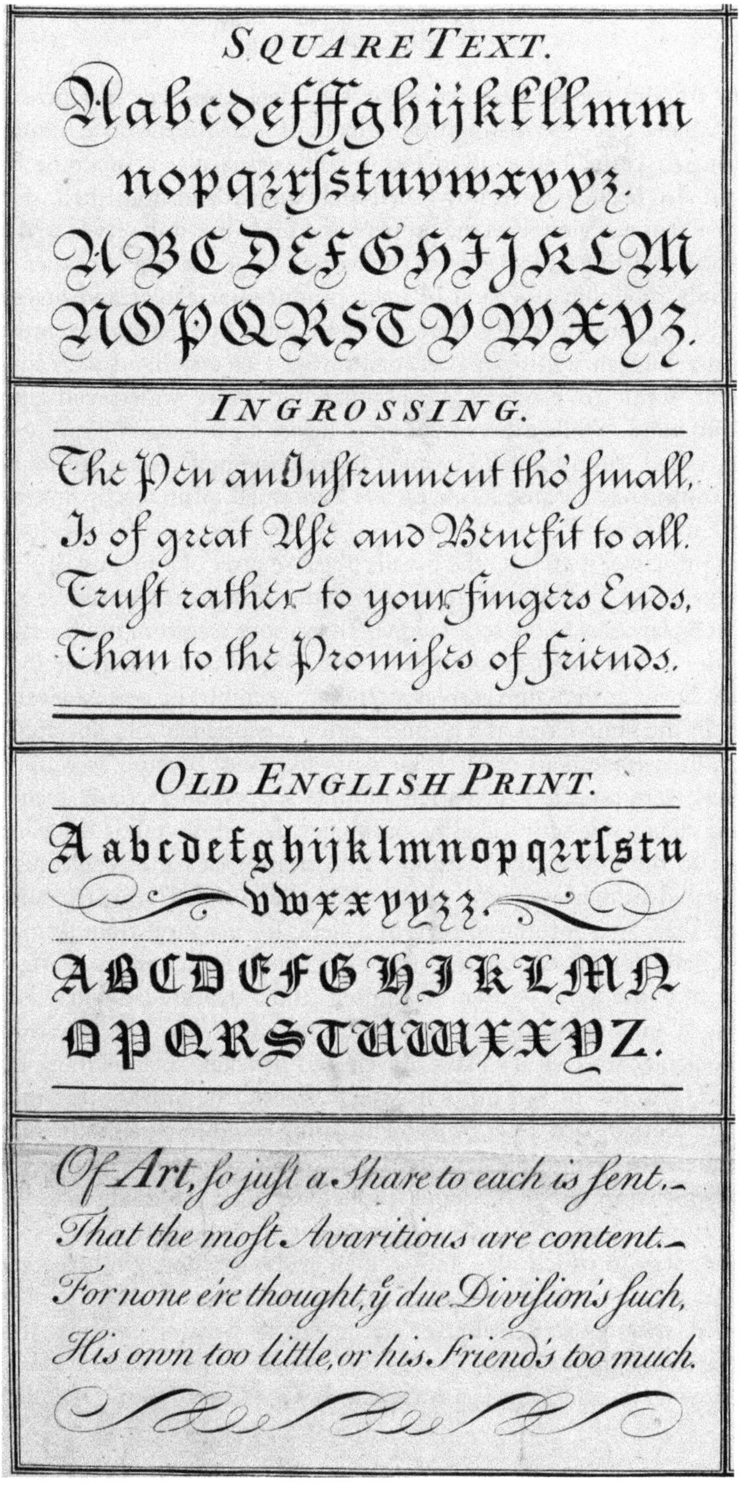
SQUARE TEXT.

Aabcdefffghijkkllmm
nopqrrſstuvwxyyz.
ABCDEFGHIJKLM
NOPQRSTVWXYZ.

INGROSSING.

The Pen an Inſtrument tho' ſmall,
Is of great Uſe and Benefit to all.
Truſt rather to your Fingers Ends,
Than to the Promiſes of Friends.

OLD ENGLISH PRINT.

Aabcdefghijklmnopqrrſstu
vwxxyyzz.
ABCDEFGHIJKLMN
OPQRSTUWXXYZ.

Of Art, ſo juſt a Share to each is ſent,
That the moſt Avaritious are content.
For none e're thought, ye due Diviſion's ſuch,
His own too little, or his Friend's too much.

Figure 1.2 Detail from Bickham, *Alphabets in all the Hands…*

In Britain, scripts were classed and gendered too. For instance, italic or "Italian," once the distinguishing mark of male Renaissance humanists writing in Latin, had evolved into a bold, vernacular aristocratic hand. It had also been adapted into a delicately looped and flourished, sloping cursive that was viewed as the proper hand for ladies, and served to distinguish the writing of ladies from the writing of gentlemen. Another more carefully disciplined version of italic produced a regular and gracefully slanted copperplate, called secretary hand. John Ayres, a late seventeenth-century English writing-master, had mixed secretary hand with English Gothic script to produce the popular and more widespread upright "round hand," while others went on to devise a particularly useful variant of it, called "running hand," which became the preferred script for trade and commerce, because its characters were small, plain, easily linked and quick to write.

In principle, therefore, the broad subject-matter of a manuscript, letter or document, as well as the rank and gender of its writer, would be apparent at a glance from the script alone. The various scripts in use functioned like dress to distinguish social ranks and spheres of activity: one did not ride a horse in the same garb as attend an assembly, or write a legal contract in the same script as a business letter; a gentleman did not dress like a mariner, tradesman or clerk, or write like one. Because accomplished writers were expected to master multiple scripts, an accomplished man could change his script like his dress, and decorously tailor the hand he chose to the subject and occasion. This meant that hands could disguise the real identity of writers as effectively as the so-called "impersonality" of print: there was nothing to prevent a clerk, for instance, from using running hand for his commercial employer's business letters, a gentleman's italic in a love letter written for himself, and a delicate lady's hand when acting as amanuensis for a woman who could not write. This is why many early eighteenth-century plays, novels and novellas, such as those of the early Haywood, turned on plots which showed the unwary that judging the authenticity of a letter by its handwriting could prove a costly mistake. The presence of multiple hands did mean, however, that recognizing what was being conveyed by the script a writer was using (or failing to use) once constituted a basic and obvious component of reading literacy.

One way in which men and women evidently coped with the variety of extant hands was by learning to read and use only those they really needed, making limited literacy the norm. In Britain, specialist writing books catered to the niche markets this created. Thomas Ollyffe's *Practical Penman* (1713) and John Jarman's *System of the Court Hands...with all the*

Abbreviations explained and applied (1723) modeled the scripts required by members of the legal profession and clerks in government employ; William Banson's *The Merchant's Penman* (1702) served bookkeepers and accountants; Joseph Champion's *The Young Penman's Daily Practice* (1760) offered commercial writers "a plain, easy and practical Running Hand without that soft and formal rounding too commonly taught." Mary Johnson's *Young Woman's Companion* (1753) directed maidservants to round-hand copybooks by informing them that: "Notwithstanding the Practice of various Hands may be of singular Service to young Gentlemen, who are brought up to various Employments...yet there is but one Hand absolutely requisite for young women to improve themselves in, and that is the *Round Hand*, which is much preferable to the *Italian*, though formerly, indeed, the latter was in high Repute among the Ladies."[32] At mid-century, in a series of copybooks targeting designated American colonies and designated English counties, George Bickham informed the provinces that "Round-hand is universally received and practiced by all Degrees of Men in all Employments, the Law excepted" – which suggests that men and women in the lower and middling ranks were solving practical problems of written communication by converging on one mutually intelligible script for everyday purposes, as printers were using roman and italic print alphabets for everyday print genres.[33] But as Mary Johnson indicates, "the practice of various hands" continued to be necessary for men's various employments. Bickham's own transatlantic best-seller, *The Universal Penman* (1741), therefore included multiple scripts besides round hand. Some decades later, writing master Joseph Champion was still explaining (with mystifying arithmetic) that of the seventeen extant hands then in use, only "six or seven" really had to be learned: two for trade, three for law, and eight for what he called "ornamental purposes" – the four round hands, the three print hands and German text hand. In 1782, Ambrose Searle likewise claimed that "the Hands or particular forms of Characters, useful and ornamental, now most used, are the Round Hand, Italian Hand, Old English Text, German text, Square Text, Engrossing Hands, Greek and Roman characters."[34] By then, however, they may have been exaggerating the number of hands still in daily use.

Bickham's observation about using one script that was "universally received and practiced" described the trend and eventual solution, as well as one cause of writing masters' ultimate demise as a specialist group. The solution to limited literacies arising from the multiplication of diverse hands and fonts was ultimately simplification and standardization: one comparatively plain, all-purpose hand would be taught and used in all domains of culture, and the variety of print-fonts would be tamed into comparatively minor design variations on a uniform roman typeface. This would remain more or less constant throughout printed matter, while the olio of other font options would be reserved for ornamental purposes. It was easier for people to learn, and quicker for them to read, one unembellished script or one clear and simple typeface than many diverse and elaborate ones. This solution was emerging, but the transition was not yet made. Throughout the century, while writing masters and print-makers devoted their efforts to devising new, more legible and expeditious styles of writing and "improved," more easily legible print-fonts, reading masters, writing masters and grammarians continued to teach the public to read their letters in different print or script alphabets, as well as to decode the many additional marks "commonly met with in books."

Reading Characters and Alphabets

While the learned speculated, historicized, narrativized and argued in their attempts to explain the proliferation of alphabets from the ancient Hebrews, Greeks and Romans down to their own day, ABCs, spellers and grammars silently juxtaposed diverse alphabets on the page. The hornbook had done so since the fifteenth century. This was a sheet of printed paper stuck to a board and covered with a transparent sheet of horn from which children in England and New England still learned their letters; it generally juxtaposed lower-case and upper-case characters in black letter and roman print alphabets, to present a total of 96 figures, with four differently shaped signs for each character ("A" does not resemble "a").[35] The *New England Primer* and other American primers contained tables of upper- and lower-case print characters in three alphabets – roman, italic and black letter – until well into the nineteenth century.[36] The mid-century Church of England primer offered roman and italic print alphabets one below the other on its first page before launching directly into the Catechism. Meanwhile, copybooks juxtaposed the variety of script hands in use. In 1712, for instance, Charles Snell's *Art of Writing* presented on successive pages complete upper- and lower-case alphabets in round hand, round text and small Italian hands, engrossing and secretary hands, square secretary text hand, German text hand, court hand, set Chancery hand and running Chancery hand, as well as in roman print hand, italic print hand and Gothic or black letter. Joseph Champion calculated that learning the 52 letters in each of the seventeen English alphabets extant in 1770 meant mastering "upwards of 884 distinct Characters."[37]

Silently juxtaposing alphabets on the page provided an excellent method for ordering and managing such profusion. Juxtaposed alphabets demonstrated that a variety of different arbitrary signs could express more or less the same sound, and that these might be substituted for one another, as occasion demanded, in the same or different texts. Operating like a glossary or dictionary of letter forms, juxtaposed alphabets offered readers a convenient key to alphabetical substitutions. Some books made this clear by presenting tables structured like conversion charts: printers printed a series of "a"s in different alphabets on the same line of the same page, with each subsequent letter treated the same way beneath it. The Church of England primer did the same by printing upper and lower-case characters and print ligatures in roman and italic print alphabets symmetrically below each other on its first page: besides providing letters from which a beginner could be taught their sounds, this permitted those who could comfortably read roman print characters to refer back when they got stuck on a word in italic in the text.[38] Readers could decipher the italic letters composing the word that was giving them trouble in the Catechism and work out what those letters must be, by looking back at the alphabetical table on the first page, locating the place of each problematical letter in the alphabetical sequence of italic letters there; and read it by means of the roman character printed in the same position above (see Figure 1.3). Understanding that one had to be able read a word before one could copy it, copybooks too invited readers to consult an alphabetical table when deciphering the model text in that script which they were to copy, by printing one above the other on the same page. In an appendix to his *Universal Spelling Book* (1756), Daniel Fenning performed the same silent "Service" for "Persons that cannot read Old English Print": he presented in a table the great and small letters of the black letter alphabet, and followed that by "a letter [epistle] or two" in that alphabet, explaining that "by this any Person may soon learn to read it very well."[39] Charles Hoole had pointed out long since that once a reader knew his roman characters, he could be "made acquainted with the rest of the characters now in use…by comparing one with another, and reading over Sentences…till he have them pretty well by heart";[40] and the method stuck. One eighteenth-century method of reading, then, was to look back and forth from a text to an alphabetical table, and to translate between alphabets.

Juxtaposed tables of characters in different alphabets subjected the multiplicity of characters and shapes to order and rule. But they ordered variety without eliminating or disguising it, and governed difference by a silent logic of analogical substitution. Once taught that an upper-case A could replace a

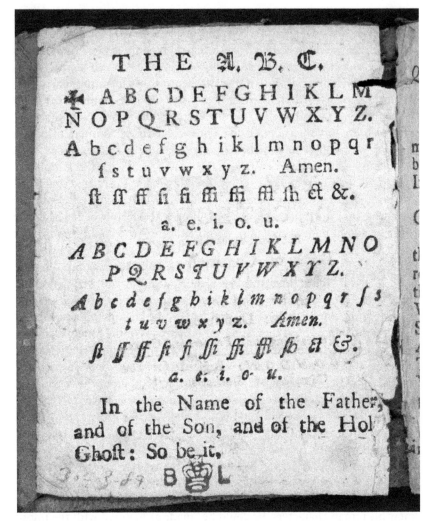

Figure 1.3 Church of England, *The Primer or Catechism, set forth agreeable to the Book of Common Prayer*, London, 1756. By Permission of the British Library.

lower-case a, or a roman A replace a Gothic 𝔄, readers were left to apply the principle of analogical substitution for themselves as required. The lacunae between and around juxtaposed alphabets meant that "learning to read meant first and foremost learning how to look";[41] it meant learning to observe and compare the strokes composing analogical letters in different alphabets, to find resemblances among the differences and establish mental connections between them. For a learner to determine that 𝔟 in Baskerville roman type was less like 𝔥 and more like 𝔟 in Gothic, and that B and 𝔅 were the same letter, demanded not only that s/he think analogically, but also that s/he exercise a modicum of judgment from his or her first exposure to written marks. Having looked and learned to identify even a small number of variations on the "same" letter, it would be hard for a reader to escape the conviction that some mental "idea" of a, b and c, however indistinct, was what was permitting him/her to connect different visible figurations of "a" "b" and "c" with "a" "b" and "c" in their minds. It was only a small step from here to the century's widespread conviction that some more stable, fundamental and universal idea or concept must underlie, and express itself in, all the variants and substitutions that one saw. One way in which this *ex pluribus unum* idea manifested itself both in scholarly texts and in popular spelling books was through the recurrent observation that the 24 alphabetic sounds offered 620,448,401, 733, 239, 439, 360,000 possible combinations without any repetition, and that alphabetical characters therefore "admit[ted] an infinity of combinations and arrangements, sufficient to represent not only all the conceptions of the mind, but all words in all languages whatsoever."[42] The imagery used for particular instantiations of this infinite *combinatoire* is noteworthy: contemporaries spoke of letters being "joined" or "conjoined," and of "conjunctions" and "disjunctions" amongst them. They also spoke of letters "meeting," as if to highlight the transitoriness of all conjunctions: letters meeting in one word parted at every instant as one read, to meet with other letters in another word, and part again.

Practices, beliefs and cultural values were attached to alphabets from the start. When the hornbook followed its alphabetical tables and short syllabery with the Invocation and the Lord's Prayer, or the primer opened directly from the alphabet onto the Catechism, they were not only providing matter on which reading could be practiced, and exposing readers to communal religious beliefs. They were also displaying, alongside the alphabet, what the benefits and rewards of reading would be: direct personal access to prayer and to the saving word of God. When spellers and copybooks designed for more secular Enlightenment readerships modeled fonts and scripts in action through short texts containing proverbs, maxims, and didactic observations on virtues and vices, they too were displaying the benefits and rewards of reading: direct personal access to the wisdom of ages and to useful lessons for life. When grammars and readers substituted entertaining didactic tales for dull proverbs and sententiae, they were conveying to their users that the reward of reading was now pleasure, as well as instruction.

Efforts to display the benefits and rewards of reading such as these formed part of a massive, and generally far less subtle, campaign to explain the purposes and utility of letters to a populace which was not yet accustomed to read, or to read very much. George Bickham, whose *Universal Penman* (1741) was perhaps the most widely used copybook of the latter half of the century both in Britain and America, used no subtlety at all. He devoted almost a third of his carefully selected, engraved plates of model writing to expressions of widely repeated contemporary commonplaces such as these:

> By the Assistance of Letters, the Memory of past things is preserved and the Foreknowledge of Things to come is Revealed. By them even Things Inanimate Instruct and Admonish us.
>
> Letters annihilate intervenient Times and make past Ages present. So that the Living and Dead Converse together...
>
> By the Arts of Reading and Writing we can sit at Home and acquaint ourselves with what is done in all the distant Part of the World, and find what our Fathers did long ago in the first Ages of Mankind.
>
> Among all the Inventions of Mankind, none is more Admirable, necessary useful or convenient than Writing, by which a Man is enabled to delineate his very Conceptions, communicate his Mind without Speaking, and correspond with his Friend at ten thousand Miles distance, and all by the Contrivance of twenty four Letters.

One learned one's letters in the different scripts along with the value of letters and the benefits they brought the individuals who mastered them. The heavy emphasis in Bickham's copybook on letters' function of annihilating time by making the dead present to the living in the act of reading, represents what was perhaps the dominant contemporary commonplace. It reminds us that, notwithstanding eighteenth-century talk of stadial progress, literate people still looked backwards more than forwards – to the Bible and the classics, to the ancient Anglo-Saxon constitution and ancient Rome, to Cicero, Shakespeare, Bacon, Harington and Locke. They cherished laws that depended upon precedent and custom, and used writing to protect ancient property rights and hereditary freedoms. They prized books for preserving knowledge of the arts and sciences acquired by previous generations, so that each generation could build on the learning of that which had gone before. Letters (characters) gave readers access to all these pasts.

The emphasis in Bickham's copybook on letters' function of annihilating distance by acquainting people at home with what was happening elsewhere, was the second most widely repeated commonplace of the period. It reminds us that this was also the great age of the letter (epistle) and that, thanks to the comparative novelty of exploration, discovery, conquest and empire (for Britons, if not for the Spanish, French and Portuguese), the period's most popular secular reading matter consisted of newspapers, letters and travel literature, followed by adventure novels and European, oriental and transatlantic tales. Letters (characters), which enabled world-wide commerce in all the contemporary significations of that word, gave readers access to the exciting, new, geographically expanding world of peoples, cultures, events and things by permitting those at a distance to communicate their otherwise concealed "minds" and experiences to those at home.

Characters or letters were thus presented to the public as the universal key to knowledge – religious, moral and practical; scientific, geographical, commercial, literary and philosophical; collective, social, private and intimately personal; present and past: "The Whole Universe is your Library: Authors, Conversation, and Remarks upon them, are your best Tutors." And if offering readers the keys to the universe did not move them to value and master their letters, there was always the appeal to self-interest:

> The Design of Learning is either to render a Man an agreeable Companion to himself, and teach him to support Solitude with Pleasure; or, if he is not born to an Estate, to supply that Defect, and furnish him with the Means of getting one.[43]

In practice, as we saw, it was a means of getting work. Often masquerading as an encomium to conceal their promotional character, paraphrases of observations about alphabetical writing that had been made by erudite sixteenth and seventeenth-century scholars and divines, were now repeated and disseminated to the public by schoolmasters, writers and scholars promoting the value of their services and the purchase of their books, and by printers interested in expanding the market for print. The more actual readers, the more potential customers. Reiterating these ideas about letters at every opportunity was sound strategy nevertheless, inasmuch as it helped to persuade more and more members of the public to undertake – and to ensure that their children undertook – the hard and unaccustomed task of reading.

Syllabic Reading

Spellers, grammars and dictionaries were designed to facilitate the pronunciation and comprehension of words and sentences; and their contents overlapped. Spelling (or "orthography") as disseminated in spelling books was the
first of the four "parts" of grammar; it looked forward to other parts of grammar and was often included in grammar books. Spellers and grammars also
did some dictionary-like things, such as alphabetization and word-definition.
Some grammars included dictionaries or long glossaries of hard words, others
referred their users to them, while dictionaries registered "correct" print spellings and gradually added from grammars, elements of prosody, etymology
and parts of speech. These conjunctions are not surprising since, for most of
the century, vernacular spellers, grammars and dictionaries generally issued
from schoolmasters' classrooms.[44] It is important to notice too that spellers,
grammars and dictionaries all focused readers' attention narrowly upon words
and word-combinations – nothing more. None addressed any unit larger
than the sentence. This fostered habits of very close reading indeed.

   In these printed books, "spelling and reading were both centered on the
syllable," as Ian Michael pointed out.[45] This is most immediately obvious
in spellers' tables of one, two, three, four and five-syllable words, and in
their practice of separating the syllables in polysyllabic words by hyphens
(am-ple, e-ter-ni-ty); early dictionaries too often separated syllables in
this way. According to modern accounts, "spelling" in eighteenth-century
usage meant sounding out a word laboriously letter by letter, then joining
the letter-sounds into monosyllables, and progressively adding syllables
one by one until one could read polysyllabic words. In fact, "to spell" was
"to divide a Word into Syllables," or "the Art of rightly dividing words into
their Syllables."[46] A great deal of importance was attached to acquiring the
ability to do this – and not, as we assume, because sounding out letters to
make syllables was as much as could be achieved by readers who never got
beyond a beginner's reading level.

   Contrary to what we suppose, eighteenth-century schoolmasters did
know that instant word recognition was essential to fluent reading, and
advised that it be introduced from the first. As one *Speller* put it: "when
the learner spells a word, it will be very proper for him to take particular
notice of it, that he may know it even by sight when he sees it again, as he
knows a man, or any other thing, at second sight, by the notice he took of
him, or it, at the first."[47] Brightland's *Grammar* observed in its notes that
the spelling book's entire method of proceeding from single vowel and
consonant, to monosyllables, dissyllables and polysyllables was designed
to "teach [students] to express every Syllable entire at first sight, without

dismembering it," that is, to foster instant syllabic recognition.[48] If he did not elaborate, it was because Charles Hoole had fully explained how this method taught readers "by often use" to pronounce words "at first sight," as early as 1661.[49] Spellers cultivated instant word recognition by filling their syllaberies with words that were identical except for one, and then two or more, letters (eat, meat, seat, cheat, treat, de-feat etc.) and by high-lighting recurrent syllables (-ship, -ing, -ate; de-, ex-, pro-) for readers to learn to recognize. They created whole-word recognition through instant-aneous recognition of the syllables they contained (Figure 1.4).

The syllabic manner of reading no doubt offered inexperienced readers a technique which they could subsequently apply to reading any unfamiliar words they encountered in the Bible or in printed periodicals and books. But its importance lay in the fact that syllables were fundamental to the "fourth part" of grammar, prosody, which measured poetic meters (called "numbers") by the number of syllables each required, and based accent and intelligibility in reading aloud (called "pronunciation") on the "quantity" of each syllable. In the *Grammar* attached to his *Dictionary of the English Language* (1755), Samuel Johnson defined "Versification [as] the arrangement of a certain number of syllables according to certain Laws"; in *A New Guide to the English Tongue* (1741), Thomas Dilworth explained that "Prosody teacheth the true Pronunciation of Syllables and Words, according to their Proper *Quantities* and *Tones or Accents";* while in *A Grammatical Institute of the English Language* (1784), Noah Webster described "syllabic accent," as "the master-key to pro-nunciation in English."[50] Working with the accenting and arrangement of syllables, prosody taught readers to read verse and prose in several other senses of read: read aloud and properly deliver, understand the mechanics of, and judge. Paradoxically, therefore, the further readers got in their grammar and the more literate (or literary) they became, the less they could leave syllables behind them, and the more useful syllabic reading became.

Based on spellers' alphabets, tidy lists of progressively more polysyllabic words and brief reading exercises, Richard Kroll described eighteenth-century reading as a process which "ascended atomically from letters to words to sentences to entire discourses," and which taught contemporaries to combine atomic constituents into ever larger and more encompassing constructs, which could be analyzed back into their elements.[51] Ronald Paulson too suggested that eighteenth-century aesthetics were based on cognate habits of making, breaking and remaking.[52] But this is not the whole story. For eighteenth-century grammarians knew that – unlike Latin or Hebrew and despite their best efforts – English writing constantly eluded orderly, Lego-like, constructions such as these. Pupils and spelling teachers could not fail to discover from their first foray into monosyllables

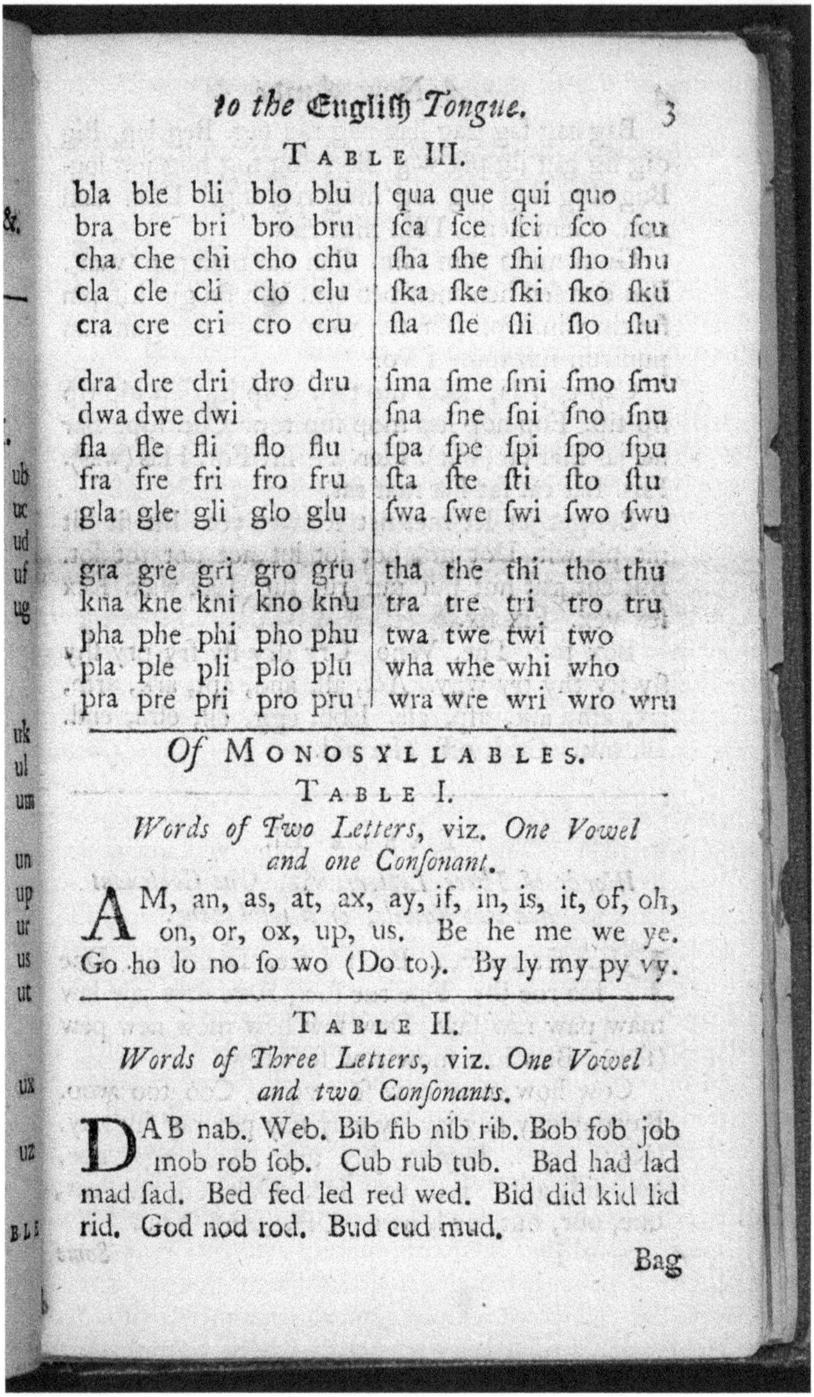

TABLE III.

bla	ble	bli	blo	blu	qua	que	qui	quo	
bra	bre	bri	bro	bru	fca	fce	fci	fco	fcu
cha	che	chi	cho	chu	fha	fhe	fhi	fho	fhu
cla	cle	cli	clo	clu	fka	fke	fki	fko	fku
cra	cre	cri	cro	cru	fla	fle	fli	flo	flu
dra	dre	dri	dro	dru	fma	fme	fmi	fmo	fmu
dwa	dwe	dwi			fna	fne	fni	fno	fnu
fla	fle	fli	flo	flu	fpa	fpe	fpi	fpo	fpu
fra	fre	fri	fro	fru	fta	fte	fti	fto	ftu
gla	gle	gli	glo	glu	fwa	fwe	fwi	fwo	fwu
gra	gre	gri	gro	gru	tha	the	thi	tho	thu
kna	kne	kni	kno	knu	tra	tre	tri	tro	tru
pha	phe	phi	pho	phu	twa	twe	twi	two	
pla	ple	pli	plo	plu	wha	whe	whi	who	
pra	pre	pri	pro	pru	wra	wre	wri	wro	wru

Of MONOSYLLABLES.

TABLE I.

Words of Two Letters, viz. One Vowel and one Confonant.

AM, an, as, at, ax, ay, if, in, is, it, of, oh, on, or, ox, up, us. Be he me we ye. Go ho lo no fo wo (Do to). By ly my py vy.

TABLE II.

Words of Three Letters, viz. One Vowel and two Confonants.

DAB nab. Web. Bib fib nib rib. Bob fob job mob rob fob. Cub rub tub. Bad had lad mad fad. Bed fed led red wed. Bid did kid lid rid. God nod rod. Bud cud mud.

Bag

Figure 1.4 Thomas Dilworth, *A New Guide to the English Tongue*, 13th edn. London, 1751.
By Permission of the British Library.

that "in writing English, we use the same Letter sometimes for one Sound, and sometimes for another, and now and then a Letter for no Sound at all; and the same Sound is sometimes written by one Letter, sometimes by another, and sometimes by two together."[53] (C), for instance, is sometimes sounded (s) ("face") and sometimes (k) ("close"); the "hard" (c) is sometimes replaced by (k) ("kind"), sometimes appears with (k) ("kick"), and sometimes doesn't sound at all ("scythe")." It therefore proved impossible in practice to read even monosyllables (much less to learn reading) without developing rules and expectations about how letters sounded in different conjunctions, "meetings" or positions relative to one another: "c before e, o, u, still sounded is/Like k; before e, i, and y, like s"; "when final (c) without an (e) is found/'Tis hard; but Silent (e) gives softer Sound"; "c sounds like k in the end of a syllable, or before a consonant or consonants in the same syllable." The rules were not tidy at all, and exceptions outnumbered every rule. But once absorbed by readers through "practical Methods of Learning," such rules and the expectations they created would "rarely miss of influencing them all their Lives."[54]

The first rule, which spelling books laid down as soon as they had separated letters into vowels and consonants, was perhaps the most influential: "As many Vowels as emit a Sound/So many Syllables in Words are found."[55] There could be no syllable without a vowel or diphthong: consonants could not form a syllable by themselves, but as many as seven or eight consonants could be joined into a syllable by a single vowel ("strength"). Together with spelling books' lists of monosyllables and monosyllabic reading exercises ("No Man may put off the Law of God"; "Who can say he has no Sin"), one effect of this first rule was to create the widespread impression that English possessed an exceptionally large number of monosyllables and of harsh, consonantal sounds. When linguists noticed that monosyllables and consonant clusters generally derived from the earliest "Saxon" stratum of the language, rather than from words that English had borrowed from the Latin or the French, they developed a theory of language which championed the "energy" embodied in harsh, clipped, "properly English" words, against the deceptively soft, smooth and mellifluous sounds of those more polysyllabic foreign tongues.[56] Scotsman James Beattie was among those who contested the argument that "English lines of monosyllables" were harsh and "dissonant" in comparison. Citing verses such as "Rise up, my Love, my fair one, and come away," he argued on the contrary, that "when two or three little words run easily into one another, the effect in point of harmony is the same, as if one word of several syllables were spoken, instead of several words of one syllable," concluding that "in English, though there is much Latin and some Greek, yet the Saxon predominates; and its Sounds are most acceptable to a British ear, because most familiar."[57] One consequence of the syllabic manner of reading, then, was that monosyllables became the focus of aesthetic and patriotic debate.

But the more important and enduring effect of the rule that "As many Vowels as emit a Sound/So many Syllables in Words are found" derived from the fact that it alerted learners to a key way in which printed writing differed from contemporary speech and manuscript writing. Printed writing reproduced all the syllables in words – each vowel-centered syllable must therefore be identified and deciphered by the reader. Manuscript writing did not; it traditionally favored abbreviations permitting "considerable saving of both time and paper."[58] Indeed, printed spelling books had to append a list of the abbreviations commonly used in manuscript writing (recd. for received, obt. for obedient, ye for the) to enable their users to read words in handwritten letters or documents. Speech too thrived on contractions, unlike printed writing, where all the syllables attributed to a word (or gratuitously added to it by the learned) lay there, extended before the reader on a line. Syllables, along with letters, were swallowed, merged or omitted by oral convention. Spelling books underlined this difference by offering lists which contrasted the way words sounded orally with the way they appeared in print (Gloster, Gloucester; villin, villain; charrit, chariot; crowner, coroner). Such juxtapositions served more to introduce speakers to the strange non-phonetic print-image of a well-known word, than to teach them how to say it. Printed writing also used orthography to distinguish syllables that were indistinguishable in speech, or indeed in phonetic manuscript writing. Spelling books stepped in here too, by providing lists and dictionary-like definitions of the homophones disambiguated visually in printed texts (altar, alter; vain, vane, vein). On occasion, of course, printed writing also incorporated contractions current in speech. But then, as spelling books made clear (again by providing lists or tables), printed writing invariably introduced an apostrophe to mark the place of each and every precious, vanished, syllable: kill'd, for killed; 'tis or it's, for it is; I'm, for I am; sha'n't for shall not.[59] By the 1740s and 1750s, printed lists of the abbreviations commonly used in manuscript writing often concluded with a warning to readers that "these Contractions ought to be avoided as much as possible, unless it be for one's own private Use" because "it argues a Disrespect and Slighting to use Contractions to our Betters, and is often puzzling to others."[60] The rules for reading aloud that were included in printed grammars, letter manuals and books of rhetoric included the injunction that "every syllable" must be clearly articulated.

And Dr. Johnson argued that people ought to start pronouncing words as they appeared in print spellings. Printed writing – which had begun its career by imitating manuscript writing and still hyped itself as the most durable way of preserving speech – now differed from contemporary speech and manuscript writing by demanding, and seeking to impose, a consistently syllabic manner of reading, writing, speaking and thinking about words.[61]

In the process, spelling books introduced readers to aspects of syllabic reading that would later be required for prosody. All spellers gave rules for determining whether vowels, and the syllables in which they figured, were "long" or "short." Most dealt with stress or accent as well. Tuite, for instance, offered a list of words that were accented on the first syllable when used as nouns, and on the second syllable when used as verbs (absent, abstract, conflict, converse, subject etc), as others did after him. Thomas Dilworth went much further in the speller occupying Part I of his *New Guide to the English Tongue,* a transatlantic best-seller that was repeatedly reprinted in London, Dublin, Boston and Philadelphia into the early nineteenth century, and that Noah Webster learned from as a boy and later sought to replace. Dilworth organized *all* words of two, three, four, five and six syllables into "Tables" according to the syllable on which the accent fell, a feature highlighted on both British and American title pages. Dilworth explained under "Prosody" in Part III that "a tone or accent denoteth the Raising or Falling of the Voice on a Syllable according to the Quantity thereof," and that syllables had three possible quantities marked by three kinds of tone or accent: the long and the short, which denoted slow or quick pronunciation of the syllable in question, and the "common," which "denotes the Tone or Stress of the Voice, to be upon that Syllable" (97).

Accent in all these senses was fundamental to "pronunciation" or reading aloud. Much simplified by Dilworth, this was the part of prosody that Dr. Johnson called "orthoepy." Basing his deductions on extant grammars rather than innovating himself (which he said would be ineffectual), Johnson's *Grammar of the English Language* gave twenty elaborate rules just for determining which syllable of polysyllabic words was accented. Since all these rules were also subject to numerous exceptions, Johnson used his *Dictionary* to forestall readerly error and confusion by marking the accented syllable in each word he defined. For Johnson, prosody was far more straightforward in "orthometry or the laws of versification," since contemporary English verse was, according to him, almost always either trochaic (accented on the first syllable) or iambic (accented on the second).

The most widely used iambic measures consisted of verses of 4, 6, or 8 syllables, the "usual measure for short poems," or of verses of 10 syllables, "the common measure of heroic and tragic poetry;' while trochaic measures generally contained 3, 5 or 7 syllables. In iambics, the accents fell on the even syllables, in trochaics, on the uneven ones. If verses contained 14 syllables, they were broken into lines consisting alternately of eight syllables and six, to produce "a soft lyric measure." There was also a "very quick and lively" anapestic measure "much used in songs…in which the accent rests on every third syllable." As Johnson pointed out, "these measures are varied in many combinations."

Terminology among grammarians was varied in many combinations too. There were differences over whether metrical numbers in English verse followed syllable length or syllabic stress, with many arguing that the two, in practice, fell together; and there were disagreements about how far syllabic rules obtaining in Latin and Greek also obtained in English. But, like variations in poetic measures, such disagreements remained rooted in the characteristics of syllables. Consequently, once readers had learned the rudiments of syllabic reading from speller and grammar, they had only to be able to count to ten – and to accustom their ear – to know what "numbers" they were reading or hearing, and to assess the technical competence of the verse. The rule was that a "just" or "harmonious" line was a "regular" line: it marched to its own, recurrent, rhythmical, beat. This did not teach ordinary readers to appreciate that "*je-ne-sais-quoi* beyond the reach of art" that Pope had reserved for the cognoscenti – as Johnson put it in his Dictionary's fourth edition (1765), "the variations necessary to pleasure belong to the art of poetry, not the rules of grammar." But grammars did equip readers with some basic poetic literacy and with ideas about versification that were widely shared until the early nineteenth century – a fact which led professional writers to complain that they encouraged everyone to "versify" and to imagine that this made them "poets." The most immediately perceptible way for Romantic poets to mark their work as "poetry" not verse was therefore obvious: it was to dispense with the familiar "grammatical" metrical rules altogether.

"For all such as Desire to Understand what they Read": Grammars and Dictionaries

Spellers created a basis for reading comprehension by teaching their users to decipher some of the many "hard" polysyllabic words (in-vi-si-bi-li-ty, dis-ad-van-ta-ge-ous) that English borrowed principally from Latin and

French during the seventeenth and eighteenth centuries. This period of "unprecedented lexical growth" flooded English with new words (especially in scientific and technical fields such as farriery, agriculture, or medicine and in sociality, food and fashion),[62] which were not widely recognized or understood. Since spellers listed but did not explain hard words, vernacular glossaries and dictionaries emerged "for the Information of the Ignorant, and for the Benefit of Young Students, Artificers, Tradesmen and Foreigners, who are desirous thorowly to understand what they Speak, Read or Write."[63] The use of dictionaries became so ubiquitous that, by mid-eighteenth century, cheaper and more portable "miniature" or pocket dictionaries of "hard words" were being mass-produced.[64] Grammars, for their part, worked extensively with the meanings and usages of common words in the context of parts of speech ("OFF signifies Separation and Distance, and has its Opposite in ON, which implies Continuation, as 'to put off;'" it also "signifies Delay, as 'he put me off.'"[65]). By mid-century, dictionaries were expanding beyond "hard words" to the meanings and usages of common ones.

Grammars contributed to the comprehension of "hard words" by teaching "etymology" or word-derivation. If people only understood how new English words were made from older ones by the addition of syllabic suffixes such as -dom or -ship (king-dom, friend-ship) or by compounding extant words (bookseller), as well as how foreign words were anglicized by means of syllabic prefixes and suffixes whose significations could be explained (un- signifies privation or want, mis- wrong or error, circum- means around), readers would be able to use their knowledge of English, and ideally of Latin and French, to identify the root of hard words and work out what they must mean. When encountering a hard word like "independent" in a sentence, readers were to parse it thus: "an Adjective, compounded of in, not, and dependent. So independent signifies not depending on any other."[66] Ironically, therefore, grammarians in the "English School" movement read and taught "hard" English words as regulated substitutions for Latin or French ones: ornament was ornamentum without the Latin inflection, and infant, infans; the prefix "ad" meaning "to" or "at" joined vocatus in "advocate" or "one called to"; English endings in -ty replaced Latin endings in -as (liberty/libertas) and the hard English <g> the soft French <j> (garden/jardin). In 1795, grammarian Lindley Murray – an American who first published in England and was massively reprinted in America until the middle of the nineteenth century – argued that "as the English scholar is not supposed to be acquainted with these languages [Latin and French], this part of derivation must be omitted" from grammar books. But, as he pointed out, "the best English dictionaries will furnish information on this head" – by then, dictionaries regularly registered etymologies too.[67]

Grammars made their major contributions to reading comprehension through syntax or "construction" and "analogy" or parts of speech, as these were oriented to respond to the crucial question raised by the putative student in *A Key to the Art of Letters* (1705), Archibald Lane's early question-and-answer grammar: "Since the Compositions of Sentences are often intricate and obscure, how may the sense and meaning of them best be found?" Lane's answer, like that of other eighteenth-century grammarians, was to show readers how to "resolve" intricate or obscure sentences by diverse forms of substitution and intra-lingual translation. "Resolving" meant "the unfolding of a Sentence, and placing all the Parts of it, whether expressed or understood, in their proper and natural Order, that the true Meaning of it may appear."[68] Lane advised readers that "the best way to find the true sense and meaning of any Sentence is to reduce transpos'd words to the Natural Order, to supply supprest words, to change Substituted words into the words for which they are Substituted, and lastly to distinguish ambiguous words." Since "the natural order" was the subject-verb-object order of words that was most easily understood, resolving a sentence into natural word order meant, in the first instance, identifying the "simple sentence" (or main clause) in intricate compound sentences by setting aside any subordinate clauses (easily identifiable, Lane said, as the words "immediately following" conjunctions or relative pronouns) and eliminating any parentheses, interjections, or vocatives. The reader could then divide the main clause into two parts, Subject and Predicate, and use what s/he had been taught about parts of speech to eliminate every word that "depends upon" another word until s/he could identify the nominative noun and principal verb. Only then could the reader set about "reducing transpos'd words" by reordering the main clause around that noun and verb in a manner that would clarify its meaning: putting the nominative noun before the verb if there was an inversion, turning s-genitives into of-genitives and passive verbal constructions into active ones, attaching adjectives to nouns and direct or indirect objects to verbs. Once the reader had translated the main clause into something comprehensible, s/he could go back to connect each sub-clause to its "antecedent" via its conjunction or relative pronoun, in a process that often transposed the order of clauses from that in the original sentence. Since sub-clauses were frequently "contracted" by the omission of key words, the next step was "to supply supprest words" to make their meaning clear. Lane devoted a large portion of his grammar to identifying the ellipses obscuring the meaning of sub-clauses, and to showing readers how to fill in the missing words. A sub-clause might be contracted, for example, by "suppressing" or "putting away the Relative and turning the Verb into a participle" or infinitive; to make the meaning plain, one supplied the missing relative pronoun and active verb, i.e. by translating "A man wanting Learning is little esteemed" into "A man who wants Learning is little esteemed" or "I know thee to be him" into "I know that thou art he." Finally, there was the matter of figurative language, which Lane defined as "Substitution" or "the using of one word for another." The solution here was to translate the substituting word/s back into the word/s it was substituting for. When an author wrote "the whole Nation are called Venetians," he explained, "the whole Nation is put for all the People of the Nation"; the meaning of "the whole Nation" became clear once the substitute was translated back into "all the People."[69]

Parsing or "resolving" a sentence "broke and remade" it in the process of translating it into comprehensible English by substituting analogical words and structures for those on the page. Lane, a schoolmaster in Herefordshire, was treating English as what his subtitle called "a learned language" by adapting techniques of translation long used in Latin grammar schools to teach Latin and Greek, into tools for the reading comprehension of printed English. Printed English may have appeared an equally foreign tongue to children and native speakers who perceived its distance both from their local dialect and from the more "natural" colloquial English into which it was being translated. What grammars gave "all such as desire to understand what they read" were tools to master the multiple, unfamiliar, uncolloquial codes of "literary" vernacular writing, so that these could become what Andrew Elfenbein too unproblematically calls "the source of commonality between author and reader."[70]

Because grammar was treated as the foundation for speaking and writing as well as for reading, some grammars angled their comments on syntax predominantly towards writers or predominantly towards "speakers" seeking guidance for reading aloud. But all integrated elements introduced by those for whom syntax was first and foremost the gateway to reading comprehension, who argued that "the Method of distinguishing the Sense in a Sentence properly belongs to that Part of Grammar that is called Syntax."[71] These grammarians appropriated from cognate disciplines whatever bore on the construction of sentences that helped to "distinguish the Sense." James Greenwood, for instance, drew on logic to identify the different forms of subordination among the clauses in a sentence: "adversative" conjunctions such as "but," "nevertheless" and "however" are "used to

couple two sentences [clauses], in marking the Opposition of the second
Sentence, with regard to the first," while "disjunctive" conjunctions such
as "or," "whether" or "either," "serve in such a manner for the Connexion
of Discourse, that they mark at the same time division or distinction in the
Sense of the Thing Spoken."[72] Verbs were another favorite location for the
introduction of logic:

> The secondary Modes are such as, when the Copula is affected by any of
> them, make the Sentence to be (as the Logicians call it) a Modal Proposition.
> This happens when the matter in Discourse, namely the being or doing or
> suffering of a thing, is considered, not *simply in itself*, but *gradually in its
> causes*, from which it proceeds contingently or necessarily. Then the thing
> seems to be left Contingent, when the Speaker expresses only the Possibility
> of it, or his own Liberty to it. The possibility of a thing depends on the
> power of its cause; and may be expressed when *Absolute or Conditional* by
> the Particle *can* or *could*; the Liberty of a thing depends upon a freedom
> from all obstacles either within or without, and is usually expressed in our
> language when *Absolute or Conditional* by the Particle *may* or *might*…the
> necessity of a thing from some external Obligation, whether Natural or
> Moral, which we call Duty, is expressed, if *Absolute or Conditional* by the
> Particle *must, ought, shall*, or *should*.[73]

Readers could determine the sense of a compound sentence by using
conjunctions to identify the logical relations between its parts, mentally
assigning each clause a conjunctive, oppositional, disjunctive, interroga-
tive, conditional, or restrictive posture towards other clauses as they read.
Likewise, they could determine whether a sentence registered something
short of certainty, by translating auxiliary verbs such as "can," "may" and
"must" into categories of possibility, liberty and necessity ("has power to,"
"free to," "can't not.") This manner of translating reading – by logical tagging and tracking – could also be used between sentences; it thus prepared
learners to trace an argument through the structure of longer compositions
and the movement of complex texts. Here again comprehension depended
on analogical substitutions – substitution of clearer, more comprehensible
or more logical word/s and structures which resembled but were not identical with those on the page, for the word/s and structures in the text.

Eighteenth-century grammars borrowed as heavily from rhetoricians as
from logicians. They not only appropriated transposition and elision from
among the figures of rhetoric to make them standard "grammatical figures," but frequently inserted some account of the "principal rhetorical
figures" in a chapter or appendix. Here, they gave short definitions of a
few, carefully selected tropes such as metaphor, metonymy, synechdoche,
antithesis and hyperbole, together with sentence-length examples. Most

interesting here was their predilection for using animal fables as reading exercises. Despite the simple language and familiar situations characteristic of this genre (and spellers' skill in narrating them even in words of one syllable), fables are not the most obvious choice of reading matter for beginning readers. For, unlike "No Man may put off the Law of God," fables do not say what they mean – a fact that early grammars underlined by articulating "The Moral" and printing it in a paragraph separated by a gap from the narrative. Latin grammar schools gave beginners fables too, usually Aesop's, in a tradition that goes back to the Ancients; so one might suppose that English-school grammarians were simply copying them. But the logic behind it, at least for English grammars teaching reading comprehension, appears to have been that fables familiarized students with a key manner of reading more advanced texts. For "Fable," the only genre regularly defined in chapters on rhetorical figures in grammars, was characterized by grammarians as "an extended metaphor" or as a discourse in which "one thing is expressed, and another understood." Since grammars made it clear that *all* tropes substituted one thing for another that had to be understood, fables demonstrated on a larger and more obvious scale the fundamental mechanism of all figurative language. They also alerted beginning readers to the possibility that whole stories or narratives could or should be read in figurative ways, as expressing one thing that another might be understood. Fables were usually characterized in grammars as akin to allegory and parable, suggesting that grammars' often programmatically religious authors saw teaching readers how to interpret figures and fables as a way of preparing them to read their bibles – as well as to understand (and accept as legitimate) non-literal interpretations of biblical verses expounded in sermons.[74]

Grammars also borrowed from rhetoricians their concern with style. Like Lane, they explained the stylistic benefits of transposition and ellipsis: "Words are transposed in a Sentence to please the Ear, by making the Contexture of words more harmonious, elegant and agreeable"; "Suppression is the most elegant and useful of all the figures of Construction [syntax], to avoid the tedious and nauseous repetition of many words that yet are necessarily understood to make up a full Construction." Some also addressed the stylistic effects of some rhetorical figures: "Antithesis... always has this effect, to make each of the contrasted objects appear in the stronger light."[75] Despite defining grammar as "the Art of rightly expressing our Thoughts in Words," Robert Lowth went even further, to turn grammar into an instrument for full-blown stylistic analysis. Not content with prefacing his mandatory grammatical sections on the various parts of speech with a five-page demonstration of how these could be deployed to explicate the meaning of a single sentence, Lowth used verses from Shakespeare, Dryden, Milton, and other British poets to illustrate the usages and grammatical constructions of each part of speech and to demonstrate their literary-stylistic effects. For instance, his standard, if minimalist, account of the cases and genders of English nouns included the following explanation about poetic substitutions:

> The English Language, with singular propriety, following nature alone, applies the distinction of Masculine and Feminine only to the names of Animals; all the rest are Neuter: except when by a Poetical or Rhetorical fiction, things inanimate and Qualities are exhibited as Persons, and consequently become either Male or Female. And this gives the English an advantage above most other languages in the Poetical and Rhetorical Style: for when Nouns naturally Neuter are converted into Masculine and Feminine, the Personification is more distinctly and forcibly remarked:

> "At his command th'uprooted hills retir'd
> Each to *his* place: they heard his voice and went
> Obsequious: Heaven *his* wonted face renew'd,
> And with fresh flowrets hill and valley smil'd. Milton, P. L. B. vi.[76]

For prose, grammars stressed the virtues and "elegance" of the simple, clear, "perspicuous" style, and later included full blown 'Essays on Style' which condemned the copious use of metaphors, the multiplication of synonyms and the imprecise use of words. One wonders whether it was grammars' championship of perspicuity, or tedious intralingual translations of complex, involuted sentences, which contributed most to the eighteenth-century demise of the long, four-part periodic sentence that readers found most "intricate and obscure." As Lindley Murray put it: "We consider him as deserving praise, who frees us from all fatigue of searching for his meaning"; consequently, "long, involved and intricate sentences, are great blemishes in composition."[77] Not coincidentally, perhaps, simplicity and perspicuity – classical virtues for the plain style – were increasingly valorized as the number of "unlearned" readers grew.

Even when designated "For Schools" on their title pages, spellers and grammars addressed several linked, but not necessarily identical, readerships by accompanying the catalogue of discontinuous rules and exceptions or the "catechetical" questions and answers which composed the text designed for learners, with often copious explanatory notes. American-authored schoolbooks often said as much on their title pages: Anthony Benezet's *Pennsylvania Spelling Book* (1782), for instance, promoted itself both as "facilitating the Instruction of Children and others," and as "More particularly calculated for the Use of Parents, Guardians and others, remote from Schools, in the private Tuition of their Children, and illiterate Domesticks, etc."[78] Grammarians used their discursive notes, which figured in smaller print on the bottom of the page and sometimes took over the page completely, to teach less scholarly teachers than themselves what they ought to know. One might say that grammars were arranged to provide the raw materials for teacher–pupil conversations much as the *Dungeons & Dragons* books did, by priming the (dungeon) master and student-players separately on the elements of the game – and sometimes modeling the game's Q & A structure, or offering a model dialogue – before leaving master and pupils, mistress and servant, governess and girls, or mother and children, to their own talk and improvisations. But this analogy falls short inasmuch as grammarians were simultaneously using the notes in their schoolbooks as we use academic books now, to highlight their novel contributions to orthography, etymology, prosody, analogy or syntax for other scholars, to devise slightly different rules and a slightly different game, and/or to argue that they were promulgating an improved method of presenting the material to learners. Female grammarians, in particular, highlighted the efficacy of the teaching methods they were imparting, as if to counter superior masculine "learning" by their superior understanding of pedagogy and children.[79]

Grammars and spellers also deployed other devices to extend their userships beyond children and schools. Title pages often openly stated that this speller or grammar would also prove useful "to all Persons who desire a better Acquaintance with their Native Language," to "adult Persons of every Profession," to "Youth in the Shop or Compting-House," or to "Foreigners." Where title pages highlighted a boys' school, prefaces stressed the importance of teaching spelling and grammar to women and girls, the origin of the schoolbook in some domestic tutoring situation, or the utility of the volume for private education in families. Grammarians also reached out more broadly by means of a rhetorical device, which Isaac Watts unmasked in the 1722 Preface to his spelling book. Having emphasized the importance of introducing verses and stories to "entertain the Child" and "entice the young Learner to the *Pleasure of Reading*," Watts continued: "But my chief Hope is to improve the Knowledge of Persons advanced beyond Childhood; though I have frequently, in the Book, address'd my Directions to Masters and other Scholars." One could "address" a particular discourse (here "directions") to one group (here "masters and other scholars"), while equally intending others whom one was not overtly addressing – the "thousands of young Persons, and many at full grown Age" learning to read and understand what they read without any other teacher than "the Directions that are here proposed."[80] Moving back and forth between the discontinuous rules and definitions that learners would be expected to memorize and the fuller discursive "directions" in the notes, these young adults had to engage in "self-converse" as they read, to put these two textual voices into dialogue. Even when their title pages indicated that children in school were their principal target audience, then, "schoolbooks" themselves were generally designed for multiple, widely divergent readerships both inside and outside schools.

During the century's last decades, realization began to dawn that these "schoolbooks" were perhaps *least* well suited to children and schools. Their guiding assumption had been that, because language signifies ideas in the mind, grammar is best conveyed by fully explaining the rational, logical and historical reasons for the constructions, rules, and manifold exceptions in the English language, and by demonstrating how grammatical strictures applied in practice to reading, speaking, and writing. But the result, as schoolmaster James Gough observed in 1760, was that grammars such as Brightland's or Greenwood's "seem to have been written for Men rather than Children." Mrs. Lovechild (Lady Ellenor Fenn) complained of Lowth that even a short "perusal" of his Grammar showed "any person conversant with [children]," that he was "much mistaken" in supposing that it was "calculated for the Use of Learners even of the lowest class." It became clear, as schoolmistress Ellin Devis said, that "the grammatical study of our own language" must be "render[ed] less difficult for children."[81] Grammars had been promoting themselves as an easy, "plaine and perfite way of teachyng children, to understand, write and speake" a language at least since Ascham's *Scholemaster* in 1570, whether they were or not. But now English schoolbooks were gradually "made easier," and conveniently "abridged," by progressively reducing grammar to the smallest possible number of general rules and definitions, and by presenting these – without rationale, history of the language, indications of immediate utility, and most exceptions – as so many facts of language. "Parsing" was reduced to "naming the parts of speech," and grammar for children became "the Art of using Words according to certain established Rules."[82]

Grammarians indicated that they were addressing a broad readership, not only to extend the elements of reading literacy more widely, but also because, in their view, grammatical correctness differed significantly from customary usage at *all* ranks. Greenwood complained in 1711 about those who "talk for the most Part just as they have heard their Parents, Nurses or Teachers (who likewise may be none of the best Speakers)," and announced that his Grammar would, instead, "call the Custom of Speech, the Agreement of the Learned." Lowth objected in 1763 that "the English language as it is spoken by the politest part of the nation and as it stands in the writing of our most approved authors offends against every part of Grammar" and set out to correct both. Anne Fisher said the same of the spoken and written English of "many Persons of all Ranks." Observing that "Custom, the grand Establisher of all things, has rendered false Concord so natural to us, that it is impossible for anyone to speak and write correctly who…has not learned the Language in a grammatical Way," she promised that her popular grammar would teach "any Person of a tolerable Capacity…to write English as properly and correctly *as if for the Press*" (my emphasis). Richard Bailey has shown that, in private manuscript writing, Lowth and Johnson themselves did not always bother to write "printer's English" but "felt free to write English in any way they chose – sometimes one way, sometimes another."[83] As Jim Milroy has observed, therefore, while "standardization [was] implemented and promoted primarily through written forms of language," it is "by no means clear that the 'standard language' at any given time [was] a direct product of the language of the highest social group."[84] The evidence suggests that linguistic "propriety" or "correctness" as it emerged in eighteenth-century Britain, was the joint and largely self-conscious, creation of the "learned" and the press – or better, of the learned *for* the press.

This was clearly the case in America. After Independence, the new Republic faced the same problem of speech communities which could not understand one another as Britain did, but in aggravated form. The distances separating American settlements and states had permitted speech communities originating in different parts of Britain to preserve their native dialects in what Noah Webster considered their original, "purer" form. And in America, religious and political oratory remained a more important means of reaching and swaying the populace than in Britain, except perhaps at election time. Noah Webster confronted this American problem after Thomas Sheridan's Elocution movement and countless rhetorical grammars and pronouncing dictionaries had begun to teach Britons to pronounce words in a more uniform fashion based, as Johnson had recommended, on the way they appeared in print. Webster's immensely popular blue-back speller addressed the problem of pronunciation by merging the speller and the pronouncing dictionary. Declaring that "the only reason we divide Syllables for Children is to lead them to the proper Pronunciation of Words," he divided syllables according to the way he heard words pronounced (hab-it and lem-on for British Spellers' ha-bit and le-mon, mo-*shun* for mo-ti-on). Webster changed the order in which words appeared, placing "easy" polysyllables (merr-i-ment) before "hard" monosyllables ("strength"). He devised a system of numerical phonetic notations to signal the different sounds made by the same vowel character and created tables of words based on vowel sounds. Promoters of his *American Spelling Book* commended it in 1784 for being "calculated to destroy the various false dialects in pronunciation in the several states, an object very desirable in a federal republic";[85] and everyone agreed that Webster's widely used speller was more effective in teaching reading and promoting uniform pronunciation than anything had been before. But to achieve these successes, Webster obliterated the connections linking "spelling" to prosody, poetics and reading aloud in the British system.

In Britain, as a new generation of historical linguists has shown, the hegemony of "Standard English" was delayed until mid-nineteenth century by lack of uniformity in the eighteenth-century spellers, grammars and dictionaries which supposedly prescribed "correct" English. The approximately 30 new grammars published in Britain between 1700 and 1750, and the approximately 155 grammars published between 1751 and 1800, often disagreed on terms, pronunciation and rules, and on what belonged to which part of grammar, which part of speech and which kind of book. Similarly, though all the elements of modern dictionaries were present by about 1800, they were not yet found all together in any single lexicon. Instead, the many seventeenth- and eighteenth-century dictionaries published before and after Samuel Johnson's *Dictionary* of 1755 were "diversified by size and price, by audience and addressees, by contents and language attitudes, as well as by their differential position within a genre which was by no means monosemic or capable of being reduced to a single representative text."[86] Something similar undercuts our long-standing conviction that great men who wrote grammars or dictionaries, such as Lowth or Johnson, were so authoritative and widely used that they succeeded in prescribing proper language use to everyone. Here diversity was introduced by print culture's proclivity for providing abridgements, epitomes and altered versions of popular or useful texts. Lowth's *Grammar*, for instance, spawned numerous other popular and much reprinted grammars which promised to "introduce" his grammar or to make it easier to understand, but which repeated him only selectively and changed him at will. A paradigmatic example is John Ash's popular and transatlantically reprinted *Grammatical Institutes* (1763), which "improved" on the Anglican Bishop's grammar by eliminating the verse and stylistics and changing some of the rules, as well as by reorienting it for a non-conformist readership. Likewise,

Johnson's expensive two-volume folio *Dictionary of the English Language* boasted a "miniature" non-identical twin compiled by Johnson himself, as well as a second cheap abridgement by another hand, which together sold ten times as many copies as the great man's great work.[87] Thus even if Lowth's *Grammar* or Johnson's *Dictionary* were authoritative and prescriptive, readers were neither gaining access to these works in a single invariable form nor receiving identical prescriptions in their name. *If* printers and booksellers were publishing a variety of spellers, grammars and dictionaries at different prices, in different sizes, with different contents, for different audiences, only to promote Standard English, they were simultaneously subverting uniformity and shooting themselves in the foot by issuing different prescriptions in different books.

But as we saw, spellers and grammars also had goals other than producing or promoting Standard English. They taught syllabic reading, conventions of printed writing and analogical thinking. They taught reading comprehension by means of diverse forms of intralingual translation, such as reordering, logical tagging and rewording through linguistic substitutions. They familiarized learners with elements of generic and aesthetic literacy through rudimentary prosody, stylistics and poetics, with particular focus on figurative language and fable. Grammars did all this consistently and well, whatever their differences in other respects. This use of grammar books to give readers strategies for deciphering printed texts, even when they did not say exactly what they mean, made grammars what printer John Newbery called "the Foundation or Groundwork of Polite Learning" and what Anne Fisher said it was generally considered: "the Basis of Literature [i.e. everything communicated through letters], being the Source from which all the other Sciences proceed."[88] Grammar was the basis of literature and the foundation of all learning not because it still figured in humanist terms as *ars recte scribendi et loquendi* (the art of writing and speaking correctly), but because it disseminated practical methods for reading and understanding all kinds of texts. Flanked by spellers and dictionaries, grammars had become the cornerstone of print's campaign to teach more and more members of society to read and understand printed writing.

"Operations of the Mind"

Isaac Watts – who made logic the art of learning and teaching others to read the books of men, as well as the book of nature[89] – is key to understanding what "operations of the mind" were displayed and exercised in spellers, grammars and dictionaries. Where Locke had derived all our ideas from sense perceptions, whether of external objects or internal acts of mind, Watts argued that we also "furnish ourselves with a rich Variety of Ideas" by reading and listening to others.[90] The best "way of attaining [that] extensive Treasure of Ideas," which is the basis of true judgments and the condition for attaining true and comprehensive knowledge, was to "read with diligence...things antient and modern; things natural, civil and religious; things domestick and national; things in your native Land, and of foreign countries; things present and past" (110–11), and to "converse with the most knowing and the wisest Men" (114). Reading and conversing with knowing people extended a person's ideas beyond his/her own direct experience in a particular time and place, and recognized that "a great part of our knowledge is both obtained and communicated" by language (68).

For Watts, reading consisted of performing rational "operations of the mind" upon language which, following Locke, stood for ideas in the mind, not for things. His *Logick or the Right Use of Reason in the Enquiry after Truth* (1724) sought to resolve the difficulty of explaining how an enquirer could discover Truth by performing mental operations upon the mind's verbal products, when neither re-present things as they really are. Though first drafted for Sir John Hartopp's son while serving as his "domestick tutor," Watts' *Logick* was almost immediately "received into the universities of both Britain and America" as a standard university text.[91] It was reprinted in Britain every three or four years until 1824, and saw five American editions after 1789. A founder of the Dissenters' famous Stoke Newington Academy, a lifelong mentor to Philip Doddridge and, in Jeremy Belknap's words, "a firm and zealous friend to New England" who "kept up a correspondence with some of our principal characters both in the civil and clerical lines," Reverend Watts was an exceptionally influential educator on both sides of the Atlantic.[92] Johnson characterized him as "provid[ing] instruction for all ages, from those who are lisping their first lessons, to the enlightened readers of Malebranche and Locke,"[93] and himself took "literally hundreds of examples and definitions" from Watts' *Logick* for his *Dictionary*.[94] Howell judges that "in the English-speaking world, more eighteenth-century students and serious general readers learned their lessons about logic from Isaac Watts than from any other source."[95] Unfortunately, Watts is remembered now, if at all, principally for his hymns, and what follows only addresses the parts of his *Logick* that are relevant to grammar and reading.

As grammars integrated elements of logic, Watts' *Logick* integrated grammar, to identify and apply to reading in search of truth, mental operations that readers had already practiced in working through their grammar book. Watts used the fourth part of his *Logick*, "Disposition or Method," to explain how grammars and his *Logick both* made their method clear and perceptible to others by *disposing* their "Subject in such an Order as is fittest to gain the clearest knowledge of it, to retain it the longest, and to explain it to others in the best manner" (9). This was a two-fold or Janus-faced method.

The first aspect of this method of disposition, the "Analytick," begins from the whole compound subject, "resolves it into its first principles or parts," and further subdivides these as necessary. The analytic method was displayed in Grammars and in Watts' *Logick* by the subject's fourfold division into parts, and by the further subdivision of these parts into topic-based chapters, and of chapters into sections, tables and/or lists (187). These analytic divisions were made visible by the table of contents and layout of printed matter within the volume. The analytic method recurred in grammatical analyses themselves, for instance in "resolving" sentences, where the sentence considered as a whole was "divided" or "resolved" into its parts and subparts; in spelling, considered as the art of dividing words into syllables; and in grammar's division of the unpunctuated and unregulated flow of spoken language into sentences, clauses, parts of speech and words. But though useful, divisions were artifices. Watts repeatedly warned readers that "one Idea or Subject may be divided in very different Manners according to the very different Purposes we have in discoursing of it":

> So if a *Printer* were to consider the several Parts of a *Book*, he must divide it into Sheets, the Sheets into Pages, the Pages into Lines, and the Lines into Letters. But a *Grammarian* divides a *Book* into Periods, Sentences and Words, or Parts of Speech as Noun, Pronoun, Verb etc. A *Logician* considers a *Book* as divided into Chapters, Sections, Arguments, Propositions and Ideas. (191–2)

The same book or subject could be divided up analytically in different ways for different purposes. A variety of different possible methods of partition obtained for any given object or subject, because such divisions were operations of the purposeful mind, rather than intrinsic to the thing itself.

The second aspect of this method of disposition, the "synthetick," was the inverted mirror image of the first, and useful primarily for purposes of instruction: it begins with parts or with the most simple principles of a subject, and "leads onward" by considering each part separately and "distinct by itself" while proceeding "successively and gradually" through "knowledge of the whole" (187, 195, 509). "So in Grammar, we learn first to know Letters, we joyn them to make Syllables, out of Syllables we compose

Words, and out of Words we make Sentences and Discourses" (310).
Grammars made their synthetic method visible on the page by means of
the blank spaces and discontinuities between juxtaposed lists and chapters.
This forced readers to address each "general idea" or principle separately
and "distinct by itself" – the general idea of a one-syllable word, the general idea of a noun or verb – even as it disposed ideas or principles in a
successive and graduated sequence of juxtaposed lists, chapters and parts.
Discontinuity was essential to enable the learner to perceive each idea or
principle distinctly. The ideas which made up the "completeness of the
subject," which were thus encountered separately, successively, gradually
and discontinuously by the reader or learner could, in principle, be conjoined once more into their original whole (184) – in principle, because
there was nothing in the disposition to oblige the learner to connect the
ideas into that original whole. This was one of Oscar Kenshur's "teleological discontinuous forms," where scattered, discontinuous units could
be reassembled into a purely implicit "higher" unity, but did not have to
be.[96] If anything, this method of disposition familiarized readers with this
method of exposition, which recurred regardless of which discipline or
subject was being "dispos'd and methodiz'd."

However, the learner considering each "idea" separately and discontinuously did have to think analogically. As Watts explained, the general idea
or principle governing each division, list or chapter, and expressed in headings, derived from comparisons, since all our abstract ideas derive from
"the Comparison of several corporeal or spiritual Ideas together" and from
a perception of their likeness and unlikeness (47). Comparison, which
Bailey's *Dictionary* defined as "a setting two things together to see wherein
they agree or disagree,"[97] was, as we saw, the Lockean basis of all reasoning. By presenting each general idea successively and "distinct by itself,"
the syncretic method based comprehension of the idea on the reader or
learner's comparisons of the items listed under it. Judgment was involved
from the first, for under the general idea or principle to which each list,
table or chapter was devoted, grammars collected disparate words which
resembled one another in the way indicated by that general idea but which
differed in most other respects. So a list of words that were accented on the
first syllable when used as nouns, and on the second syllable when used as
verbs (absent, abstract, conflict, converse, subject etc.) contained a variety
of words which resembled one another only in that feature, and differed in
other respects. The same held for parts of speech. Learners had to perceive
where the disparate words collected under each idea agreed and disagreed
to grasp the general idea. Analogical thinking was key. Learners also had

to compare words they encountered while reading other things to words
they already knew from one of the grammar's chapters or tables to determine (for instance) whether the word they were reading in a sentence was
a noun or verb, and regular or irregular in its declension. In grammar, one
was constantly "setting two things together to see wherein they agree or
disagree."

Like ABCs and spellers, then, grammars taught readers to manage variety without eliminating it, through a system of regulated substitutions.
Since no list or set of examples was, or could be, exhaustive, every general
idea contained words which could easily be replaced by others as long
as the resemblance held: any one-syllable word could be added, or substituted for another, on the list of one-syllable words, any regular verb
for another on tables of declension. At the same time, general ideas were
substituted for one another as the learner moved gradually and successively
from general idea to general idea. This meant that learners encountered
the same marks or words under different general ideas in different lists or
chapters: <a> for instance, reappeared under the idea of alphabets; under
the idea that every mark was sounded differently according to which letters
it met with in different words; under the idea of accent in pronunciation
(long a, short a); under the idea of one-syllable words; and in "analogy"
and syntax, as an article or part of speech. Resemblances depended on
what <a> was compared to, and different resemblances pertained in each
case: resemblances were substituted for each other according to the lesson
(i.e. purpose) in view. This "set the [Matter] before the Reader in several
Lights" and "turn[ed] the various Sides of it to View, in order to give a
full Idea" of it (526), while keeping each "side" or perspective distinct; but
it also concretized the idea that each word or idea resembled a variety of
others in diverse ways. One might say that words appeared in grammars
in different lights according to the particular words or ideas with which
they were conjoined, and that this repeated on a different level, the behavior of letters which met and joined with other letters and parted again in
successive words.

Comparison among analogical entities as a rational and logical act productive of general ideas found paradigmatic expression in definition – a
form of rewording extensively used in grammars and dictionaries, as we
saw. Watts' instructions for creating short definitions explained what these
instructional books did without explanation: begin by "comparing the
thing to be defined with other things that are most like to itself"; seeing
where its nature "agrees with them" will discover its genus or the general
idea that it has in common with like things (160 ff.): wine is compared to

cider and perry and found to be a sort of juice. Next, consider the thing's most essential and specific difference from those other things that are most like it: so wine differs from cider or perry by being pressed from grapes not apples or pears. Finally, join the specific difference to the genus to create the definition: wine is a juice pressed from grapes. For more complete definitions, the things "most like" to which a thing was compared must include "what are the Opposites or Contrarian to it," since "many things are to be known both by their contrary and their kindred Ideas" (196). Thus the complete definition of a virtue included comparison to "the false virtues that counterfeit it and real vices that oppose it," description of the specific principles and tendencies which distinguish it from these and from kindred virtues, and some account of "the evils attending neglect of that virtue, and of the rewards for practicing it both here and hereafter" (197). Watts was describing best practices for writers and readers in the same terms: to know how to read a short definition was also to know how to write one, and vice versa. His instructions for short definitions explained to learners the components of the dictionary and grammar book definitions they read, and how to define their own words when they wrote or spoke, as they were advised to do. Watts' instructions for complete definitions laid bare for readers and potential writers the formula for a certain kind of periodical essay, beginning with some of Addison's *Spectators*, which explained the right understanding of a virtue or idea by trailing it through all the kindred ideas or virtues which counterfeited it and could be mistaken for it, as well as through its opposites and contraries.

Definition made words, and the ideas they evoked, clear and distinct. They were yet another form of regulated substitution. But they too were artificial and dependent upon the purpose one had in view (one's "End" or "Design") rather than on the nature of things themselves. For "the several species of beings are seldom precisely limited in the Nature of things by any certain and unalterable Bounds" but "resemble others of a kindred nature" and "by various Degrees…approach nearer to [them]" as "the colours of a rainbow are sufficiently distinguished in the middle, but near the borders of each colour, run into each other" (172). Things were not in reality clearly separate or distinct; they bled into one another – or better, into a variety of others, since they could be compared to any number of different things which they resembled in different ways. For instance, rather than compare wine to other juices, we compare it to alcoholic beverages, and distinguish it from beer and hard liquors, for the purpose of making it liable for licensing and taxation; here wine "is" an alcoholic drink, not a juice. Words and ideas offered an almost infinite *combinatoire*. As different analytical partitions suited different purposes, so different ways of joining and disjoining words or ideas were equally good, depending on one's "end," design or goal. For language – like definition and grammatical operations of the mind – fell short of reflecting things themselves: "the infinite Variety of Things and Ideas is beyond all the Words invented" (75); one must "not suppose that the Nature or Essences of Things always differ from one another as much as their Names do" (139).

The fact that definitions were artificial and purely instrumental products of the thinking mind, rather than true reflections of anything in nature, was precisely what gave definition an important function in reading comprehension. For "Words have different Significations according to the Ideas of the various Persons, Sects and Parties who use them" (108) – with the consequence that writer and readers, or speaker and hearers, might easily deploy the same words with different ideas in mind:

> So when I hear a Man use the Words Church and Sacrament, if I understand by these Words, a Congregation of faithful Men who profess Christianity, and the two Ordinances, Baptism and the Lord's Supper, I have a true Idea of those Words in the common Sense of Protestants; but if the Man who speaks them be a Papist, he means the Church of Rome, and the Seven Sacraments, and then I have a *mistaken* Idea of these Words, as spoken by him, for he has a different Sense of the Meaning. (66)

Watts held this responsible for the misunderstandings and ubiquitous religious and political "contests" among men. It followed that the primary task "in Conversation or Reading [was to] be diligent to find out the true Sense or distinct Idea which the Speaker or Writer affixes to his words; especially those Words which are the chief Subject of his Discourse," and to "endeavour that your Ideas of every Word may be the same as his were" (146–7). Understanding what another person said or wrote literally meant determining exactly what that person had in mind. The words that were the chief subject of a person's discourse went to the heart of what they were saying – to what was at issue, and to the thesis or opinion they were propounding – as well as to their purpose in speaking or writing. The assumption was that no one speaks or writes without a purpose and that every speaker or writer therefore "directs his Expressions generally to his designed End."[98] The path to determining exactly what idea/s a speaker or writer had in mind in using the words which represented "the chief Subject of his Discourse," ran directly through the different parts of grammar:

> In order to attain clear and distinct Ideas of what we read or hear, we must search the *Sense of Words*; we must consider what is their Original and Derivation in our own or foreign Languages; what is their common

> Sense amongst Mankind, or in other Authors, especially such as write in
> the same Country, in the same Age, about the same time, and upon the
> same Subjects: We must consider in what Sense the same Author uses any
> particular Word or Phrase, and that when he is discoursing on the same
> Matter, especially about the same Points or Paragraphs of his Writing: We
> must consider, whether the Word be used in a strict and limited, or in a
> large and general Sense; whether in a literal, in a figurative, or in a prophetic
> Sense; whether it has any secondary Idea answering to it beside the primary
> or chief Sense: We must enquire farther what is the Scope and design of the
> Writer; what is the Connexion of that Sense with those that go before it and
> those which follow it. By these and other Methods we are to search out the
> Definition of Names, i.e. the true Sense and Meaning, in which any Author
> or Speaker uses any word which may be the chief Subject of Discourse, or
> may carry considerable Importance with it. (148–9)

Here definition was reoriented for the purpose of determining the author's
"sense of the words" by reference to larger contexts. One was textual: the
word in the context of the sentence, in the context of the sentences before
and after it; in different parts of the whole text; in different parts of the
author's opus; and in the context of other authors writing on the same subject at the same time and place. Since authors and speakers often "affix different Ideas to their own Words, in different Parts of their Discourses, and
hereby…confound their Hearers" or readers (150), definition was an aid to
discovering whether the speaker/author used key words consistently. When
he did, "comparing the words and Phrases in one Place of an Author with
the same or kindred Words in other Places of the same Author" enabled
the reader to use one to explain the Author's meaning in the other, on the
principle that "a Writer best interprets himself."[99] Discovering whether the
speaker or author was using key words in ways that were consonant with
other contemporary authors was not only, or so much, a way of using contemporary usage to clarify his meaning, as a way of discovering which contemporary controversies turned on different meanings attached to the same
words, and thus what meanings (and whose views) one's speaker or writer
was using them to contest. This was advanced by examining the writer's
words in another type of context, that consisting of the historical circumstances in which the discourse or writing had been produced and received.
For these enabled the reader to "examine the Reach, Force and Coherence
of what is said," and determine how far it held true. Like speaking, writing
was always produced on a particular occasion for a particular purpose. As
authors' purposes, "ends" or "designs" differed in different circumstances, so
did the reach and meaning of their key words. To "penetrate as far as possible into the Design of the Speaker or Writer," it was therefore necessary

to "consider the Time, Place, Occasion, Circumstances of the Matter" (244). In Watts' example above, knowing whether the words, "Church" and "Sacrament" were spoken or written by a Protestant or Catholic for Catholics or Protestants, and what religious controversies turned on the meanings attributed to these words, enabled the reader to determine what the speaker or writer meant by them, and what his "end" in using them was. Discovering that these words were being used by a Catholic demonstrated the reach or "scope" of his words. As a "foot" signifies different things in books of different scopes – a body-part in a treatise of anatomy, twelve inches in a book of geometry – so "Church" and "Sacrament" signified different things in Catholic and Protestant theology. "Penetrat[ing] as far as possible into the Design of the Speaker or Writer," positively contributed to the readers' "sagacity and wariness" by showing them what "knowledge" to take away from a text: in Watts' example, how Catholics used the words "Church" and "Sacrament" as opposed to Protestants, and by extension, what in the text was true for Catholics but not necessarily for Protestants.

Contemporaries called this manner of reading "Grammatical Criticism," because it deployed grammatical and contextual methods of exegesis that ancient Roman grammarians had practiced and taught, that Christian fathers and Renaissance humanists had used in their wake, and that eighteenth-century editors of Milton and Shakespeare were beginning to use on them, to resolve the obscurities in ancient texts, as well as to correct scribal errors in manuscripts.[100] Watts' *Logick* selected from among the methods that "grammatical critics" used "to explain what is obscure in Authors" and adapted them for readers who, without being erudite scholars, sought fuller understanding both of what they read and of whether it held true.[101] He showed readers how using grammatical taxonomies incorporating logical ideas enabled them to make other clarifying distinctions too – to determine, for instance, whether an author was using words in a general or particular, literal or figurative, univocal or ambiguous sense, and with or without implicit connotations or secondary ideas. This too would help readers or hearers both to clarify what was being said, and to judge the truth or falsity, consistency and reach, of the assertions being made.

The fact that grammar helped to "teach the Mind Sagacity and Wariness" in its search for "real and substantial knowledge" was important in reading because, as Locke had pointed out, "there is no part wherein the Understanding needs more careful and wary Conduct than in the Use of Books."[102] Books gave readers knowledge (for instance of "civil and natural history") in the form of what Locke called "hearsay" and William Duncan "testimony" – facts and events filtered through other men's eyes, minds and words. As Duncan put it, echoing Locke, "it is necessary to admit many things upon the Testimony of others, which by this Means become the Foundation of a great part of our Knowledge"; and when testimony is the source of our knowledge, as it is in reading, "the Possibility of our being deceived, is still greater than in the Case of Experience."[103] Indeed, as Watts complained, through words, "Not-Being may be proposed to our Thoughts as well as that which has real Being" (16). If the goal of reading was to acquire real and substantial knowledge, then reading was also a matter of judging what part/s of a book contained truths that were worth extracting and remembering.

The problem here, however, was that peoples' thinking was "confused," and their judgments "led into frequent Mistakes" (4) by the mind's own shortcomings. Following Locke's "Of The Conduct of the Understanding," which became available in his *Posthumous Works* in 1706, Watts' *Logick* took pains to instill in readers salutary suspicions about the rationality of the operations of their own reading or listening minds. As Locke had observed, "great Care should be taken of the Understanding, to conduct it aright in the search for knowledge, and in the Judgments it makes" because, misled by our own psyches, we "impose upon ourselves, which is the worst and most dangerous imposition of all."[104] We are liable to be led into misreadings and misjudgments of what we receive on the "testimony of others," by the faculties, bent and contents of our own psyches – our imagination and passions; the ideas, "knowledge" and prepossessions already in our minds; our temperament or disposition. Owing to prejudices imbibed in infancy or in the course of our education, or because we are swayed by custom, authority or fashion, we make the "Writings of any venerable Authors, and especially of the sacred Books of Scripture…speak our own Sense" and confirm "our own Schemes or Hypotheses" (322); or we "stand ready to oppose everything that is said…when [we] read or hear a Discourse different from [our] own Sentiments" (328). We also "judge in a Lump." So "when we read a Book that has many excellent Truths in it and Divine Sentiments, we are tempted to approve not only that whole Book, but even all the Writings of that Author"; and conversely, when we judge that a book contains rubbish, we forget that "some very excellent Sayings are found in very silly Books, and some silly Thoughts appear in Books of Value" (301). Our imagination is so susceptible to oratory and fine words that when a "Man of Eloquence" writes or speaks on any subject, "we are too ready to run into all his Sentiments" (309). As our perception is deceived when we "see" the sun as a flat disk about two inches in diameter, so our susceptibility to language makes us credulous when falsehood puts on a fair disguise. Susceptibility to language was precisely what traditional rhetoric taught speakers and writers to exploit: rhetorically trained speakers used imagery, word-choices, cadences and arrangement of matter to persuade others to assent to a view or pursue a course of action. Hearers and readers seeking Truth must be aware and beware.

Watts added to Locke's laundry list of causes of misreading and errors in judgment in the quest for truth, and organized the results according to: "Prejudices arising from the Things about which we judge," "Prejudices arising from words," "Prejudices arising from ourselves"; and "Prejudices arising from other People." The first group included "a Mixture of different Qualities in the same Thing," the "Different Lights in which an object may be placed" and "False Associations of Ideas." The second addressed rhetoric and equivocal or meaningless words; the third, prejudices imbibed in infancy or arising from the faculties – the senses, the imagination, the passions, one's temperament – and from self-love. The last addressed education, custom, fashion, the authority of the writer or speaker, and the assurance with which they wrote or spoke. Unlike Locke and earlier attempts to explain his "Conduct of the Understanding," such as Ambrose Philips' unexpectedly popular periodical, *The Free Thinker* (1718–19), Watts' *Logick* also gave misreading and errors in judgment social grounding. He explained that persons, sects, parties and ranks of people often misread and misjudged because they conversed with only one kind of people, read only one sort of book, and heard only one sort of idea, noting that "the ways of discourse and reasoning are very different, even concerning the same matter, at Court and in the University," at Westminster and in the Exchange.

This was a formidable list of prejudices and prepossessions; and Watts made it clear that no one was entirely free of all of them. Enquirers after Truth would therefore do best to "suspend Judgment," as the Pyrrhonists did, until they could "keep [their]Mind open to receive Truth" (387). One can see why Reverend Watts had to fall back on innate ideas, and thus on the argument that we can all somehow recognize Truth when we see it, if only our minds are open to receive it. The echo of religious language here was not fortuitous. For this also conveniently resolved a key problem that many Christians had with Lockean epistemology: that "Virtue according to Mr. Locke has no other Measure, Law or Rule, than Fashion and Custom: Morality, Justice, Equity, depend only on Law and Will"; faith and religion too.[105] Introducing into his Lockean framework elements of de Crousaz's Cartesian *Art of Thinking*[106] in order to admit innate ideas of God and Virtue, and claim that these instinctively gave us "a true knowledge" of both, safeguarded religion and morality (9). It put some received ideas *hors de combat* – beyond fashion, custom, cultural relativity, and attack – by pretending or assuming that they were not customary ideas at all. One might say that Watts' integration of Descartes with Locke, and of innate ideas with empiricism, anticipated and likely influenced fellow dissenter Frances Hutcheson and the course of Scottish moral sense and common sense philosophy.[107]

But for our purposes, Watts' *Logick* made readers aware of "operations of the mind" they had employed, and of the utility of categories and techniques to which they had been exposed, in their grammar books. He showed readers how to apply these to reading comprehension and elucidation, and alerted readers to their epistemological limitations. Watts' *Logick* freed rational, analogical operations of the mind from within the covers of elementary schoolbooks, by showing how grammar's intrinsic alliance with logic could be applied critically in all reading to determine whether a writer was using language in indeterminate, sectarian, rhetorical or otherwise illegitimate ways, how far he spoke truth, and whether he was practicing to deceive. Watts' *Logick* also laid the groundwork for further learning by supplying readers with prompts for a hermeneutics of suspicion not only about what they read or heard, but also about the contents, convictions and operations of their own minds.

NOTES

1 John Locke, *Essay Concerning Human Understanding* (5th edn. London, 1705): IV: 1.
2 Daniel Defoe, *Essay Upon Literature* (New York: AMS Press, 1999): 112, 113.
3 Green, *Print and Protestantism*: 40; Barker, "The Morphology of the Page": 250; Morison, *Politics and Script*: 323.
4 N. Bailey, *An Universal Etymological English Dictionary* (London, 1727): title page.
5 Quoted in Fox, *Oral and Literate Culture*, 82. Also Jones, *English Pronunciation*.
6 Chancery scribes and professional scriptoria had settled on habitual spellings since the fifteenth century. See Scragg, *English Spelling*. Osselton argues that some eighteenth-century epistolary networks had distinctive spellings of their own. See "Informal Spelling Systems."
7 Quoted in Salmon, "Orthography and Punctuation": 46.
8 Smollett, *Humphrey Clinker*: 34.
9 Thomas Blount, *Glossographia* (London, 1707 [1656]): title page; John Wesley, *The Complete English dictionary* (London, 1753): Preface.
10 *The Spectator*, Tuesday, June 24, 1712 in *Papers of Joseph Addison*: 3: 252.
11 Philip Allwood, *Remarks on Some Observations edited in* The British Critic... (London, 1800): 183.
12 For anxiety about language, Dawson, *Locke, Language and Early Modern Philosophy*; for a political view of the detachment of words from things, Zwicker, "Politics and Literary Practice."
13 Cohen, *Sensible Words*: xxiv.

14 Francis Brokesby, *Of Education with Respect to Grammar Schools and the Universities* (London, 1701): 191.

15 Thomas, "Meaning of Literacy": 100.

16 Street, *Literacy*.

17 Mrs. Lovechild, *The Mother's Grammar* (London, 1798): Preface.

18 Grenby, *Child Reader*: 49, 50, 103; St. Clair, *Reading Nation*.

19 Massey, *Origin and Progress of Letters*, Part II: 83.

20 *The Guardian*, 2 vols. (London, 1794): #94: ii, 47, 48, 49.

21 Spufford, "Women Teaching Reading to Poor Children"; Whyman, *The Pen and the People*: Chap. 3; Simonton, "Schooling the Poor": 195; Fergus, *Provincial Servants*.

22 Monaghan, *Learning to Read and Write*: 145 ff.; Wyss, *English Letters and Indian Literacies*; Round, *Removable Type*.

23 Quoted in Mandelbrote, "The English Bible and its Readers": 52.

24 Massey, *Origin and Progress of Letters*: II: 121.

25 Willliam Robertson to Charlotte Lennox, Edinburgh 6th April, 1759 in Schürer (ed.) *Charlotte Lennox*: 98.

26 Okie, *Augustan Historical Writing*; Kenyon, *The History Men*.

27 "English Language Law Bill," in Cobbett, *Parliamentary History of England*: viii: 858–9. Also Hector, *Handwriting of English Documents*: 67 ff.

28 Ambrose Searle, *A Treatise on the Art of Writing* (London, 1782): vi.

29 Morison, "Development of Handwriting"; Backscheider, *Spectacular Politics*; Hector, *English Documents*: 66.

30 Monaghan, *Learning to Read*: 287, 26. A necessary demand, since Laetitia Yeandle ("Evolution of Handwriting") found that even prominent, highly literate Americans continued to insert Gothic characters into their roman scripts throughout the century.

31 Thornton, *Handwriting in America*: 17. Also Dierks, *In my Power*.

32 Mary Johnson, *The Young Woman's Companion or the Serving Maid's Assistant* (London, 1753): 63–4. Bickham's round-hand copybooks, London, c. 1760: "To the Men of Business." (The copy texts here were bills of sale, promissory notes, receipts, and other commercial forms.)

33 To be taken with some caution, since Bickham was puffing round-hand copybooks that he or his father had engraved and published.

34 Joseph Champion, *Penmanship or the Art of Fair Writing: A New Essay* (London, 1770?): 6; Searle, *Art of Writing*: 2.

35 There were only 24 letters in the alphabet, though some grammarians were already making it 26.

36 Tuer, *Horn Book*: 332; Crain, *Story of A*: 42.

37 Champion, *Penmanship*: 5.

38 Green, *The Christian's ABC*: 174 ff.

39 Daniel Fenning, *The Universal Spelling Book; Or a New and Easy Guide to the English Language* (London, 1756): 173.

40 Charles Hoole, *A New Discovery of the old Art of Teaching Schoole* (London, 1661): 22.

41 Crain, *Story of A*: 7.

42 Thomas Astle, *The Origin and Progress of Writing* (London, 1784): 19.

43 George Bickham, *The Universal Penman; Or, the Art of Writing* (London, 1741). This and all the quotations above in the text are taken from here. Since the book was compiled from extant plates, there is no continuous pagination.

44 Starnes and Noyes, *The English Dictionary*.

45 Michael, *Early Textbooks*: 14.

46 James Greenwood, *An Essay towards a Practical English Grammar* (London, 1711): 191; Lindley Murray, *English Grammar Adapted to the Different Classes of Learners* (York, 1795): 15. Lowth too defined it as the art of "rightly dividing words into their syllables" *A Short Introduction to English Grammar with Critical Notes* (2nd edn. corrected. London, 1763): 6.

47 Thomas Tuite, *The Oxford Spelling Book* (London, 1726): 79.

48 Brightland, *Grammar*, note p. 57. Believing that Charles Gildon wrote Brightland's Grammar, modern grammarians call this the Brightland-Gildon grammar.

49 "The ordinary way of teaching children to read...is to make them name the Letters, and spell the words, till by often use they can pronounce (at least) the shortest words at first sight...If any where he stick at any word (as seeming too hard) let him mark it with a pin, or the dint of his nayle, and by looking upon it again, he will remember it." Charles Hoole, *A New Discovery of the old Art of Teaching Schoole* (London, 1661): 20, 22. For the rationale for the method, see the chapters on Petty-School.

50 Samuel Johnson, *Grammar of the English Tongue* in his *Dictionary* (1755): prosody section (n.p.); Thomas Dilworth, *A New Guide to the English Tongue* (13th edn., London 1757): 96. Noah Webster, *A Grammatical Institute of the English Language*, Part II (Hartford, 1784): 5. Also Crystal, *Prosodic Systems* and Jones, *English Pronunciation*.

51 Kroll, *Material Word*.

52 Paulson, *Breaking and Remaking*.

53 William Tiffin, *A New Help and Improvement of the Art of Swiftly Writing* (1751), quoted in Jones, *English Pronunciation*: 43.

54 S. Harland, *The English Spelling Book Revis'd* (3rd edn., London, 1719): 4, iv; Brightland, *Grammar*: 32; Tuite, *Oxford Spelling Book*: 49.

55 Harland, *The English Spelling Book*: 5.

56 Lauzon, *Signs of Light*, esp. Ch. 6.

57 James Beattie, "The Theory of Language," in *Dissertations Moral and Critical* (London and Edinburgh, 1783): 272.

58 Beattie noted that contractions were "much affected by the first printers, in imitation no doubt of the manuscript writers, to whom they were a considerable saving both of time and paper" "Theory of Language," in *Dissertations Moral*: 319.

59 For other differences between speech and written representations of it, Culpeper and Kyto, *Early Modern English Dialogues*.

60 Dilworth, *New Guide*: 126. Beattie still told university students in Aberdeen during the 1780s that "in writing for one's own use one may employ abbreviations, or the ciphers of shorthand, or any other characters one is acquainted

with; but what is to be laid before the public or any other superior, should have all possible clearness, and ought therefore to be free from contractions, and the like peculiarities." "Theory of Language," 319–20.

61 *Spectator* #135, on "laconic" Englishmen who spoke exclusively in monosyllables and contracted all their words, can be read as a joke on these aspects of the spelling book.

62 Nevalain, "Early Modern English Lexis and Semantics": 332.

63 N. Bailey, *An Universal Etymological English Dictionary*: title page.

64 Spellers and dictionaries also cooperated in highlighting the utility of the abc as an ordering device and in enforcing "correct" orthography since, as Vivian Salmon has pointed out, "only with a consistent spelling for each entry would dictionaries become viable." Salmon, "Orthography and Punctuation": 36.

65 Brightland, *Grammar*: 107.

66 James Gough, *A Practical Grammar of the English Tongue* (2nd edn., Dublin, 1760): 111.

67 Murray, *English Grammar*: 85.

68 James Buchanan, *A Regular English Syntax, wherein is Exhibited the Whole Variety of English Construction* (London, 1767): xix.

69 A. Lane, *A Key to the Art of Letters; or English a Learned Language* (2nd edn., London, 1706): 108–110, 107, 88, 91, 104, 106.

70 Elfenbein, *Romanticism and the Rise of English*: 20.

71 Greenwood, *Grammar*: 225.

72 Ibid.: 163.

73 Lowth, *A Short Introduction*: 65–6.

74 But see Chapter 5 of this book.

75 Murray, *English Grammar*: 221, 220.

76 Lowth, *Short Introduction*: 1, 28.

77 Murray, *English Grammar*: 198, 176.

78 Anthony Benezet, *The Pennsylvania Spelling Book; or Youth's Friendly Instructor and Monitor* (3rd edn., Providence, RI, 1782): title page.

79 Percy, "Learning and Virtue": 92 ff.

80 Isaac Watts, *The Art of Reading and Writing English* (2nd edn., London, 1722): xvi. There were still American and British editions in 1796 and 1797.

81 Gough, *Practical Grammar*: 4; Mrs Lovechild, *The Child's Grammar* (Dublin, 1790): Preface; Ellin Devis, *The Accidence… Designed for the Use of Young Ladies* (8th edn. London, 1795): iii.

82 Devis, *Accidence*: 1. For efforts to make learning fun for children and for home schooling, see Hilton et al., *Opening the Nursery Door* and Styles and Arizpe, *Acts of Reading*.

83 Bailey, "Variation and Change in Eighteenth-Century English": 199.

84 Milroy, "Historical Description and the Ideology of Standard Language." Also Cummings, *Literary Culture of the Reformation*; and Barrell, "The Language Properly So Called."

85 Greenwood, *Grammar*: i, 37; Lowth, *Short Introduction*: vii; Anne Fisher, *A Practical New Grammar* (8th edn., London, 1763): xii, vii; Noah Webster, *The American Spelling Book* (2nd edn., Boston, 1790): xiii.

86 Mugglestone, "Registering the Language." See also essays by Tieken-Boon on "Lowth as an Icon of Prescriptivism," Bailey on "Variation and Change" and Jones on "Nationality and Standardisation" in Hickey (ed.), *Eighteenth-Century English*; Tieken-Boon (ed.), *Grammar*; Wright, *Development of Standard English*; and Sundby, *Dictionary of English Normative Grammar*.

87 Dille, "The Dictionary in Abstract," in Lynch and McDermott (eds.), *Anniversary Essays*.

88 For the prehistory of this architectural image, Mitchell, *Grammar Wars*, Ch. 2; for its humanist origins, Elsky, *Authorizing Words*, Ch. 1; for the foundational role of grammar in humanism and Protestantism, Cummings, *Literary Culture of the Reformation*.

89 For science and nature, see Howell, *Eighteenth-Century British Logic and Rhetoric*: 331–45.

90 Watts, *Logick: or the Right Use of Reason in Enquiry after Truth* (2nd edn., London, 1725): 114. Page numbers to this edition will hereafter be in the text.

91 Jeremy Belknap, *Memoirs of the Life, Character and Writings of Dr. Isaac Watts* (Boston, 1793): 23; but compare Samuel Johnson, *Lives of the Most Eminent English Poets*, 4 vols. (London, 1779): 4: 279. Belknap copied, corrected and added to Johnson's *Life of Watts*, which non-conformists thought biased by the fact that Johnson adhered to "the Episcopalian communion established by law in *South* Britain" (119). See for instance, Samuel Palmer's abridgment of *Johnson's Lives of the English Poets* (London, 1787) and *Vindication of the Modern Dissenters against the Aspersions of the Revd. William Hawkins, MA* (London, 1790).

92 Belknap, *Memoirs*: 31.

93 Johnson, *Lives*: 4: 282.

94 Davis, *Isaac Watts*: 87.

95 Howell, *Logic and Rhetoric*: 342.

96 Kenshur, *Open Form*: 120.

97 Nathan Bailey, *An Universal English Dictionary* (London, 1721).

98 Watts, *Improvement of the Mind*: 121.

99 Ibid.: 120.

100 See Eden, *Hermeneutics*.

101 Watts reduced circumstances, from seven *topoi* – who, what, where, by whose help, why, how and when – to three – who, when and why. Circumstance, definition, comparison, similitude, dissimilitude, and division were among the traditional *topoi* of both dialectical logic and invention. This was compatible with Locke, who had privileged, and extended the scope of, comparison.

102 John Locke, "Of the Conduct of the Understanding," in *Posthumous Writings* (London, 1706): 58, 125, 74. This was subsequently reprinted at least ten times as a separate text before 1800.

103 *The Preceptor* (London, 1754): 11: 84, 179.

104 Locke, "Conduct of the Understanding": 4, 45.

105 [Anon], *Several Letters Written by a Noble Lord to a Young Man at the University* (London, 1716): 41.

106 De Crousaz was only translated into English from the French as *A New Treatise of the Art of Thinking* in 1724; but Watts could read French. Shaftesbury spoke of a moral sense without relation to Lockean epistemology.

107 Watts was made an honorary doctor of divinity at the Universities of Edinburgh and Aberdeen in 1728. For analogy in Scottish Enlightenment thinking, Manning, *Poetics of Character*, Chap. 1; for analogy in Newton and Locke, Bannet, "Analogy as Translation." Watts' influence may also be seen in Scottish efforts to defend Watts' most dubious philosophical proposition: that "a clear and distinct Perception, or full Evidence of the Agreement and Disagreement of our Ideas to one another or to Things, is a certain Criterion of Truth" (272). For why this is dubious, see Hoyles, *Waning of the Renaissance 1640–1740*. Unfortunately, the ideas Watts used in exemplifying syllogisms show that there is nothing to prevent prejudices from appearing to the mind as clear and distinct ideas.

CHAPTER 2

Arts of Reading

The oral dimensions of reading centered on character and sociality. For the eighteenth century, speech was always situated – it transpired between an "I" and a "You" about a "he," "she" or "it"; it was addressed by an "I" to a "You" or many "You's," and anticipated a response. This was as true of the "silent speech" of writing as of orations or conversations, and held for printed writing as much as for manuscript. To read was to hear someone speaking to you through the medium of a letter, essay, or book. Reading a writer's words nullified distance, time, death and physical absence by revivifying his/her words in the present and permitting readers to "converse" with the person who had written them. To read was thus to acquire a companion for one's solitary hours whose "Character" one could come to know.

"Giving the Character of an Author" was therefore a serious critical act. Critics continued to practice a form of criticism inherited from the Ancients, which consisted of comparing the "Characters" of paired authors – Homer and Virgil, or Richardson and Fielding.[1] As John Boswell explained, "giving the Character of each Writer" told a reader "what he is to expect in the respective Authors" and "the peculiar Excellences for which they are remarkable," in order to indicate "the Manner in which the Authors recommended may be read with Advantage."[2] Using his intimate knowledge of the author's opus and reflections upon his characteristic style and contents made over years, enabled learned critics to "give the Character of an Author" as one might give that of a person with whom one was intimately acquainted when introducing them to an unwary stranger under one's protection – describing and vouching for their writerly virtues, warning readers of their faults. New print genres designed for a broad readership made it quicker and easier for readers to discern the character of the author who was addressing them. Periodicals provided an eidolon – a manifest authorial persona with a few stated character traits and a distinctive "voice," who "spoke" to readers and occasionally addressed, invoked or characterized them directly. "Letters from a Gentleman in Town to his Friend in the Country" did much the same.[3] Printed collections of non-fictional letters or voyages were often prefaced instead by some account of the character and situation of their author, if not by a full-blown "Life." And there was a brisk market in first-person memoirs, true and fictional autobiographies, and epistolary novels where characters spoke directly through their letters, as characters did through speeches in plays. These methods of presentation confirmed readers in the view that they were reading what someone in particular was saying to them – and that conversing with or about them was the appropriate response.

The conviction that every text communicates a particular person's character and sentiments to others, underlay the instructions for reading aloud that were disseminated to the public. The reader aloud was supposed to turn that person's written speech back into oral speech, by using all the resources of his/her voice, as well as his/her posture, facial expressions and gestures, to "express the full Sense and Spirit" of the writer, and fully convey his/her "design." The reader made his/her voice and body the vehicle for someone else's meanings and feelings. As James Burgh put it in *The Art of Speaking*, "Reading is nothing but speaking what one sees in the book, as if he were expressing his *own* Sentiments as they rise in his mind" (8). To read aloud was to use one's understanding of the sense and sensibility of a writer and one's technical skill, to produce what Africans in the New World correctly called a "talking book."

"Delivery" had long been taught in Latin grammar schools and colleges as part of rhetoric, to train young men destined for the bar, the pulpit, the camp, or the Senate to pronounce their orations. Learning to speak in public and political venues – to deliver one's sentiments to a parliamentary assembly, or to a crowd on election day, in powerfully persuasive and moving ways – remained important for men of rank throughout the century. Particularly in New England, where pulpit oratory had been more extensively used to generate religious conversions, eloquent delivery of impassioned public orations played a key role from Revolution to Constitution, both in persuading the populace to accept or enact these political conversions and in symbolizing the republican character of American political regimes.[4] But something else emerged alongside this, both in Britain and America. Separated from the rest of rhetoric, "Pronunciation" or "the Art of Reading" adapted delivery for an era when there was occasion for everyone to read aloud from letters, books and papers in social, domestic and working situations and when, instead of speaking extempore, many clergymen and barristers read sermons and briefs aloud from a written or printed text.

Some books continued to offer specialized instruction in reading aloud for clergy or lawyers; but the art of "pronouncing" texts was disseminated to the generality of readers in a multitude of venues – through grammars, books of rhetoric, preceptors and arts of reading; through encyclopedias and dictionaries of the arts and sciences; through periodicals, reviews and letter manuals. Most printed matter tried to "methodize" pronunciation to make it easier for people to read aloud in a manner that would not tax the politeness of everyone condemned to listen to them. But as we will see in the first section below, pronunciation was methodized differently in discursive texts, and by printers through "printers' marks" which included punctuation. The art of reading also spawned a small industry in pronouncing dictionaries and in miscellanies of select pieces from "the best writers" which were designed primarily for use in practicing the art, but often served subsidiary purposes as well. Americans began compiling their own pronouncing-anthologies after Independence.

Samuel Johnson's *bon mot* – that reading and conversation "should be mixed like eating and exercise; the one digests the other"[5] – described best practices both in education and in social life. During the seventeenth and eighteenth centuries, "education was performative" and heavily dependent upon speech and dialogue, and "women, particularly mothers…had a much wider involvement in education than past scholarship suggests," particularly in the home.[6] Conversation was widely used pedagogically, in schools and by women instructing children at home.[7] A growing body of scholarship also demonstrates the persistence into the nineteenth century of literary coteries, which made sharing writing and conversation about reading important parts of their sociality. This scholarship suggests that both in Britain and America, seventeenth-century coterie practices, or versions thereof, spread down the social hierarchy from the aristocracy and gentry to provincial mixed-rank reading groups attached to subscription libraries, to circles of writers and aspiring offspring of the middling sort, and ultimately to popular debating societies and working men's clubs.[8] The focus in the second section of this chapter is on how printers and booksellers contributed to this development by publishing printed "conversation-pieces."

"Conversation-pieces" were a stylized print genre which used the familiar form of conversation to transmit knowledge relevant to the reading and judgment of texts, as well as to model ways in which polite conversations about reading was or should be conducted in pedagogical or social situations. Informally set in gardens and parlors, by firesides and at tea- or dinner-tables, as well as in classrooms, "conversations-pieces" included (and/or were included in) works that we now classify as periodicals, novels, children's literature, dialogues and literary criticism, as well as works that remain unplaced. Some elaborated their characters and settings, others resembled disembodied dialogues. Some were devoted entirely to matters of pronunciation and reading, others integrated these with conversation about other subjects. Many were designed for a dual or triple readership. As Mary Wollstonecraft observed, being "accommodated to the present state of society," they were "intended to assist the teacher as well as the pupil" and the mother as well as the child.[9] Conversation-pieces which modeled politely sociable conversations about reading often demonstrated, in addition, how readers could take knowledge applicable to themselves and their own experience from character-focused reading. Since book learning was supposed to be supplemented by knowledge of the world in matters such as this, the stylized printed conversation-pieces in the second section are balanced in the third section by some lively contemporary accounts of extant practices.

Guides to Reading Aloud

"To read, is to express written (or printed) Words by their proper Sound."[10] Reciting words aloud from a written or printed text was perhaps the most immediately obvious meaning of "read" during the eighteenth century – we still use reading in this sense when we speak of reading for a part. Reading aloud was both intimately connected to reading comprehension, and somewhat distinguished from it. "Pronunciation" dealt with the proper sounding of words and periods. But since "good Reading is that which conveys the Sense and Meaning of what is read to the Hearer fully and clearly and effectively," it was evident that the reader must "manage his Voice according to the Sense." Since writing was "silent speech," to express written words by their "*proper* Sound," was to convey another person's "sense and meaning" orally as their representative, and thus to transmit "what is the Chief Design of the Speaker or Writer."[11] Fully transmitting the author's design also meant transmitting the feeling/s that his words sought to convey. As John Mason put it in 1740: "a good Pronunciation in Reading, is the Art of managing and governing the Voice so as to express the full Sense and Spirit of your Author in that just, decent, and graceful Manner, which will not only instruct but affect the Hearers; and will not only raise in them the same Ideas he intended to convey, but the same Passions he really felt."[12] Reading aloud was impersonation – the physical and material embodiment of the reader's fullest comprehension of an author's (or in plays, a character's) meanings and feelings.

A widely recommended technique for managing the voice according to the sense, began by identifying "the Emphatical Word" in each sentence. This was seen as the equivalent, on the level of the sentence, of identifying the accented syllable in each word. The emphatical word was defined as "that Word which shows the Chief Design of the Sentence," or, the word or words "for the sake [of which] the whole Sentence seems to be made."[13] To identify the emphatical word was thus to determine the main point each sentence was making, and the word or words on which it primarily turned. When reading aloud, the voice must convey that point by marking the emphatical word with an "emphasis," i.e. by pronouncing it more forcefully and with a slight rise in the voice, or by introducing an "emphatical pause" before or after it. Elocutionists tried to give rules for identifying emphatical words: in questions, it was usually the questioning word ("*Who* said so?"); in antitheses, the words set in opposition to one another ("He is a *tyrant*, not a *father*, to his People"); in lists or invocations, parallel words ("Ye *hills* and *dales*, ye *rivers, woods*, and *plains*"). But it was impossible to give rules for sentences where "we may present to the hearers quite different views of the same sentiment by placing the emphasis differently." As Lindley Murray explained (repeating Hugh Blair verbatim) emphasis became a purely interpretative act in a sentence such as "Judas, betrayest thou the Son of Man with a kiss?"

> "*Betrayest* thou," makes the reproach turn on the infamy of treachery; "Betrayest *thou*," makes it rest upon Judas's connection with his master; "Betrayest thou the *Son of Man*," rests it upon our Saviour's personal character and eminence; "Betrayest thou the Son of Man *with a kiss?*" turns it upon his prostituting a signal of peace and friendship to the purposes of a mark of destruction.[14]

Emphasis in reading aloud made the meaning of texts intelligible; it prevented the reading from becoming monotonous, lifeless and dull; and it affected how all other parts of a sentence were pronounced. But interpretative latitude such as this made educators nervous. They sternly warned that "the Reader should not make new Emphases beyond the Design of the Writer," and that "if the emphasis be placed wrong, we pervert and confound the meaning wholly."[15] And they referred readers for safety to the punctuation in printed texts which, in principle, served both to guide oral reading and to disambiguate sense.

Punctuation was another feature that distinguished printed writing from most people's handwritten texts, including authors' – it was usually inserted into authors' scripts by compositors at the press. Spellers, grammars and letter manuals therefore included a chapter on "the Marks principally met with in Books," in which punctuation points were explained to readers together with apostrophe, brackets, brace, hyphen, quotation marks and the marks that printers used for chapter division, section division, paragraph division, marginal notes, footnotes, index, and appendix. The assumption appears to have been that users would have absolutely no familiarity with such practices. For quotation marks, for instance, one grammarian wrote: "Quotation is a Thing, or Subject, borrowed from another Author, and quoted Word for Word; and then the Author that borrows it puts, or should put, two commas made backwards thus (") to let the Reader know 'tis not his own Words, or Opinion, only."[16] Punctuation "points" were universally described, by contrast, as so many "pauses" or "stops," which showed readers how to manage their voice when reading words aloud: commas indicated that the reader aloud must pause for a count of 1, semi-colons for a count of 2, colons for a count of 3, full stops for a count of 4. Parentheses demanded a shorter than comma-length pause at each end, and that the words between be spoken with "a moderate depression of the voice." Colons and semi-colons held the voice in suspension. Full stops called for a drop in cadence to convey the closure of the period, while exclamation and interrogation points respectively required a modulation and elevation of the voice. Printers also had other visual methods of pointing such things out: they located for readers those pesky emphatical words which required emphasis in pronunciation "by printing the Emphatical Word in Italick or beginning it with a Capital."[17] They introduced paragraph breaks to indicate where a "double period pause" was required (count of 8). They left the gap of an empty line between two paragraphs to indicate the need for a "double paragraph pause" (count of 16). And the line-endings in their layout of verse acted as prompts for readers to pause for a beat, to enable their hearers to keep track of the "numbers." Printers were punctuating writing to make reading aloud easier by turning the printed page into something like a musical score.

Since sound and sense were connected, the same points helped readers to disentangle intricate compound sentences, by clarifying their syntax. Colons and semi-colons dismembered compound sentences into their two, three or four major segments. Commas marked groups of words or phrases that belonged together within these. Parentheses indicated segments that could be omitted without injuring the sense. This was a genuine aid to reading comprehension as well as to reading aloud, as Daniel Fenning, among others, stressed: "nothing contributes more to clearness of style than accurate pointing…it is possible for pointing to be so very inaccurate as to render even a good writer obscure, and a bad one absolutely unintelligible."[18] By the 1760s, James Burgh was bitterly (but as yet inaccurately) complaining that printers had stopped italicizing the emphatical word despite "the great advantage it was to understanding the sense of an author," because "we have grown so nice, that we have found the intermixture of two characters deforms the page, and gives it a speckled appearance."[19] Other forms of punctuation dropped away too, or changed their functions once sentences became shorter and more perspicuous, and after schoolmasters finally managed to persuade the public that punctuation was also needed in handwritten texts. But meanwhile, printers were facilitating reading – and giving print an edge over script – by using "the Marks commonly met with in Books" to do some of their readers' work for them. The corollary, of course, was that printers and compositors were using pointers (points, marks, italics, capital letters, layout) to determine for readers how texts should be transmitted, and understood. But since editions of the same text by different printers often differed precisely on these points, and since the "learned" regularly complained that the punctuation in printed books was "often capricious and false,"[20] pointing in printed matter can still be regarded as a series of unregulated and fairly individual interpretative acts.

The difficulty in rendering the tone, moods and passions communicated by written texts, as Thomas Sheridan complained, lay in "the want of sufficient signs and marks, in the art of writing, to point them out."[21] Printers had not managed to develop a method of pointing to do readers' work for them with regard to tone, mood and passions, as they had with the regard to sense; and the complex notation systems devised by eighteenth-century phoneticians did not catch on. The effort to provide readers with readily applicable rules instead, produced a veritable barrage of printed matter. While differing on one point or another or emphasizing one point over another, instructional matter offered readers three imperfect approaches.

One approach relied on the cue (or clue) of genre. It was considered as improper to indite all genres in the same style, as it was to use the same script alphabet in different domains of culture. Newspapers, poems, speeches, letters, satires, sermons, history, philosophy, drama and fiction demanded different styles of writing, and different modes of pronunciation as a result. To read a text aloud correctly, readers had be able to distinguish among genres, know which style belonged to which genre, and learn how each style should be pronounced. Printers helped by listing books by genre in their catalogues, and by indicating a book's genre on its title page or a text's genre in the sub-headings of miscellanies and periodicals. There were at least two versions of this taxonomy. The first was based on a more or less traditional division of styles into high, middle and low. The plain or simple style, which eschewed ornamental tropes and figures and aimed at perspicuity and exactness, was described as the style in which "common subjects" were rendered, principally in newspapers, letters, narratives and representations of ordinary conversation or dialogues. Texts in the plain style must be rendered plainly and simply, without drama or declamation, ensuring only that each word was pronounced distinctly and that the pauses and emphases were correctly observed. The sublime style, by contrast, was full of lofty thoughts, rich expressions, bold figures and lively passions; it belonged chiefly to tragedy and epic poetry, and to sermons and orations. Here "the different Passions of the Mind are to be expressed by a different Sound or Tone of Voice, *Love*, by a soft, smooth, languishing Voice; *Anger*, by a strong, vehement, and elevated Voice; *Joy*, by a quick, sweet, and clear voice; *Sorrow*, by a low, flexible, interrupted Voice; *Fear*, by a dejected, tremulous, hesitating Voice; *Courage*, hath a full, bold, and loud Voice; and *Perplexity*, a grave, steady and earnest one." In speeches and orations, structure too must be conveyed through the voice: this must be low in the exordium, distinct in the narration, slow in the reasoning, and strong in the peroration; in a "climax"(an argument or expression of feelings which ascends by steps from the weakest to the strongest), the voice must progressively rise; in a *prosopoeia*, where speech is given to a thing, the voice must be changed to reflect that. The middle style, a mixture of the plain and sublime, was to be found wherever the subject was neither so lofty nor so common as to warrant the other two, namely almost everywhere else. Here readers were left to mix and match instructions for reading the other two styles as appropriate. Another version of this taxonomy, promoted by Robert Dodsley's popular *Preceptor* (1748), divided styles instead into the Familiar, the Solemn and the Pathetic,

> each of which demands its particular Mode of Elocution: in the *Familiar*, he that reads is only to talk with a Paper in his Hand, and to indulge himself in all the lighter Liberties of the Voice, as when he reads the common Articles of a Newspaper, or a cursory Letter of Intelligence or Business. The *Solemn* Stile, such as that of a serious Narrative, expects an universal Steddiness [sic] of Speech, equal, clear and calm. For the *Pathetic*, such as an animated Oration, it is necessary the Voice be regulated by the Sense, varying and rising with the Passions.[22]

The shortcoming of this cue was that, if the sound was to suit the sense, every part of a text in any genre could not necessarily be pronounced in the same way. In satire, for instance, the fact that "we sneeringly say one thing and mean the contrary" is "discovered by the Tone of Voice";[23] but a satire might contain gently ironical passages as well bitingly sarcastic ones, and heavily affected dialogue besides. A matter-of-fact newspaper article might be satirical in places. A text might be grave and solemn, matter-of-fact, and cheerful or sprightly in different places. And was "an universal Steddiness" universally appropriate to a "factual" historical narrative which, in its effort to "transport the attentive reader back to the very time" and enable him to "live with the men who lived before [him]," displayed the motives and passions of historical characters through the speeches it put into their mouths?[24]

It therefore required supplementation by a second approach, which may be called the cue (or clue) by matter. In a narrative or discursive text, the reader must determine whether the subject was grave and solemn, cheerful and lively, droll or serious, important or trivial, and regulate his voice accordingly. One did not want to deliver something with solemnity that had nothing solemn about it, or to make something sound important that was really rather trivial. In a descriptive text or passage, the simplest mode of pronunciation, based on clear articulation and proper emphases, sufficed; but in animated or pathetic poetic descriptions, the mood or pathos of the scene must be conveyed by the voice. In a public speech or address, the important thing was to speak the words with honest and heartfelt conviction, as if inspired by every thought and entering into every emotion that was being expressed. In the more informal address of a letter, the voice must remain easy and genteel throughout. In a text or passage that showed rather than told, as in drama or dialogue, different rules applied. As John Rice explained, in narratives, essays, descriptions or letters, "the Reader stands in the Place, and speaks in the Person of the Writer; but in the Rehearsal of Conversation-Pieces, he must diversify not only his Mode of reciting, in Conformity to the Subject, but also in Conformity to the Character. Thus the same Narrative and Description, if spoken by different Personages, must be differently recited."[25] Here reading aloud intersected with acting on the stage.

The third approach may be called the cue from experience. This was founded on the argument that, in ordinary conversation, people automatically (or "naturally") pronounced sentences correctly, successfully conveying their passions, mood, and emphases along with their thoughts; and that everyone knew how it feels to grieve or fear, to love or be joyful. Readers had only to make the thoughts and passions of the author they were reading their own, and to reproduce in reading from a text, the speech patterns that they and others used in similar situations in ordinary life, to correctly convey an author's mood and passions in pronouncing his words.

Readers might usefully "study Nature," in the form of their own "natural dispositions and Affections" and those of others, or observe how people spoke in conversation and in different states of mind. Since art was only "Nature methodiz'd," readers might also study books on the Arts of rhetoric or elocution that delineated the nature of each passion and described how each "naturally" expressed itself in characteristic tones of voice and "action" – distinctive motions of the head, countenance, hands and body that had been used by orators and actors for centuries. But "the great, general and most important Rule of all…in reading [is] to attend to your Subject, and deliver it just in such a Manner as you would do if you were talking it." Once the rhythms and tones used in talking were the thing to be imitated in reading everything aloud, including poetry, the reader had only to "enter into the Spirit of [his] Author" and to "bring himself to have those Affections which he desires to infuse into others" for the words to come out just as they should.[26] The reader would, in Pope's words, "*read each work of Wit/With the same Spirit that its Author writ.*"[27]

The shift from "unnatural" forms of declamation to a more "natural," conversational style of delivery is now often associated with the famous actor, Garrick, or with Thomas Sheridan and the elocution movement of the 1760s. But for contemporaries such as John Mason, who was already touting this idea during the 1740s, its source was Isaac Watts, whose *Art of Reading and Writing English* (1720) remained a transatlantic best-seller throughout the century.[28] Grammars and letter-manuals were emphasizing that reading must imitate conversation and everyday speech by borrowing paragraphs from Mason's *Essay on Elocution* for their chapters on pronunciation before and after Garrick and Sheridan came on the scene. Though an important promoter of standardized pronunciation, Sheridan was concerned with the same issues in reading aloud as everyone else: "A just delivery consists in a distinct articulation of words, pronunciation in the proper tones, suitably varied to the sense and the emotions of the mind; with due observation of accent; of emphasis in its several gradations; of rests and pauses in the voice, in proper places and well-measured degrees of time; and the whole accompanied with expressive looks and significant gesture."[29]

Instructing the generality of readers to model their cadences, tones and expressivity in reading aloud on ordinary conversation and on the ways in which they would normally express their feelings when talking, while touching more lightly on the more technical aspects of the art, was a sensible fall-back position for schoolmasters and elocutionists addressing the public at large in print. There was far too much for most people to

remember and apply as they read aloud, and it was impossible to use written or printed words to describe tone of voice in a manner that invariably
produced the same uttered sounds. The main difficulty, however, was that
"no man can read an Author he does not perfectly understand and taste":[30]
no rules could be devised to ensure that readers fully understood and
"taste[d]" the varying and diversely interacting moods, passions, styles and
matter that the sounds they uttered were supposed to express, or even that
they would correctly identify in texts the features that were supposed to act
as their cues. Everyone could, however, understand and follow a list of general and purely formal rules for pronunciation which, accordingly, recurred
in most instructional books: Do not read too fast (or your hearers will not
be able to absorb what you are saying). Do not read too slow (your hearers
will find that tedious). Do not shout or mumble, but pitch your voice to
reach the furthest extent of your hearers in the room or open space. Do
not cant, chant, whine, chitter, hemm and haw, sneeze, cough or yawn as
you read. Stand up straight. Be careful to observe the emphases and pauses.
Articulate every syllable and every word distinctly. Articulation included
getting the accent right, both in the sense of accenting the right syllable
in each word and in the sense of not speaking in a "low" or provincial
accent. Getting the accent wrong in either sense made the reader hard for
hearers to understand outside his/her own speech community. Rhetorical
grammars and pronouncing dictionaries were therefore produced – and
suggested throughout this literature – as aids to correct pronunciation in
reading aloud, as other vernacular dictionaries were suggested in grammars
as aids to analogy, etymology and word comprehension.

Reading aloud was an "Art," a skill or craft based on special knowledge
but acquired primarily through practice. All guides to reading aloud therefore emphasized that "Practice is the principal thing,"[31] and that readers
could best learn or improve their skill in reading aloud by listening to the
"best readers" and imitating how they read. English-school masters too
were sometimes advised to model the just and graceful reading of passages
for their students' imitation. Readers of all ages were told, in addition, that
they must practice reading aloud to themselves every day, and take every
opportunity to read aloud to a friend, colleague or teacher who was capable
of correcting their errors. Several of the most popular manuals on pronunciation therefore coupled relatively brief theoretical essays with extensive
"lessons" or "exercises" in the form of extracts from the "best" ancient
and modern authors for learners to practice upon. Recognizing that "the
Connection of one Sentence with the rest, or the Sense of the Context,
determines the particular Sense of every Sentence in the Discourse,"[32] some

manual-anthologies prefaced speeches or orations with circumstantial accounts of when, where and why they had first been spoken, or how they figured in the play from which they had been extracted, to enable readers to perceive how each ought to be pronounced. Other manual-anthologies, such as James Burgh's *Art of Reading* (1762) accompanied chosen extracts with marginal notes "showing the various passions and emotion of the mind…as they change from one to another in the course of the speeches," to enable readers to identify which passion or emotion they were supposed to be conveying where, and see how frequently these might shift, even in the course of a single extract.

Many pronouncing-anthologies gave readers little guidance, beyond announcing their function on their title pages and including among their extracts, short pieces about orating, taste, criticism or the passions. Those that did offer guidance explained that their principal goal was to ensure that they were providing readers with "a competent variety of passages out of the best writers in prose and verse, for adapting the general manner of delivery to the spirit and humour of the various matter there may be occasion to pronounce."[33] Readers required opportunities to practice all the different kinds of text that they were ever likely to have to read aloud in public, social or domestic situations. In *The Speaker* (1774), a much reprinted pronouncing-anthology originally designed for the Warrington Academy, William Enfield accordingly divided a variety of practice pieces into sections by kinds of writing: "Narrative Pieces," "Didactic Pieces," "Argumentative Pieces," "Orations and Harangues," "Dialogues," "Descriptive Pieces," "Pathetic Pieces." *The Preceptor's* "Lessons in Reading" were sectioned by style: didactic and narrative pieces for the "solemn style"; letters for the "familiar style"; poetry and moving speeches from the classics and from Shakespeare for the "pathetic style." Burgh's pronouncing-anthology in *The Art of Reading* followed Latin arts of rhetoric such as John Holmes', by selecting practice texts that illustrated each of the different passions or emotions.[34] William Scott's, *Lessons in Elocution* (1778), which contained "examples from almost every Species of Composition, and such as may exercise all those feelings of the soul, and all that diversity of voice and gesture, upon which a just and graceful elocution depends," was broadly divided into prose and verse, and ordered by level of difficulty.[35] Together with Vicesimus Knox's very popular *Elegant Extracts* in prose and poetry (1784, 1789), these pronouncing-anthologies were all reprinted in America into the nineteenth century.

Different collections also had different subsidiary goals and accordingly different principles of organization and selection. Where Enfield's

The Speaker (1774) was dominated by moral pieces on the conduct of life and learning, Dodsley's *The Preceptor* (1754) had an underlying patriotic agenda; where Newbery's *Rhetoric Made Familiar and Easy* (1769) sought primarily to give vernacular-only readers access to Greek and Latin classics in translation, Walker's *Exercises for Improvement of Elocution, being select Extracts from the Best Authors for the Use of those who study the Art of Reading and Speaking* (1777) offered readers "in some degree, a system of polite knowledge" by showing them who were the most highly-rated modern authors and where their "beauties" lay.

In British pronouncing-anthologies, youth and masters in schools, and adults wishing to practice or improve their skills in reading aloud, were often not the only target audiences. As *Elegant Extracts: or useful and entertaining Passages in Prose, Selected for the Improvement of Scholars at Classical and other Schools in the Art of Speaking* (1784) explained: though the compilation "may be employed in various methods for the use of learners," it may also "be read…at any age with pleasure and improvement" – "all readers may find it an agreeable companion."[36] Or as William Scott observed: "the compiler does not wish this Selection should be considered *merely* as a schoolbook" but "is encouraged to hope that it will contribute also to the amusement of every person of Taste, who may give it a perusal."[37] For the amusement of this other projected market of silent perusers, the variety of short, discontinuous pieces and the different fictional and non-fictional styles, genres, subjects and authors served an entirely different purpose: it ensured that "in so various a Collection, it will not be difficult [for each] to find something correspondent to his Taste and Humour."[38] Variety broadened the anthology's potential buying public by appealing to readers with different interests and tastes. Some compilers added that the variety of matter in their collection provided readers with "a little English library" by assembling in one place extracts from diverse books that were too voluminous to read, or too expensive to buy individually.

American-authored or adapted pronouncing-anthologies of the 1780s and 1790s, by contrast, were principally designed for children or schools, and took a more consistently moral and patriotic line. Noah Webster's popular *American Selection of Lessons in Reading and Speaking…Being the Third Part of a Grammatical Institute* (3rd edn, enlarged, 1787) was a manual-anthology prefaced by "Rules of Elocution and Directions for Expressing the principal Passions of the Mind." Others followed Webster in using the word "Selection" in their titles to indicate that, though based on British copy-texts, their American pronouncing-anthologies only included extracts that their compilers judged were still useful or relevant to

American readers. Most also took pains to include American authors and American themes.

Relatively few extracts cropped up repeatedly across pronouncing-anthologies: Shakespeare's "Seven Ages of Man" speech from *As You Like It* and the speech by Antony, "Friends, Romans, Countrymen," from *Julius Caesar*, an oration or two from Demosthenes, and something from the *Tatlers* or *Spectators*. But oral genres such as orations, speeches from plays, dialogues, and letters (a genre in which a person was said to "show himself") often figured large, perhaps because these genres facilitated access to the "Character" of their real or putative authors. The contents of these otherwise very various British and American pronouncing-anthologies also had one other important characteristic in common. Partly because ancient rhetoricians stressed the superior persuasive power of public orators who knew how to express the passions or emotions, and partly because rightly expressing the passions and emotions was the most demanding because most indeterminate aspect of reading aloud, pronouncing-anthologies included large numbers of "pathetic" pieces as reading exercises. That is to say, at least from the 1740s on, and in the context of pronouncing the "best" writing with proper feeling, vernacular rhetorical manuals and pronouncing-anthologies were dwelling on pathos, and requiring each reader to "enter into the Spirit of [his] Author" by "bring[ing] himself to have those Affections which he desires to infuse into others." Teachers and pronouncing-anthologies were demanding from the 1740s that readers exercise sympathy, and what would later be called their "sensibility," in reading aloud. This practice may have played a neglected role in producing and disseminating that taste for literary representations of the passions that gave readers opportunities to feel a variety of emotions, which became so characteristic of sentimental literature during the century's last decades. It did not hurt either that, unlike plain, dispassionate, perspicuous prose, sentimental texts supplied good readers aloud with opportunities to display their superior interpretative and expressive talents, and to distinguish themselves from inferior readers, through their lively and emotionally rousing renderings of the most challenging kind of text.

It appears that there was initially some resistance in England to extending instruction in the useful masculine art of reading aloud to girls and women. Writing from High Wickham in Buckinghamshire in 1726, Mrs. Bellamy vigorously defended her practice (imported from boys' grammar schools) of having the young ladies at her boarding school mount private theatricals to practice and exhibit their skills, against the "many…who are of opinion, that the Art of Pronunciation is no Female Accomplishment."

Pronunciation was, she said, "an Exercise of their Rational Faculties," which permitted girls to "improve their Judgment" and exhibit "the Endowments of their Minds." Private theatricals gave ladies an opportunity to "display the Beauties of their Mind, and demonstrate, by a due Emphasis, a proper Accent, and an apposite Variation of Voice, that they are Judges of Good Sense, as well as good Manners."[39] The short essay on pronunciation that followed explained how much was involved, when the lady's voice had to "sympathize" with the writer's "Thoughts," and her "Action" (expressions of face, hands and body) had to follow her voice, in ways conformable to the Art of Pronunciation, where "there are distinct and proper Tones to all the Tropes and Figures of Speech"; and where "all the Passions have their proper Variations" as well as their appropriate actions. Mrs. Bellamy silently indicated why it required "a judicious person" to "employ every distinct Tone to great Advantage and, as the Painter does his Colours, shew [a writer's "Thoughts"] in their proper light" by introducing long and complex speeches from *Macbeth, Julius Caesar, Tamberlaine, Cato, Paradise Lost* and *The Orphan*. These selections showed how much grammatical reasoning, reading comprehension, sympathy and judgment, as well as elocutionary skill, a lady needed to recognize and adequately render (for instance) "the debate of mind with itself upon a pressing difficulty" in "a very grave and earnest, but not bemoaning voice"; or "an Irony…in a smooth voice with an artful Insinuation, and an Excess of Complaisance, by which the Dissimulation is discover'd" – while "letting [her] Looks correspond with [her] Subject."[40] Mrs. Bellamy also gives us insight into why private theatricals in country houses became so popular during the eighteenth century: in addition to serving as an entertaining pastime, they offered ladies an opportunity to "display the Beauties of their Mind" through the manner in which they pronounced a text. By the end of the century in New England, though not, it seems, in England, young women were regularly pronouncing essays and orations of their own composition to a public on school prize days.[41] But in 1726, in the English provinces, Mrs. Bellamy complained that "Fools are all the Fashion," and that parents thought that ladies were "designed by nature" to be "nothing but moving Pictures" and "Objects of Sight only."

"Conversation-Pieces": Exemplifying Book Talk

Because "no man can read an Author he does not perfectly understand and taste," analyzing issues of character, genre and style went hand in hand with reading aloud, especially in pedagogical situations which themselves used conversation as an instructional tool. Readers' analytical skills could be improved, along with their oral performance, by using their pronunciation of passages to teach them to better understand the author they were reading aloud. Having students read aloud gave teachers a useful diagnostic tool, and an opportunity to converse with students on a variety of relevant topics, as schoolmaster, James Buchanan, explained. Echoing Mason by arguing that "no grown person can convey the force and fullness of his author's ideas to another, till he feels them himself, or read a discourse to advantage, he does not understand and taste," Buchanan described how a competent master taught pupils who were "learning to pronounce elegantly," and trying to become "masters of all the graceful variations of the voice peculiar to each subject":

> When they come to any period which the master thinks they do not understand, he should accustom them to stop, till they discern, or are taught its full meaning. This is a rule of great importance; as it early opens the capacity, and improves the judgment, at the same time that it enables them in all the progress to read with understanding and propriety.[42]

Halting students to give them time to "discern" the full meaning of a sentence which they had not adequately pronounced, taught them that they must "attend to what they read," stretched the limits of their understanding, and gave them an opportunity to revise mistaken judgments. When the meaning assumed information they lacked, explaining it to them enabled the master to "acquaint [them] with things themselves, Arts and Useful Sciences," or with "principles of religion and morality." Asking pupils to read from the works of "our best English classics, both in prose and verse," permitted masters to "point out to them the beauties in style and sentiment, and give them a taste for poetry."[43] Both reading exercises taught them "Knowledge of the World" and "the Characters of Men." Using reading aloud at once as a measure of reading comprehension and as a display of taste was also the means of developing more sophisticated readings of the genre that pupils would most frequently encounter in their working and social lives:

> The Method I take, and find it so far effectual to the End proposed, is, having got what I judged the best Book of Letters, I make several young Gentlemen stand up, and one of them read a Letter gracefully; after which I read it to them myself, making Observations on the Sentiment and Style, and asking their Opinions with Respect to both. And if the Letter has an answer, I ask them before they read it, what Answer they would make to this or that Passage? If their Answer happens to tally with that of the Author, it gives them great Spirits. And on the whole, a deep and lasting Impression is made on their Memories, and their Understandings improved.[44]

Here, having permitted his students to read the letter aloud, Buchanan corrected their pronunciation of it by modeling the proper reading himself,
while pausing to make observations about the style and sentiments – in the
dual eighteenth-century sense of thoughts and emotions – which explained
why he gracefully varied his voice in the different parts of the letter as he
did. Students were then engaged again by asking how they judged the letter's sentiments and style, and how they would answer the points it made.[45]

Richard Cumberland provided even more detail when describing how
his mother (daughter of scholar, Richard Bentley) taught him to read
aloud in English during school holidays from Westminster, where he was
given the traditional classical education in Latin and Greek:

> It was in these intervals from school that my mother began to form both
> my taste and my ear for poetry, by employing me every evening to read to
> her, of which art she was a very able mistress. Our readings were with few
> exceptions confined to the chosen plays of Shakespeare, whom she both
> admired and understood in the true spirit and sense of the author. Under
> her instruction I became passionately fond of these our evening entertain-
> ments. She was attentive to model my recitation, and correct my manner
> with exact precision. Her comments and illustrations were such aids and
> instructions to a pupil in poetry as few could have given. What I could
> not else have understood, she could aptly explain, and what I ought to
> admire and feel nobody could more happily select and recommend. I well
> remember the care she took to mark out for my observation the peculiar
> excellence of that unrivalled poet in the consistency and preservation of his
> characters; and wherever instances occurred amongst the starts and sallies of
> his unfettered fancy of the extravagant and false sublime, her discernment
> oftentimes prevented me from being so dazzled by the glitter of the period
> as to misapply my admiration, and betray my want of taste. With all her
> father's critical acumen, she could trace, and teach me to unravel, all the
> meanders of his metaphor, and point out where it illuminated or where it
> only loaded and obscured the meaning; these were happy hours and inter-
> esting lectures to me.[46]

Treating young Richard's initial reading of Shakespeare aloud as a diagnostic for what he had understood from the text, his mother "corrected his
manner" by explaining and illustrating what he had not understood of the
"true spirit and sense of the author." She also taught him how to unravel
and thus understand Shakespeare's meandering metaphors; drew his attention to the qualities and consistency of each of the characters; and showed
him what emotions their speeches required him to feel and express. This
enabled Richard to better see how he ought to "model the recitation."
His mother sometimes also "modeled the recitation" herself by reading a

speech or passage aloud for him, confident that he now understood why she pronounced each part of each speech as she did. As he practiced his "lectures" (readings), his mother could turn their attention "with exact precision" to how he pronounced every phrase, and to whatever further elucidation was necessary to ensure that Richard's delivery "illuminated" rather than "obscured the meaning" of his author and highlighted what was most worthy of admiration.

"Conversation-pieces" provided stylized printed models of conversations such as these, that centered on reading aloud. They represented orally delivered texts and conversations about them that focused on issues of character, genre and style – the three textual features most crucial to successful reading aloud – while also acquainting readers with "Arts and Useful Sciences," or with "principles of religion and morality." In addition, conversation-pieces exemplified manners used in polite conversation – such as turn-taking, listening to others attentively without interruption, speaking calmly, and deferring to one's elders or superiors – polite manners that the period's many "Essays on Conversation" disseminated in another form. Here conversation-pieces modeled what James Buchanan and Richard Cumberland left unsaid, both to mark literary conversation as a pastime of the polite, and to show the would-be polite how to engage in genteel literary conversations.

The most popular of the conversation-pieces was undoubtedly Sarah Fielding's *The Governess or Little Female Academy* (1749), which exemplified instruction by "pronunciation" and "familiar conversation" for girls and female teachers, professional or maternal. By figuring the latter as a head-girl, and showing that instructive conversation about orally delivered texts could be conducted by girls in conversation amongst themselves, Fielding also tapped into the contemporary conviction that conversation among peers even without a teacher constituted an acceptable form of "study" (see Chapter 3). And while explaining how to read for ideas that could be discussed, she demonstrated how sociable conversations about reading should be conducted. For instance, the girls cannot begin to have politely sociable conversations until they stop quarreling and fighting amongst themselves, and conduct themselves as young ladies rather than hoydens. Each must be sure she "keeps Command enough over [her]self" to suppress pride, anger or resentment in the interests of order, harmony and peace; each must listen to the others and give everyone their turn to speak. *The Governess* was hugely popular: "Calculated for the Entertainment and Instruction of Young Ladies in their EDUCATION," as each title page emphasized, it saw fourteen editions in London, Ireland and Philadelphia before 1800.

The Preface opens by asking: "What is the true Use of Reading?" Its answer, that "the true Use of Books…is to make you wiser and better," points in two, partly overlapping, directions, which are reflected in the two stories attached to each girl. On the one hand, one reads to learn. Readers desirous to learn must "attend with a Desire of Learning" – must neither "fansy yourselves too wise to be taught" nor "say that you are incapable of understanding [books] at all, and therefore, from Laziness, and sooner than take any Pains, sit yourselves down contented to be ignorant."[47] On the other hand, one reads to "make Application" of one's reading to one's own character, life and experience. Histories, both true and fictional, taught by example rather than precept; they made "stories the vehicle to convey…wholesome truths that [readers] refused to receive under the form of precept and instructions," or found it difficult to grasp in abstract form, by entertaining them with accounts of other "People."[48] Readers became "wiser and better" in the conduct of their own lives by extrapolating and applying the practical wisdom embedded in positive and negative examples of characters and their conduct.

The text consists of a frame story about girls at Mrs. Teachum's academy who are encouraged to settle down in the garden of an afternoon, to listen to orally pronounced texts and engage in instructive conversation about them under the direction of the oldest girl, Miss Jenny. "That [they] should know something about all kinds of writings," (101) the texts, which are read aloud and embedded in the printed narrative, take a variety of generic forms – allegory, fairy tale, letter, story, fable, drama. Except for the play, each of these texts is read aloud by a different girl, and accompanied by a short oral history of her life, which is subsequently written down by Miss Jenny for Mrs. Teachum to read. Each oral reading and life-story is followed by a conversation about the text that has been read aloud, in which the girls are shown how to "look further than present Amusement" in order to "understand what [they] read," "improve [their] Mind" and "make just Remarks" about texts (36). "Looking further" involves understanding how genres work. The girls are told, for instance, that allegories and fairy tales use "Giants, Magic, Fairies and all sorts of supernatural Assistances" to "amuse and divert"; but that they must look beyond these, to understand that the Giants in "The Story of the Cruel Giant Barbico [and] the good Giant Benefico" are "called so only to express a Man of great Power" (34), and that a complex moral about the uses and abuses of power is contained in the story's contrasts between a tyrannical ruler and a beneficent one. Or again: the girls are told that when asked to give an account of a play, they must "not tell you the Acts and Scenes as they followed one another" (101), but "describe the chief People in the Play, and the Plots and Contrivances that are carry'd on among them" (102); and that the moral of a comedy "lies deeper" than its happy ending, and "is to be deduced from a Proof throughout the Play..." (106). Analysis, reflection and looking beyond the mere sequence of events are required just to tell someone the play's "story," never mind to discern its moral. Significantly, the girls are also told that when telling oral histories about themselves, some people "made up dismal Stories without much Foundation" (60).

The girls are informed that "In order to make what you read of any Use to you, you must not only think of it thus in general, but make the Application to yourselves" (37). This is applied to the conduct of conversations about reading, through the interplay between the frame story and the embedded stories. The girls cannot use sociable conversations for the purpose of learning until they are willing to "look up to [Miss Jenny] as the most proper person to direct them in their Amusements" (20). But refusing to defer to 13-year-old Miss Jenny, 11-year-old Miss Sukey objects that Jenny "always wants to be tutoring and governing" just "because you are the oldest in the school"; and she sets her "rights" against the doctrine that "it is wisest to submit to everybody that would impose upon me" to keep the peace (6, 7). Miss Jenny's two embedded stories constitute her responses to Miss Sukey's objection in the frame story. Jenny's oral history tells of her mother teaching her that she "owed Respect to my Brother, as the Eldest"; and that "remember[ing] how much my Brother's superior Strength might assist me in being my Protector," she should oblige and assist him in her turn. Acting as "mutual Assistants" through the exchange of good offices was considered the cement of Britain's hierarchical society. The relevant point in the allegorical giant story is analogical: unlike the cruel tyrant Barbico, the beneficent giant is accepted by the people as "their Governor...and their kind Protector," because he obeys the social compact by governing them "to their Good" and with their consent (32). In the frame-story, Miss Jenny must earn the girls' "Respect" by showing that she is doing the same before they consent to defer to her and willingly "follow her Example in the paths to goodness" (10) as Jenny willingly follows the example of the admirable Mrs. Teachum. In other words, no one is expected to submit willingly to a governor or governess who would "impose" upon them, as Miss Sukey fears. But voluntary deference to elders acting as wise guides and benevolent governesses (female governors) was as requisite to peace and harmony in polite conversation, as to peace and harmony in schools, families, and states.

Despite their different genres, Miss Jenny's autobiographical and allegorical stories both centered on characters and their conduct, and contained other practical lessons for life and conduct that a reader could
apply to and for herself. Miss Sukey, the next girl to speak autobiographi-
cally, demonstrates this by "making the Application" of Miss Jenny's stories to herself. She compares herself to the characters in both stories, and
again uses the long-standing family–state analogy to apply the allegorical
story of giant rulers to her own domestic conduct. This enables her to see
that, like the evil giant Barbico in his government of the realm, she had
abused her power over a servant girl at home, and "quarrel[ed], fought,
and contend[ed] for everything" at school (39–40). Acknowledging her
faults opens the way to correcting them by "follow[ing] the Example of
the Giant Benefico" whenever she has power over her inferiors, and following Miss Jenny's "Example in the path to Goodness" in relation to
her peers. Stories made readers "wiser and better" in their everyday lives
if they followed Miss Sukey's example by reading to extract lessons for
their own lives from the example of fictional "People," instead of reading only for present "Amusement." As the story of Barbico and Benefico
showed, the pedagogy of example did not require documentary realism. It
could occur in any genre as long as there was a "moral" that readers could
perceive as applicable to themselves, to their society, and to the course of
common life.[49]

Writers also embedded literary conversations within a framing fable that
modeled literary conversations among adults, and showed readers how to
discourse about literature "as if they taught them not." Of these, Eliza
Haywood's *The Tea-Table; or A Conversation between Polite Persons of both
Sexes at a Lady's Visiting Day* (1725) is the most neglected and most interesting. Like Sarah Fielding's later *Remarks on Clarissa* (1749), Haywood
addressed the value of fiction and the conduct of adult conversations about
it. But Haywood also showed why literary coteries formed as self-selecting
groups of cognoscenti meeting privately, within but separate from the
larger society, and offered good readers aloud a splendid text for displaying
the broadest possible range of elocutionary skills.

The Tea-Table begins by portraying fashionable conversation among the
beaus and belles at Amania's tea-table on her visiting day. The narrative
satirizes a variety of visitors: ladies who came only for scandal and gossip
about "the Intrigues of the Town"; a lady who "draws attention to herself
by having fits, rather than taking interest in any Conversation" (4); and a
"titled Coxcomb" or "Lord Critick" who makes "ridiculous Remarks on
the Scenery, Plot and Diction" of a play he has seen in rehearsal, for three

quarters of an hour without letting anyone get a word in.[50] Substantive conversation can begin only when these fashionable fools depart. The two men and two women who remain, observe very different "polite" protocols when they embark on a "discourse of the Passions" which naturally turns to love. Opinions differ. Each participant illustrates their opinion by adducing a literary text, which they read aloud to the company and which is embedded in the printed text – a poem, a story in a letter, and a "Manuscript Novel." Each opinion and illustrative text is heard by the others with attention and pleasure, and respectfully discussed; there is no "titled Coxcomb" here, hogging the floor and imposing his views on everyone, and no one seeks to draw attention to themselves. Indeed, reading the poem or stories aloud deflects attention from the reader to the text, even as it gives the company matter for conversation and "useful Reflections" (19). And though scandalous in themselves – like most of Haywood's amatory histories, they describe women seduced and betrayed by their supposed lovers – the poem and stories are not scandal of the sort that the beaux and belles come to Amania's visiting day to hear, namely mean-spirited detraction and slanderous suppositions about people they know.

The scandalous poem and stories appeal to the same "curiosity" which impels fashionable society to seek an "Opportunity to inform themselves of the Intrigues of the Town"; but, as the coterie's conversation demonstrates, they enable listeners and readers to observe and reflect upon the causes, conduct and consequences of such Intrigues, and to learn from them. Sharing the poem and stories permits participants to consider and discuss the character of characters and the consequences of their conduct; to reflect upon the part played by the passions in preventing women from recognizing false lovers; to address the very different costs of "love" for women and for men; to judge whether the authors' representations of characters and situations are just (the poem, for instance, is judged to portray only "imaginary ills"); and to learn a practical lesson or "Moral" – that women must not "allow our reason to be debilitated by passion," but must instead "make use of their Penetration" to avoid "fall[ing] Prey to [men's] Villainy and Deceit."[51]

The conversation itself thereby illustrates what it is teaching readers about reading novels as a genre: that "these kind of Writings are not so trifling, as by many Persons they are thought. Nor are they design'd, as some imagine, for *Amusement* only; but *Instruction* also, most of them containing Morals, which if well observ'd, would be of no small service." Readers are once again being shown how to look past Amusement, to the Instruction within. Novels may "cloath Instruction with Delight,"[52] to make it more palatable; but readers who read only for delight, overlook their utility and purpose. This information about the genre is presented by the two male cognoscenti at the end. Their masculine consensus marks the position of the "instructor" who leads the ignorant to knowledge and truth, while the participants' resolution to meet at Amenia's tea-table next day for more literary conversation, marks this as good conversation. Haywood was inculcating a character-focused manner of reading that made stories about other "People" more than gossip, while showing how polite conversation could enhance readers' understanding of the value and practical applications of what they read.

In principle, extra-diegetic readers were supposed to imitate intra-diagetic readers like Miss Sukey or Haywood's cognoscenti, and "make Application" of their reading in reflection and/or conversation for themselves. For as one conversation-piece observed, citing a common conviction: where "the maxims that arise from [reading] are conceived through the reader's own reflections, [they] have much more weight than they could derive, either from argument or authority...the lessons of his own mind are lessons that no one suspects or disregards."[53] In the writing, however, authority figures within conversation-pieces sometimes led discussants to the "Truth" about the texts discussed and the practical wisdom they contained, as surely as Cumberland's mother led her son to a right reading of Shakespeare speeches, leaving little room for readers to think for themselves. On other occasions – particularly when they included conversation-pieces about reading in their novels – women writers showed readers how, and left them to do more of the work for themselves.

To take an example almost at random, characters in Elizabeth Griffith's epistolary *History of Lady Barton* (1771) model reflective conversations to counter what Griffith described in her Preface as the tendency of readers to read only for amusement, and to "feel their affections or curiosity so interested, either in the characters or the events, that it is with difficulty they can be diverted to any other study or amusement till they have got to the end of the story." Characters tell each other that they must take breaks from reading the suspenseful and emotionally wrenching narratives about acquaintances' adulterous marriages that they receive in letters, to give themselves "opportunity for reflection"; and they recommend conversation as a way for readers to further distance themselves from their immediate emotional reactions to what they read. In the conversations about these epistolary narratives that fill breaks in reading them, the characters compare the analogical situations they have been reading about to make judgments and draw conclusions about how marriage affected women;

they also separately make application of these written stories about other women to their own lives and experiences, and consider the life-lessons they can learn.[54] The "self-reflexivity" characteristic of so much eighteenth-century fiction did not serve "aesthetic" functions only, as under the influence of belletrism we still suppose; it also served to show readers how to read a novel otherwise than "just for the story" and, as here, often bore on current reading habits as well.

In *The Boarding School* (1798), Hannah Webster Foster adapted such conversation-pieces to early republican New England by invoking some contemporary American circumstances. During the 1780s, after daughters of the middling sort joined daughters of the elite in boarding schools and Young Ladies Academies, dyadic or small group versions of literary coteries, based on intimate sentimental friendships and involving the sharing of letters and writing, spread from the gentry to the aspiring offspring of artisans, small farmers, tradesmen and lesser professionals. At the same time, girls who had been exposed at school to reading circles and literary societies, began to preserve and deepen intimate school friendships after leaving boarding schools for their far-flung homes, by corresponding with one another, often for the rest of their lives.[55] *The Boarding School* briefly portrays girls conversing with their teacher prior to returning to their homes, to establish what they had learned; but the focus is on the letters they subsequently exchange to preserve their friendships and support each other in maintaining interests and values imbibed at school. The girls demonstrate their "thinking powers...merit and abilities" through epistolary "written conversations" in which personal news is accompanied, coterie-like, by discussion and judgment of books, rational comments on the social scene, and manuscript exchanges of self-authored poems. Lauding the delights of reading, retirement, and simple rural pastimes, and warning each other of "the deceptions which love and courtship impose upon their votaries," their letters model "rational and improving conversation" among virtuous women with literary tastes and "cultivated minds," and the "elegant, simple style," marked by "frankness, simplicity and sincerity" that Foster deemed appropriate to everyone in America.[56]

In Britain, printed conversation-pieces also became a popular means of exemplifying and conveying instruction on all manner of school subjects during the second half of the eighteenth century. Here, questions of pronunciation and observations about how to look beyond the entertaining surfaces of genres to the substance within were often introduced into or alongside instructive conversations on other subjects – the natural history of fish, animals and plants, and their uses in manufactures in Priscilla Wakefield's

Mental Improvement (1794); natural and human history in Charlotte Smith's *Minor Morals* (1799); grammar, civility, geography, history and science in Ann Murray's much reprinted *Mentoria or The Young Ladies Instructor* (1779); history and famous women in *The Female Mentor; or Select Conversations* (1793). Most of these conversation-pieces were set in domestic or familial situations, one in a virtual classroom. Some represented men in egalitarian terms, as participating in the conversations, and/or sharing the tasks of domestic instruction. They simultaneously gave readers access to knowledge of subjects through the medium of conversations, and modeled how such conversations might be conducted to best advantage in happy families, where benevolent, attentive and infinitely patient parental instructors conversed with respectful, attentive and well-behaved offspring. In America, Enos Hitchcock integrated conversation-pieces into *Memoirs of the Bloomsgrove Family* (1790), his fictionalized conduct book for parental educators in early republican families. Convinced that "impressions favorable to Virtue may be made with ease, by familiar stories founded on fact," Hitchcock inserted extra-diegetic exemplary anecdotes into his fictional accounts of the exemplary Bloomsgroves' educational practices. He framed each exemplary anecdote with conversation directed to Boston readers explaining how it demonstrated the form of domestic education best suited to "a state of society, government and manners in their own country" where republican principles required a virtuous population and people were expected to work.[57]

In Britain, the authors of instructional conversation-pieces (as opposed to philosophical dialogues distantly imitating Plato[58]) were overwhelmingly female; a surprising number were also authors we now know as novelists, perhaps because many had themselves been teachers. Murray, who originally wrote *Mentoria* "for the use of her pupils," also suggests another reason: "dialogue and fable, are in general esteemed the best vehicles for conveying instruction, as they lure the mind into knowledge, and imperceptibly conduct it to the goal of wisdom."[59] This was a genre that permitted novelists to pair "dialogue and fable." Some novelists, such as Mary Wollstonecraft in *Original Stories*, or Sarah Scott in *A Journey through Every Stage of Life* (1754) made this pairing central to their conversation-pieces: Scott framed original stories in diverse genres orally delivered by a female mentor to her young protégé with conversations between them about the merits and demerits of each genre; while Wollstonecraft, whose embedded stories were designed to "illustrate the moral" of conversations on such topics as humanity in the treatment of animals, or the danger of delay in bringing someone charitable aid, introduced observations about how such stories should be read. Conversation-pieces were effective pedagogically, as Priscilla Wakefield explained, because: "Dr Watts says that there are four methods of attaining knowledge: observation, reading, conversation and meditation," and printed conversations employed two of these to foster the other two.[60]

The method and goals of conversation-pieces were down-to-earth. Instructors sought to instill sufficient understanding about how genres, literary language and narratives worked to enable readers aloud and silent readers or listeners to look beyond amusement or emotional engagement with the text, to discover what it indicated about an authorial or fictional character and "the secret springs" and beneficial or harmful effects of his/her actions. This was key to their sense of the practical utility of reading. Readers aloud and silent readers were both supposed to read with a view to thought and action – the former, in the rhetorical sense of varying their voice and physical motions according to the character and designs that, upon reflection, the words expressed; the latter, in the moral sense of reflecting upon, and making personal "Application" of, life-lessons derived from the characters and conduct represented in the text to their own character, actions and experience.

Social Practices

As this section briefly illustrates, there is much more to be learned about unwritten conventions and their circumstantial complexities, from contemporary accounts of situations in which reading aloud and conversation actually occurred.

The fact that in reading aloud, a person was displaying their "parts" – their understanding, judgment and taste, their sensibility, and their education and skill in pronunciation – could substantially complicate the mores and dynamics of evening entertainments which consisted of reading aloud to one's "friends" (family, patrons or guests). Most obviously, there was potential conflict between reading aloud for self-display and accommodating one's reading to the tastes and pleasure of one's auditors. In the passage below, Cumberland begins from this dichotomy, and goes on to show how complex and multi-faceted the dynamics of reading aloud to company could become. He was describing how Bub Doddington read to him and to the Dowager Ladies Stafford and Hervey while they were all staying at Doddington's house in Eastbury:

> as the trivial amusement of cards was never resorted to in Mr. Dodington's house, it was his custom in the evenings to entertain his company with reading, and in this art he excelled; his selections, however, were curious, for

he treated these ladies with the whole of Fielding's *Jonathan Wild*, in which he certainly consulted his own turn for irony rather than theirs for elegance, but he set it off with much humour after his manner, and they were polite enough to be pleased, or at least to appear as if they were.

His readings from Shakespeare were altogether as whimsical, for he chose his passages only where buffoonery was the character of the scene; one of these I remember was of the clown, who brings the asp to Cleopatra. He had, however, a manuscript copy of Glover's Medea, which he gave us *con amore*, for he was extremely warm in his praises of that classical drama, which Mrs. Yates afterwards brought upon the stage, and played in it with her accustomed excellence; he did me also the honour to devote an evening to the reading of some lines, which I had hastily written to the amount of about four hundred, partly complimentary to him as my host, and in part consolatory to Lord Halifax upon the event of his retiring from public office; they flattered the politics then in favour with Mr. Dodington, and coincided with his wishes for detaching Lord Halifax from the administration of the Duke of Newcastle.[61]

One convention attached to reading aloud was that the person offering the entertainment by doing the reading got to choose what was read. On the face of it, Doddington was using this prerogative to display his excellence as a reader: he displayed the range of which he was capable by entertaining his guests with prose, drama and verse, chosen to demonstrate his skill in rendering the comic, the tragic, and the sentimental, as expressed through exposition, narration, personation, and description. He also displayed the breadth of his taste and reading, by offering his auditors a variety of whole pieces and selected extracts, modern and ancient, from both manuscript and print sources – a recent popular novel, a putative English classic, a classical drama, and a topical occasional poem. Doddington was sustaining the character he presented to the world, where he was "generally courted and admired as a gay companion rather than as a grave one," by providing entertainments filled with variety, irony and humor which were consistent with that persona. At first sight, then, his desire to display his "parts" appears to have silenced all consideration for the listening Ladies, who preferred more elegant fare. But Doddington clearly had the address to use his readings to compliment, please or flatter his guests when he chose, since he devoted an entire evening to reading young Cumberland's poem, apparently with this end in view.

Cumberland invites us to look beyond the obvious conclusion that Doddington's failure to take the tastes of the Ladies Stafford and Hervey into account was due to his vanity or social ineptness, by describing the political moment and the deal that Doddington was trying to broker between Halifax and the Opposition. Cumberland was staying at Doddington's house as the envoy of his patron, Lord Halifax, who had instructed him to cultivate Doddington's society, so that Halifax could, without raising suspicion, employ Cumberland as a go-between in political negotiations which were being conducted in secret. Behind the gay companion that society saw, then, Doddington was a serious political player, and one who delighted in intrigue. Doddington's choice of texts – which were as political as they were humorous – also reflected this doubleness in his character. Where Newcastle's projected downfall was concerned, Doddington was himself the clown with the asp (or planned to be). Cumberland's poem, *Jonathan Wild*, Shakespeare's clown with the asp and Glover's *Medea* all offered commentary on the political situation in which Doddington, Halifax and Cumberland were secretly engaged.

What delighted Cumberland about these readings, was that all this was being communicated under the noses of the Ladies Stafford and Hervey, who did not notice, or were polite enough to pretend not to notice, what was going on. If the ladies were already in Doddington's confidence and had been invited for that reason, or if they realized what was happening from Cumberland's poem, there was also more than one covert dynamic going on in the room. But duplicity on the part of the ladies was not a possibility that Cumberland considered. Ironically, he also "forgot" these ladies' notable politeness, and the duplicity politeness often entailed, when he sat covertly listening in the next room to Doddington reading out his poem and to the ladies' approving comments upon it, and was "not a little gratified by what I overheard."

Another convention of reading "entertainments,' clearly demonstrated by the Ladies Stafford and Hervey, was that politeness required hearers, especially female ones, to display their complaisance by appearing attentive and pleased, whether they were or not. This could turn such entertainments into occasions when, as Catherine Talbot put it, the "social duties" were "mixed with pain," since "Justice and Gratitude demand often, that our kindest Affections should be excited and expressed, where natural Temper and Inclination do not prompt them."[62] At the inception of their correspondence during the 1740s, Talbot and Elizabeth Carter exchanged confidences about reading entertainments that demanded such duplicity. Carter described a visit to a family at Deal, during which she had been "dragged in at last and condemned by my perverse fortune, to hear part of a satyre ready for the press" being read aloud by its author, Paul Whitehead. Since Carter had "as strong an antipathy to a wit, as some people have to a cat," and disliked satire besides, she had "much ado to sit with any kind of patience and hear it out."[63] But Carter's patience on this visit bore no comparison to that which Talbot was obliged to demonstrate during the seven months each year she and her mother spent in Bedfordshire with Mrs. Secker, and Lady Mary Grey listening to Dr Secker's "family books." These were "read to us every day after breakfast and supper, ten o'clock is the hour that generally concludes them at both those times." Talbot was watching the clock as she listened twice a day for the whole summer, autumn and winter of 1743/4 to "Sir Richard Steele's papers" ("though I thought we had been perfectly acquainted with them before"); to a string of Greek and Roman historians during 1745 (including Thucydides, who failed to mention a single Grecian lady, and Xiphilin, who even Carter had never heard of); and to a whole dreadful winter of *Don Quixote*, which was supposed to make the family laugh.[64] Steele's *Tatlers* and *Spectators*, *Don Quixote* and ancient history represented what the learned Dr. Secker, like other right-thinking gentlemen and conservative conduct-book writers, considered appropriate, instructive and entertaining reading for women. In exercising his prerogative as reader and master of the family to select the "family books," this kindly Anglican clergyman failed to consider – or perhaps even realize – that once alone in her own apartments, Talbot delighted in reading Montaigne and Machiavelli, Mme de Sevigny, Milton, Dante and Akenside.

As both Cumberland and Carter indicate, it was a convention for authors to read their new work aloud to friends and possible patrons before it went to press so that it "became known to a circle that was always increasing." The author's hope was that the work's more prestigious auditors would like it enough to recommend it to their acquaintances; to facilitate its publication or production on stage by recommending it to a publisher or theatre manager; or to create enough buzz around it to make it "take." But clearly, not everyone was as respectful at such readings as Carter's account suggests. John Hawkesworth burlesqued an author's "shame and confusion" when invited to read his play to "a very great lady" and the "select company" she had invited to hear it. He gave a humorous account both of the nervous author's social gaffes, and of how difficult he found it to attend to his text in order to "pronounce it with emphasis and propriety" and move his hearers to the proper emotions, when he was constantly being interrupted – by comments on the whining of the great lady's pet dog, by a gentleman's anecdote about the auction of an ox, by a snuff box clumsily opened which made him sneeze, and by the sudden appearance at the end of the fourth act of two new visitors. At length:

> To atone for the mortification I had suffered, the ladies expressed the utmost impatience to hear the conclusion, and I was encouraged by repeated encomiums to proceed; but though I once more attempted to recollect myself,

and again began the speech in which I had been interrupted, yet my thoughts were still distracted, my voice faltered, and I had scarce breath to finish the first period. This was remarked by my tormentor the Buck, who suddenly snatched the manuscript out of my hands, declared that I did not do my play justice, and that he would finish it himself. He then began to read; but the affected gravity of his countenance, the unnatural tone of his voice, and the remembrance of his late anecdote of the ox, excited sensations that were incompatible both with pity and terror, and rendered me extremely wretched by keeping the company perpetually on the brink of laughter.[65]

Politeness and reading aloud could both be used to make an author and his "performance objects only of merriment and sport." But the buck who parodied the author's pronunciation of the play to keep the company on the brink of laughter also had it right. For Hawkesworth's sub-text was about the incompatibility between the learned author, whose serious play was modeled on the classics, and members of high society, who had short attention spans, were easily distracted, and sought company for entertainment, hilarity and diversions. A learned author was bound to be plunged into "shame, perplexity and confusion" by the responses of tonnish auditors such as these to a tragedy that was designed to elicit pity and fear through a single complete action which demonstrated by a "natural" sequence of events, how "virtue had been sustained by her own dignity and exalted in the enjoyment of intellectual and independent happiness," and "vice, by the success of her own projects had been betrayed into shame, perplexity and confusion." Hawkesworth was using a short and anecdotal piece of burlesque to make a serious point about the importance of matching one's choice of text – both when reading aloud in company and when writing for the public – to the tastes and pleasure of one's hearers.

As Hawkesworth indicates, the oral arts of reading discussed in this chapter also delineated (or produced) its bad readers and hearers. We have met several: bad readers aloud who misjudged the taste and patience of their hearers; failed to "understand and taste" what they were reading; mumbled, chanted, chittered, whispered, yawned or speeded; spoke in unintelligible dialects; or bungled pronunciation. We also met bad hearers who did not listen to anyone but themselves; were too lazy to attend; did attend but not with any desire to learn; or cared only for amusement and recreation. Bad hearers also became too involved emotionally to be able to reflect; wished only to be transported by the story and rushed upon the end; or failed to apply what they heard or read to their own lives and experiences. These were not just *ad hominem* attacks on certain kinds of readers and hearers, but bore directly on why it mattered that this manner of reading turned on issues of character and sociality: for according to this conception, the practical utility of such genres as history, letters, voyages, poetry, plays, periodicals and novels lay in diffusing "knowledge of the world" and of "the characters of men," to convey what philosophers called "practical wisdom" and Johnson "instructions into life."

The ability to discern and evaluate "the characters of men" in social situations was not a negligible skill in hierarchical, face-to-face societies like eighteenth-century Britain and America, where most things depended on who one was dealing with, and on being able to see what people were really like, what their words really meant, and how they might be expected to act. As contemporaries emphasized, discerning character mattered in a person's choice of companions as well as in dealings with superiors, who still exercised inordinate power over their dependents and inferiors. Character was also an existential issue in many ranks. The artisan, tradesman, shopkeeper or merchant who lost his character lost his financial, with his social, credit. Servants who lost their character, could not get domestic work. Young ladies who lost their character, fell out of the marriage mart (unless they were exceptionally rich). There was a great deal of pressure to seem better than one was. The ability to discern a person's *ethos* was a skill, acquired and practiced through the manner of reading delineated here, that was useful both in the arts of reading and in those of life.

NOTES

1 For a digest of these, John Pointer, *Miscellanea in usum juventis academicae* (Oxford, 1718): "Characters of the Classick Authors and some of our English Writers: Collected from Kennet, Addison, Pope, Garth, Dryden, Rapin etc."
2 John Boswell, *A Method of Study, or a Useful Library*, 2 vols. (London 1738): 1: v.
3 Powell, *Performing Authorship*; Brant, *Eighteenth-Century Letters*.
4 Gustafson, *Eloquence is Power*; Fliegelman, *Declaring Independence*; Grasso, *Speaking Aristocracy*.
5 [Anon] *Dr Johnson's Table-Talk* (London, 1785): 50.
6 Moncrieff and McPherson (eds.), *Performing Pedagogy*, 7.
7 Cohen, "Familiar Conversation"; Janowitz, "Amiable and radical sociability."
8 Trolander and Tenger, *Sociable Criticism*; Prescott, *Women, Authorship and Literary Culture*; Schellenberg, "The Society of Agreeable and Worthy Companions"; Piper, "Art of Sharing"; Kelley, *Learning to Stand and Speak*; McMahon, *Mere Equals*; Knott, *Sensibility and the American Revolution*: Chap. 5; Mee, *Conversable Worlds*; Allan, *A Nation of Readers*; Russell and Tuite, *Romantic Sociability*; Rose, *Intellectual Life of the British Working Classes*.
9 Mary Wollstonecraft, *Original Stories from Real Life* (London, 1788): v, xiii.

10 Isaac Watts, *The Art of Reading and Writing English* (2nd edn., London, 1722): 1. Also Bartine, *Early English Reading Theory*.

11 James Gough, *A Practical Grammar of the English Tongue* (2nd edn., Dublin, 1760): 94; Watts, *Art of Reading*: 39, 57.

12 John Mason, *An Essay on Elocution or Pronunciation* (2nd edn., London, 1748): 22.

13 Watts, *Art of Reading*: 57.

14 Lindley Murray, *English Grammar Adapted to the Different Classes of Learners* (York, 1795): 152, 153.

15 Ibid.: 153; Watts, *Art of Reading*: 61.

16 Daniel Fenning, *The Universal Spelling Book: Or a New and Easy Guide to the English Language* (London, 1756): 61.

17 Gough, *Practical Grammar*: 13.

18 Daniel Fenning, *A New Grammar of the English Language* (London, 1771): 162.

19 James Burgh, *The Art of Speaking* (2nd edn., London, 1768): 10. For unevenness in abandoning capitals, Wendorf, "Abandoning the Capital."

20 Hugh Blair, *Lectures on Rhetoric and Belles Lettres*, 2 vols. (London, 1783): ii: 214.

21 Thomas Sheridan, *A Course of Lectures on Elocution* (2nd edn., Dublin, 1764): 31.

22 [Dodsley] *The Preceptor: Containing a General Course of Education. Wherein the First Principles of Polite Learning are Laid Down* (London, 1748): xvi–xvii.

23 [John Newbery] *Rhetoric Made Familiar and Easy to Young Gentlemen and Ladies, Being the Third Volume of the Circle of the Sciences* (3rd London edn., 1769): 35.

24 Bolingbroke, *Letters on the Study and Use of History* (London, 1752): 186.

25 John Rice, *An Introduction to the Art of Reading with Energy and Propriety* (London, 1765): 291–2.

26 Mason, *Essay on Elocution*: 20, 31–5.

27 Alexander Pope, *Essay on Criticism* (London, 1711): 15.

28 Also Bartine, *Early English Reading Theory*: 43.

29 Sheridan, *Course of Lectures*: 27.

30 Mason, *Essay on Elocution*: 31.

31 [Dodsley] *The Preceptor*: 4.

32 Rice, *Art of Reading*: 199.

33 Burgh, *Art of Speaking*: 4, 5.

34 John Holmes, *The Art of Rhetoric Made Easy: or the Elements of Oratory briefly stated* (London, 1739).

35 William Scott, *Lessons in Elocution; or Miscellaneous Pieces in Prose and Verse selected from the Best Authors* (Edinburgh, 1779): v.

36 Vicesimus Knox, *Elegant Extract: or Useful and Entertaining Passages in Prose, Selected for the Improvement of Scholars at Classical and other Schools in the Art of Speaking* (London, 1784): iv.

37 Scott, *Lessons in Elocution*: vii–viii.

38 Anon, *A Help to Elocution and Eloquence* (London, 1770): iv.

39 Mrs. Bellamy, *The Young Ladies' Miscellany… To which is Prefixed a short Essay on the Art of Pronunciation* (London, 1726): Preface, n.p.

40 Ibid.: ii, x, v.
41 Kelley, *Learning to Stand and Speak.*
42 James Buchanan, *A Plan of an English Grammar School Education* (London, 1770): 109.
43 Buchanan, *Plan*: 116; James Buchanan, *The British Grammar* (London, 1762): xvii.
44 Buchanan, *British Grammar*: xxviii–xxix.
45 Also Janowitz, "Amiable and radical sociability."
46 Richard Cumberland, *Memoirs of Richard Cumberland* (Boston, 1806): 28.
47 Sarah Fielding, *The Governess* (London: Pandora, 1987): xii, xiv. Subsequent references to this edition will be in the text.
48 Clara Reeve, *The Progress of Romance* (London, 1785): 85.
49 For the pedagogy of example, Bannet, *Domestic Revolution*: Chap. 2.
50 Eliza Haywood, *The Tea-Table* (London, 1725): 6.
51 *Tea-Table*: 2, 18, 48, 49.
52 *Tea-Table*: 49, 50.
53 [Anon] *Constantia; Or a True Picture of Human Life, Represented in Fifteen Evening Conversations*, 2 vols. (Dublin, 1751): 1: xix.
54 Elizabeth Griffith, *The History of Lady Barton* (London, 1771): v–vi, I: 240.
55 Knott, *Sensibility and the American Revolution*: Chap. 3; Kelley, *Learning to Stand and Speak*; McMahon, *Mere Equals.*
56 Hannah Webster Foster, *The Coquette* and *The Boarding School* (Boston, 1797, 1798): 201, 203, 149, 150.
57 Enos Hitchcock, *Memoirs of the Bloomsgrove Family* (Boston, 1790): 204, 48.
58 See Prince, *Philosophical Dialogue.*
59 Ann Murray, *Mentoria, or The Young Ladies Instructor, in Familiar Conversations on Moral and Entertaining Subjects* (Dublin, 1779): vi.
60 Priscilla Wakefield, *Mental Improvement, or the Beauties and Wonders of Nature and Art conveyed in a Series of Instructive Conversations* (London, 1794): i.
61 *Memoirs of Richard Cumberland*: 83.
62 Catherine Talbot, *Essays on Various Subjects in Prose and Verse*, 2 vols. (Dublin, 1773): 1: 109.
63 Elizabeth Carter, *A Series of Letters between Mrs. Elizabeth Carter and Miss Catherine Talbot from the Year 1741 to 1770*, 4 vols. (London, 1809): 1: 95.
64 Ibid.: 1: 42, 86, 102, 40,
65 John Hawkesworth, *The Adventurer*, No. LII, Saturday, May 5, 1753 (London, 1800): 136.

CHAPTER 3

Polite Reading

"The World is full of Books" – some sound, others not, some useful, others not. Or as Thomas Baker put it as early as 1708: "Learning is already so voluminous that it begins to sink under its own Weight: Books crowd in daily, and are heap'd upon Books, and by the Multitude of them, both distract our Minds, and discourage our Endeavors."[1] It followed, at least for the learned, that the reading public needed a "judicious friend" to advise them on which books were most proper for them to read after their Grammar, and to direct them in how to do the recommended reading effectively during their idle hours. For those personally unacquainted with a suitable prodigy, print manufactured a host of virtual friends who vied with one another to perform these roles: mentors on study and "improvement of the mind"; preceptors in the Arts and Sciences; parental or clerical monitors on the proper conduct of reading; the "gentlemen" of the Reviews. Whether in stand-alone books, conduct books, encyclopedias, or miscellany essays, guides to study told their users what subjects they ought to learn about and why, recommended suitable books, and gave "directions how to study them to advantage." Here "Study" meant reading with a view to acquiring new knowledge, to retaining it in "the storehouse of memory," and to "enlarging the mind" – we still use "read" as a synonym for "study" when we say that someone is reading a subject at University. Guides to study had been a Renaissance humanist phenomenon, designed for the use of scholars and teachers and "shaped by the pressures of training gentlemen destined for careers in public service or the administration of their estates."[2] Their methods of study were adapted and translated in Britain during the eighteenth century for a far broader reading public, which included the ambitious, the fashionable, the unlearned, and women.

Guides to study made it clear that what was being proposed was a course of reading for every man's leisure hours, to enable him to acquire the kinds of general knowledge he needed to make him a useful and productive citizen, a moral, Christian and social being, and a man of sense who could judge and discourse in a useful and instructive manner about a variety of subjects. The recommended course of reading would supplement schooling, familiarize men and youths with subjects not yet taught in schools, and/or entirely supply the place of schooling, since after early education, books were "the most sovereign Remedy against Ignorance and Error that human Wit can propose."[3] Most guides to masculine study sent their users a double message: the suggested course of reading would benefit them in their working or public lives, but must come a distant second to their properly professional studies and public or professional duties. There was more than a suggestion too that, whatever one's birth, to be a true gentleman and take one's place among the "polite" required a range of reading, and accumulation from it of a "stock" of "approved" knowledge and ideas, beyond what was needed for work-a-day purposes. Guides to study were guides to "polite learning" and "polite knowledge" produced by the learned, which relayed to the public, and helped to determine, which subjects and which books it was "polite," as well as useful, to know.

Guides to study were gendered in the sense that they were usually directed either to men or to women, and gendered again, according to whether guides for women's reading were authored by women or by men. Male authors generally treated "the female sex" as a species unto itself, which required advice different from that given to youths and men. They often differed from their female counterparts in the goals they set for women's studious reading, as well as in the subjects and books they recommended. For instance, where Hester Chapone advised young ladies to acquire knowledge of the Ancients by reading Rollin's *L'Histoire Ancienne*, John Bennett pronounced Rollin, and other multi-volume books, "too voluminous" for ladies because "the perusal would require more time, than would consist with your other various engagements," and recommended that they read biographies full of "domestick anecdotes and events" instead. Bennett, whose letters of advice to young ladies were reprinted more often in America than in Britain, thought biographies "far more useful and interesting to a woman" than history, with its accounts of "wars, victories or great achievements, which are not so much within the province of a female."[4] But Bennett was positively broad-minded compared to the "Gentleman of Cambridge" who "adapted" Abbé d'Ancourt "to the Religion, Customs and Manners of the English Nation" during the 1740s: he described the "Learning proper to a young Lady" as consisting of her own language, French and Italian, sufficient Arithmetic to cast accounts, and the ability to write a good hand.[5]

Like guides to men's study, female-authored guides to women's study were designed for their leisure hours. Ladies (and would-be ladies) too were enjoined not to let reading interfere with the performance of their duties; but in their case, this injunction resonated as an Awful Warning, given men's long-standing objection to women's learning on the grounds that "they have other things to do [which] they will not mind if they be once Bookish."[6] Ladies, young and old, were told that reading for self-improvement would give them a pleasant way of occupying the many dull hours which lay heavy on their hands, redeem them from the vacuous round of visits and diversions with which they currently filled their time, and guard them from the temptations to dissipation and vice attendant upon such flighty pastimes. Female-authored guides more frequently presented the course of study they prescribed as a *substitute* for schooling while girls' education centered on "accomplishments," such as deportment, dancing, sewing, drawing, music, and French.

In part because they were most detailed and complete, the century's two most influential guides to study were Revd Isaac Watt's *The Improvement of the Mind* (1741) and clergyman's widow, blue-stocking Hester Chapone's rewrite of it as a program of independent study for young women between 15 and 18, *Letters on the Improvement of the Mind* (1773). Chapone too advised her putative "niece" to read in order to "store your mind with as many ideas as you will know how to manage" in order to "enlarge your Mind," insisting that "with regard to accomplishments, the chief of these is a competent share of reading, regulated and well chosen." Echoing Watts again,[7] she told young ladies they needed to know that "philosophical inventions" such as the microscope or telescope made it possible to see "what is unavailable to the eye and by the ignorant not known to have existence," and that they must overcome their initial "astonishment" in private, rather than demonstrate shameful "ignorance" in public. Young ladies should attain sufficient knowledge of diverse subjects to be able to "ask now and then a pertinent question" when they arose in conversation, and to be able to "mention any circumstances relating to it that have not before been taken notice of."[8] They might learn music and drawing if they had the aptitude or inclination, but French or Italian were useful principally for "the multitude of original Authors which they furnish"; indeed, several of the books Chapone recommended were in French. She excluded Latin and Greek because it was unhelpful for a woman to provoke men's "jealousy" of her learning, and unnecessary to do so when the principal Greek and Roman texts could be read in translations.[9] The course of reading Chapone proposed covered history (beginning with the Bible considered as history), chronology, biography and geography; natural philosophy, with emphasis on astronomy and natural history; moral philosophy; modern languages, poetry and criticism. Chapone excluded from Watts' list, subjects such as "Mechanicks" or "Opticks" which required a higher knowledge of mathematics than the "common arithmetic" which was "an indispensible requisite" for women and which was – realistically – as much math as most women were likely to be allowed to learn. Chapone privileged history as a subject for young women to study, because it could be made to encompass and mask learning about philosophy and rhetoric, metaphysics, natural religion, government, the law of nations and other "manly" subjects. As Hume had observed, history "opens the door to many other Parts of Knowledge, and affords material to most of the Sciences."[10] Like Watts' *Improvement of the Mind*, which was reissued 22 times between 1741 and 1800 in London, and seven times in America between 1793 and 1813, Chapone's *Letters on the Improvement of the Mind* rapidly became a transatlantic best-seller: her book saw 15 London editions, as well as 5 American, 5 Irish and 4 Scottish editions before 1800. It was even more popular during the early nineteenth century, when it was reprinted 29 times in Britain, 21 times in America, and 3 times in France before the mid-1840s.

Gender politics were not the only politics to play out in the pages of guides to study. Party politics figured here as they did everywhere else. For instance, in its review of William Smith's *The Student's Vade Mecum*, which gave "directions how to proceed in the Study of each Branch of Learning, and an Account of the proper Books to read on each Subject," *The Critical Review* complained that Smith's "political opinions are repugnant to the sentiments of a free people" and that his recommendations were distorted by them.[11] More fundamentally, until mid-century, there was basic disagreement about which subjects the generality of readers ought to know. Guides to study such as Henry Felton's *Dissertation on Reading the Classics* (1713) or Anthony Blackwall's, *An Introduction to the Classics: containing a short discourse on their excellencies; and directions how to study them to advantage* (1737) promoted the classical and humanist curriculum of Latin grammar schools and English Universities, sometimes extended to include English "classics." Guides such as Rollin's *Method of Teaching and Studying the Belles Lettres* (translated 1734, 11th edition in 1778) and Watts' *Improvement of the Mind* reoriented study towards subjects in the Circle of the Sciences that were more typical of Dissenter academies, Scottish universities, and the new "English" schools. The subjects Watts recommended were represented in widely-used mid-century digests such as Newbery's *Circle of the Sciences* or Dodsley's *Preceptor*, which offered themselves as aids to schoolmasters as well as to "Young Gentlemen, and Ladies" studying on their own.

However, the focus here is not on such disputes. In the first section below, it is on the methods of reading that guides to study recommended both for individual books and for whole subjects, and on the different methods of reading demanded by digests or handbooks that endeavored to make study "more easie." The second section examines a subset of guides to study, guides to taste, which were digests from the first, and more closely allied both to professional training and to schools.

For all the period's changes in taste, guides to taste show remarkable continuity of conception and consistency in approach. The two most influential guides to taste were Charles Gildon's essays on "The Art of Rhetoric" and "The Art of Poetry," which were appended to Brightland's best-selling *Grammar* in 1712 and regularly plundered by other grammars and instructional books before Blair's *Lectures* were plundered instead; and Hugh Blair's *Lectures on Rhetoric and Belles Lettres* (1783), which were constantly reprinted, as well as abridged, adapted, imitated, extracted and quoted without attribution by grammarians, Latin-school masters, English-school teachers, university professors, periodical writers and compilers on both sides of the Atlantic throughout the late eighteenth and nineteenth centuries.[12] Based on lectures he had delivered at the University of Edinburgh since 1759 to students in their early teens, Blair's *Lectures* represented a sort of *summum* of the instruction we have tracked so far. Though not viewed now as a schoolmaster among schoolmasters, Blair revisited all that English-school books taught, or were supposed to have taught, their pupils about reading and writing: alphabets and the development of the English language, syllabic accent, versification and "Latinized English," parts of speech, and syntax, rhetorical figures, the virtues and faults of style, the construction of orations, and questions of pronunciation and delivery. Gildon's "Art of Rhetoric" had also covered this ground, but more rapidly. Like Gildon's "Art of Poetry," Blair provided an overview of what was known about genres together with a sketch of their ancient and modern histories, and modeled those forms of critical reading which Blair's contemporaries called "corrective criticism," "historical criticism" and "philosophical criticism." Blair correctly claimed that he had "availed himself of the ideas and reflections of others," rather than "deliver merely what was new," in order to offer Youth "a more comprehensive view" of the subject than "[wa]s to be received from any one Book in our Language" at that time.[13] The *Lectures'* clarity, conventionality and amazing comprehensiveness rapidly turned this schoolbook into an immensely popular handbook for British and American adults and the would-be polite.[14] Guides to taste offered the public an overview of ideas about "belles lettres" upon which the learned largely agreed, which the learned dubbed "polite" and compre-hended under "Criticism."

Guides to study and guides to taste proposed different manners of reading. But both were "intensive" – requiring close reading and multi-ple rereadings of texts – and both confronted an "extensive" world full of newly accessible books to engage new unlearned readerships. The story of studious and tasteful reading was therefore soon doubled by what many contemporaries perceived as its other: the story of convenient but disem-powering shortcuts.

Guides to Study

Guides to study urged "all Persons of Leisure, of what Rank or Condition soever they be…to apply some Part of their Leisure-Hours to the Improvement of their Minds in useful Knowledge."[15] This had been preached to "Gentlemen such as live upon their Estates" at least since the turn of the century. But John Clarke extended it in 1731 to "Persons in the genteel Professions or Trades…that have a pretty good deal of empty time upon their Hands," such as lawyers, physicians, divines and mer-chants, and to "Ladies of Fortune," all of whom he accused of a lamen-table "Narrowness of Mind" for knowing nothing beyond their peculiar "Calling." While people would naturally "make a thorough Acquaintance with such Parts of Learning, as their Station and Business require," they could and should read to "take a general view of the rest," in order to "enlarge the Capacity and strengthen the rational Faculties of the Mind."[16] Echoing and extending Clarke, Isaac Watts not only called on "every man who pretends to be a Scholar or a Gentleman," but also on "everyone who has Leisure and Opportunity" to read all around "the Circle of the Sciences," to "attain some general and superficial Ideas of most or all of the Sciences" and "enlarge the Capacity of his Mind." The circle of the sciences included the natural sciences (astronomy, optics, mechanics, chemistry and natural history); history (beginning with the Bible considered as his-tory), chronology, biography and geography; natural religion and the law of nations; logic, ontology and metaphysics; and the various "philological subjects" – languages and their grammars, rhetoric, poetry, criticism, and history again.[17]

The difficulty was to get the public on board. Guides to study represented the reading public as restless, inattentive, unmotivated, undisciplined and easily distracted. They complained that most women were more interested in trivia, gossip, dress, balls and diversions than in serious reading; and that most men read only "by fits and starts," unselectively, superficially and "without due Attention." Here, for instance, is John Clarke's description of the reading public in 1731: "Some Men have so little Appetite for a Book, that it lasts not long; they are soon weary with Reading, upon which they fly to Company or Diversion, and spend their Time that Way," until losing their appetite for company, they again take up a book. Others, who read only to display their learning and taste in company, get through a variety of matter rapidly and superficially "in hopes of being quickly enabled, as Occasion or no Occasion offers, in Company, to throw out Hints, and give little Glances, upon the several Arts and Sciences, which...pass them upon such as know no more, or not so much as themselves." A "great many" others "read anything they light upon, all is Fish with them that comes to the Net." Clarke complained that readers were reading "without Thought," without "proper Recollection of what [they] have read," and without that "close Application of the Mind to Reading or Thinking" which produces "solid useful knowledge" and which he, like others, called "Study."[18]

Guides to study therefore explained the utility of studying particular subjects to the lives and/or labors of people in different stations. History was particularly useful "for Gentlemen who deal in Politicks," since it behoved them to know something about "the Government of Nations, and the distressful and desolating Events which have in all Ages attended the Mistakes of Politicians" in order to avoid making the same mistakes themselves. Chapone argued that young ladies needed to study history to know (among other things) "the history of that empire, of which you are a subject," particularly "something of the East and West Indies, where so great a part of it is situated" (199) and something of the "American Settlements," which "seem likely, in some future period, to be as much the seat of empire and of the sciences as Europe is at Present." Watts argued that some knowledge of astronomy and natural history was necessary to give divines "a wider and more delightful View of the Works of God," as well as "lively and happy Images" to draw upon in their sermons; but that physicians primarily needed to read natural history because some acquaintance with the animal body would give them a fuller understanding of the health and sickness of the human body. Blackwall insisted that gentlemen required knowledge of the "sublime" ancient classics because "there are inexhaustible Stores of noble Sense and suitable Expression in the best Greek and Latin classics," which would enable them to "supply the lacks of English" when they were obliged to speak in public, or write in the course of their public offices.[19] But Watts argued that besides "furnish[ing] our Tongues with the richest and most polite Variety of Phrases and Words upon all Occasions of Life or Religion," ancient and modern poetry was "of great Use to be read at Hours of Leisure," both for divines and for those suffering from "narrowness of soul," because it "convey[ed] to the Soul, most exalted and magnificent Images and sublime Sentiments" which "raise and aggrandize our Conceptions" and "elevate them even to a divine Pitch," in a manner particularly useful for "devotional purposes."

Guides to study agreed that the recommended course of reading must be broad and "regular": it must be pursued according to a plan, in an orderly and methodical fashion. They debated how many subjects a reader could profitably study concurrently – too few would "fatigue" (i.e. bore) the reader and discourage him from continuing; too many would get confused in his mind. But they tended to ignore the question of how much leisure-time any segment of society really had to read all the books and subjects they proposed. Initially, the assumption seems to have been that reading for self-improvement was something profitably pursued throughout a man's life: the course of reading proposed would take more years or fewer years to get through, depending on how much time a man was willing or able to devote to his leisure-time studies, but that did not matter because a man would be going back to books he valued throughout his life, and continuing to expand his knowledge by reading anyway. James Burgh opined that, if a youth managed to acquire some knowledge of "instrumental" subjects such as languages, numbers, geography, chronology and logic before he was eighteen or twenty, and proceeded in "a judicious manner" thereafter, he might expect to see "an improvement in most branches of science to a masterly degree by thirty or forty years of age."[20] After mid-century, digests targeting tutors and schools began to disseminate the idea that such studies were best completed during youth, before the onset of adult responsibilities, and short, question and answer introductions to individual subjects designed for schools began to appear.[21]

Guides to study highlighted four elements of "study": attention, method, memory and reflection.

All agreed that to benefit from reading, readers must learn to "attend." Though "the Mind, at first, through a Corruption of Nature and Custom together may…take it much amiss to be confined from rambling," it must be taught to "fix its Attention steadily upon any Object it has Occasion to survey," and "pinned down" to "a constant steady Pursuit of one single Subject only."[22] Guides usually suggested that readers train their attention by gently bringing it back to the matter at hand whenever it "rambled," assuring them that their concentration would improve with time and practice. Guides did a better job of showing readers how to process what they were reading, how to use writing and conversation to ensure that they could recall it afterwards, and how to reflect on what they had learned. In these regards, their instructions for reading individual books and for reading whole subjects were analogical.

The way to begin reading any book or treatise was with a "survey" of it to get a general and comprehensive "view" of the whole. These analogies taken from surveying, a standard subject in English schools, suggested that the contents of books were, like landed property, a landscape whose topography and major landmarks the surveyor-reader could map. They implied that reading, considered as the mental process of abstracting general ideas from the indeterminate mass of language and information in a book, was like the mental processes involved in creating a platt (plan) or abstract of a landed estate in the form of an organized, visual and spatial geographical field.[23] Watts advised readers to begin with a book's obvious landmarks, by "surveying" its title, table of contents, index (if there was one) and Preface in a "general and cursory manner, to learn…what you may expect from the writer" (60). The author's name, if known, would provide some indication of "the Manner it is done." This was also the time to dip into a chapter or two, to decide if the book was worth reading all the way through. If it was, the reader should devote his "first perusal" of the book as a whole to going rapidly through the text – marking in the margin with a pencil but skipping over any obscure or difficult passages – in order to take a "superficial and cursory Survey" of the book's main points or features. A general sense of the book's argument and "geography" would prepare him to peruse the book for a second time "with greater Attention and Deliberation." Understanding the author's overall "scheme," would help the reader resolve some of the difficult passages upon this second reading, enable him to pay more "studious Attention" to the complexities and details, and permit him to "learn with more Ease and Readiness what the Author pretends to teach" (60). Chapone made similar recommendations: the first time a young woman perused the Bible, she should do so chronologically beginning with Genesis, skipping non-historical chapters and passages she found difficult or obscure, to get a clear idea of the main events of biblical history and of the life and character of Jesus. Upon a second reading at some later date, she should include the hard parts she had skipped, and use one of the many available biblical "expositions" to help her understand them.

Memory was a major issue for guides to study, because nothing was known that was not remembered. The memory was a great "treasury" or "storehouse" – as traditional commonplace books collected and stored useful knowledge from a variety of sources in durable material form, so the reader's memory was supposed to collect knowledge from a variety of reading and store it, like the wares in a warehouse, for future retrieval and use. "Study" was the process of collecting selectively what one had seen inscribed on the pages of a manuscript, periodical or book, and "inscrib-ing" it on the tablets of one's memory in an organized fashion. The meta-phors could be varied, the meaning and upshot were the same: learning was not about knowing where to locate information should one happen to need it, but about absorbing it (another metaphor) into one's mind and body in such a way that one could recall it at will. Guides to study there-fore showed readers how to use a *third* perusal, along with writing, conver-sation, and reflection, to ensure that what had been learned was retained. "Nothing," as John Mason said, "helps the Memory more than often Thinking, Writing, or Talking on those Subjects you would remember."[24] There is evidence that readers did use these helps, though each reader did not necessarily use them all.

When using writing as an aid to recollection, the reader was advised to mark what was new or unknown to him in the margins of the book he was reading during his second perusal of it and then, during a third, more selective, rereading, to go back to re-view the pages, paragraphs or chapters he had marked. Later, when he had laid the book aside, the reader should mentally review the passages he had marked and reread, to see what he remembered; indeed, the reader should do this several times on differ-ent occasions until he was sure he had the new information fixed in his memory.

Another method involving more writing required a man to go back during that third rereading to copy the passages he had marked – and more significantly, to inscribe summaries, sketches or epitomes of chapters and arguments – into his commonplace book. Readers were advised to write down what they wished to remember in their commonplace books, because inscribing words and expressions, ideas and sentiments, on a page with one's own hand was said to help one remember them. Indeed, when "recur[ring] to the Help of a Commonplace book," readers were warned that they must "take care that, by confiding to your Minutes or Memorial Aids, you do not excuse the Labour of Memory."[25] Transcribing passages and summaries of one's reading into one's commonplace book made them more readily available for the regular rereading and review that were recommended to ensure that they were not forgotten. However, as Henry Felton observed in 1713, despite "the Pains and Labour to record what other Persons have said, that is taken by those, who have Nothing to say themselves," this exercise was useless "where the Brain is to be exercised."[26] In an essay "On the Means of Reading with the most Advantage" of 1782, Vicesimus Knox likewise complained that students "who spend their days in extracting passages from Authors, and fairly transcribing them in their commonplace book" on the assumption that "the exercise of the hand can impress ideas on the brain," were wasting their time because this exercise had become too "manual and mechanical" to be effective. Since "nothing really serves us in reading, but what the mind makes its own by reflection and memory," the best way of returning commonplace books to their proper function, was "to express the author's ideas, after shutting his book, in our own words," because "in this exercise, the memory is exerted and the style improved."[27] Readers might then compare what they had written down in their own words with the matter contained in the printed book, to see what they had forgotten.

Conversation was highly recommended as an aid to memory, as well as to attention and comprehension. Repeating in conversation what one had learned from a book was a way of impressing it upon one's memory. When three or four equals conversed on different books each had read and each repeated the main points he had learned from it, their "mutually improving conversation" allowed each to fix one book's contents more firmly in his memory, while sharing its ideas with others and adding to everyone's general knowledge. In conversation of this sort, each participant might answer the others' questions so fully as to make it unnecessary for them to peruse the book themselves. Their sketch of a book's main points also provided others with an idea of what they might expect from it, saving them from having to work that out for themselves from the paratext and first rapid perusal. On the other hand, when three or four equals conversed about a book which they had all agreed to read, each could find out from the others how much he had retained of what he had read, and learn to better select which ideas, facts or arguments were most worth retaining. By bringing his own observations and remarks about it to the conversation, each helped the others to understand or notice aspects of the book which they might have missed and to attain fuller comprehension of it. The prospect of debating or defending their different opinions of the book or of the subject it addressed "animated" reading for each of them: it made them return to the same book with more "eager attention," or peruse a book recommended by the others with more interest and attention, than they otherwise would. Chapone argued that conversation was particularly well suited to women's learning; indeed, she nowhere suggested any manner of reading, learning or study that involved writing.

Guides to study mentioned that bookish conversations were enhanced by conversing with people who had greater knowledge and wider reading than oneself. But they made it clear that conversation with one's "equals in attainment" would do perfectly well. While it would be an oversimplification to say that dissemination of this idea "caused" the proliferation among adults, during the eighteenth and early nineteenth centuries, of subscription library reading clubs, provincial philosophical societies, debating societies, and working men's adult-education clubs, it does explain why participants thought that conversing with each other without a teacher made good educational sense.

Most guides to study supplied the place of a book's first cursory perusal, like the participants in the first sort of conversation described above, by providing brief summaries, surveys or sketches of what readers could expect from the books they recommended. A survey or sketch described the text's principal features or main points in general terms in order to prepare the reader to read or study it themselves. Chapone provided a short sketch of each book of the Old and New Testaments because "short sketches of the matter contained in different Books of the Bible" would provide her "niece" with "a general notion of what to expect from each book [which] may help you understand them and increase your relish of them" (28–9). Summaries or sketches of a book's contents were aids to reading comprehension since they directed and organized the reader's reading by telling him/her what features of the narrative or argument to look for. At the same time, while giving her niece a "general notion of what to expect from each book" of the Bible, Chapone conveyed the "views and sentiments" with which each book "must be read" (28), and indicated, both implicitly and explicitly, what features the reader ought to admire or condemn.

Reviewers were in the same line of business as guides to study when it came to telling readers "what to expect from each book." As Robin Valenza has shown, a number of now neglected early periodicals, such as *Memoirs of Literature* (1710–14), *The History of the Works of the Learned* (1735–43) and *The Literary Magazine or Select British Library* (1735 onwards) undertook to guide readers who were scattered throughout the British empire far from the "Marts of Learning" in London, in what they needed to read to be considered polite and "learned" in metropolitan terms. Explicitly targeting readers who were "addicted to study," reading for "agreeable and useful amusement" or "people of much leisure, who read *pour tuer le temps*," they tried to "overcome the discouragement to learning" caused by the seeming "Impossibility of making any considerable Progress in Knowledge, without a constant and laborious Attendance upon Study." They did this by selecting and "digesting" books recently written in the modern languages "that could be deemed useful for a generality of readers."[28] Here, as in review periodicals established during the 1750s such as *The Monthly Review* or *The Critical Review*, a large part of each printed review of a non-fictional work consisted of a sketch of its main points. Jan Fergus and David Allan have shown that provincial readers often read review periodicals such as *The Monthly* or *The Critical* in place of the volumes whose main points they summarized, or used them to select the titles they would order for themselves or for their subscription libraries;[29] but the utility of review periodicals did not end there. The reviewer's sketch of a book's main features, and summary of its major points, also informed readers "what to expect" from it, and thus enabled them to "learn with more Ease and Readiness what the Author pretends to teach" when they came to read it; and reviewers were never shy about instructing readers in the "views and sentiments" with which a book should be read. We know of at least one reader, Joseph Hunter, an apprentice cutlery-maker in Sheffield, whose diary "mimic[ked] the structure of reviews by including a summary of a text followed by an extract or discussion of a scene" and by "a balanced account of the 'merits' and defects of the work." As Stephen Colclough observes, "summary and transcription were thus very important elements in Hunter's reading experience."[30]

Inevitably, different "views and sentiments" of the same texts were presented in different printed outlets. Readers who read in compliance with them would be led to read the same text differently. It made a difference whether one read the Bible (for instance) to view it as an historical and biographical narrative (Chapone); as divine revelation which knowledge drawn from the circle of the sciences only supported and confirmed (Watts); or as a book which rivaled the Ancients' greatest productions in its "striking passages of the pathetic and sublime, the vehement and impassioned" and in its "lofty images, grand conceptions, or…picturesque and animated descriptions" (Bennett).[31] Each view or perspective came paired with appropriate reader responses – fitting thoughts and emotions ("sentiments") that were either hinted or spelled out by the guide: read as history, the Bible was "interesting and affecting" and gave the reader rational "evidences of the Christian religion"; read as moral and spiritual instruction, it awakened humility and required "frequent perusal" to better understand one's duties; read as rivaling the Ancients in style, the Bible inspired "the admiration of the most accomplished scholars, orators and critics in the world" and was a vehicle for the exercise of the reader's sensibility and taste. To borrow Genette's image, the "views and sentiments" delineated by guides to study and review periodicals were so many "thresholds to interpretation":[32] each opened onto a different understanding, different reflections, different emotions and a different experience of the text; and each demanded of the reader its own, well-defined intellectual and emotional responses. To read the Bible for "evidences of the Christian religion" was to seek in it evidence of Jesus' historical existence, to place his life in a sequence of true events that began with Creation, to consider it in relation to the history of the Jews as recounted in the Old Testament, and to enter into debates about Christianity's proper dates. But to read the Bible as a model of sensibility and taste was to seek out the ""bold images, metaphors, allusions and descriptions with which [it] abounds," and admire how language was used to create its rhetorical effects. As their language shows, the "views and sentiments" expressed in guides to study, conduct books and reviews were prescriptive and regulatory: what ordinary reader would dare *not* admire where the greatest scholars and orators did, or not produce the proper response? But contemporaries' acceptance of variety, as long as piety was there somewhere in the mix, tended to water down the regulatory effect of these prescriptions. Different "views and sentiments" were quite often juxtaposed in the same guides without apparent concern about inconsistencies amongst them. For many guides, it seems, the variety of possible views and sentiments was something to be celebrated as a form of *copia* or abundance which testified to the value of particular texts, and to the many uses and benefits of reading, rather than something to be decried.

As readers were advised to begin studying a book by taking a general survey of it, so they were advised to begin acquiring knowledge of a subject by reading a general survey of that. I will take my examples from history. This not only appeared, as here, among the subjects in the circle of the sciences, but as we will see in the next section, as a form of writing among the *Belles Lettres*, and as a form of subsidiary knowledge required by readers of other kinds of texts.[33] There are some surprises here for those who believe, following Foucault, that in this period the *episteme* was already thoroughly historicized in the modern way.

The problem for both scholars and readers was how to "methodize" the historical materials they read so that what mattered could be distinguished and remembered. Sir William Temple was among those who complained during the 1690s that to discover the history even of his own country, "a

Man must read over a Library rather than a Book, and after all, must be content to forget more than he remembers." Men in the governing ranks needed a book which judiciously selected and "collected…what was fit to be told" from the multitude of historians dating back to the Romans, who had documented or recorded small bits of England's past. Such a book must "make an Abridgment" of the material and "digest [it] with good Order" so that its readers could remember what they read.[34] This was not a call to popularize or disseminate some extant story of England's past to all and sundry – that came later. It was a call for someone to provide "the nobility and gentry" with a quicker and easier means of learning (in the sense of discovering or coming to know) what had happened in England's past, by producing a survey or "general history" which selected and identified the most important people and events, condensed what was known about them, and presented the major landmarks methodically in such a way as to fix them in the reader's memory. As one eighteenth-century guide to study put it, without such a method, "History is a meer Chaos, a jumble of Words and Facts heap'd together, that can neither be read with Pleasure nor Advantage."

This kind of thinking led to two manners of studying history during the eighteenth century, both of which – ironically, given their subsequent history – arose more from efforts to devise solutions to the shortcomings of memory, than from any pretense that they represented anything intrinsically true either about the subject-matter or about "reality." Both turned on the idea that history (like any other subject) must be "digested into a regular Method" for readers to be able to learn and remember it. The method chosen for digesting and organizing historical materials consisted of treating chronology and geography as "the two Eyes of History," and of dividing each up "analytically," as grammars divided up language, into parts or units. Chronology and geography, time and place, were the coordinates that would methodize historical information to make it retrievable by the memory. Dates and geographical locations were mnemonics, divisions or partitions of chronology and geography which functioned like an index, or if one prefers, like the "house of memory" used by Renaissance orators.[35] *Epocha* were so many houses, countries so many rooms within them, with each conveniently subdivided again – *epocha* into intervals, decades, years, months and days; place into continents, countries, regions, towns, villages, rivers and mountains. Historical information had only to be mentally attached in the proper place under the proper "head," and thus associated with a particular time and location, to be remembered when one "looked" there. As Thomas Hearne said, "When one is thoroughly acquainted with the time and place, when and where Matters have been transacted, it is almost Impossible to forget them."[36] Or as John Mason explained, in the "Storehouse of the Mind," facts and information must be "laye[d] up in their Order, digested or ranged under proper Subjects or Classes," as in an index, so that "whatever Subject you have occasion to think or talk upon, you may have recourse immediately to a good Thought, which you heretofore laid up there under that Subject."[37] For the purposes of memory, it did not matter how *epocha*, never mind "countries," were identified, named or circumscribed. People with different interests or professions might periodize differently – princes and governors, by the reigns of kings; soldiers, by wars; lawyers, by pivotal legislation; or, as Chapone said, each reader could pick out a few remarkable events for herself, and order other events in relation to them. European countries were in any case constantly changing their borders, the empire to which they belonged, even their place names, while large parts of other continents were blank. Chronological and geographical divisions were "purely *technical*" – "the Circumstance that assists the Memory, and puts the Reader in a Capacity to retain the Accounts of Things."[38] As "the thread of history," chronology merely ensured that no room, no *epocha*, was forgotten between Creation and the present day.

This is why guides to study recommended that readers begin their study of history by reading general histories such as Rollin's *Ancient History* or Rapin de Thoyras, *History of England*, which conveniently "digested [the historical materials] into a regular Method," according to the time and place in which men had lived and events had occurred. Ideally, such general histories functioned both as an introduction and as a notebook. Their general and methodical "survey" of the historical material provided an introduction in the form of an overarching, systematic narrative framework for the more specialized, localized and detailed histories, documents, memoirs or biographies that readers were advised to peruse afterwards. But printed narrative surveys were also notebooks: they bound together partly blank pages, stamped in the middle with printed text which the reader was supposed to supplement, correct and complete with his own handwritten notes in the margins as he read. As they read more on the subject, readers were advised to go back to insert in the blank margins of their general history book, references to other books which confirmed or disproved particular passages; objections or corrections to the sentiments expressed; comments about the justice of the author's argument, about the probability of his narrative, or about the virtues and faults of his style; inferences that might be drawn in particular places; clarifications of obscure words or ideas; information lacking in the text; and/or amplifications of important points.[39] In other words, readers were advised to use the blank space in the margins of each printed page to "converse with the book" in light of what they knew or subsequently learned from other books or other people, and thus to record their reflections upon what the book said. Conversing with the book in the margins of the printed text enabled the reader to judge "what he [the author] writes so well as to approve itself" and what the reader ought to "treasure in [his] memory."[40] This also made the printed book more useful for subsequent readers, who now had the benefit of a previous reader's (or several previous readers') notes and corrections as well as the general survey in the printed text.

The problem with multi-volume histories such as Rollin's, Rapin's or Hume's *History of England*, was that they were still too prolix and detailed for the purposes of memory. Their narratives had to be abridged, and "methodized" again, before the principal people and events could be placed and recalled. Chapone advised her niece to use her second perusal of Rollin's *Ancient History* to "fix the ancient chronology in your mind" (64). Since Rollin treated the history of each ancient empire separately, one after another, this involved collating the histories of different empires in different volumes to see where they overlapped in time, and abstracting from the narrative a largely implicit chronological line on which simultaneous events in different geographical locations could be placed. The chronology had to be worked out mentally before it could be fixed in the mind; but working it out helped to fix it there. Watts urged his male readers to use writing in their commonplace books to "abridge [such books] into a lesser form"; and, "if several things relating to the same Subject are scattered up and down through the Treatise," to abridge the book in such a way as to "bring them all into one View" (65). Things had to be condensed, reorganized and mapped to be remembered. As Boswell said, "To assist the Memory of the Student, all kinds of Epitome [are] serviceable."[41] While methodically observing chronology and geography, the reader's abridgment must highlight the principal characters, events or issues to provide "a full Survey," which could be used for purposes of memory, as a matrix for reflection and further reading, and as a basis for subsequent conversation with the book. James Burgh provided particularly full instructions on these points:

> To draw up in writing an epitome or abstract of the most shining parts of history, the eminent characters, as one proceeds, adjusting the chronology and geography all along, will contribute greatly to fixing in the mind a general comprehensive view of the whole thread of story from the oldest

accounts of time downwards, disposed according to the several ages and countries which make a figure in history...Among the abridged facts, might with great advantage be disposed a set of reflections moral, political and theological, as they occurred in the course of reading, which would in the whole amount to a very great number and variety; and would prove an agreeable and improving amusement in advanced life, to peruse, add to, and correct, as one's judgment matured, and views enlarged.[42]

Using one's commonplace book for abridgments and summary-surveys of one's reading, and/or to "converse" with books, was a departure from earlier uses of commonplace books, that was inspired more by guides to study than by Locke, who had merely devised a more efficient way of indexing traditional commonplace books. This underlay the gradual shift to what he calls "note-taking" that David Allan found in his empirical study of eighteenth-century commonplace books.[43] Conceived as a pocket library for those who lacked easy access to books, traditional commonplace books had contained short passages, that were remarkable as *sententiae* or wise sayings and/or as models worthy of imitation in one's writing. In principle, each reader selected these for him/herself as they read, transcribed them into their commonplace book from a variety of sources and organized them for easy retrieval under topics or headings, such as love, jealousy, or idleness. This manner of reading had long been portrayed as a process of selecting and gathering "flowers" from the gardens of others, while the reader was compared to a bee collecting honey.[44] The traditional commonplace book did not disappear in the eighteenth century as we once supposed. Some people continued to use it, though it may have been affected by guides' recommendation to appropriate reading-matter by rewording. Victor Watson found, for instance, that Jane Johnston personalized sententiae by rewording as she transcribed them (writing "I" for "man" or "he").[45] Traditional commonplace books also entered print culture both in alphabetized printed collections of the "beauties" culled from eminent authors, and in such philosophical and ethical olios as Kames' *Introduction to the Art of Thinking* (1761), or *The Hive*, which was reprinted in America multiple times between 1794 and 1814. If nothing else, Felton's and Knox's complaints about students' spending their days laboriously transcribing passages into their commonplace books tells us where print got such copy from.

In recommending that readers use their commonplace books to summarize and reflect upon their reading, eighteenth-century guides to study recommended uses of the commonplace book that were laborious in an entirely different way. Extending to the work of the mind Locke's argument that men made what they took from nature's common stock their own property by adding their own physical labor to it, they argued that a man must "make the several Parts of Learning his own Property by reading, by reasoning, by judging for himself, and by remembering what he has read."[46] Even more adamantly, they insisted that once a man had worked up the words and ideas of others himself, they *were* his own. To reword, abridge or enlarge a thought taken from another, to apply it to a different object, to reflect upon it, and to write all this down, was "to "convert to our own use, what we have observed and treasured up from others" and "so to digest it, as to make it [our] own."[47] It did not matter that "we can say nothing Better, than hath been said before," for "we may nevertheless make what we say our *Own*" by "mix[ing] and incorporate[ing] with what we read"; for though your mind will be "infused" and "improved" by your reading, "yet the Spirit, the Thought, the Fancy, the Expression which shall flow from your Pen, will be entirely your Own."[48] Guides also made these points by reverting to the old metaphor of food: "Reading is, indeed, most justly called the food of the mind. Like food, it must be digested and assimilated; it must show its nutritive power by promoting growth and strength, and by enabling the mind to bring forth sound and vigorous productions. It must be converted *in succum et sanguine*, into juice and blood, and not make its appearance again in the form in which it was originally imbibed."[49] By using his own judgment to produce summaries, epitomes, abridgements and surveys of his reading in his own words, a man was adding his labor to what he had taken from the common stock of words and ideas, changing the form in which his reading was originally imbibed, digesting it into a form in which he could more readily assimilate and remember it, adding his own comments and reflections as he went, and rendering it "his own." This was also how a man showed that he was a "man of learning" in essays, treatises, letters or conversation: by repeating in his own words, and in altered form, what he had gleaned from his reading on a given topic, and adding his own reflections. "What oft was thought, but ne'er so well express'd," plus a little something of one's own for the common pot.

This method of study led to diversity in what readers chose to take away from their reading. Chesterfield's letters to his young son, for instance, supplied him with an epitome of Roman history, which showed him what to learn from it. As Chesterfield explained (in French):

> Of all the ancient histories, the Roman is the most interesting and instructive. It abounds with most accounts of illustrious men, and presents us

with the greatest number of important events. It likewise spurs us on, more than any other, to virtuous actions, by showing how a small city like Rome, founded by a handful of shepherds and vagabonds, could, even in the space of seven hundred years, render herself mistress of the world by courage and virtue.

Hence it is, that I have resolved to form a small abridgement of that history, in order to facilitate your acquiring the knowledge of it; and for the better imprinting it in your mind, I desire that, by little and little, you would translate, and copy it fair into a book, which you must not fail to bring to me every Sunday.[50]

The utility of Roman history was that Rome could serve as a model for Britain's growing empire, and illustrious Romans for the conduct of Britain's great men. The survey of that history that Chesterfield's letters provided in conveniently abridged narrative form would facilitate and guide his son's reading by sketching out and highlighting what mattered in Roman history in these regards. Asking his son to translate his letters from the French would improve the latter's skill in both languages, and together with copying his English translation into a commonplace book, provide the boy with two ways of imprinting both the major characters and events, and his father's framework and values, upon his memory. By contrast, in his commonplace book, Ashley Cowper tried to reconstruct how the English had obtained their religious liberties. He composed a long historical narrative on the subject from material gleaned from a printed general history and several subsidiary books, complete with additions and corrections in the margins.[51] Guides to study showed readers how to "trawl" books to "create meanings that were informed by their professional interests, political loyalties, existing commitments, worries and deeply held beliefs."[52]

Though permitting wide diversity in what readers took from their reading and facilitating what we now call "student-centered learning," these studious methods of reading for the purpose of acquiring useful knowledge and making it one's own were laborious and time-consuming. Because they involved a great deal of rereading, reorganizing or rewriting, and "reflection" or "meditation" on what one had read, as well as the acquisition of expensive books, guides themselves came to recognize that they were better suited to "men of leisure and fortune" than to working stiffs. Consequently – to provide for readers with less leisure and fewer funds, to enlarge the market for their services, and to disseminate knowledge more efficiently – booksellers and educators offered another, shorter and easier, path to knowledge through printed "helps to study": chronological tables, maps, digests of the various subjects, and dictionaries of the arts and sciences. These fundamentally changed how one read to acquire useful general knowledge. Printed chronological tables, maps and globes provided readers with the architectonics for methodization and memorization *a priori*; and digests of "the particulars necessary to be known" in any subject provided readers with *a priori* selections and summaries of what ought to be remembered. Here reading or study consisted largely of attaching one to the other, and of memorizing the result.

One application of this method of study began by getting the architectonics for memory by heart. Readers, and increasingly pupils in schools, were advised to memorize printed chronological tables which contained "all the Epochs and some of the most remarkable Occurrences that have happen'd since the Creation," all "rang'd in their proper Order with their Dates affix'd to them," and to make themselves familiar enough with geographical maps containing all the towns, villages, mountains, seas and rivers, properly labeled, preferably with both their ancient and modern names, to be able to see them in their mind's eye. The first order of business was to understand and memorize the scaffolding for memory. Then, as one read a survey or digest to acquire information about terrains, towns, people or events, one was supposed to mentally attach this information to its proper place on one's mental map with its memorized chronological thread and memorized geographical maps. Writing could help here: readers were advised to use their pens to add people or events in their proper places to those already printed on the chronological table, and to insert newly-discovered places in the vacant spots on the printed maps.

Chronological tables created useful knowledge: they allowed "the generality of readers" to literally see for the first time how different personages and events related temporally, whether in the same or in different countries, and to discover, quite shockingly, just how long ago things they had often heard about had occurred. In principle, it was still possible to proceed to the reading of more specialized and detailed histories, memoirs or biographies after attaching the information from a short survey or digest of "approved" historical or geographical matter to one's chronological table. Information gleaned from contemporary newspapers, which were said to record "the history of the times," could be added to that already inserted in the maps and chronological table too.

Providing readers and students with a chronological table was also useful, because scholars themselves were struggling for most of the century to create a single time-line that reconciled the different temporal measures of the Greeks, Romans, Christians and Jews, and that ascertained how events in different countries or places might have related to one another

temporally. It did not help that Britain itself changed her calendar a third
of the way through the century, or that chronological tables produced by
the learned disagreed – until Joseph Priestley's chronological tables at century's end began to command the field.[53] But even if they were uncertain,
subject to revision and more "technical" than true, printed chronological
tables did save readers and students personal effort and study-time; as *aide-
memoires*, they were "useful" whether they were correct or not.

The shortcoming noted by contemporaries was that they encouraged
learning that stopped short of the reflection required to make the content of books one's own. As the author to one *Introduction to the Study of
History* complained after this method of study began to establish itself in
schools: "Young Gentlemen burthen their memories with a great number of dates, names and events; and provided they can but repeat what
they have heard or read, they are generally esteemed for their knowledge.
The true purpose of history, however, consists not in the remembrance
of a number of events and actions, without making proper reflections
thereon." This method of using chronological tables and other aids to
study led "ignorant" parents, teachers and students to mistake memorization for knowledge, and chronology for history, and to defend what they
were doing by arguing, equally erroneously, that students were too young
to reflect.[54]

Guides to study also recommended a second method of using printed
aids to acquire historical and geographical knowledge. This was to read a
general history or historical digest with a chronological table and a map
open before one, and to pause in one's reading to consult them whenever
one came to a place-name one did not recognize or to an event one could
not place in time. James Burgh explained the upmarket version:

> To be master of antient history, let a person first peruse carefully the universal
> history, consulting all along the maps of several countries which have been
> the scenes of action, and referring every character and event to its proper
> date. After this general view of the whole body of antient history, those who
> have leisure and other advantages, may read as many of the originals as they
> please, especially upon the most important characters and facts.[55]

Burgh went on to advise "gentlemen of leisure and fortune" that they
ought to have "a little acquaintance" with Herodotus, Thucydides,
Polybius, Xenophon, Diodorus Siculus and Plutarch among the ancient
Greek historians; and Justin, Livy, Tacitus, Caesar, Sallus, Suetonius and
Curtius among the Romans. This manner of reading was adapted for ladies
by those who assumed they would not be following a "regular" course of

study, and for men in the same case who lacked a fortune to spend on books. Readers of historical digests, newspapers and/or travel literature were advised to read with a map and chronological table open before them, and to consult these as they went along in the manner Burgh described. They were also advised to take this opportunity to turn from their map and chronological table to a compendium (Dictionary of Arts and Sciences or Encyclopedia) to look up what was known about the history, government, customs, manners, commerce, agriculture and arts of the place they had seen mentioned and then found on the map. Readers were advised to do the same when they came to any "terms of art" (disciplinary jargon) they did not know. Reading digests and compendia was a quicker and easier way of acquiring "approved" knowledge; therefore, according to Oliver Goldsmith, "the generality of readers fly from the scholar to the compiler, who offers them more safe and speedy conveyance."[56]

As modern scholars have explained, eighteenth-century encyclopedias and dictionaries of the arts and sciences go back to the medieval *speculum*, and were modeled on commonplace books – or perhaps more accurately, on a cross between alphabetical indexes and newer-style commonplace books which contained summaries and abridgements.[57] But eighteenth-century compilers made it clear that the audience they had in mind no longer consisted primarily of learned scholars who were concerned about the unmanageable volume of knowledge, and anxious to have it reduced in volume and organized so that it could be comprehended in a single, Cyclops-like view. Ephraim Chambers, whose *Cyclopaedia* (1728) Benjamin Franklin famously mocked a rival printer for reprinting serially in his paper, promised that his "universal dictionary of the arts and sciences" would "answer all the Purposes of a Library, except Parade and Incumbrance; and contribute more to the propagating of useful Knowledge through the Body of a People, than any, I had said almost all, the Books extant."[58] The "Society of Gentlemen" which added a supplement to Harris' *Dictionary of the Arts and Sciences* in 1744 said the same thing, adding that "a Work such as this was to be instead of a Library to a great many People, who, tho' Lovers of Learning, might not have wherewithal to purchase Books; and others who had Books, not Leisure enough to consult them; and even those who have both these Advantages, would not chuse to be continually seeking out the Information referr'd to." These gentlemen kept the entries brief, to ensure that their dictionary would not be "inconsistent with the Pocket, as well as the Patience of the Generality of Readers."[59] The primary goal of these compilers, then, was dissemination of knowledge to a wider public by giving those without the interest, fortune or leisure to prosecute a regular course of study, direct and immediate access to the kinds of general knowledge they were thought to need. When Scotland's *Encyclopaedia Britannica* described itself as "a comprehensive library in itself; alike adapted to the profound Scholar, the accomplished Gentleman, and the Inquisitive Trader,"[60] it was targeting the three most influential segments of Scottish society: the clerisy, the landed gentry, and the commercial classes.

Dictionaries of the arts and sciences also endeavored to insert themselves into the course of study and manners of reading described by guides to study. Some represented themselves as a first survey of each topic by attaching a list of books for further reading to each entry. Almost all ensured that their diverse entries covered the entire circle of the sciences – the Society of Gentlemen, for instance, added their Supplement to Harris' dictionary because Harris had favored the "mathematical" subjects at the expense of subjects such as theology, history, antiquity, poetry and government. Recognizing that the goal was to give the public "some general and superficial Ideas of most or all of the Sciences," compilers also struggled against the miscellaneous, disconnected and "un-scientific" character of a genre that ordered fragments of information merely alphabetically. They made desperate efforts not to produce "a book of shreds and patches," but to make the dictionary form give readers "the advantages of a continued discourse" which would enable them to see each subject "whole."[61] Chambers in effect tried to make his dictionary work like a hypertext, by listing in a designated order the terms that readers should look up to work their way around each subject, and by referring them to related entries at the end of each topic. One could, in principle, piece a subject together by following the links to entries in different parts of the *Cyclopaedia*. The *Britannia*, which doubted that anyone would take the trouble to do that, tried to "digest" each subject into a "a treatise or system comprehending the history, theory and practice of each," while finding ingenious ways of preserving the convenience of being able to look up terms of art, countries, and other topics alphabetically. But in each case, as in the grammar book, the way to a sense of the "whole" subject lay through a series of discontinuous entries that had to be reconnected by the reader's mind.

Guides to Taste

Guides to taste were guides to the "liberal arts": to painting, sculpture, architecture or music, as well as to the language-based arts of oratory (speeches and sermons), poetry (including drama), history (sacred, prophane, true and fictional – the narrative arts), and philosophy (moral philosophy and argument). These language-based arts, which were initially described as "philological" and later as "polite literature" or "belles lettres," are what will concern us here.[62] Guides to taste in the language-based arts took the form of digests, which taught "critical" manners of reading. The authors of guides to taste were characterized by contemporaries as "philosophical" or "conjectural" critics, and (mockingly by their detractors) as "men of taste." We often mistake them for "practical critics" because they exemplified their precepts through close reading of literary works, but they were viewed (often negatively) as the "Theorists" of their day. Since many of them were or became teachers or university professors, we might also think of them as academic critics.

Guides to taste for the language-based arts were centered on genres or "kinds." Centering guides to taste on genres was said to conform to the practice of ancient "philosophical critics" such as Aristotle, and to learned seventeenth-century European precedents. But it also conveniently made "literary knowledge" a "rational science" and a branch of learning like all others. Genres constituted "a system of knowledge." They represented divisions of literary knowledge into parts which, like the parts of grammar or logic, contained "the doctrine, reason and theory of the thing"[63] and could be successively and cumulatively studied. Like the parts of other subjects, genres were kept separate and distinct. This ignored British writers' long-standing practice of mixing genres, marginalized or proscribed the many discontinuous and miscellarian forms that will be addressed in the next chapter, and suppressed key controversies among the learned. But keeping genres pure and distinct enabled critics to encapsulate the most obvious generic features of each in ways that were clear and relatively easy to remember. Keeping each genre pure and distinct also enabled genre to serve as a convenient fulcrum for a variety of contemporary methods of critical reading – corrective, historical, and philosophical – as well as for the uphill work of teaching students and the general public to read and appreciate what philosophical or conjectural critics deemed the "best" ancient and modern writing.

Because they also served as professional training, guides to taste in the language-based arts were more closely aligned to schoolbooks and to their authors' "liberal" or classical education, than guides to study generally were. Hugh Blair, for instance, told students at the University of Edinburgh who would be entering "the learned professions" that the reading practices comprised under "Criticism" would "prepare them for the pursuits they have in view" because they would have to write "in consequence of their profession." Guides to taste taught students what was *ab ovo* a belletristic manner of reading that was designed to teach them to write as gentlemen should. Belletristic critical reading had been taught in conjunction with writing and speaking, and as their precondition, at least since the Renaissance when, following Horace and Quintilian, humanists deemed that "the Judgment and Skill" to speak or write well was to be acquired by "reading or hearing whatever is best in its kind," and by imitating the best models.[64] For Henry Felton, the principal reason for a young lord to develop his taste by reading the classics in 1709 was still to "form a just style."[65] As John Boswell put it in 1738, students required "such Intimacy with the best Greek, Latin and English Writers, as shall capacitate the Student not only to see and admire the Beauties of their several Compositions, but to imitate their Manner of Writing…and make their Diction and their Sentiments his own."[66] Belletrism, or the identification of "beauties," was built into reading for the purpose of writing or orating: one had to determine what was worthy of imitation and what was not; one had to read critically to distinguish the "beauties" worth imitating. In guides to taste, critical reading continued to be the means of teaching students to "write perspicuously and agreeably" since guides "pointed out proper models for imitation" and "br[ought] into view the chief beauties that ought to be studied, and the principle faults that ought to be avoided" in one's writing, as Blair confirmed. But here it was the teacher-critic's critical reading and determination of beauties that prevailed. Guides to taste presented their subjects as "arts" – "collection[s] of rules and precepts for doing a thing surely"[67] – that were designed to teach readers how to judge and write or perform well in each genre.

This was one important way in which guides to taste distinguished themselves from guides to study: they "proceeded upon known Rules, and established Measures," as Joseph Spence put it, supplying readers with rules and models for imitation and standards for appreciation or "taste." Guides to study, by contrast, held that "true Taste…must rise from every Man's own Apprehension and Notion of what he heareth and readeth."[68] In his guide to study, Anthony Blackwall told "Gentlemen" and "young scholars" how to set about determining rules, standards and models of imitation for themselves on the basis of a formidable list of ancient and modern authors. Having read *all* "the best and most approv'd Classics" once, he explained, they must compare authors who were fellow citizens, those who were contemporaries, and those who wrote on the same subject, in order to determine which authors "deserve to be read several times," which required only "one careful Perusal," which "cannot be studied too much or gone over too often," and which they would have "frequent Occasions to consult…[only] in some of their particular Passages." By the same token, "careful Comparison of the Greek and Latin writers" would enable them to "see how judiciously the latter imitated the former," and "qualify [them] with greater Pleasure and Success to read and imitate both."[69] Comparison would enable readers to decide which texts, or parts of texts, contained true beauties of sentiment and style. Discovering the causes of beauties and faults – or what had worked well and what had not in each genre, and why – required what Blair called "comparisons of lower and higher degrees of the same beauties," as did the long, slow, reading-based, education which led to "the refinement of taste."[70] In principle, then, taste was developed and refined by using both "extensive" and "intensive" modes of reading. One read extensively and comparatively in order to determine which texts, or which parts of which texts, deserved intensive and repeated rereadings. One read intensively and comparatively to determine what one text had imitated from another, how what was borrowed had been (re) used, how different expressions compared, and where the superiority in beauty or wisdom lay.

Guides to taste reserved this kind of reading for philosophical critics, teachers, and the authors of guides to taste, who, as Joseph Spence observed in 1726, now assumed the role of "Ancient Criticks" like Aristotle or Horace, who had "distinguished the beauties of Language or Sentiments, from the defects and vices of either…that their Remarks might serve as Buoys to shew where former ventures had miscarried, and to prevent others from running upon the same Shallows."[71] The standards of genre and taste in this "liberal and humane art" were no longer to be established by studious readers for themselves, much less by "the approbation of the majority," but by "true critics" – men with a liberal education, who knew the ancient philosophical critics and were capable of comparing ancient and modern writers in their respective tongues. Comparison was fundamental to the teacher-critic's philosophical, evaluative and corrective tasks because "all human excellence stands merely on Comparison."[72] After Locke, it was also the foundation of reasoning, as we saw. This made criticism what Spence called "a Study highly rational" because, unlike the "common, vulgar passionate" method of reading which allowed "the Soul…to be hurried away by[its] vehemence of delight," criticism was a "method in reading" that required the reader to stand back and reflect in order to "balance" faults against beauties, and provide a rationale for each. The "improved taste" of "true critics" based on wide and repeated rereading and comparison of classical and modern authors, not only made their judgments just and true, it also gave them knowledge of what was "most enduring" in literature, enabling them to separate transitory historical manners and beliefs and fashionable prepossessions, from what "coincided" timelessly with universal human nature and with "the general sentiments of men." The enlightened and educated taste of true critics must therefore "correct the caprice of unenlightened taste" wherever that was found"[73] and guide the taste of the majority. Those who professed belles lettres distinguished themselves from other readers and showed where they added value by stressing their superior belletristic taste, and knowledge of supposedly universal truths.

As John Baillie observed, "the genuine work of *Criticism* is to define the *Limits* of each *Kind* of Writing, and to prescribe their proper Distinctions" by establishing and disseminating "Rules" for how they ought to be conducted.[74] This created an efficient, streamlined, philosophical and rational method of teaching reading, writing and taste: guides articulated *a priori* generic rules and standards of taste for each genre, and then illustrated them by offering examples of writings, ancient and modern, that met or failed to meet these tests. They modeled a controlled and limited version of the comparative method of reading by adducing and comparing positive and negative exemplars of each genre.

Gildon's essay on "the Art of Poetry," for instance, followed its account of syllabic accent and versification with succinct accounts of the rules and standards for six literary genres – epigram, pastoral, satire, comedy, tragedy and heroic poetry – a selection that appears to have been dictated by the writing exercises in Latin Grammar schools. Gildon articulated the "principles" of comedy: it "imitates common Life in its Actions and Humors, laughing at, and rend'ring Vice and Folly ridiculous; and recommending Virtue. It is indeed an Imitation of Life, the Mirrour of Custom, and the Image of Truth; whatever Comedy follows not this Track, is unworthy of the name." He supplied the associated rules: because comedy was a mirror of custom, writers must ensure that the manners and speech of each character were "agreeable to every Man's Station, Quality or Years," and reflective of contemporary life. Some lower-class characters should be included, because "humour is essential to English Comedy," and humors are "more visible in the lower sort of Persons"; but, for the comic representation of other ranks, "affectation is thought to be a Character fit for Comedy, as being highly ridiculous, and capable of being corrected by it."[75] This smacked of providing "receipts [recipes] for making all sorts of poems according to the modern taste," to borrow a phrase from the self-promoting title of another guide.[76] But as Gildon intimated, it also served to form the horizons of expectations of readers and spectators:

Our plays being divided into Acts, I shall add a word about them. There must be no more, nor less than five Acts…The first contains the Matter or Argument of the Fable, with the shewing the principal Characters. The second brings the Affairs or Business into Act. The third furnishes Obstacles and Difficulties. The fourth either shews how those Difficulties may be remov'd, or finds new in the Attempt. The fifth puts an end to them all, in a fortunate discovery, and settles all as it should be.[77]

Explaining what a comedy was supposed to do, how it was supposed to do it, and what we now call 'five-act structure' also showed readers and audiences what to expect of a comedy, how to organize it in their heads as they read or watched, what to look out for, what to admire and what to condemn. A play that failed to follow five-act structure correctly, to give characters manners and diction suitable to their station or their years, or to recommend virtue by rendering vice, humors or affectations ridiculous, was clearly an ill-made comedy and "unworthy of the name." Here reading was the other face of writing both in the sense that writing correctly depended on a right reading of the right models, and in the sense that reading and judging correctly depended on understanding what the "Art of Poesie" required of writers in each genre. Gildon and Blair were in entire agreement here. Blair expanded on Gildon's accounts of the genres he did tackle, and added others – historical, philosophical and epistolary writing, sermons and descriptive poetry, the novel and the biblical poetry of the Hebrews – thus extending the "philosophical criticism" of Ancient Criticks beyond their traditional objects.

Poised on the cusp between reading and writing, "criticism" as the "just application" of the accepted standards, rules and devices of the poetical genres and rhetorical arts, provided a more rational and efficient means of guiding "imitation" – the conventional seventeenth- and eighteenth-century method of teaching composition and of producing new publishable writings – than traditional approaches had done. There, imitating precedents had involved striving for osmosis by "reading [the models] over and over" and "daily Exercise of the Pen." As the following directions suggest, this could prove slow, tortuous and uncertain:

To read a Sermon, *Spectator* or Chapter of Locke, two or three times very attentively over; after that to set Pen to Paper, upon the same Subject; and in the doing it, recollect as much as possible, the Thoughts and Language of the Author. This, if any thing, will work a Man in time into a Way of thinking and writing, like that of the Models he proposes to form himself upon. And this Method, I think, it will be best for him to pursue for some Time; till he finds his Invention more free and nimble, with regard to both Thoughts and Language; after which, he may now and then give it a more Severe Exercise by composing without the Help of Reading to prepare himself for it.[78]

The rules and standards articulated by Philosophical Criticism streamlined, regulated and simplified this process of working oneself over time into a proper way of thinking and writing according to the author/s of one's choice. They were a shortcut, as William Milns' account of how he used them illustrates. Milns was a member of St Mary's Hall, Oxford and Master of the City Commercial School in London, who migrated to teach in America during the 1790s, as did his *The Well-bred Scholar, or Practical Essays on the best method of improving the Taste and assisting the exertions of Youth in their Literary Pursuits* (1794).[79]

In this book, which was dedicated to the Inspector of Schools, Milns described how he prepared "young gentlemen destined for a commercial or military life" to understand and write the genres they might principally need: letter, fable, theme and speeches. He explained how the ancient and modern models that he had selected for students' imitation exemplified the standards and rules for each genre, to alert pupils to what their imitations of the model should re-present. For fable, for instance, Milns discussed the "nature, form and essential qualities of fables," explaining that "the simplicity of its air" was only a "shallow disguise, under which human passions and manners are represented," the disguise being designed to "surprise us" into accepting without resistance the revelation at the end of its application or moral. Milns used close readings of fables by Phaedrus, Gray and Merrick to illustrate the "essential qualities of narration" (conciseness, clarity, probability, pertinency and interest, which "include in themselves all the principles of fine writing,") as well as "the proper ornaments of fictional narration" (images and descriptions, thoughts, allusions and expression). He paid attention not only to authors' "strokes of wit or fancy," but also to "the more important succession of just ideas…which form, as it were the tissue of the work." Milns' instructions on style were punctuated by negative examples: "Diffuseness is not only liable to become languid and tiresome, but often obscure, from the very details that are intended to make it perspicuous" was exemplified by the fable of "The Old Man and the Ass."[80] Reading, informed by the master's just applications of generic rules and standards of taste to the model or models he had selected, was the prelude to writing in which boys practiced doing the thing themselves. Like those who are taught to play sports at school most of which they will enjoy only as spectators in later life, practicing different genres of writing under the direction of a critic-coach gave boys an inside view of the rules of each generic game, together with an appreciation of its better moves and sorrier passes.

The reading could be done without the writing, but they remained fundamentally conjoined. The bridge both to students who expected to inherit wealth or estates and to the wider public lay in the assurance that "the same instructions which assist others in composing, will assist them [readers] in judging and relishing the beauties of composition," as Blair put it. The same critical manners of reading that were used to teach writing and composition would provide those "who may wish only to improve their taste with respect to writing and discourse," with the "principles" and "standards of taste" to "admire and blame with judgment."[81] Knowing how to "admire and blame with judgment," would provide them with a useful social skill:

> In an age when works of genius and literature are so frequently the subjects of discourse, when everyone erects himself into a judge, and when we can hardly mingle in polite society without bearing a share in such discussions; studies of this kind, it is not to be doubted, will appear to derive part of their importance from the use to which they may be applied in furnishing materials for those fashionable topics of discourse, and thereby enable us to support a proper rank in social life.

Demonstrating judgment and taste in discussing works of literature would support the gentry, as well as young professional men and upwardly mobile members of the public, in their pretensions to be or become members of polite society, by distinguishing them from "the vulgar," who were capable of "relish[ing] only coarser beauties," and by demonstrating their superiority to idle persons of fashion who merely "follow the crowd blindly."[82] Here criticism was a manner of reading that intersected with conversation, sociality and manners and helped to define them. It was a branch of "polite learning" that enabled a man to mingle in polite society and to show him/herself to advantage there. Presenting information about genres, standards and beauties as "polite learning" – things one needed to know to be or appear genteel – was also an effective way for academic critics to market "Taste" to the public. It belonged to what I called in the Introduction the "commercial politics" of academic criticism.

Some printed digests of polite learning therefore confined themselves to teaching readers how to read in an informed and judicious manner. John Newbery's popular *Poetry Made Easy to Young Gentlemen and Ladies* (1748), which served as volume 4 of *The Circle of the Sciences*, was an elaboration of Gildon's "Art of Poetry," which highlighted "the distinguishing Characters" of each genre only to show readers how to read and judge particular exemplars of it. The "distinguishing Characters" of epigram, for instance, were "Brevity, Beauty and Point." This meant, dear Reader, that an epigram "ought to be expressed in a little Compass, or else it loses its Force and Strength"; that its beauty "consists of a Harmony and apt Agreement of all its Parts, a sweet Simplicity, and polite Language"; and that the point to be looked for is the "sharp, lively, unexpected Turn of Wit, with which the Epigram ought to be concluded." Any epigram which lacked these features could safely be condemned. Similarly, the distinguishing characters of pastoral "consist in *Simplicity, Brevity, and Delicacy*, the two first of which render an Eclogue *natural*, and the last, *delightful*." Inculcating what was natural, never mind beautiful or delightful, in this fashion demonstrates the artificial and socially constructed character of "taste." But Newbery's "Short View of the Nature of Poetry" was doing what he said it was designed to do: provide readers with the accepted rules and standards of polite taste for each genre, along with suitable examples, "by which they will soon entertain an adequate Idea of its Real Beauties."[83] One could learn to read unfamiliar genres and their proper "beauties," as one did unfamiliar alphabets, by looking back from a text to a table or checklist. Other instructional books suggested that teachers could intervene at this point by requiring pupils to "make just Applications of the Rules" for themselves. Having read out and elaborated on a rule from its pages, *The Preceptor* explained, teachers "should require [students] to exemplify it by their own Observations, point to them the Poem or, in longer Works, the Book or Canto, in which an Example may be found, and leave them to discover the particular Passage by the Light of the Rules which they have lately learned."[84] There was, as Blair said, "a good and bad, right and wrong in taste, as in other things."[85]

The questions of language, grammar and style which occupied "corrective criticism" also intersected conveniently with genre, since different genres and subject-matter required different styles. Here again, guides to taste proceeded by articulating the relevant standard of taste for each genre, described what writers must do and avoid in order to achieve it, and illustrated their points through positive and negative examples. Gildon, for instance, explained that the standard of taste for speeches and expository writing was "*Elegance* [which] comprehends the *Purity* of the Language, and *Perspicuity* in the Choice of Words." To achieve purity of language, writers must avoid obsolete, rustic, vulgar and low words ("the language of the mob"), as well as obscure foreign words (Blair's "Latinized English") – which Gildon showed that Roger L'Estrange and several divines had notably failed to do. To achieve perspicuity, the best writers rejected empty verbiage and always sought *le mot juste*. Tropes too "must be clear and contribute to the understanding of what we intend" – consequently, they must not be too copious, too unfamiliar or too remotely connected to the object described.[86] Such standards were also, as we saw, increasingly propounded by grammarians. Blair laid out similar standards of taste for expository writing –"Perspicuity, Strength, Neatness and Simplicity are beauties to be always aimed at."(214) He explained what each of these stylistic virtues required, and gave examples. He also used four lectures devoted to Addison and Swift, to model and inculcate the work of "corrective criticism," which identified "beauties" but actively corrected "faults," largely on the level of the sentence. Here Blair is exemplifying this kind of criticism by correcting a sentence from Addison's *Spectator* (issue number 411) for grammar and "neatness" or economy of expression:

> *There are few words in the English Language, which are employed in a more loose and uncircumscribed sense than those of the Fancy and the Imagination.*
>
> *There are few words – which are employed.* It had been better if our author here had said more simply – *Few words in the English Language are employed.* – Mr Addison, whose style is of the free and full, rather than of the nervous kind, deals, on all occasions, in this extended sort of phraseology. But it is proper only when some assertion of consequence is advanced... *Those of the Fancy and the Imagination.* The Article ought to have been omitted here. As he does not mean the powers of *the Fancy and the Imagination*, but the words only, the article certainly had no proper place; neither indeed was there any occasion for two other words, *those of.* Better, if the sentence had run thus: "Few words in the English Language are employed in a more loose and uncircumscribed sense, than Fancy and Imagination. (223)

Corrective or "grammatical" criticism was associated in the minds of many, as we saw, with the "corrective" linguistic, textual work of humanist editors and "grammarians." But corrective criticism also had an early history in the "sociable critical judgment" of literary coteries whose members read each others' works and rectified prosody, amended sentences, and reworked passages to make each others' numbers or phrasing more euphonious, more perspicuous, more memorable or more correct.[87] These practices flowed directly into eighteenth-century methods of teaching and improving grammar and style. We are most likely to recognize them where a teacher describes how he corrected a student's work: for instance, William Milns described how he used corrective criticism when his students handed in their imitations of a particular model or genre, to show them sentence by sentence how to correct the awkward syntax, imprecision, verbosity and diffuseness which he said were characteristic of young and inexperienced writers. However, corrective criticism became a manner of reading with virtues of its own when pupils in English schools were given grammatically incorrect English sentences to "correct," when Spence analyzed and "corrected" Pope's translation of Homer, or when Robert Lowth demonstrated in his *Grammar* how the verse and prose of eminent English authors could be improved by the corrections of a master. For here, as in Blair's "critical examination of the style" of Addison and Swift, everyone was being accustomed to reading closely with a view to noticing and correcting "faults" in other peoples' word-choice, grammar and style, not merely in their own. Reading authors "with a view to Style" (216) involved comparing different versions of sentences or passages to indicate where the greater beauties lay. It is worth noting that, while purporting to lead to an appreciation of the single "most beautiful" form of expression, this practice opened a Pandora's box by drawing readers' and writers' attention to the variety of different ways in which it was possible to say the same thing. It taught writers to vary their expressions, and readers to notice and appreciate such variations, as much as to judge the most felicitous one. It also once again fragmented texts into lexes composed of sentences and short passages.

Guides to taste also provided a shortcut to historical knowledge. Recognizing that grasping differences in culture, values and historical circumstances was essential for situating a text, as well as for understanding its allusions and assumptions, and the events or debates to which orators and writers were responding, Blackwall's Guide to Study directed readers to supplement their reading of ancient histories and literatures with scholarly books on the Greek or Roman "Antiquities." Guides to taste, by contrast, provided a cursory, general historical background to the examples they selected in each genre, which they linked across historical times and national frontiers. Gildon presented select moderns as variations on the best Ancients in each genre; Blair did the same, while making the temporal lacunae this supposed and permitted even more blatant. The "History of Eloquence" in Lecture 26, for instance, "passed" directly from the eloquence of the Greeks and Romans "to the state of eloquence in modern times" and to the establishment of "a new profession…which gives peculiar advantages to oratory and affords it the noblest field." Blair linked the eloquence of the Ancients to that of the eighteenth-century pulpit, and oratory in the Athenian polis and Roman Senate to that in the eighteenth-century British Parliament, ignoring everything between. In Lecture 4, he taught that the sublime style in writing appears pre-eminently in the Holy Scriptures, and more sporadically in Homer's *Iliad,* Virgil's *Aeneid,* Ossian, Shakespeare, and Milton's *Paradise Lost.* Critical judgments based on the standards of taste, which determined which exemplars were the "best" in each genre, supplied the principle of historical selection, and justified the temporal gaps. Literary history was thus not, like history, a complete, methodized and chronologically continuous narrative of all that had come before. Because guides to taste were engaged in collecting what true critics considered the best models for admiration and imitation in the present, their histories contained only what each considered immediately reusable of the past. Once this method of selecting and attaching texts to each other was disconnected from the practice of imitation and from the teaching of professional writing, literary history of this sort lost its utilitarian ground- ing, and became merely "aesthetic." Lacking history's method as well as much of its explicatory value, "literary history" began what April London calls "its slow migration from historiographical affiliate to a lesser branch of literary criticism."[88]

"Criticism" ruthlessly subordinated character/s to generic and bellet- ristic considerations, in sharp contrast to the character-focused manner of reading, considered in Chapter 2, which invited each reader to discern the character of the author addressing him/her and to make personal "Application" of life-lessons learned from the example of characters in an immediately socially and culturally relevant story. As in Gildon's account of comedy above, critics offered general rules for the kinds of character appropriate to each genre, and for the way they were to be represented. Describing criticism as a "humane" enquiry because "the End [of poetic texts] is to stir up the Soul, by true representations of Nature," Spence, like others, focused belletristic reading on characters' truth to nature and on whether the poetic language related to them sufficiently stirs up the soul. Spence argued that, epic poetry was like drama inasmuch as "the Author is to disappear as much as possible" and use his "Art…to deceive us into an imagination, that we hear the very characters speaking, and see them acting before us." (I, 125) As in drama, therefore, most of the language in the *Aeneid* pertains to characters not to "Virgil." The proper method of considering character in both cases was to analyze how a given char- acter was represented in a key speech at a critical moment of the action. Spence would select a particularly "Pathetick" moment – "the last Efforts of dying Heroes," Calypso's speech at Ulysses defection – and show how accurately this portrayed some universal aspect of human nature, how noble or ignoble his/her "sentiments" were (in the dual eighteenth-century sense of thoughts and emotions) and how well the language (by its broken cadences, images, or sublime simplicity) rendered the play of thoughts and/or conflict of passions in the character's mind and heart. Comparisons based on the standards of taste (here: truth to human nature and power to move) showed up faulty renderings of the same kinds of characters and situations – for instance, in moderns like Tasso or Ariosto, who "go beyond Nature" and make themselves ridiculous by portraying dying heroes fight- ing on with one half their bodies to avenge the wounded, incapacitated other half. This method of discussing individual characters – describing how well a character and his/her sentiments represented universal traits of human nature, and how well this was rendered by the verbal arts – was something of a set piece. The Reverend Joseph Spence's *Essay on Pope's Odyssey* (1726) earned him the Oxford Chair of Poetry in 1728; it was reprinted five times in London and Oxford before 1747, and many of its rules were repeated in schoolbooks and guides to taste long after that.

Identification of beauty of sentiment with beauty of form and expression, as represented by guides to taste, already had a long history in commonplace books and in the English humanist tradition, and so did the demand that poesie be moral, didactic and exemplary. What eighteenth-century philosophical critics added was an insistence that a nothing could be beautiful that did *not* both conform to noble, moral or religious sentiments and offer a "just" or "true" and probable, representation of human nature and of the physical world. Form and content, beauties of sentiment and beauties of style, were supposed to be so inseparably linked that Blair could argue that an author such as Chesterfield, whose works were "filled… with so many oblique and invidious insinuations against the Christian religion" (212), could not possibly be admired by men of taste despite his felicities of style. "The moral beauties" (13) were the true "test of what is to be accounted beautiful in the arts" (18). Emphasis on the Platonic idea that beauty is truth, and truth beauty – where truth meant both moral truth and truth to nature – was not new with Blair (much less with Keats). As recent scholars have shown, it had a prehistory in the Renaissance,[89] and by 1776, it was being disseminated as doggerel in the magazines:

Beauty and virtue are the same;
They differ only in the name;
What to the soul is pure and bright,
Is beauty in a moral light;
And what to sense does charms convey,
Is beauty in the natural way.
Each from one source its essence draw,
And both conform to Nature's Laws.[90]

According to one guide for young ladies, "Taste…may be defined at Large as a clear sense of the noble, the beautiful, and the affecting, through nature and art."[91] Circular identifications of nature, truth, beauty, justness and morality sanctioned, naturalized and universalized moral and religious didacticism. Modern scholars have demonstrated the ideological character and manifold shortcomings of these concepts. But the important point here is that philosophical critics used them to re-present the argument of all guides to polite learning: that reading the polite literature they recommended in the manner they recommended, would be useful and improving both to individuals and to society. Developing a taste for the beauties in rhetoric and belles lettres would make readers more moral, more Christian, more dutiful, and more civilized.

Andrew Ashfield and Peter de Bolla rightly observe that British aestheticism's "concatenation" of the aesthetic with the moral assumed that "elevated states…need not be divorced from those standards we invoke to govern our conduct," since "'ideal presence'…might become 'ideal being.'"[92] One might add that aestheticizing, abstracting and universalizing moral values elevated morality above the contentious party politics in which it was generally engaged during this period,[93] in order to permit "men of taste" to commodify and re-politicize morality, together with this manner of reading, from a different, and supposedly more high-minded place.

The moral beauties that Blair listed and that "true critics" identified in texts were broadly Christian ideas of virtue, benevolence and "contempt of external fortune," and whatever other "elevated sentiments and high examples" of personal morality, exalted friendship, private piety, patriotism and "public spirit," (8–9) could be found in ancient or modern classics. This enabled Blair to make essentially the same arguments in his *Lectures* about the advantages to society of educating people to have a "cultivated taste" in literature that he had made about promulgating Christianity in *The Importance of Religious Knowledge to the Happiness of Mankind* (1750). For instance, as Christianity "tames the Fierceness of [Men's] Passions, and wears off the Barbarity of their Manners,"[94] so a taste cultivated by education "increases sensibility to all the tender and humane passions" and "tends to weaken the more violent and fierce emotions" (8). And as Christianity "civilizes Mankind,"[95] so an educated taste for belles lettres gives "immense superiority…to civilized, above barbarous nations" (11). Richard Sher has shown that Reverend Blair's *Lectures* embodied the position of the Moderate party of the Scottish kirk which, as he put it, "shift[ed] the emphasis of Scottish Presbyterianism from predestination and election to individual and social morality."[96] This dovetailed with the practice of divines of all stripes in England. Ian Green found that in catechisms, primers, books of meditation and introductions to the Scriptures that were designed for schools or for the multitude, English clergy consistently evaded divisive issues of grace and salvation to focus on matters of holy living and moral conduct. Educators passed over disputed Christian and political doctrines and embattled questions of salvation and inwardness,

in favor of *sententiae* and *exemplae* on practical morality and godly living about which Protestants could, by and large, agree.[97] Blair's *Lectures*
steered belles lettres into this wider and less doctrinaire Christian camp. By
showing how the "concurrent sentiments of [Christian] men" could be discerned in pagan and secular texts, he showed how Christian teachers could
use belles lettres to teach readers to admire and value that love of neighbor,
restraint of the fiercer passions, and admirable social and personal morality
which constituted civilized Christian conduct. As Edmund drily observed
in Jane Austen's most Blairian novel, *Mansfield Park*, assigning to clergymen "the guardianship of religion and morals, and consequently of the
manners which result from their influence" gave them "the charge of all
that is of the first importance to mankind, individually or collectively considered, temporally and eternally." As Austen ironically indicates, this was
commercial politics: a monopolistic bid by clerics (many of whom were,
like Blair, engaged in teaching and professional writing) to increase their
importance and influence.

The "influence" of "philosophical critics" depended in at least two senses
on their standard of taste for form. Their standard of taste for form, which
served as the handmaid of the moral beauties, was the requirement that the
text as a whole demonstrate the "beauty" of unity, understood as involving
regularity, order and simplicity. Blair asserted that "Unity" was "of the greatest
consequence in every Composition" because "Nature herself" accounted for
"the superior pleasure which we receive from the relation of an action which
is one and entire, beyond what we receive from the relation of scattered and
unconnected facts"(21). Unity manifested itself in "Simplicity of Composition,
as opposed to too great a variety of parts," and might be found in:

> the Simplicity of plan in a tragedy, as distinguished from double plots and
> crowded incidents; the Simplicity of the *Iliad*, or *Aeneid*, in opposition to
> the digressions of Lucan and the scattered tales of Ariosto; the Simplicity of
> Grecian architecture, in opposition to the irregular variety of the Gothic. In
> this sense, Simplicity is the same with Unity. (208)

Blair was not promoting an earlier eighteenth-century neo-classical aesthetic, so much as demanding that all works "preserve...so much Union
and Connection [between parts] as to make the whole concur in some one
impression" (319). Unity of impression was a key correlate of aesthetic-moral
didacticism because it made all parts of the text tend towards impressing
the reader with one clear moral idea. As we saw from Watts, the mind was
capable of comparing and connecting anything to anything according to its
disposition or particular purpose at any time. Texts composed of "scattered

and unconnected facts" set such operations of the readerly mind in motion. Since they enabled different readers to make different connections between unconnected elements, and reach different conclusions as a result, there was no guarantee that any reader would get the "right" moral lesson. Texts whose unity impressed the reader with one clear impression avoided this problem. As Kames said: "it ought not to be overlooked, that regularity, uniformity, order and simplicity, contribute each of them to readiness of apprehension, and enable us to form more distinct images of objects…"[98] For philosophical critics and guides to taste, effective moral didacticism depended on limiting the reader's interpretative options and on exerting as much control as possible over the reader's response. Since eighteenth-century definitions of the classical genres already had morality built into them (as in Gildon's description of comedy as "rend'ring Vice and Folly ridiculous and recommending Virtue" or Spence's "the design of the Epick Muse was to paint the Successes of Vertue or the Punishment of Vice"), the conjunction of purity of genre and simplicity of composition made the work's moral tenor plain.

Unity and simplicity of composition also had moral valence in its own right. As Charles Rollin declared: "The good taste of literature reaches to the public customs and the manner of living…As is their life, so is their discourse…A licentiousness of style, when it becomes public and general, shows evidently a depravation and corruption of the understanding of mankind…This should awaken the diligence of the master in the University to prevent and hinder, as much as in them lies, the ruin of good taste."[99] Taste not only made the man; it made the nation. If "a taste in the fine arts goes hand in hand with the moral sense," as Kames said, philosophical critics could claim that their critical judgments and selections of the greatest "beauties" of the "best authors" would have a "beneficial influence in society." Unity and simplicity of composition gave works "the beauty of utility" as well as whatever "intrinsic beauty" they possessed.[100] It gave guides to taste the beauty of utility too: critical good taste pronounced on the morality and form of texts and steered readers towards those demonstrating the proper "beauty, truth and justness of thoughts and expressions." This supported the period's perennial Societies for the Reformation of Manners, by permitting learned critics who were "men of taste" to act as moral censors of the nation's reading and guardians of the nation's virtue. Philosophical critics would fashion the public's taste and morals, promote harmony, virtue and simplicity of manners, and as Lord Kames put it in his dedication of *Elements of Criticism* to the King, demonstrate that criticism "studied as a rational science" would "cherish love of order" and "enforce submission to government."[101]

Textual unity also had allegorical valence. It was at once a figure for the kind of *United* Kingdom or *United* States that Lowland Scots envisioned and early republican patriots desired to create, and the means of achieving that ideal by uniting a country in the same tastes, judgments and texts. In an early version of France's "one culture, one nation" idea, Kames argued that criticism "studied as a rational science" would "unite different ranks in the same elegant pleasures." By articulating, teaching, and helping to establish shared standards of taste and horizons of expectations, criticism would put readers and "approved" writers or speakers on the same page. Philosophical or conjectural critics would play a glorious national role by creating from among those who lacked "learning," the wider "polite" readership and paying public that would have a taste for the same kinds of "literary entertainments"; they would thus unite diverse ranks in Britain's heterogeneous, composite empire through a conformity of judgment and taste. As all Britons would learn to conduct themselves by the same polite manners, so all would acquire the same polite taste for the same kind of reading.

In all these regards, belletrist efforts to create a need or justification for their services that could give them a public, and indeed national, role of "the first importance" beyond the narrow confines of their educational or ecclesiastical institutions, was clever commercial politics. "True criticism" made the "learned" (clergy and other men with a liberal education) the masters and self-appointed legislators, as well as the teachers, of unlearned mankind. This made criticism a Janus-faced public endeavor. It aided printers in their efforts to spread manners of reading to all segments of society by disseminating certain kinds of rhetorical, literary-historical and aesthetic-moral literacy to anyone who would read it, as well as to anyone who was taught the rules at school. But it also reintroduced distinction, hierarchy and prerogative into reading: the judgments and tastes of the vulgar, of the fashionably polite, and of men of liberal education (who had not been "idle" like the gentry Addison condemned) were *a priori* not going to be the same. And further distinctions within each class of readers (the more vulgar, or more learned and well read; those with more "delicate" tastes or sounder judgment) were not only possible, but required, for true critics to "support a proper rank" and compete for ascendancy in the literary marketplace and in the social game.

Criticism's most effective ploy in this regard was to characterize men of learning's favorite reading and characteristic methods of approaching literary texts as "polite learning" and to insist that this was as essential as polite manners to those who hoped to pass as "genteel." True criticism – the commodification of learned "good taste" – was marketed to the politely unlearned, as well as to provincials, rising professionals, the vulgar, the innocently unwary and the would-be genteel, by elitism and snob appeal. Criticism's master-terms were accordingly value-laden and emotive. Terms marked positive and desirable, such as taste, nature, beauty, the "best" authors and "polite literature" persuaded learners and the public not only that the "standards of taste" that critics promoted were the "best," the most "refined," the most "natural' and "polite," but also that those who adopted them would be part of an elite and aristocratic club. Pejorative rhetoric was deployed to dismiss contemporaries who did not share critics' tastes, or would not go along, as "vulgar," "unrefined," "unenlightened" and "untaught"; as well as to censure of the "prepossessions and Opinions" that had led earlier and less "refined" ages to be so strangely (and mistakenly) pleased by works which, judging by critics' universal standard of taste, they should have found displeasing. The rhetoric of men of taste was designed to make readers believe that "polite literature" and "the language of politeness grew out of the lived experience" of an aristocratic "elite"[102] and that "taste" was a means for common readers to pass through rank's glass ceiling into this elite.

There is reason to view this with skepticism, at least in Britain. Here men of learning and of taste themselves complained throughout the century that good taste and a bent for reading were lacking not only among the "vulgar" but also among "idle persons of fashion" and among most members of the upper ranks. During the 1720s, for instance, Dean Swift complained that every young noble was "taught from the Nursery, that he must inherit a great Estate, and hath no need to mind his Book, which is a Lesson he never forgets to the End of his Life."[103] A tutor in 1748 complained (in a piece entitled *The Polite Student!*) that "Young Gentlemen are too apt…to think Wit, Knowledge and Learning are by no Means necessary Ingredients in the Composition of a Gentleman, but entirely calculated for low Life and ought to be confined to the Schools of Pedants, distant Cloisters and unpracticed Cells."[104] Dedicating his *Essay on the Study of Literature* to his father in 1764, Edward Gibbon Jr informed this notable classical historian that "in those days [his father's], it was thought a fine accomplishment to study and admire the Ancients; in ours it is judged more easy and polite to neglect and despise them."[105] In 1775, Edward Harwood complained that "Of late years, books have been converted into a species of furniture; an apartment, much frequented, hath been ornamented with…a long order of splendid volumes which no prophane curiosity hath disarranged…principally with a view, I suppose, of giving the spectator a suitable system of sentiments in regard

to the taste and erudition of the illustrious possessor of these literary treas-
ures."[106] By the 1780s, characterizing what they were inculcating as polite
good taste while disparaging the fashionably polite for their lack of reading
and lack of taste, had become such a commonplace of critical discourse that
Vicesimus Knox devoted a whole essay to reflecting upon these "Complaints
of Men of Learning." He pointed out that their complaints only showed how
out of touch they were with "the rest of the world [who] devote the greatest
share of their time to ease, merriment and diversion."[107] In bemoaning the
unenlightened pleasures of the fashionably polite and readers' lamentably
unlearned tastes, men of learning were bearing witness to their own marginality. The critical discourse of taste and politeness was the effort of marginalized men – whose cultural capital consisted principally of divinity and/or of
that traditional classical education which was everywhere being represented
as irrelevant to the needs of a commercial empire and to the purposes and
pleasures of most ranks – to give themselves a viable, and thus respectable,
national and public role in Britain's vibrantly powerful, and relentlessly practical, vernacular, commercial culture.

   In America, by contrast, belief that the "standards of taste" promoted
by British (and especially Scottish) men of learning were the "best," the
most "refined" and the most "polite," and that adopting them made
one part of an elite and aristocratic British club, helped to turn newly
wealthy provincial landowners, merchants and successful professionals
into an American elite or "aristocracy." Still under the influence of this
belief, Americanist scholars have tirelessly documented the presence of
the "best" British books in American libraries and on American book-
shelves; the frequency with which American writers imitated the "best"
British authors and genres, both in scribal publications and in print; the
way the refinement of America on British lines accompanied increases
in population and wealth; and the ubiquity of American "Anglophilia"
well into the nineteenth century. It may be, as has been argued, that
prosperous American gentry pursued British refinements because they
wanted British gentry to acknowledge them as equals. But their adoption
(and adaptation) of these was far shrewder considered as a strategic move
on the American scene. Marking displays of "polite" British tastes and
manners as signifiers of status and wealth supplied American elites with
a convenient means of distinguishing themselves from the "vulgar." It
helped them maintain the ascendancy of their own Anglophone cultures
over rival cultural forms (Francophone, Hispanic, Indian, African, West
Indian, Celtic, etc.). And it distinguished America's new "aristocracy of
merit" from Britain's "aristocracy of birth." Crudely put, a well-born

Briton was well-born even if s/he never read a book, displayed elegant taste, or bothered to be polite. That was precisely what British men of taste complained about.

Unfortunately for both American and British men of taste, neither their prerogative nor their judgments went unopposed. As we will see in the next chapter, Quintilian's dicta that "works have their different Admirers as well as Authors" and that "no Style has yet been found out that is agreeable to all Mankind" proved true of their present, as well as of their past.

NOTES

1 Thomas Baker, *Reflections upon Learning* (1708) (8th edn., London, 1756): Preface (n.p.).

2 Bushnell, *A Culture of Teaching*: 118; Ann Blair, "Reading Strategies"; Yeo, "A Solution to the Multitude of Books."

3 Thomas Fuller, *Introductio ad Sapientiem; or the Art of Right Thinking*, 2 vols. (London, 1731): 1: iv.

4 John Bennett, *Letters to a Young Lady*, 2 vols. (Warrington, 1789): 1: 202, 206, 180–1, 185.

5 Abbé d'Ancourt, *The Lady's Preceptor; or a Letter to a Young Lady of Distinction upon Politeness* (2nd edn., London, 1743): 62.

6 Bathsua Makin, *An Essay to revive the Antient Education of Gentlewomen in Religion, Manners, Arts and Tongues* (London, 1673): 6.

7 See Introduction, pp. 27–8.

8 Hester Chapone, *Letters on the Improvement of the Mind* (London, 1773): 115, 121, 141, 105.

9 For women's study of Latin, Michele Cohen, "A Little Learning"; D. R. Woolf, "A Feminine Past?"

10 David Hume, *Essays, Moral and Philosophical* (Edinburgh, 1742): 74.

11 *The Critical Review* 28 (December 1769): 430.

12 See Ferreira-Buckely and Halloran (eds.), "Introduction" in *Lectures in Rhetoric and Belles Lettres by Hugh Blair*; for Blair's influence, Crawford, *The Scottish Invention of English Literature*; Court, *Institutionalizing English Literature*; Crawford, *Devolving English Literature*; for biography and context, Schmitz, *Hugh Blair*; Law, *Education in Edinburgh*; Meikle, "The Chair of Rhetoric and Belles Lettres."

13 Hugh Blair, *Lectures on Rhetoric and Belles Lettres* (London, 1783): 1: iv.

14 Golden and Ehninger, "Extrinsic Sources of Blair's Popularity."

15 John Clarke, *An Essay Upon Study* (London, 1731): 219.

16 Clarke, *Essay*: 29, 28.

17 Isaac Watts, *The Improvement of the Mind; or a Supplement to The Art of Logick*, 1741 (2nd edn., London, 1743): note, p. 6, 217, 325.

18 Clarke, *Essay*: 74, 81, 120, 98, 103, 3, 97, 82.

19 Watts, *Improvement*: 330, 356–7, 355; Anthony Blackwall, *Introduction to the Classics* (London, 1737): 4; Chapone, *Letters*: 206.
20 James Burgh, *The Dignity of Human Nature* (London, 1754): 125.
21 For instance, [Anon] *Education for Children and Young Students in all its Branches, with a Short Catalogue of the best books in polite learning* (2nd edn. corrected, London, 1752); R. Turner, *An Easy Introduction to the Arts and Sciences, being a short but comprehensive system of useful and polite learning* (London, 1783) – in its 7th edition by 1800; Daniel Jaudon, *A Short System of Polite Learning: being a Concise Introduction to the Arts and Sciences and Other Branches of Useful Knowledge, Adapted for Schools* (London, 1789).
22 Clarke, *Essay*: 82.
23 For surveying, Bruckner, *Geographic Revolution*.
24 John Mason, *Self-Knowledge* (London, 1745): 133.
25 Ibid.: 131.
26 Henry Felton, *Dissertation on Reading the Classics* (1713): 37.
27 Vicesimus Knox, *Essays Moral and Literary*, 2 vols. (London, 1782): II: 3–4.
28 Valenza, *Intellectual Disciplines*: 98, 99.
29 Fergus, *Provincial Readers*; Allan, *A Nation of Readers*.
30 Colclough, "Procuring Books and Consuming Texts": 35, 36, 38.
31 Bennett, *Letters*: 37–8.
32 Genette, *Paratexts:* subtitle.
33 Woolf, *Social Circulation of the Past*.
34 Sir William Temple, *Introduction to the History of England* (1695) (London: 1708): Preface.
35 Yates, *Art of Memory*.
36 Hearne, *Ductor Historicus* (2nd edn., London, 1704): 128.
37 Mason, *Self Knowledge*: 133.
38 John Boswell, *Method of Study*, 2 vols. (London, 1737): 85, 105.
39 The classic modern studies here are Tribble, *Margins and Marginality*; Jackson, *Marginalia*; and Jackson, *Romantic Readers*.
40 Watts, *Improvement*: 64.
41 Boswell, *Method of Study*: 135.
42 Burgh, *Dignity*: 128.
43 Allan, *Commonplace Books and Reading*.
44 Moss, *Printed Commonplace Books*; Crane, *Framing Authority*; Guillory, "The English Commonplace."
45 Watson, "Illuminating Shadows": 21 ff.
46 Watts, *Improvement*: 78.
47 John Ward, *A System of Oratory*, 2 vols. (London, 1754): 435, 405, 398.
48 Felton, *Dissertation*: 39, 40.
49 Knox, *Essays*: 2: 4.
50 Chesterfield, *Letters to His Son*, 4 vols. (London, 1776): I: 49–50.
51 *Commonplace Book of Ashley Cowper*, begun 1735 in *British Literary Manuscripts Online*.
52 Towsey, *Reading the Scottish Enlightenment*: 231.
53 For the transformative impact of establishing a single, universal time-line in the early nineteenth century, Chandler, *England in 1819*.

54 R. Johnson, *An Introduction to the Study of History: Wherein is considered the proper Method of Reading Historical Works...* (London, 1772): 2.

55 Burgh, *Dignity*: 127.

56 Oliver Goldsmith, *Enquiry into the Present State of Polite Learning in Europe* (1759) (2nd edn. revised, London, 1774): 82.

57 Yeo, "Ephraim Chambers"; Dacome, "Noting the Mind."

58 Ephraim Chambers, *Cyclopedia: or an Universal Dictionary of the Arts and Sciences*, 2 vols. (London, 1728): Preface, ii.

59 Anon/Society of Gentlemen, *A Supplement to Dr. Harris's Dictionary of the Arts and Sciences* (London, 1744): Preface, 1, 2.

60 *Encyclopaedia Britannica; or a Dictionary of Arts, Sciences and Miscellaneous Literature* (Dublin, 1790): 1: To the Public.

61 Preface to the 3rd edition of the *Encyclopaedia Britannica*, reprinted in *Encyclopaedia, or a Dictionary of Arts, Sciences and Miscellaneous Literature* (Philadelphia, 1798): vi, v.

62 The term belles lettres was in use since 1703; dictionaries defined it as "polite literature"; the *Supplement to Dr. Harris's Dictionary of the Arts and Sciences* ([Anon/Society of Gentlemen], 1744) explained under "Philology" that "Philology makes what the French call the *Belles Lettres.*"

63 Daniel Jaudon, *A Short System of Polite Learning* (London, 1789): 1.

64 Quintilian (M. Fabius Quintilianus) *Quintilianus his Institutes of Eloquence*, tr. William Guthrie, 2 vols. (London, 1756): II: 330.

65 Felton, *Dissertation*, Title. There were 5 editions between 1709 and 1753.

66 Boswell, *Method of Study*: 243.

67 Ibid.

68 Felton, *Dissertation*: 131.

69 Blackwall, *Introduction*: 126, 117, 125.

70 Blair, *Lectures*: 1: 20.

71 Joseph Spence, *Essay on Pope's Odyssey* (London, 1726–7): 1: 145.

72 Spence, *Essay*: 1: 104, 101, 143; II: 8.

73 Blair, *Lectures*: 9, 31, 19.

74 John Baillie, *Essay on the Sublime* (London, 1747): 3.

75 Charles Gildon, "The Art of Poetry," in John Brightland, *Grammar of the English Tongue* (London, 1714): 148, 150.

76 [Anon] *Boeoticum Liber: or a New Art of Poetry, Containing the Best Receipts for Making All Sorts of Poems, According to Modern Taste* (London, 1732).

77 Gildon, *Art of Poetry*: 152.

78 Clarke, *Essay*: 194–5.

79 Retitled *The Columbian Library* in New York, 1797.

80 William Milns, *The Well-Bred Scholar* (London, 1794): 3, 61, 62, 31, 73.

81 Blair, *Lectures*: 5, 9.

82 Ibid.

83 John Newbery, *Poetry Made Easy to Young Gentlemen and Ladies* (2nd edn., London, 1748): 57, 39, 41, Preface (n.p.).

84 [Robert Dodsley] *The Preceptor: Containing a General Course of Education. Wherein the First Principles of Polite Learning are Laid Down* (London, 1748): xxiii.

85 Blair, *Lectures*: 1: 27.

86 Brightland, *A Grammar of the English Tongue with notes* (2nd edn., London, 1712): 182, 185. An expanded version of the essay on poetry was also printed separately, as *The Complete Art of Poetry*, 2 vols. (London, 1718).

87 Trolander and Tenger, *Sociable Criticism*.

88 London, *Literary History Writing*: 3.

89 Galisyer and Pennell (eds.), *Didactic Literature*; Dolven, *Scenes of Instruction*; Grantley, *Wit's Pilgrimage*; Grafton and Jardine, *From Humanism to Humanities*.

90 *The Westminster Magazine* (London, 1776): IV: 414.

91 James Ussher, *Clio; or a Discourse on Taste, addressed to a Young Lady* (Dublin 1778): 3.

92 Ashfield and Bolla, "Introduction," 3.

93 See Introduction above, 18 ff. and Chapter 5.

94 Hugh Blair, *The Importance of Religious Knowledge to the Happiness of Mankind* (Edinburgh, 1750): 23.

95 Ibid.

96 Sher, *Church and University*: 35.

97 Green, *Humanism and Protestantism*: 293. Also Sullivan, "The Transformation of Anglican Political Theology"; and Goldie, "Civil Religion and the English Enlightenment."

98 Lord Kames, *Elements of Criticism*, 2 vols. (3rd edn. with additions, Edinburgh, 1765): 190.

99 Charles Rollin, *The Method of Teaching and Studying the Belles Lettres*, 4 vols. (London, 1774): I: 54–5, 57, 60.

100 Kames, *Elements*: x, 5, 196.

101 Kames, *Elements*: x, 5.

102 Klein, "Political Significance of Politeness": 88, 89.

103 Jonathan Swift, "An Essay on Education," in *Miscellanies in Prose and Verse* (Dublin, 1733): 3: 134.

104 [Anon] *The Polite Student* (London, 1748): 12.

105 Edward Gibbon Jun., *An Essay on the Study of Literature* (London, 1764): 6.

106 Edward Harwood, D.D., *A View of the Various Editions of the Greek and Roman Classics with Remarks* (London, 1775): xii.

107 Knox, *Essays*, I: 19.

CHAPTER 4

Ordinary Discontinuous Reading

Eighteenth-century readers were far less tractable than philosophical critics' confident, imperious tones, suggest. While they touted the beauty of
unity, and of connected discursive sequences with a beginning, middle and
end, the taste among readers for what Shaftesbury called "the miscellaneous
manner of writing," which privileged variety, discontinuity and the shock of
novelty and surprise, continued to prevail. While men of taste insisted that
pure, classical genres and classicizing vernacular authors were *universally*
pleasing, the tastes of readers both in the propertied classes and in the lower
ranks continued to run to the new, miscellaneous and discontinuous, generically mixed, non-classical forms – the popular periodicals, puppet shows,
ballad operas, jest books, miscellanies, romances, newspapers, magazines
and novels of the day. And while conjectural philosophical minds argued
that literature imitates "nature" both in her Horatian and Aristotelian
forms, readers continued to enjoy wonders and enchantments, improbable
marvels and romance. Along with sermon-collections, manuals and schoolbooks, these miscellarian genres dominated the eighteenth-century market
for print both in Britain and America. American printers worked almost
exclusively with miscellarian genres; however, until the 1780s, newspapers,
almanacs, practical how-to manuals and sectarian religious matter figured
larger on their reprint and publication lists than other miscellarian genres.

In Britain throughout the century, men of learning who wrote for the market sided with the reading public in this stand-off with philosophical critics
and men of taste, who sought to "unite different ranks" by having everyone
read and admire the same pure genres and formally unified texts. Philip
Skelton sardonically summed up the position of opponents to these "super-
cilious Critics," who promoted "a Parcel of dry Rules concerning Unity,
Uniformity and Probability." Opponents criticized these critics for "thinking
in Trammels" and trying to deprive a "huge Body of Persons...of their right"
to read whatever they liked. By contrast, those whom Shaftesbury called

"miscellarian" preached "Toleration of all sorts of Readers to indulge themselves uncensored and uncontrouled, in the Perusal of all such Writings as
their various Humours and Tastes shall respectively dispose them to." They
praised writers who catered to the "infinite Variety of Tastes and Capacities
among Men"; and argued that "as we freely live, so let us freely read."[1]
Mr. Spectator too mocked philosophical critics in his capacity as a Man
of Learning, by announcing that he would tell "the Blanks of Society...
what to Think." John Hawkesworth observed that "the speculative and
recluse are apt to forget that the business and the entertainment of others
are not the same as their own," and are therefore "often surprised and disappointed" to find that what they communicate "is heard with too much
Indifference to be understood, and wearies those whom it was expected to
delight and instruct."[2] Vicesimus Knox, as we saw, said much the same.
Goldsmith described criticism as "the natural destroyer of polite learning" and blamed its proscription of novelty for the decay of writing.[3] John
Aikin objected that by "endeavouring to pursue to the first principles of
an abstract philosophy every speculative conclusion in the fine arts," "men
of taste" had "narrowed the range of pleasurable sensations" and "inspired
a fastidious disrelish for many efforts of ingenuity" that others enjoyed
and admired.[4] Belletristic criticism's philosophical principles and narrow
tastes were at variance with much that was being published throughout
the century, and with the pleasure that others took in it; and of the two,
reading fastidiously according to narrow principles was the more artificial and *recherché*. Isaac Disraeli observed that "conjectural critics," whom
he called "Pedants," "make their peculiar taste a standard by which they
judge the sentiments of others," and cut themselves off from the generality
of readers as a result: "Miscellanists satirize the Pedants; and the Pedants
abuse the Miscellanists; but little has hitherto been gained by this inglori-
ous contest; since Pedants will be read by Pedants, and Miscellanists by
the tasteful, the volatile and the amiable."[5] Like Samuel Johnson before
him, he characterized the situation as a split between antithetical groups
of readers and writers. Johnson had addressed the divide between men
of learning and men of who lived by their wit/s in *The Rambler* (#22)
by means of an allegorical fable in which Wit and Learning are represented as "rivals," who had "a hatred and contempt of each other," "har-
assed each other by incessant contests," and embraced opposite principles:
"Novelty was the darling of Wit, and Antiquity of Learning"; Wit's
weapon of choice was satire, and Learning's, Criticism; Wit had a retinue
of smiles and jests and danced among the graces, Learning, "a train of
the severer virtues, Chastity, Temperance, Fortitude and Labour"; theatres

were built for Wit, and colleges for Learning; but while the public had "veneration for Learning," they had "greater Kindness for Wit."[6] The fact that the printing trade stood behind the miscellanists is particularly clear in America, where printers rarely published non-miscellarian works and generally left American belletrists to circulate their writing in script.[7]

Like printers and booksellers, miscellanists who wrote for the market understood that "as it is in no man's interest to write that which the public is not disposed to read, the productions of the press will always be accommodated to popular taste,"[8] and that whatever learning or instruction they hoped to convey to "common readers" must likewise be accommodated to them. This meant appealing to the public's love of amusement and promising to entertain,[9] while using their quest for diversion for more instructive and improving ends. As "Constantia" explained: "the majority of mankind, as experience shews, are very far from having any passion for reading, neither do they esteem it a thing necessary…If business constrains, men apply themselves to books without exhortations. But with respect to those who are unimpelled and uninclined to study, books of amusement alone have a chance of coming into their hands." Consequently, it was up to books of amusement to "be of some utility" both in "conquer[ing] that aversion which some young persons have to reading" and in "serv[ing] to open the mind."[10] While catering to the variety of tastes and capacities among readers, miscellanists too sought to instruct the public in useful knowledge. But they sought to "open the mind" by appealing to readers' curiosity, rather than to snobbery and social ambition. As we will see in the first section below, they theorized and legitimized curiosity as the universal motive for reading and linked it to the public's taste for novelty, variety and discontinuous, miscellaneous genres. The taste for "patchwork" writings had a long, now largely forgotten, series of classically educated Grub Street champions and of popular female defenders. Miscellanists taught readers to read miscellaneous fragments both in selective and in rational and reflective ways; but their guidance to readers was, as one might expect, scattered discontinuously about their texts, appearing as hints, as headnotes and as shreds of information in essays and prefaces rather than in philosophical treatises or long, analytical surveys.

For contemporaries, novels and romances belonged on the list of miscellarian writings because they were composed of fragments (letters or short chapters); because they were prized for containing variety of character and incident; because they mixed genres, most obviously by including embedded narratives, poems, dialogues, sermons and letters; and because they were often published serially or in extracts, and written episodically as a result. But they faced a challenge that other miscellarian genres did not: how to attract and hold readers' attention through long narratives. As we will see in the second section, many of the eighteenth-century novel's characteristic features derived from methods devised to keep readers "chained by the ears and fascinated by curiosity" through longer, miscellarian texts, as indeed they explained.

Despite Johnson's and Disraeli's binary opposition between miscellanists and men of taste, the boundary between the two was porous: some writers wrote for both sides depending on print outlet; others theorized with the "men of taste" while reading and writing like miscellanists; others changed course in the course of their careers. There were Tories and Whigs in both camps; and it did not follow from being a miscellanist, that a writer was also a deist, political radical, religious skeptic, or patriot. But form mattered: presenting a belletristic position, however magisterially, in a miscellaneous genre where it jostled against other magisterially presented views, demoted it to a taste among others; and, as we will see in the last section, it was by co-opting, reorienting and eviscerating ideas and manners of reading promoted by their more popular and successful rivals, that men of taste developed what became academic criticism's most familiar concepts and rules.

Reading Miscellaneous Fragments

Shaftesbury highlighted the key issue at the beginning of our period by mocking the "revolution in letters" that had substituted "patchwork" for the Ancients' supposedly exemplary unity, regularity and harmony of design. He observed that contemporary writers were giving the world "cuttings and shreds of learning, with various fragments and points of wit…drawn together and tacked in any fantastic form," which booksellers called "*Letter, Essay, Miscellany* or anything else," in an attempt to "conform themselves to the rude taste of unpolished mankind." This "random way of miscellaneous writing" appealed to a public composed of readers who had short attention spans and were easily bored – readers who found the "capricious and odd" diverting, and needed frequent stops, changes of direction and promises of further diversion to keep their interest alive. Consequently, even narratives and arguments were being fragmented: "miscellarian authors, being fearful of the natural lassitude and satiety of our indolent reader, have prudently betaken ourselves to the way of chapters and contents, that, as the reader proceeds, by frequent intervals of repose contrived on purpose for him, he may from time to time be advertised of what is yet to come and be tempted thus to renew his application." This "post way" of writing (with frequent breaks for a change of horses, subjects or direction) which was "the manner of writing so much admired and imitated in our age" was particularly favorable to commercial writers. Editors and compilers could more conveniently "change and manage" texts "at [their] pleasure" when letters, essays, or other pieces could be "divide[d] into five or six" or "tacked to another, and that to another and so on." The work of epitomizers and abridgers was easier when sentences succeeded one another so loosely that they could be "taken asunder, transposed, postponed, anticipated or set in any new order [they] fancy." And it was certainly quicker for an author to write "as many pages as he likes or as his run of fancy would permit," by mixing or alternating genres so as to "render almost every soil productive," and by digressions that "vary often from [his] proposed subject." Besides conforming to the taste of the public, then, the miscellaneous manner of writing permitted "more hands" to be "taken into the work" of providing copy for the ever-expanding print trade.[11] As Shaftesbury's "prudently betaken *ourselves*" indicates, he wrote his own *Characteristics* in the miscellarian manner and openly included himself among "miscellarian authors."[12] Though giving a recognizable and largely accurate account of popular print culture, he framed this as what he called "sober raillery."

For miscellaneous, fragmentary and discontinuous writing did not represent the "revolution in letters" that Shaftesbury pretended in this satirical dig at upstart neo-classicists. If anything, it was the older, and in some ways the more respectable, learned tradition. Peter Stallybrass has shown that miscellaneous discontinuous contents were characteristic of the codex (or book) from the first centuries of the common era. He argues that Christianity adopted the codex as its "privileged form" rather than the scroll which antiquity preferred, precisely because the codex was "a technology that takes the reader easily from place to place" and "not only allows discontinuous reading" but even "encourages" and "enforces it": "In a book, unlike a scroll, one does not need to read from page 1 to page 2 to page 3 continuously." Christianity took full advantage of the codex's navigability to combine extracts from different source-texts into missals and primers, lectionaries and books of common prayer: here the book's binding served merely to hold together the miscellaneous texts required on diverse religious occasions, so that users could move quickly and easily back and forth between them at will. During the course of the early modern period, Stallybrass explains, printers highlighted this technical advantage of the codex over the scroll by introducing chapter and section breaks, sub-titles, tables of contents, indexes and other means of "navigating" books without reading them from cover to cover. One might add that from the Middle Ages well into the eighteenth century, while script and print were still bought in unbound sheets and binding was done separately from printing, readers likewise regularly bound together in one binding or "book" a variety of disparate matter and genres. Counter-intuitive as it may seem to us today, this suggests that "miscellaneous" and "discontinuous" once seemed the most familiar and natural things for a book to be; and that what Stallybrass calls "reading as a practice of discontinuity" was the way in which, for centuries, one mostly expected to read.[13]

Eighteenth-century miscellanists shared Stallybrass' sense of the antiquity of reading as a practice of discontinuity. But they made the point by showing that discontinuous, miscellarian writing, and narratives that were varied by multifarious discrete, self-contained episodes and enlivened by long, apparently irrelevant digressions, had been characteristic of the Ancients from the first. Thomas Gordon and Abbé Trublet, whose essays were popular between the 1720s and 1740s, insisted that "the detached way of writing" practiced by Ancients such as Marcus Aurelius and imitated by moderns such as Montaigne, Pascal, La Bruyere and Rochefoucault had numerous advantages over "the too strict and over-scrupulous Care of Connexions [which] renders the modern Compositions oftentimes tedious and flat." The detached way of writing was "copying after Nature itself"; it was a "refined way of writing"; it was "a great help to memory" since "the best way of retaining what is material, in a work of any length, is to reduce it to maxims and sentences"; and it saved readers from having to work their way through fillers and commonplaces in "books of great bulk" to find the few enlightening thoughts they contained.[14] Fifty years later, observing that "the Ancients were great admirers of Miscellanies," Isaac Disraeli was still reminding belletrist critics that they were suppressing a long and *learned* tradition of miscellarian writing, which led from Ancients such as Plutarch and Seneca through Montaigne, Petrarch, Boethius, Montesquieu, La Bruyere and Rochefoucault, to Addison, Defoe's *Essay on Projects* and Bolingbroke's *Reflections upon Exile*.[15] Vicesimus Knox devoted a long and learned essay to listing and explaining twenty different titles that the Ancients had used to distinguish among types of miscellany: *Silvae* or *Hyle*, the wood, for "the multiplicity and variety of matter it contains," which Ben Jonson had appropriated for his *Timber* and *Underwoods*; *Peplon* or *Peplos*, a mantle embroidered with different scenes, that was mostly used for books and poems memorializing the achievements of great heroes; *Cornucopia*, the horn, from Jupiter's gift to his nurse of a horn "from which she would be able to take whatever she wanted"; *The Hive* or *Honeycomb*, "which conveyed at once the idea of industry and taste in the collector, and of sweetness in the collection"; and all kinds of bouquets of flowers – Anthera, Florigilegium, Anthologia, Polyanthea" which had been appropriated in the humanists' common-placing tradition, as "The Nosegay, The Garland, The Wreath, The Chaplet and The Festoon."[16] Elsewhere, observing that "Miscellanies...are not without sanction by antient examples," Knox pointed out that "all works which bear the title *Saturae* are miscellaneous. What are Seneca's but moral miscellanies? What are Plutarch's *Opuscula*?"[17]

Plutarch was particularly prized by miscellanists for showing how it was possible to impart practical ethics for everyday life, and to "teach us how to demean ourselves by the Examples of others"[18] in brief and concise miscellarian forms: collections of discrete *Lives*, each including other genres; and *Moralia* composed of "unconnected" essays, dialogues, orations, anecdotes, poetry and moral tales. Plutarch's late seventeenth-century translator described his writings "taken together" as "a piece of Mosaick Work." Plutarch himself not only emphasized that brevity "is requisite to move and astonish the Minds of Men," but argued that poetry "Beautifies its Fictions with Variety and Multiplicity of Contrivance; for Variety bestows upon Fables, all that is pathetical, unusual and surprising, and thereby makes it more taking and graceful, whereas if it is void of Variety...so it raiseth no Passions at all."[19] Good miscellanies, as Disraeli said, were "various" and "unconnected," "multifarious and concise": this enabled them to serve as "literary recreations" which provided "intestitial pleasures for our listless hours" and permitted "knowledge [to be] acquired without tedious Study."[20]

The same points were made in more coded fashion by appealing to Homer's *Odyssey* rather than to his *Iliad*. Miscellanists tapped into a learned critical tradition, first contested and then suppressed by "true" philosophical critics, which took its authority from an observation of Cicero's: that when Pisistratus found them, and put them in their present order, Homer's poems were "only so many Songs or Ballads upon the Gods and Heroes, and the Siege of Troy." This critical tradition argued that *The Odyssey*, in particular, still consisted of "loose, independent Pieces tacked together."[21] Henry Fielding observed, for instance, that though the *Iliad* was certainly "entire and uniform," Virgil and Milton were its "only pure Imitators." The other classical "Original," *The Odyssey*, which had been brilliantly imitated by Ariosto, Cervantes and Butler, offered the model of a "Fable consist[ing] of a Series of Separate Adventures detached from and independent of each other."[22] While everything tended to the great end of Odysseus' return to the home from which he set out, *The Odyssey* was filled with miscellaneous, largely self-contained adventures. This proved that classical form could not simply be equated with Iliadic unity of action, and that Fielding's own "comic epics in prose" – which were written on the Odyssean model and highlighted their own "post way of writing" (frequent stops, changes of direction and promises of further diversion) – were equally in the classical tradition. Similarly, writing anonymously on this occasion as "The Adventurer," Joseph Warton criticized "the common practice of our instructors of youth in making their pupils far more intimately acquainted with the *Iliad* than the *Odyssey*," before devoting two periodical papers to the latter's superior "excellencies." He argued that "the vast variety of scenes perpetually shifting before us, the train of unexpected events, and the many sudden turns of fortune in this diversified poem, must more deeply engage the reader and keep his attention more alive, than the martial uniformity of the *Iliad*"; and that "the Speciosa Miracula of the *Odyssey* are better calculated to excite our curiosity and wonder, and allure us forward with unextinguished impatience to the catastrophe, than the perpetual tumult and terror that reigns in the *Iliad*." Complaining that in the *Iliad* "the continual glare of a single colour that unchangeably predominates throughout the whole piece" is "apt to disgust," Warton dismissed its contents as "a Manual for Monarchs" – unlike *The Odyssey*, which "descends and diffuses its influence over common life and daily practice" through "the amiable pictures it affords of private affections and domestic tenderness."[23] The *Odyssey* taught practical ethics that were applicable to most readers' lives in ways that were better calculated to excite their curiosity and hold their attention than *The Iliad*. In other words, as we have again discovered, *The Odyssey* prefigured the romance and the novel.[24]

For his eighteenth-century peers, Addison was the great theorist and practitioner of miscellarian writing. Most subsequent discussion of the manners of reading associated with it (including Warton's) are related to him. His influence both in Britain and America, as we know, was enormous: his *Spectator* essays were not only reprinted throughout the century on both sides of the Atlantic; they were reproduced individually and in fragments in miscellanies and "beauties," and used as models in schools. Following Blair who described him as "a high example of delicate taste,"[25] we now think of Addison as that embodiment of polite good taste who demonstrated his critical acumen in his *Spectator* essays on *Paradise Lost* and his belletristic aesthetic values through his accounts of beauty and the sublime in essays on "The Pleasures of the Imagination." But this is to overlook how cleverly Blair marginalized Addison's pronouncements on miscellarian writings by confining them to lectures devoted to corrective criticism, where Addison's defective grammar and style were the only points at issue. It is also to overlook what is staring us in the face. A fervent champion of Illiadic unity, Blair condemned as negative examples all the ancient writers who had produced "irregular" and discontinuous texts; but all those negative examples embedded in his text stand as monuments to the ubiquity among the Greeks and Romans of complex, discontinuous, digressive, non-unified works.

For Addison's miscellanarian "Grub Street" peers, *The Spectator*, which consisted of a series of discontinuous papers that embraced a seemingly endless variety of topics, genres, styles, and characters, was the miscellany of all miscellanies – Addison was, as Disraeli put it, the "periodical miscellanist" par excellence.[26] His capacious curiosity-based miscellarian aesthetic accommodated Milton's Illiadic unity and Shakespeare's famous lack of it, Xenophon and nursery tales, ballads like *Chevy Chase* and all the visual arts. There was room in it for men of taste's valorization of beauty and the sublime. But it modeled, championed and theorized the novelty and variety pursued by miscellaneous, discontinuous texts, which printers and editors agreed were the principal sources of their commercial advantage and huge contemporary appeal: "in so various a Collection, it will not be difficult [for each reader] to find something correspondent to his Taste and Humour."[27]

Printers' paratextual and authors' metacritical observations affirm that offering a variety of short and diverse texts increased a book or periodical's potential market share by appealing to diverse readers with diverse interests and tastes – and diverse levels of education too, since short pieces were less intimidating to a newly literate public than lengthy tomes, however unified and tending towards a single unified impression. As William Dover observed: "Among the Variety of matter treated of, every Reader may find something worth laying up; Let him be Prince or Peasant, Master or Servant, Parent or Child, Rich or Poor…"[28] Dividing printed matter into relatively short units – paragraphs in newspapers; essays and letters in periodicals; extracts in anthologies, "beauties" or miscellanies; letters or chapters in novels – also had a practical function in an era where print was read aloud in domestic or social settings, since these breaks conveniently marked places where readers might pause for conversation or halt the reading till another day. Mixing subjects and genres was a wholly traditional means of producing novelty, or the appearance thereof. And there was widespread agreement throughout the century that "there is no way to gain reception in the world, but by the commendation of novelty"; that "what is new, finds better Acceptation/Than what is good and great"; and that "novelty is the surest and readiest road to fame."[29] An essay entitled "Reflections on Novelty" in *the Gentleman's Magazine* opened with the verse: "For Novelty alone, he knew, could charm/the Lawless Crowd."[30] It is interesting to note in this connection that what others called "intelligence" or "the history of the times" was touted in the public prints as "News"; and that prose fiction underwent a similar change of name. Leah Orr found that until about 1770, the vast majority of prose fictions were characterized on their title pages as "histories," "lives," "memoirs" or "accounts"; after 1770, by contrast, a full 30 percent were designated as "Novels" instead.[31] "Novel" highlighted what was for readers their most attractive feature: that, unlike biblical stories and classical legends, the stories they told were always new. Printers also exploited the appeal of the new in other ways, for instance by making "large additions" to every "new" edition to persuade readers to buy it again. Addison was not only highly responsive to the public's taste for novelty and variety, and to printers' interest in catering to it; he modeled it, explained and justified it, and put it to good and "improving" use.

Addison's curiosity-based miscellarian aesthetic spoke to the contemplative and readerly perspective of those who, like Mr. Spectator, have "no Character or Significancy" in the world, and for whom "ever looking on new Objects with an endless Curiosity is a Delight." *The Spectator* modeled, described and tried to foster the kind of reading, observing and enquiring that might be done for pleasure, by those who could afford to "value things only as they are Objects of Speculation [i.e. Observation], without drawing any worldly Advantage to themselves from them, but just as they are what contribute to their Amusement, or the Improvement of the Mind."[32] Though evidently not without its utility, this was not reading to "study," or for the fixed purpose of professional training, gaining preferment, or rising in the world. It was the kind of desultory and unstructured reading, observing and enquiring, that a person might do at their leisure without any very pressing or specific end in view, other than their own enjoyment and benefit. Here, "the new or uncommon" held a privileged place. It not only stood alongside the beautiful and the sublime as one of the three principal pleasures of the imagination, but was said to accompany and increase our pleasure in beauty and sublimity too – novelty "improves what is great or beautiful, and makes it afford the mind a double entertainment." Addison made our pleasure in novelty more ubiquitous than any other pleasure derived from reading, hearing, viewing or observing; but he attached it most directly to various, constantly changing scenes and to multifarious, miscellarian texts. Readers' and spectators' pleasure in all that was new or uncommon underpinned the pleasure they took in variety: novelty "recommends variety, where the mind is every instant called off to something new, and the attention is not suffered to dwell too long, and waste itself on any object."[33] Constantly diverting the attention to new and different objects, addressed the problem of gaining and holding readers' attention that scholars grappled with in their efforts to promote "study." And, as Mr. Spectator pointed out, that could be turned to advantage both for purposes of entertainment and for "Improvement of the Mind."

Considering "the remarkable Curiosity of his Countrymen" as manifested in "the general Curiosity" after such news of the latest war as could be gleaned from the newspapers, Mr. Spectator observed that "if rightly directed, [this] might be of good Use to a Person who has such a Thirst awakened in him." For "why should not a Man, who takes Delight in reading everything that is new, apply himself to History, Travels, and other Writings of the same kind, where he will find perpetual Fuel for his Curiosity, and meet with much more Pleasure and Improvement, than in these Papers of the Week?" As long as they were designed to ensure that "the Reader's Curiosity is raised and satisfied at every moment," history, travel, and other such writings could offer readers all the novelty their "yearning Curiosity" craved, since "All Matters of Fact, which a Man did not know before, are News to him."[34]

Here Addison was bringing "Philosophy" out of libraries and colleges to dwell in coffee-houses and assemblies. For Hobbes and Locke had both defined curiosity as "an Appetite after Knowledge" (Addison's "Thirst"), that was intimately associated with delight, with novelty, and with whatever a person encountered that was strange, surprising, rare or uncommon. Here is Hobbes:

> Forasmuch as all Knowledge beginneth from Experience, therefore also new Experience is the beginning of new Knowledge…Whatsoever therefore happeneth new to a Man, giveth him Matter of Hope of Knowing something that he knew not before. And this Hope and Expectation of future knowledge from anything that happeneth new and strange, is that Passion we commonly call Admiration; and the same considered as an Appetite, is called Curiosity, which is the Appetite of Knowledge…Because Curiosity is Delight, therefore also Novelty is so.[35]

The new was always strange in the sense that it was always unfamiliar – it had not been met with before, it was the unknown *par excellence*. For the same reasons, the new might be cause for wonder, astonishment or surprise (the strong meaning of "Admiration" in seventeenth-century English). For Hobbes, this appetite for knowledge about new things that stimulated enquiry or "the desire to know why and how," distinguished man from beasts as much as speech did. For the curiosity of beasts was exhausted when they had discovered if something was likely to harm or serve them, whereas human curiosity was the "beginning" from which "all Philosophy [natural, civic and moral] is derived." Human curiosity was "a Lust of the Mind, that by a Perseverance of Delight in the continual and indefatigable generation of Knowledge, exceedeth the short Vehemence of any carnal Pleasure." It was better than sex. Hobbes acknowledged that not everyone shared this "Lust of the Mind" to the same extent, and therefore that "from the Degrees of Curiosity, proceed also the Degrees of Knowledge among Men." But he argued that "they that want the Curiosity of furnishing their Memories with Rarities of Nature in their Youth, and pass their time making Provision only for their Ease and sensual Delight, are Children still, at what years soever."[36] Ignorant adults were like children in this regard.

Locke made the same points more tactfully – thus not in *Essay Concerning Human Understanding*, where he described what a learned and highly literate, adult man could know and how he could know it, but in *Thoughts on Education*, where curiosity could figure as the "Appetite after Knowledge" which leads children to ask questions and motivates them to learn. Here Locke described curiosity as "the great Instrument Nature has provided to remove that Ignorance they were born with; and which, without this busy Inquisitiveness will make them dull and useless Creatures," and advised parents and tutors to "excite their Curiosity by bringing strange and new Things in their Way, on purpose to engage their Enquiry, and give them Occasion to inform themselves about them." Children were like "Travellers newly arrived in a strange country, of which they know nothing…Strangers to all we are acquainted with," who were naturally curious about all that they saw and heard. Things that were not new in themselves, were new to them, and therefore naturally awakened their curiosity. Consequently, if children "abandon themselves wholly to silly sports, and trifle away all their time," it was only because they had "found their Curiosity bawk'd." If their curiosity were stimulated and encouraged, and their questions answered by their parents and teachers, children would "take more Pleasure in Learning and Improving their knowledge, wherein there would be still Newness and Variety, which is what they are delighted with, than in returning over and over to the same Play and Playthings."[37] Novelty and variety were key to exciting children's curiosity and to making them delight in learning; and the fact that curiosity was natural to children only proved Aristotle's dictum that "All men by nature desire to know."[38]

One might therefore legitimately conclude, as Addison evidently did, that adults were "dull and useless creatures" only because their curiosity was not "awakened" by "bringing strange and new things in their Way." Treating the generality of readers as "Children of a larger growth" who were strangers to what the learned knew ("All Matters of Fact, which a Man did not know before, are News to him"), Mr. Spectator both modeled the conduct of the curious man, and used it to "gratify this Curiosity which is so natural to a Reader." Characterizing himself as a man of learning, Mr. Spectator described "Curiosity [as] being my prevailing Passion, and indeed the sole Entertainment of my Life."[39] As he repeatedly reminded his "curious Readers," his curiosity was invariably "raised" by "new objects" – whether in the form of the "odd," "strange" or "whimsical" characters, "uncommon sights" and "sudden Surprises" that he met with in common life, or in the form of the "curious observations," "pieces of Curiosity," "curious pieces of Antiquity," "curious letters," "remarkable anecdotes" and "uncommon remarks" that he met with in the course of his reading or conversations. Barbara Benedict observed that during this period, the word "curiosity" was used both for the subjective appetite and for the objects that attracted it, and thus for all those odd, rare, uncommon, or exotic material objects ("curiosities") that people collected and displayed in their "cabinets of curiosities." Neil Kenny has shown that from the seventeenth century, there was a parallel "culture of printed curiosities" – miscellaneous compilations, books and periodicals which "turned a wide range of knowledge and matter into curiosities…discursive fragments that did not add up to a coherent systematic whole." Often self-described as containing "curious" items, miscellanies on such subjects as history, antiquities, nature, medicine or travel "were presented as figurative cabinets of curiosities, or as collections of recipes, facts, anecdotes, views and so on."[40] *The Spectator*'s patchwork of "curious observations," curious characters, "curious Pieces of Antiquity," "curious letters," curious clubs, and curious correspondents – who, like Mr. Spectator, have "the Curiosity to ask after" or "enquire into" all manner of subjects – offered readers just such a cabinet of printed curiosities to excite and "fuel their curiosity" – which Addison defined, like Hobbes and Locke, as the "Appetite the Mind has to Knowledge."[41]

Organizing *The Spectator* as a collection of printed curiosities enabled Addison and Steele to present anecdotes from ancient history, disquisitions on spelling or English grammar, lucubrations on the immortality of the soul, criticism of *Paradise Lost*, philosophical reflections on sententiae, classical letters or orations, anecdotes exemplifying practical ethics, and other "cuttings and shreds of learning," as curiosities among other curiosities – the astonishing sights, strange characters, curious "adventures" and odd brick-a-brack of everyday London life. Cuttings and shreds of learning thus figured along with the rest as strange, new, surprising or uncommon objects, which gave the mind "an idea of which it was not possessed before" and which readers were invited to collect for the cabinet of curiosities in their heads, while they collected *The Spectator Papers* for that in their bookcases. More ingeniously, perhaps, this also meant that the pleasure to be derived from the new or uncommon was attached to Mr. Spectator's every paper – including to papers about things beautiful or sublime, which thereby "afforded a double Entertainment."

The curiosity-awakening novelty in question was not new in the modern sense of new as opposed to old – unprecedented or appearing for the first time. Nor, as Helene Merlin has pointed out, was "the apprehension of the new always accompanied by the thought of progress," as it would be in the nineteenth century.[42] *The Spectator* and the periodicals and magazines which followed it, were composed of a miscellany of extant knowledge-fragments – learning in the arts and sciences (moral, political and natural philosophy, history, cultural geography, theology and religion, classical learning, literary, dramatic and art criticism), factual information, practical receipts, political and commercial intelligence, "knowledge of the world, "instructions unto life," summaries of domestic, foreign and American news – as well as of poems, letters and stories in a variety of genres, including the exotic and the marvelous. All periodicals and magazines were not equally instructive, or even instructive on all the same topics. But their reiterated promises to "disseminate useful knowledge among all ranks of people at small expence"[43] and to serve as "Museums" and "Repositories of Instruction" as well as "Amusement" should not be dismissed as trivial or marginal to more important party-political and/or conduct-book functions – as they went out of their way to explain. Like Mr. Spectator, subsequent periodicals and magazines disseminated the principles by which different genres (including popular ones, such as biography or the novel) should be read and judged. They also instructed readers in how to read and use periodicals and other discontinuous miscellaneous texts.

Mr. Spectator proceeded by "hints" and metaphors. As Ronald Paulson observed, *The Spectator* figured the process of collecting curiosities as a kind of hunt or chase, in a clever variation on Locke's observation that "searches after truth are a sort of hawking and hunting, wherein the very pursuit makes great part of the pleasure."[44] In *Spectator* issue number 131, for instance, Mr. Spectator compared his own search for "game" to that of Sir Roger "beating about in search of a Hare or Partridge" on his country estate where game "does not lie so thick as to produce any Perplexity or Confusion in the Pursuit":

> In the same manner, I have made a Month's Excursion out of the Town, which is the great Field of Game for Sportsmen of my Species, to try my Fortune in the Country, where I have started several Subjects, and hunted them down, with some Pleasure to myself, and I hope to others. I am here forced to use a great deal of Diligence before I can spring anything to my Mind, whereas in Town, while I am following one Character, it is ten to one but I am crossed in my Way by another, and put up such of Variety of odd Creatures in both Sexes, that they soil the Scent of one another, and puzzle the chace. My greatest Difficulty in the Country is to find Sport, and in Town, to chuse it.[45]

Points about writing and reading discontinuous texts are made by the ways in which Addison varied Locke's metaphor: Mr. Spectator's pursuit (and that of those "others" who are his readers), is not that of a hawk scouring the landscape for his prey ("Truth") and purposefully swooping down to capture it, nor that of a huntsman doggedly pursuing a deer (or single subject) until he has killed and consumed it. It is that of a sportsman beating about in search of game until he finds a subject (in both senses) that appeals to "his Mind" which he will enjoy pursuing for a while. Unlike the philosopher hunting after Truth, then, for the sportsman, neither the path to be pursued, nor the object of pursuit (a hare or partridge, odd creatures of both sexes, several subjects), nor even the time to be devoted to it, are fixed in advance; and much is left to chance. It all depends upon what one happens to come upon, in life, papers or books. The sportsman-like writer and reader was intrigued by any number of curious subjects, any of which s/he might start after – and stop following when wearied by it or if something more intriguing happened along. As the miscellarian writer was free to write about subjects in any order and manner he pleased, just as the fancy took him, so (once the *Spectator* papers were bound into volumes) the reader was free to read the papers in any order and manner s/he pleased. S/he could read piecemeal or pursue papers on the same or similar subjects across diverse volumes. S/he need follow a subject from paper to discontinuous paper only for as long as it appealed, and could change course if attracted by some other issue along the way. The difficulty was only to keep objects of curiosity separate and distinct – as they were in cabinets of curiosity and in Mr. Spectator's unconnected papers – to prevent things from falling into confusion and creating perplexity in the mind. But "indulging Curiosity" in the desultory, unstructured, miscellaneous manner of readers and spectators who were always on the hunt for whatever was new and strange to them, and "ever looking on new Objects with an endless Curiosity," was "a Delight" that "contribute[d] to their Amusement" and to "the Improvement of [their] Mind."[46]

Some periodical essayists were more direct. *The Free Thinker* (1718–19), for instance, explained that it was the "Business" of periodical writers to "endeavour to please every Body by suiting [their] Discourse, and varying [their] Subjects to the different Tastes of their Readers" in order to "gratifie every Gusto." This was why "today we are a Philosopher, tomorrow a Divine, the third a Stoick, and the fourth perhaps a Whining Lover," and why "there is no kind of Art, Science or Profession but [we are] suspected of having a Smattering of it." Variety of subjects and knowledge-fragments made periodicals "like an elegant Feast, where every Guest may find his Palate gratify'd in his Turn." "Lighter fare" accommodated readers who "can neither relish nor digest, substantial Dishes," and "contribute[d] to Diversify an Undertaking which, pursued without Interruption would soon grow too serious for any but the Wise." Like other periodicals, Mr. Free Thinker made it clear that he expected selective and discontinuous reading by inviting and modeling it: he excused readers from "the lighter fare" if their tastes ran to more "substantial dishes" and vice versa. Meanwhile, letters to the editor showed correspondents' reading piecemeal and judging the utility of a particular issue, essay or story to themselves. Since *The Free Thinker* was designed to teach women and the unlearned to read and reflect upon political and religious arguments in rational, dispassionate ways, it also provided lists of the numbers (issues) in which "lectures" on the same topic occurred, and advised readers in which order to read them. The periodical thus showed readers that they were free to read and use the periodical in different discontinuous ways: by selecting whatever appealed to them piecemeal and skipping issues or essays that were not to their taste, or by skipping issues in pursuit of discontinuous essays connected by subject.

Other periodical writers couched their instruction on the reading and use of periodicals and miscellanies in observations on the genre. Johnson, for instance, explained that abridgments, compilations, versions, translations, biographies, newspapers, essays, and all the literary "manufactures" of miscellanists were useful because they were tailored to the intellectual girth of readers who would be "overpowered" if exposed directly to a learned author's sentiments or prose. Johnson disparaged guides to study, criticizing "the discoverers of a new art of education, by which all languages and sciences might be taught to all capacities and inclinations, without…any obstruction to the necessary progress of dress, dancing or cards" (*Rambler* #105) and objecting that "the mental diseases of the present generation are impatience of study" and "a disposition to rely wholly upon [their own] unassisted genius and natural sagacity"(*Rambler* #154). Offering readers cuttings and shreds of learning in discontinuous, miscellarian forms was better than trying to persuade them to study because "every size of readers requires a genius correspondent to their capacity".[47] Miscellarian genres were adapted to the capacities and needs of readers who were incapable of remembering "long details" and of following distant causes; to readers who thought it mattered more to read about the times in which they lived than to learn about antiquity; and to "the greater part of mankind [whose] duties of life are inconsistent with much study" (*Idler* #94). The manufactures of miscellanists therefore had "uses often more adequate to the purposes of common life, than more pompous and durable volumes." "Diurnal Writers" like Johnson wrote for ramblers and idlers – those readers, condemned by guides to study, whose minds "rambled" from subject to subject and diversion to diversion, and who were unwilling or unable to devote their "idle hours" to any regular and laborious course of study.[48]

Johnson added a version of Abbé Trublet's argument that every size of author needs a size of publication corresponding to his knowledge and abilities. He explained that the short unconnected pieces of which miscellarian writings consisted were conveniently tailored to the girth of the author who either wished to "escape many inconveniences of long works – long trains of consequences, perusal of antiquated volumes, accumulations of preparatory knowledge" or who, when "turn[ing] over the repositories of his memory…finds his collection too small for a volume" but "enough to furnish out an essay." The author who was not a practicing scholar was well served by the brevity of each component in miscellarian publications. He was well served by their variety too, for "confined to no single subject," and free to "follow the national taste through all its variations," he could easily "quit" a subject "without confessing ignorance, and pass to other topics less dangerous or more tractable".[49] Short essays could also make a writer look more learned, and more competent, than he was. Johnson deprecated curiosity because he considered it a "thirst of the soul" which, like the imagination and with its aid, "enflames and torments us" by conjuring expectations, possibilities, and hopes beyond the present, that were likely to make people disorderly and discontented with the status quo.[50] But in practice, Johnson – who wrote as a "hack" for booksellers throughout his writing career – knowingly offered readers of his periodicals the same order of pleasure and instruction that Addison had described. Indeed, Johnson published only in miscellarian genres – periodicals; Plutarchian collections of unconnected *Lives;* reviews; a dictionary; a grammar. More tellingly perhaps, he modeled his "philosophical fable" on *The Odyssey,* not the *Iliad. Rasselas* consists of a series of separate scenes or adventures, "detached from and independent of each other," which exemplify a variety of different "modes of life," all tending to one great end – that of returning Rasselas and Pequot to the Happy Valley from which they started out. The scenes or chapters in this fable, which range from the serious to the ridiculous, can easily be extracted and read independently – they still often appear singly in anthologies today. Scenes or chapters can also be skipped, or read in a different order, without loss of intelligibility. The same is true, of course, of the periodical essays and *Lives.*

American printers, who often acted as editors and compilers themselves, eagerly reprinted miscellanist "manufactures" for similar reasons, arguing well into the nineteenth century that "the proliferation of general interest periodicals and affordable editions of foreign books was…proof of democratic institutions' remarkable powers of enlightenment."[51] Offering American publics printed matter in "small Parcels" at affordable prices ("cheap print") enabled printers who initially survived by job-printing (tickets, legal forms, matter for local authorities) to keep their presses running and expand their customer-base without risking overlarge capital investments. But miscellanist manufactures were also particularly well suited to provincial printers' "culture of reprinting." What Adrian John calls "the Miscellaneous Method" enabled printers and editors to "change and manage texts at their pleasure." As Martha Milcah Moore explained, a "Miscellaneous Compilation" was composed of "extracts…collected from a variety of Authors," whose names were lost or ignored; and "Alterations" were "made in some of the extracts, the better to adapt them to the present design."[52] Extracts could be reworded or "amended," eliminated and introduced; fragments from American authors could be added; and in the process of (re)compilation, extracts could be given new import by reordering and recontextualizing them in meaningfully different ways. Miscellarian writing favored reprinters because it was preeminently adaptable to the needs and tastes of diverse local or regional readerships.[53] And compilation was a traditional writerly skill, which both displayed the judgment and designs of the compiler, and "invited readers to practice their judgment on those displays."[54] Newspapers, periodicals and magazines flourished in eighteenth-century America, along with other miscellarian forms (almanacs, letter-manuals, preceptors, essay or sermon-collections, beauties, miscellanies) both because they met the financial constraints of printers and readers, and because they enabled printer-compilers to "distinguish themselves" from their British counterparts by "specifically addressing the needs and interests of their various readerships during the colonial and early national periods"[55] in ways compatible with readers' liberty to choose and judge for themselves. Especially in early republican America, where creating an informed citizenry became a patriotic duty, dissemination of useful information, general knowledge and exhortations to virtuous action figured large among those needs and designs.

Miscellanists everywhere affirmed the value of transmitting knowledge and information to the public in brief, self-contained, miscellaneous "shreds." Knox, for instance, argued that their brevity was precisely what enabled essays to instruct the public. Addison's *Spectator* was "universally read," he said, because its short papers were tailored to "numerous classes of the community" which only had "the short interval which the pursuit of gain and the practice of mechanic arts affords" to devote to reading. "Common readers" did not have time to read "a long tedious treatise, divided and subdivided, and requiring at least the unsuspended attention of half a day fully to comprehend the whole." But they could easily fit in an essay "of a few pages," which "satisfies the subject, without fatiguing the attention or overburdening the memory"; and this gave them "the advantages of study, unmixed with the toil of formal application." Periodical miscellanies and collections of short, detached essays which amused and entertained their readers by "treat[ing] a variety of subjects in various manners," were best suited to bring learning and "truth" home to the "heart and imagination" of men "engaged in the employments of common life" because they made learning, moral and/or religious instruction and the pleasures of reading available to anyone with "the advantage of a common education."[56] By a "common education," Knox meant an English-school education that might – or might not – have proceeded beyond the grammar book to such practical subjects as writing, ciphering, book-keeping, history, geography and surveying. By explaining this, he was, of course, also informing readers with a common education when and why to read the short detached essays on a variety of subjects that he and others wrote.

Elsewhere, Knox made his case for discontinuous, miscellarian reading by anatomizing contemporary readerships. There were three kinds

of reader: "the professional, the philosophical and the miscellaneous."
Professional readers "read as a duty," either to qualify for a profession or
to regulate their conduct within one; they were obliged to work their way
through long, methodical treatises, whether they enjoyed them or not,
"like the stage coach, whatever the weather." Philosophical readers, by contrast, were ambitious to advance knowledge: "their very toil is a delight,
and they come forth at last Bacons, Boyles, Lockes and Newtons." But
their delight in the toil of learning was shared by few. The vast majority of members of the public were "miscellaneous readers," who had little
more than "a common education" and found learned treatises unintelligible. This group was not middle class as we often suppose. According
to Knox, it included people "of all conditions: the young and the old,
the gentleman and the merchant, the soldier, the mariner, the subordinate
practitioner in medicine and law, those who hold places in public offices,
philosophers and professors in their leisure hours; and lastly, though not
least numerous or important, the ladies." Knox argued that "the literary
wants" of this "very respectable part of mankind" were eminently "worthy
of supply," and criticized the erudite for pretending that it was beneath
them to write for "common readers." The works the learned wrote, which
were "only intelligible to a few" and stood as "useless lumber on dusty
shelves," were far less useful than the miscellarian writings of those who
had the skill to "instruct the people at large" in novel and pleasing miscellarian ways. For these were the writings that were read by "the majority
of mankind, who have hearts and understandings capable of happiness
and improvement."[57] Miscellanists therefore had greater impact upon a
nation than the learned: "the taste and morals of the nation have been
more generally improved by these excellent, though short and detached
compositions, than by long regular elaborate systems."[58] Knox's observations are particularly interesting because he began, as one might expect
of the master of a Latin-grammar school, as a classicist and belletrist, and
used the first volume of his *Essays, Moral and Literary*, to show why he
became a committed miscellanist. These discontinuous essays also explain
why he thought the miscellanists of the 1780s and 1790s would do better
to offer the public learning, moral or religious instruction and miscellarian
pleasures, in essays on diverse subjects, written in simple, conversational,
expository prose, than in now exhausted periodical forms.[59]

By practicing what he preached, explaining what he was doing, and
showing readers that they could read and use his essays in miscellaneous
ways, Knox succeeded in hitting the public taste. All Knox's publications
were reprinted multiple times; but his *Essays, Moral and Literary* were

reissued in ever-expanding form almost annually in London between 1778 and 1795, and reprinted in Dublin, Philadelphia and New York. Two of his anthologies of *Elegant Extracts* – the prose anthology (1784) and the poetry anthology (1789) – were reissued at least sixteen times in London before 1812 and 1816, reprinted in America several times before 1826, and variously abridged and combined.

It is important to notice too that, following *The Spectator*, periodicals and magazines continued to instruct the public in, and provide it with, non-belletristic genres – what Knox described as "Allegories, Diaries, Eastern Tales, little Novels, Letters from Correspondents, Humour, Irony, Argument and Declamation." Mr. Spectator had observed that these appealed to readers who sought relief during their idle hours, from the "continual sameness" of their everyday lives. Against "men of cold fancies and philosophical dispositions" who belittled popular tastes, Addison extended his argument that "everything that is new or uncommon raises a pleasure in the imagination because it fills the soul with an agreeable surprise, gratifies its curiosity, and gives it an idea of which it was not before possessed" to the "strangeness and novelty" of fairies, witches, ghosts, monsters, prodigies and enchantments as these were found in nursery stories, old wives' tales, antiquated romances, and Shakespeare's plays. Mr. Spectator offered his readers pleasures of this sort through the medium of dreams, allegories and exotic fictions: there was a place for wonder among the pleasures of the imagination, and for the marvelous or supernatural in the patchwork miscellarian text. In scholarship, "every new idea brings such pleasure along with it as rewards any pain we have taken in its acquisition, and consequently serves as a motive to put us upon fresh discoveries"; if it did not, scholars would not study. The curiosity and delight that readers and hearers evinced for fairies, monsters, prodigies and wonders, was no different in principle, from that which drove the scholar's "pursuit after knowledge" or "the general thirst after news." The marvelous or supernatural was strange and uncommon, and gave pleasure because all discovery "serves us for a kind of refreshment, and takes off that satiety we are apt to complain of in our usual and ordinary entertainments."[60] Everyone sought novelty from their reading and pastimes, because, by awakening curiosity, novelty provided relief from the boredom generated by the tedium and humdrum repetitiveness of everyday life.

Among subsequent writers, it became something of a commonplace to speak of the attraction that novelty held for those who were trapped in dull familiar routines, engaged in numbingly repetitive work, or leading idle, boring, fashionable lives. Even Kames mentioned that in any profession or calling, "a train of operation that is simple, and reiterated without inter-mission, makes the operator languish…and regret…the being obliged to do the same thing over and over." Others said, with more enthusiasm, that seeking novelty in consumption, travel, adventure or the marvelous ("fantasy"), was "a remedy of the *taedium vitae*" that was experienced both by "the inhabitant of a great city, imprisoned within its walls by business or necessity" and by "the villager" who found that the "familiar prospect" about him "pall[ed] upon his sense." They pointed out that "the insati-able demand for new gratifications" among the fashionably idle, who were said to experience *taedium vitae* in its extremest forms, found an outlet in "the importation of exotic fashions, exotic wonders, and exotic man-ners." "Desire/Of objects new and strange" also moved "daring youth" to leave their familiar home "in foreign climes to rove," just as it explained why "the virgin follows, with inchanted step/The mazes of some wild and wond'rous tale," and "the village-matron, round the blazing hearth/ Suspends the infant audience with her tales,/Breathing astonishment, of witching rhimes and evil spirits." Desire of objects new and strange also drove the universal passion for newspapers: "When "a Man…is doomed to drudge perpetually at an attorney's desk, or is fated to take his stand behind a merchant's counter from day to day, and from year to year," and "has very few opportunities to gratify the innate desire for novelty," he was bound to "gratify the humour for novelty" by "tak[ing] delight in reading about murders and massacres," hurricanes and earthquakes, distant insur-rections and sudden deaths, in the *new*spapers.[61] Looking to miscellaneous print genres for diversion and entertainment, as relief from the "continual sameness" of everyday life, was a legitimate use of reading that the public embraced.

Reading Novels

Miscellanists conceived of curiosity as a dynamic motive force with (at least) two distinct, but sometimes interconnected, modalities. The first, which was paradigmatically represented and invoked by periodical miscel-lanies and essay collections, was, as we saw, digressive, ephemeral, sub-ject to chance encounters, and apt to change its objects. Curious writers and readers delighted in collecting and examining any singular, uncon-nected objects that succeeded in capturing their attention for a while. The second modality of curiosity was more purposive. Like Locke's hunt for truths that were as yet unknown, here curiosity extended to an object just beyond its reach, and pursued it with persistence regardless of difficulties or obstacles. As such, it was paradigmatically invoked and represented by narrative: curiosity was capable of driving a story "line" and of exciting in readers the desire to pursue it. The key point here is that curiosity was quintessentially an act of imagination, for it carried the mind beyond what presented itself empirically to the physical eye to something beyond it, that was as yet only envisioned in the mind's eye. As such, it was mobile and multidirectional. When pursuing the causes and origins of things, curiosity carried the mind back in time. When moving the mind to inquire into what it did not yet know, it carried thought forward into a future when its object would be attained. When turning the mind to the false, but enchanting face presented by the natural or social world, curiosity sought out the secret laws, motives or acts hidden behind appearances which determined the forms they took. When attached to a person, a character or a life, curiosity hung on the unfolding of situations and on the outcome of events. Curiosity carried the questing, inquisitive mind beyond the immediacy and solidity of present empirical existence into alterity, ideality, and past or future time, and thus into what Johnson called "the realms of possibility which fiction takes as her domain." Wherever it was headed, curiosity always led away from the place it started from, to some farther destination. Consequently, curiosity was often figured through metaphors involving movement, travel, or transportation – as, indeed, by analogy, was the experience of reading or writing miscellarian texts. Shaftesbury, as we saw, spoke of a "post-way" of carrying readers from chapter to chapter and text to miscellaneous text, while Addison twinned writerly and readerly chases after a delightful variety of chance-met game. But novelists with an eye to the story-line were more apt to suggest irregular movement along a road: Henry Fielding, for instance, offered curious and judicious readers of *Tom Jones* inns for repose upon a readerly highway, and digressions from it for temporary diversion and relief.

This association of curiosity with physical mobility along an irregular road or path was not new. Michele Gally showed that curiosity was represented in medieval romances as a quest for a mysterious, saving object like the Grail – or a mage like the Green Knight – whose true nature was unknown and remained imperfectly known even at story's end. Quest romances narrativized curiosity as a series of adventures which took the hero outside the boundaries of the civilized, orderly world he knew. Gally argues that physical movement out and away from all that was familiar, together with the danger of the adventures and the risks involved, served to distinguish the knowledge of new, strange and wonder-ful things that was obtained by searching, by courageous pursuit, and by "curious or questioning dialogue," from the authorized, fixed and predetermined knowledge of the Roman Church, which proscribed curiosity and dictated what counted as truth.[62] Other modern scholars have shown that medieval romances, now redacted into chapbooks, continued to be popular throughout the seventeenth and eighteenth centuries; William St. Clair and David Hall found that during the Romantic period, they were read and enjoyed by Britons and Americans at all ranks.[63]

Whether derived from this native tradition or from *The Odyssey* as miscellanists inferred, the link between curiosity and physical adventure into strange, new, dangerous, and frighteningly unfamiliar territories, where new and curious objects might be found, remained equally strong in the newer seventeenth- and eighteenth-century travel genres based on observation and fact: "Voyages," "Life and Suffering" narratives, captivity narratives and "Life and Adventure" stories. As Britain expanded her empire abroad, these genres again narrativized curiosity as a quest for knowledge as much as for conquest or wealth. Following a hero's perilous adventures into regions that remained mysterious and largely unknown – the Atlantic, the Barbary states, the Indies, the Americas, Indian country, or the far East – such narratives excited and gratified readers' curiosity by admitting them to the experiences and (often imperfect) knowledge gained by heroes who had left the familiar confines of "home" to venture into foreign climes, and regions beyond the bounds of English life. Some guides to study recommended travel narratives as an easy way of acquiring historical, cultural and geographical knowledge, precisely because they provided "armchair travelers" with knowledge about unknown places, unfamiliar peoples, unseen dangers and unexpected opportunities beyond Britain's shores.

Eighteenth-century travel narratives were marketed by highlighting this long-standing link between curiosity and adventure. This was particularly blatant in fictional "Life and Adventure" narratives that were "founded in fact," where the connection was often made on title pages. Titles invoked some or all of the accepted stimuli to curiosity (the strange, new, uncommon, surprising, unfamiliar) – as in Defoe's *Life and Strange, Surprising Adventures of Robinson Crusoe* (1719), Edward Kimber's *Life, Extraordinary Adventures, Voyages, and Surprising Escapes* of Captain Neville Frowde (1758), or Isaac Bickerstaff's *Life, Strange Voyages and Uncommon Adventures of Ambrose Gwinnett* (Glasgow, 1800). "Adventure" too inspired curiosity, since it still meant a risky venture with an uncertain outcome. Book descriptions and tables of contents on title pages likewise invoked readers' "yearning curiosity" by describing whatever was new, strange, surprising, or uncommon about the hero (a lapdog), the heroine (a female soldier), or their adventures (escaped Indian captivity, survived their own hanging, lived in a cave for twenty years, or alone on a desert island for forty). Other paratextual material might also be used for this purpose. For instance, Aphra Behn's Dedication told readers that *Oronooko* (1688) would take them to "countries [which] do in all things, so far differ from ours, that they produce inconceivable Wonders; at least they appear so to us, because New and Strange."

The challenge facing what Johnson in *Rambler* #4 (1752) called "familiar histories" – narratives "exhibit[ing] life in its true state, diversified only by the accidents [incidents] that daily happen in the world" – was, as he pointed out, "to keep up curiosity without the help of wonder," while providing the young, ignorant and idle with "lectures of conduct, and instructions into life." *Rambler* #4 conveniently marks the "didactic turn" at mid-century from what we call amatory fiction and secret history to what we call courtship, seduction, domestic, sentimental and Gothic novels. But *Rambler* #4 is not the useful theory of the novel we have supposed, especially when divorced from novelist-essayists such as Eliza Haywood whom it contested and novelist-essayists such as John Hawkesworth who contested it.

All novels provided "instructions into life." Woman-authored amatory fiction before Johnson did so by revealing what he referred to dismissively as the "frauds" practiced in society, the "hazards" to which women were exposed, and "the snares which are laid by Treachery for Innocence" (29). Amatory fiction taught the young, the naïve and the unwary knowledge of the world and practical wisdom by showing them how to recognize and avoid the snares society created by hypocrisy and vice. As Jane Barker declared, "opening the understanding of young Readers, to distinguish between real Worth and superficial Appearances" prevented them from "mak[ing] Shipwreck of their Fortune"; or as Haywood indicated, "pluck[ing] off the mask of hypocrisy" and revealing "the Secret Springs which gave rise to Actions" taught readers to better "regulate their Conduct."[64] Women novelists after mid-century stressed their moral probity, and wrote in support of a reformation of manners based on Enlightenment and/or traditional religious virtues, such as benevolence, charity to the poor, protection of the weak, patience and fortitude under suffering, and faithful performance of all the relative duties of life. But their "negative examples" of fallen women and positive examples of male or female virtue in distress continued to teach innocents knowledge of the world by making visible the evils perpetrated by powerful patriarchs, hypocritical suitors, greedy or lustful guardians, violent and abusive husbands, ambitious stepmothers or jealous friends, and the snares presented by seduction, abduction, forced marriages, incest, family greed or ambition, and the silences, depredations and injustices of the law. *Rambler* #4, by contrast, demanded that novels use their characters to exemplify moral ideas in their best, purest and most universal form, in the manner of medieval morality plays where good characters "exhibit the most perfect idea of virtue" while bad characters display such unmitigated vice that they can only disgust, and each explains themselves at length. In arguing that familiar history ought to exemplify abstract ideas of moral philosophy, Johnson was creating a blueprint not for familiar histories, but for *Rasselas* and other philosophical fables. As his friend, John Hawkesworth, gently indicated in *Adventurer* #4, his answer to *Rambler* #4, Johnson rejected or eviscerated all that novels used to engage readers: his idea of narrative failed to excite curiosity or the passions, left invention and the imagination too little to do, and was too cerebral to give readers pleasure or delight.[65] This is also the case made by modern critics against *Rasselas*.

The difference between Johnson and eighteenth-century novelists is that they did not simply equate fiction with "lectures of conduct and instructions into life"; they said instead that their mission was, in Samuel Richardson's words, "to *Divert* and *Entertain*, and at the same time, *Instruct* and *Improve* the Minds of the Youth of both Sexes."[66] Like periodicals, novels must both entertain and instruct; indeed, they must entertain *in order* to instruct. Being entertaining distinguished novels from sermons and moral or philosophical treatises, and enabled them to convey prudential moral, religious, and philosophical teachings to readers who were unwilling or incapable of reading the latter for themselves. Entertainment was therefore their *raison d'etre*. But novelists faced a problem that periodical writers were spared: how to ensure that "the curiosity is kept alive through the whole progress of the narrative."[67] Long narratives had not only to capture, but also to hold, readers' attention, to keep them reading, to have their effect.

Hawkesworth highlighted one long-standing method of doing this by explaining why "those narratives are most pleasing which not only excite and gratify curiosity, but engage the passions." History, voyages and travels were less "universally read" than epic poems, the old romances or novels, he claimed, because the former only gratify our curiosity, while the latter both "gratify Curiosity and move the passions" by exciting our "solicitude" for the hero or heroine. The fate of nations does not move us, but "whatever concerns the hero engages the passions...[and] compels us to follow him with reverence and solicitude, to tremble when he is in danger, to weep when he suffers, and to burn when he is wronged." Once a reader cares about a character, his or her attention can be held by "such a series of facts as will perpetually vary the scene, and gratify the fancy, with new views of life," while curiosity is kept in a constant state of excitement by "such complications of circumstances, as hold the mind in anxious but pleasing suspense, and gradually unfold in the production of some unforeseen and important event."[68] In other words, while agreeing with Addison that "fancy [constantly] requires new gratifications" in the form of novel views, varying scenes and surprising or unexpected events, Hawkesworth argued that in prose fictions, our curiosity is attached to a principal character by solicitude, and can be kept pleasurably alive and "unsatisfied" by variety and suspense. Solicitude for the character engages our passions, while suspense holds our curiosity captive as, by varying the scenes and events, the narrative rings changes on the passions that we feel.

Hawkesworth was defending and giving fuller expression to what many women novelists had been, and would go on telling readers in their Prefaces. In 1711, Delarivier Manley explained that creating characters who move readers to "enter into all the Motions and Disquiets of the Actor" and in whom they could see something of themselves, was necessary to "inspire the Reader with Curiosity, and a certain impatient Desire to see the end of Accidents." Mary Davys observed that novels engage readers by "work[ing] upon the Reader's Passions, sometimes keep[ing] him in Suspense between Fear and Hope, and at last send[ing] him satisfied away."[69] Similar arguments were made by Smollett, Richardson, Jane Collier and Sarah Fielding: "sympathy [for a character] is necessary to raise a desire of our farther acquaintance with them"; and "accidents" (incidents) which keep us in suspense until we know the outcome of events keep our curiosity alive.[70]

Because, on this view, readers felt with and for characters they cared about, novels modeled in their chief protagonists and/or in ancillary characters the passions they wished readers to feel. Different sub-genres of the novel presented and evoked different passions, as modern scholarship has shown. Amatory fiction centered on love and associated passions such as the lust that passed for it among gallants, and the fury, despair and appetite for revenge of betrayed women. Fearing that its vivid accounts of these passions succeeded in "heating" readers more than in warning them of the disastrous consequences of uncontrolled desire, courtship, seduction and domestic novels ceased to describe amatory passions in any detail. Instead, they sought to evoke what, following Aristotle, contemporaries sometimes described as pity and fear or terror – pity for the fallen, suffering heroine or for oppressed masculine virtue, fear or terror that the reader might inadvertently find her/himself in like case. To engage the reader's increasingly jaded passions and solicitude on the protagonist's behalf, the passions evoked in the reader "by a sort of contagion" had constantly to be ratcheted up – for instance, by portraying in vivid detail the virtuous heroine's undeserved and almost unbearable sufferings at the hands of cruel fathers, vicious lovers, jealous stepmothers and faithless friends. One might say very sketchily that sentimental novels grew out of an intensification of pity and of the altruistic "social affections" associated with it, while Gothic romance heightened the fear or terror and suspense. But the point is that though they described and evoked different passions to different extents, virtually all novels proceeded on the assumption that to keep readers' attention, long narratives must "not only excite and gratify curiosity, but engage the passions."

This was also key to their instructional mission. As Hawkesworth explained, once engaged and "agitated" by the fate of the hero or heroine, our passions "naturally" become the vehicle of our moral education: "the passions are aroused; we approve, we emulate, and we honour or love; we detest, we despise, or we condemn, as fit objects are successively held up to the mind; the affections…learn their exercise in a mock fight, and are trained in the service of virtue." Hawkesworth therefore argued, as Manley had before him, against introducing "moral Reflections, Maxims and Sentences" which "discourage the Impatient Reader who is in haste to see the End of Intrigues."[71] Novelists were defeating their own instructional purposes when they tried to make stories the vehicles of moral instruction by using events only "to introduce declamations and argument." For "if the events excite curiosity, all the fine reflections which are interspersed, are passed over; if the events do not excite curiosity, the whole is rejected together." Curious readers skipped the moralizing bits to get on with the story; if the moralizing was read at all, it was "read as a task" and would not be remembered. But moral ideas that emerge "naturally" from the story and are impressed on the mind by the passions are remembered along with the facts of the story, because everyone remembers and likes to repeat a good story. Or as Letitia Barbauld and John Aikin put it, "few can reason, but all can feel."[72] Aided by their novelty – not knowing exactly what would happen fed curiosity and heightened suspense – novels used "the Impulse of Curiosity" which few could resist, to teach, reform and "humanize" readers through their feelings.

Another method that novelists used to hold readers' attention was to excite and gratify their curiosity about things that were normally kept secret. Haywood, the great theorist here, agreed that curiosity was the principal motive for reading: "From my Observations of human Nature, I found that Curiosity had, more or less, a Share in every Deed; and my business was to hit this reigning Humour in such a Manner, as that the Gratification it should receive from being made acquainted with other People's Affairs, should at the same Time teach everyone to regulate their own." But she argued that novels and secret histories excited readers' curiosity by penetrating into "the secrets of families and characters of persons," and revealing "the Secret Springs which gave rise to [the] Actions" that publicly appeared.[73] She used a spy, her eidolon in *The Invisible Spy*, to make visible the conduct of the observer-narrator of secret histories and amatory fictions, who explored what was secretly going on behind closed doors, and made public what others hid in the recesses of private life. Like Mr. Spectator, Mr. Invisible is possessed of "the most insatiable curiosity of knowing all that can be known"; but instead of going to public places as a man about town as Mr. Spectator did, Mr. Invisible "avoids all crouds" and uses a figurative belt of invisibility to introduce himself into families and private spaces in such a way that s/he can perceive what is going on while remaining unperceived. Instead of pretending to the invisibility of one who has "no Character or Significancy in the world" while keeping himself constantly before the reader's eye as Mr. Spectator did, Mr. Invisible disappears into the process of sharing with readers "the advantage of those discoveries [his] invisibility enabled [him] to make."[74] As in *The New Atalantis* (1709), Delarivier Manley had disappeared behind an "Intelligence" that discovered the secrets of the great and recounted the scandals in high places, so Mr. Invisible narrates what he sees in the recesses of private life, repeats what he hears, and summarizes or recopies what he reads, without appearing himself. When Mr. Invisible does not entirely disappear behind characters' letters or dramatic dialogue, he becomes the anonymous third-person narrator who enables readers to peer through his invisible spying eye into the recesses of private life and perceive all that is carefully hidden from the world.

The third-person narrator in Haywood's amatory fictions, early and late, and in many subsequent novels, was like Mr. Invisible, an anonymous "intelligence" or invisible "unbodied mind" which, while keeping his/her own identity secret, recounts the scandalous secrets of others, and brings to light the hidden passions driving them to act as they do. This narrating intelligence knows things about protagonists' "Thoughts and Reflections," about their real characters and designs, and about the dynamics of interactions, that most of the characters in the narrative do not, and gives readers all the "Gratification" of spies (we say *voyeurs*) who "keep Company" with those they spy upon and secretly participate in all their adventures. The invisible narrator spies into "other People's Affairs" in order to excite and gratify readers' curiosity about what is happening privately in other people's families and lives, and thus to spur them to thought and action. For spying into other peoples' affairs gave readers an understanding of the passions, ploys, threats and machinations at work in domestic and social intercourse, as well as of the potential dangers of acting thoughtlessly on their own desires. This was precisely what enabled readers to determine how to "regulate" their own conduct – not by ideal standards of virtue or vice, but in light of extant social realities and their hidden pitfalls.

Haywood called her amatory fictions "secret histories" while later novelists spoke of "histories of private life"; but the two expressions were synonymous, since the primary meaning of "private" was still "secret," and both true and fictional narratives were still considered "(hi)stories."[75] Secrecy too persisted across different sub-genres of the novel, as April London has shown.[76] In Britain after the "didactic turn," woman-centered courtship, seduction and domestic fiction continued to excite and gratify readers' curiosity just as Behn, Manley and Haywood had done – by making readers privy to "the secrets of families and characters of persons," and enabling them to spy into matters that respectable families would normally keep hidden from the world. In America, novelists of the 1790s revived, reinvigorated and implicitly or explicitly invoked secret history in novels such as *The Coquette* by Hannah Webster Foster, Charles Brockden Brown's *Wieland* (1798) and Leonora Sansay *Secret History or The Horrors of San Domingo* (1808), which were founded on the facts of real scandals, often involving prominent people, that had been reported in the American press. In Gothic romances, secrecy was given a new lease of life by making families' buried secrets darker, more mysterious, and more deeply hidden (in dungeons, vaults, ancient documents, the past). As in Haywood, hidden secrets had to be ferreted out; but now the quest for essential, missing knowledge became the plot itself. As we will see in the next chapter, questions of secrecy went to the heart to all forms of eighteenth-century communication and of many aspects of eighteenth-century life; and print taught readers how to recognize and read secret writing. But it is important here to recognize that one reason for its recurrence in novels of different kinds was the power that secrecy was thought to exercise over readers' curiosity.

A third method of engaging readers' curiosity in narratives and novels, as Addison had suggested, was by resorting to the marvelous. In defending the marvelous against Johnson and providing a rationale for the kind of fictions which he proposed to insert in his own periodical, as well as for the sensational wonder-filled stories most often reprinted in American periodicals and magazines, Hawkesworth described features of prose narratives that, twenty years later, would become fundamental to Gothic romance.[77] Hawkesworth argued against Johnson that familiar history fell short of epics and antiquated romances because it was too probable and too familiar: "confined within the narrow bounds of probability...it surprises us less; the distress is indeed frequently tender, but the narrative often stands still; the lovers compliment each other in tedious letters...[and] trivial circumstances are enumerated with a minute exactness." Most people's lives contained few, if any, surprising or uncommon adventures. Probability and truth to life deprived novels of valuable resources of novelty, strangeness, surprise, wonder and suspense which the *Speciosa Miracula* in epics like *The Odyssey* and the marvelous characters and improbable events in the old romances had exploited to the full. Being freer from the constraints of reality than novels, stories involving the supernatural were better able to ensure that the reader's fancy was "captivated with variety" and his/her passions "agitated with the fate of imaginary beings." This was why the stories that were still "read by almost every taste and capacity with eagerness and delight" were tales like *The Arabian Nights* or *The Tempest*, where "supernatural events are at every moment produced by Genii and Fairies" and where the story "contradicts all experience" in "open violation of the most known and obvious truths." Lack of verisimilitude was no impediment, because once we grant the possibility of supernatural agency (Henry James would say the *donnée*), and admit the marvelous, we accept as probable everything that follows from it in the story-world; and "we are abundantly rewarded by the new scenes to which we are admitted, and the unbounded prospect that is thrown open before us."[78]

While intimating that the marvelous resembled the sublime in this regard, Hawkesworth was inverting the hierarchy of arts in Addison's essays on "Pleasures of the Imagination," which rose from those imitating nature most closely to the "superstitious" tales of fairies and witches that were furthest from reality. For the cold, rational, empirical mind, what was furthest from reality was least admirable. But Hawkesworth was arguing in 1752 that, as stories involving the supernatural were "much more difficult and laborious to invent" than stories which imitated nature, so they were more properly works of pure imagination, that offered to readers' imaginations all the novelty, variety, agitation, suspense, enchantment, and delightful escape from the *taedium vitae* of everyday life that readers sought. He was also legitimating the continuing popularity among readers of the "wonder" tradition in chapbooks based on "the old romances," as opposed to chap-book tales of monstrous births and "remarkable Deliverances" targeting popular piety. Though we seldom read him today, Hawkesworth was not a negligible eighteenth-century voice: at least thirteen London editions and five Dublin editions of *The Adventurer* were issued between 1752–4 and 1800; it was widely available in America and reprinted there in 1803; and miscellanists frequently repeated, alluded to or answered its aesthetic arguments.

Discontinuous Readers and Miscellarian Method

Variety also remained a constant of eighteenth-century British novels. These regularly promised and were regularly praised for their "very entertaining Variety of Incidents," and for "lead[ing] on the reader's imagination, with an eagerness of Curiosity, through scenes of prodigious Variety" and "a great Diversity of Characters."[79] Periodical miscellanies derived such unity as they possessed from the eidolon, or fictional persona, whose "voice" was carried from paper to paper by a variety of different authors writing on different subjects for the same periodical, all speaking as one persona. As one eidolon put it, "I am no more than the packthread which ties these articles together."[80] British novels generally derived such "unity of design" as they possessed, in analogical fashion, from what might be sup-posed to happen in the life of the title character. Men of taste and learn-ing liked to remind their readers that Aristotle considered unity derived from a character's life inferior to that derived from unity of action. But this supposedly inferior form of unity permitted a great deal more variety of incident, and inclusion of a larger variety of characters and plot lines than did Iliadic unity of action. This was the case even when the life of the title character followed a more or less conventional, courtship, marriage, seduction or treason plot. A plot line could be condensed, and narrated very briefly, when relating the history of a minor character. But it could also be amplified and extended as much as one wished in the main plot by introducing any number of diverse interviews, unexpected obstacles, new trials, and unpredictable events, or in epistolary novels, any number of descriptive, analytical, meditative, misunderstood, deceptive, intercepted, or interpolated letters on those or any other subject. A plot line could be doubled or multiplied analogically, and varied that way – as in Charlotte Lennox's "two sisters" version of the courtship plot in *Henrietta* (1758), Eliza Inchbald's two-generational *Simple Story* (1791) or Susanna Rowson's multi-generational *Reuben and Rachel* (Boston, 1798). Above all, a plot-line could be delayed or interrupted by accounts of what was befalling, or had befallen, a variety of other characters who were in some way connected to the title character/s, or introduced into the story by a chance encounter with one of the characters already in it. Since it was perfectly permissible to introduce long digressions about other characters, and to add any number of analogical sub-plots, this served to add further delightful variety to the mix. After mid-century, many novels of familiar life were more probable, more openly didactic, and less obviously miscellarian than Jane Barker's "patchwork screens for the ladies," Defoe's amazing "Variety" of strange and wonderful adventures "exceeding all that is to be found extant" in a single life, or Manley's olio of political and sexual scandals in *Atalantis*; but as their authors assured readers in their prefaces, they had not surrendered the pleasures, advantages and market appeal that Variety afforded.

Because variety made novels what Leah Price felicitously calls "an aggregate of modular parts,"[81] they also lent themselves to diverse manners of discontinuous reading, as they indicated to readers themselves. Print culture also catered separately to each of these discontinuous manners of reading novels.

One way of reading a novel discontinuously was to read it in the manner that conjuring readers' curiosity seemed to invite: by focusing on a lead character and his/her fate and to that end, largely ignoring the variety and irregular architectonics of the whole. To hasten through a novel to find out what would happen to a favorite character, while skipping unrelated, uninteresting or inessential matter as one read, was to read a text discontinuously in the sense that one was only reading selected and often non-contiguous parts of the text. This was also a way of giving long novels something of the brevity that recommended other miscellarian genres.

Print culture catered to headlong readers in two principal ways. The most obvious was through abridgments, which eliminated the variety of extraneous matter to reduce novels to one principal story-line. Shortening novels by paring them down to the bare essentials of a single character's story saved readers the trouble of deciding what to skip. Less obvious, perhaps, were the extended chapter titles, and later the verse epigraphs, that novelists placed at the beginning of each chapter to indicate its contents and enable readers to decide, as they turned the pages, whether to read the chapter they had just reached or to skip over it. "True histories," philosophical texts and other learned tomes also used keyword summaries printed under chapter heads to alert readers to each chapter's contents and enable them to decide whether to read it when they came to it. But novelists sometimes liked to tease their readers by playing with this manner of reading in their titles – for instance by suggesting that a chapter could safely be skipped because it did not advance the story, or by describing its contents through circumlocutions (or, later, verse epigrams) that could only be decoded by reading the chapter itself.[82] Prefaces too sometimes informed readers that skipping was an acceptable option, as Jane Barker did in her preface to *Exilius* (1715): "those who love not Description may pass it over unread, without any Prejudice to the substantial Part of the Story."[83]

One method of reading novels discontinuously, then, was to read for the main character's story, skipping or ignoring whatever did not appeal or pertain to that. Another was to skip whole books of multi-volume novels. This was possible because, when a novel was sold in separate volumes, each contained fairly self-contained "books," to permit each volume to be read independently of the others, or in a different order, without failing to constitute a story. This is most obvious in episodic narratives with several "parts" like *Robinson Crusoe* or *Gulliver's Travels*, and in novels that fall into two distinct halves, such as Eliza Inchbald's *Nature and Art* (1796) and *A Simple Story* (1791), Perdita Robinson's *A Natural Daughter* (1799), or Susanna Rowson's *Reuben and Rachel* (1798). But it was certainly not restricted to these. It has been suggested that rural readers in America often read only one volume of a multi-volume novel because this was all they were able to obtain. Early republican novelists made that a non-issue by publishing novellas and single-volume novels. But readers might also read a single volume of a novel when others were accessible. Jan Fergus discovered, for instance, that even when all volumes were available in a library, many provincial British readers read only one or two volumes of a multi-volume novel, without necessarily including the first (e.g. Vols 2 and 3 of five).[84] And I discovered by chance, the first time I read Charlotte Smith's *The Young Philosopher* (1798), that multi-volume novels could be written to be read in this way. For I read the first volume of the novel with interest, only to discover when I had finished it and picked up the next volume, that what I had been reading was in fact Volume II. Reading the volumes out of order – Volumes II, then I, then III – presented no problem; each supplied an engrossing story by itself. Keeping volumes more or less self-contained served readers well, especially after the rise of book clubs and circulating libraries which permitted borrowers to check out only one volume of multi-volume novels at a time. When most of the volumes of recent or popular multi-volume novels had already been checked out to other readers, this permitted borrowers to "begin" a novel at whatever volume they could obtain.

The variety of loosely connected matter in eighteenth-century novels meant that they could also be fragmented by extracting segments from them. Subsidiary narratives were extracted and turned into stand-alone texts, by printers or editors who, when necessary, added scenes or endings of their own invention. Likewise, as David Brewer has shown, a small cottage industry grew up around providing popular characters extracted from novels with new chapters, scenes and volumes, that their creators had never conceived.[85] The relatively short and fairly self-contained units – letters or chapters – of which narratives were composed could often be further subdivided. Richardson extracted the "moral sentiments" and religious meditations from the letters in *Clarissa* (1748) to anthologize them in separate publications. When reviewers included extracts from novels as samples for their readers, they often selected a single letter or part of a scene taken from a chapter – a bit of descriptive context and part of a conversation, a vivid portrayal of a character in a moment of intense suffering and some improving reflections upon it – and their selections proved remarkably self-contained too.

Readers also made their own extracts from novels and other longer texts (such as histories) as they read, especially when they read aloud to family or friends. Naomi Tadmor discovered that the Turners, mercers in a Sussex village, and Samuel Richardson's London household read diverse texts simultaneously and "intermittently." Parts of one text were read on one evening and parts of other texts were read on the next. The reading of any text might stretch over months, entwined with the reading of other texts in diverse genres. Many volumes were not read in a linear way from beginning to end, or not read "throughout," in part because "texts were also read in combination with, or while doing, other things," as when Mrs. Turner read segments from different books to her husband while he worked.[86] As we saw in Chapter 2, Richard Cumberland recalled how Bubb Dodington would entertain him and other guests at his country house every evening, by reading them extracts that he had selected from diverse novels and plays; and Catherine Talbot described how Dr. Secker would read segments from different "family books" to the women in his household after breakfast and dinner. Daniel Woolf found that even readers whose diaries and commonplace books showed that they knew how to read in the manner recommended by guides to study, rarely read historical narratives this way from beginning to end. They generally practiced "a much more haphazard perusal of works in no particular order," "dipping into" diverse histories, picking them up and putting them down at infrequent intervals, returning to some and leaving others unfinished or largely unread.[87] Mark Towsey found the same. Readers also read in a "haphazard," discontinuous and fragmentary manner because they read at odd times and places: during a carriage-ride, or on a boat to Deptford; at a meal; over a pint in a tavern; in the shop when business was slow; or *in situ* standing at a bookstall or in a bookseller's shop. Readers were thus making their own oral and mental as well as written anthologies from the various books and periodicals they chose to read or to read aloud to others and heard read aloud to them. Printed anthologies, collections of elegant extracts and miscellanies of all sorts catered to this manner of reading, as abridgments catered to readers who read for the story-line. They provided readers with "a little English Library" by assembling in one place extracts from diverse books that were too voluminous to read or too expensive to buy individually; and they invited readers to read them, silently or aloud, in the same, selective, extractive and discontinuous manner that they were catering to: "The great Variety of Entertaining Subjects of which [these Volumes] consist, will render them agreeable to all Sorts of Readers."[88]

Miscellanists and true critics both condemned reading headlong "for the story" as an unthinking manner of reading – albeit for different reasons. As we saw in Chapter 3, true critics sought to unite the nation by means of narratives which conveyed a single impression, and inculcated the same incontrovertible moral judgments. One might say that if true critics and men of taste attached reading novels headlong for the story to ignorant, unreflective girls – and thus to readers furthest removed from men of learning – it was partly to elide the awkward fact that reading for the single story-line of a character and his/her fate reduced any novel, no matter how various, to something approaching Iliadic unity of action. As modern critics have discovered, eighteenth-century novels were far more complex and demanding than true critics pretended in their efforts to disparage them by portraying them as the reading matter of girls, servants and the vulgar multitude. Another reason for the proliferation of extracts, abridgments, and epitomes was certainly that some novels were too long, too complex and too demanding for some readers in their original form. This may also be one reason for the frequency with which American printers reprinted abridgements of British novels instead of the originals, and for the tendency of American novelists to focus on a single story-line. While precluding the need for over-simplifying abridgements of their own narratives, short American novels with a single story-line could also reach segments of the public accustomed to reading American reprints of abridgements.

Miscellanists, by contrast, saw reading headlong for the principal story-line as missing the point of introducing variety in the first place. Novelists advised their readers to pause in their reading and reflect upon they had read. Manley explained in a Preface that novelists' business was to show, not to distribute praise or blame. Novelists left "an entire Liberty to the Reader to judge as he pleases," because it was up to the reader to reflect and judge. Henry Fielding famously interrupted readers' forward progress by introducing coldly analytical essays at the beginning of each volume, and pausing the narration to describe how different readers might inter- pret and judge the same characters and scenes. And as we saw in Chapter 2, Elizabeth Griffith used characters in her epistolary novel, *The History of Lady Barton* (1771), to show readers pausing in between other characters' letters to calm their emotions, distance themselves from what they had read, and discuss the issues their reading had raised. She demonstrated that chopping up engrossing narratives into letter-sized episodes enabled read- ers to stop between letters in order to recover from the intensity of their sympathetic emotion and provide "opportunity for reflection," conversa- tion and debate about what they had read or heard.[89]

Miscellanist essayists supported and theorized such injunctions by familiarizing readers with a version of Joseph Spence's distinction between the "common, vulgar passionate" method of reading which allowed "the Soul…to be hurried away by[its] vehemence of delight," and a miscel- larian "method in reading" which involved standing back and reasoning about what one had read. Disraeli explained, for instance, that while the common manner of reading narratives consisted in "indulging in the facile pleasures of perceptions," a superior manner of reading involved "the laborious habit of forming them into ideas." Since words stand for ideas in the mind, what happens initially when we are reading a narrative is that "in idea we perceive persons acting and suffering, precisely as in an original survey."[90] Readers who indulged in the pleasures of perception were simply watching characters acting and suffering as the mental percep- tions of them created by the words they were reading flowed past in their mind's eye, and allowing themselves to be variously moved and affected by what they "saw." Engrossed in the way the story-line unfolded and in their emotional reactions to it, they were not bothering to turn percep- tions into ideas through "an art of combination, and an exertion of the reasoning powers," as they would if they paused to reflect upon the resem- blances and differences among characters, actions and scenes. Reading passively or "facilely" by letting the story-line unfold before the mind's eye, gave "the numerous class of readers" "temporary pleasure," enjoyment during the time of reading, but it did not produce knowledge or general ideas.[91] For the ideas in miscellarian novels were not necessarily presented as declamations of moral sentiments, or embedded in the poetic justice of a story-line. They emerged, instead, from the reader's comparisons among analogical characters, scenes and story-lines, and "combination" of what they found. Miscellarian novels were often constructed like a tapestry, on "a general plan" in which analogical parental or mentoring figures, analogical suitors, and analogical young women, each embodying different character-types, conduct and/or ranks, faced analogical situations, often in series of analogical scenes (balls, proposals, courtships, visits, carriage rides). To ignore "variety" was to fail to reflect on what conclusions might be drawn from comparison, combination, judgment and discussion with one's friends about these analogical characters and situations. It was therefore to miss what novels did not openly express, but left to be "understood" upon reflection and decided by each reader on their own and/or in discussion with friends. One might say that analogical characters and scenes were tailored to readers who had learned from their first introduction to alphabets to reason and reflect by considering "the agreement and connection or disjunction and disagreement of ideas." But it is important to note that the conclusions that readers might draw from comparing analogical characters, situations and scenes might differ widely both from each other, and from the conventional morality that prefaces or narrators pretended to teach. In this sense, novels invited "open" reading practices too.

Unlike "true critics" also, miscellanists insisted that practicing discontinuous reading by extracting only the pieces one wanted from novels, books and periodicals was a normal, natural and profitable way to read. Knox pointed out that *Legere*, "to read" in Latin, meant to pick and choose, and disparaged "the insipidity of universal consent" and "the death-repose of unvaried uniformity."[92] Citing the elder Pliny – "who having been a voluminous compiler, must have had great experience in the art of reading," Disraeli observed that "to read every book [entire] would be fatal to the interest of most readers"; and that with so much in print to choose from, "those who attempt to read everything…miss the most interesting performances." The art of reading was the art of picking and choosing – within books as much as among them. For, regardless of how continuous it appeared, every book could be broken up into pieces. And scattered among the bad or boring pieces, every book "contained something good."[93] That was the part that readers were after, regardless of what they considered "good." Miscellanists accepted that readers defined good quite variously according to their interests, tastes and motives for reading. "Some read for style, and some for argument: one has little care about the sentiment, he observes only how it is expressed; another regards not the conclusion, but is diligent to mark how it is inferred…Some read that they may embellish their conversation, or shine in dispute; some that they may not be detected in ignorance, or want the reputation of literary accomplishment."[94]

Interestingly, miscellanists made the point that the selective, discontinuous reading practices of the generality of readers were not substantively different from "learned" and "polite" manners of reading that we saw guides to study delineating. Selecting and extracting the parts of novels or periodicals that interested them as common readers did, was no different in principle from what students and men of learning did in pursuing their studies when they used the indexes in books, or tables of contents, to find the parts of books they wanted. Nor was it intrinsically different from what "the reader of taste" did, who "restrict[ed] himself to the paths of cultivated pleasure grounds" in his quest of beauties or sublime passages by reading the parts of a book that others had approved and recommended in advance.[95] Whether they were learned or untaught, and reading erudite tomes, sublime poems, newspapers, periodicals or popular novels, everyone selected and extracted the parts of texts they wanted. Navigating books in highly personal ways by reading only the fragments one selected, and extracting only what one wanted, was practiced by all types and levels of readers – by scholars and men of liberal education; by readers of taste; and by the common readers of periodicals, miscellanies and novels. Their manners of discontinuous reading differed. But in all cases, discontinuous reading was precisely what permitted readers to "fix on proper aliment for their insatiable curiosity." Instead of assuming like philosophical critics and some modern scholars that schoolbooks, anthologies and collections of beauties inevitably determined the public's taste in reading, miscellanists recognized that, in reality, it was a case of "Every Man his own Miscellanist" as well as of *Every Man his own Physician*.[96]

Miscellanist readers were free to pick and choose what, and how much of anything, they read. They skipped chapters, letters and whole volumes of novels when they wished, just as they skipped paragraphs, entries, essays or subjects in newspapers, periodicals, encyclopedias and compilations. Miscellanist readers would go on reading a single or continuous text only as long as they found it interesting, instructive or enjoyable, so they did not necessarily read anything in its entirety, even novels – especially if they were long. Miscellarian by virtue of their own personal, selective and discontinuous reading practices, and those of others who read aloud to them, miscellanist readers created anthologies of disparate fragments of story, knowledge and event in their heads as they went.

But miscellanist readers were also free to piece together in their own heads whatever fragments their reading had collected – and if they paused to reflect, to make something of it. Though himself advocating a different manner of reading, Coleridge perfectly expressed the sentiments of eighteenth-century miscellanists when he wrote that "the reader should be carried forward, not merely or chiefly by the mechanical impulse of curiosity, or by a restless desire to arrive at the final solution, but by the pleasurable activity of mind excited by the journey itself."[97] As Knox observed, ancient authors had called their miscellanies *Sylvae*, to "intimate by it, that they had collected a store of timber, which themselves, or others, might hereafter use in erecting a regular structure."[98] And as we saw, miscellanists went out of their way to explain to the generality of readers that they must not "hastily pass from scene to scene, with too much volatility to admit thought and reflection,"[99] but use what they read to erect a mental structure of their own through "an art of combination, and an exertion of their own reasoning powers." Hawkesworth warned readers not to "tamely" rely on the "second hand knowledge" to be gained from critics such Rapin, Felton, Blackwell or Rollin, but "to eagerly press forward to the great originals" themselves.[100] Disraeli told readers that they must "converse" with authors as they read them: "There is something in composition, like the game of shuttlecock, where, if the reader does not quickly rebound the feathered cork to the author, the game is destroyed, and the whole spirit of the work falls extinct."[101] Miscellanists thought that persuading even the "half-learned" that they must extract, reflect, compare, and put things together for themselves was important because they identified "the art of combining [the] fragments" of knowledge and experience that readers encountered, and each reader's use of his/her own reflective and reasoning powers to do so, with the kind of freedom that Kant would later argue was central to Enlightenment: the freedom to think for oneself. "As we freely live, so let us freely read."[102] In Stallybrass' terms, one might say that miscellanists encouraged readers to exploit all the freedom of "navigation" permitted by the codex, while belletristic philosophical critics tried to turn the codex back into a scroll.

By offering readers a story-line and a variety of other characters, story-lines, and digressive incidents, familiar novels and Gothic romances combined the pleasures of curiosity's two principal modalities: they fed the purposive curiosity which followed a character into the hidden recesses of private life and shadowed him/her through the events determining his/her fate to their unknown conclusion; and they fed the digressive curiosity which delighted in variety, multiplicity, and in whatever strange, uncommon, new or chance-met characters, narratives and events that were encountered along the way. This may also be why novels proved so popular with readers – and so unstoppable by philosophical critics – and why they lived on, constantly renewing themselves, long after other genres went out of fashion.

The Vocabulary of Taste

Philosophical critics fought a rearguard action both against miscellarian arguments and against the discontinuous manners of reading practiced by the public and promoted by miscellarian texts. They went for the jugular by discrediting and virtually eliminating curiosity from the motives they gave for reading, and promised readers other – safer, muted and sanitized – versions of the pleasures miscellanists claimed for discontinuous texts. Their Lockean epistemology made it difficult for them to offer cogent philosophical arguments for privileging unity of action and design in continuous texts where beginning, middle and end were connected by cause and effect. So, to make the unified and morally perspicuous literature they prized more palatable, they argued that belletrism's more limited pleasures were superior and infinitely more refined than those they sought to discredit.

Miscellarian variety was an obvious problem for philosophical critics who viewed it through the tenets of associationist psychology. For, as we saw from Isaac Watts, they knew that the mind could, in principle, connect anything to anything that it happened upon, depending on its purpose, interests, preconceptions, or goals. As Martin Kallich has shown, the century's principle philosophical critics – Hobbes, Locke, Addison, Watts, Hutcheson, Turnbull, Baillie, Hartley, Burke, Shenstone, Brown, Hume, Hurd, Gerrard, Priestley, Beattie and Alison – attributed readers' diversity of views and tastes to the variety of connections that people made among discrete ideas. Some, like George Turnbull, argued that "various associations must produce various tempers and dispositions of the mind," others that people's various tempers, dispositions, educations, passions or interests gave rise to diverse associations of ideas.[103] Whichever was the chicken or the egg, the variety of connections that could be made not only accounted for the diversity of readings or interpretations that could be derived from the same text. It also indicated that variety of views and opinions was only promoted by discontinuous miscellaneous texts, which left common readers free to connect anything to anything as they wished, and might enable the "half-learned" to cobble together from dispersed and undirected elements, any number of new and unwelcome ideas. It thus clarified why associationism did not "naturally" put everyone on the same page and create that *consensus gentium* of taste and opinion which seemed so desirable to those who sought stability and national unity after the civil war, and who were finding both elusive in the long eighteenth-century climate of ongoing political and religious disputes, recurrent provincial riots and insurrections, commercial competition, social mobility and redistributions of rank and wealth. The mind's "natural" freedom to make connections among discrete ideas only promoted a maddening diversity of tastes and opinions. Adam Smith argued in his Glasgow lectures that being frequently confronted with "irregular and discordant" ideas, which constantly "follow one another in a [new or] uncommon order," produces "giddiness and confusion," and was likely to "bring on lunacy."[104] It was lunacy, in a supposedly *United Kingdom*, to admit a wildly proliferating diversity of opinions and ideas.

However, it was hard for eighteenth-century philosophical critics to make a clear, rational case for insisting that texts must "preserve...so much Union and Connection [between parts] as to make the whole concur in some one impression," because they were not entirely sure themselves how this was done. Lockean epistemology had left it to the understanding to connect and combine detached singular impressions into more comprehensive and meaningful constructs. But it had not satisfactorily explained how the understanding determined "the Connection of Ideas" and developed a continuous "Train of Ideas" in order to grasp the "Reach, Force and Coherence of what is said."[105] As Kallich explains, how the understanding made connections was debated throughout the century. Hobbes' argument that the mind uses resemblance, contiguity in time or space, and cause and effect, to connect discrete ideas into a rational "Trayne of Thought" was already under attack in Locke, who highlighted the danger of making false, irrational, imaginary, arbitrary, or fanciful connections which hinder understanding of the object one is looking at.[106] Hume deconstructed Locke's binary between rational trains of thought and their arbitrary or irrational other, by showing that irrational passions drove apparently rational trains of thought, and that Hobbes' supposedly rational modes of connection were far from that: relations of cause and effect were in reality only "constant conjunctions" between ideas, acts or objects which happened to appear contiguously in time or space, and which we imagine to have a "secret tie" or connection. And nothing could be freer than the imagination in placing resemblances wherever it wished, as the copia and variety of similes and metaphors showed. Novelists such as Defoe,

Fielding and Sterne demonstrated in their turn how easily connecting perceptions by resemblance, contiguity, and cause and effect might produce faulty readings of literature and life. In *Moll Flanders*, for instance, the causal connection Moll repeatedly makes between money, gentility and her own physical beauty, stemming from early experiences in which they appeared contiguously to her view, lead to polygamy, penury and crime; and making natural but erroneous connections between perceived effects (real conduct) and probable causes (motives) leads Allworthy to misjudge Partridge, Blifil, Tom and his own sister in *Tom Jones*.[107] Connections that people might make between perceptions or ideas were various, unpredictable and not necessarily uniform or "correct."

Supposing that children were born *tabula rasa* meant that everything had to be learned. This made education appear the solution to problems of conduct and opinion: "Tis Education forms the common Mind;/Just as the Twig is bent, the Tree's inclined." Building on Locke's idea of habit or custom, one could use iterated sententiae and little moral tales to try to create regular, habitual and automatic associations of ideas in the mind and thereby "train up a child in the way he should go." Exposing learners and readers to repeated conjunctions between virtue and socially desirable conduct, and between socially undesirable conduct and vice, would ensure that sight of an action in fiction or in life automatically summoned up in the mind the idea of virtue or vice associated with it. Repeated use of poetic justice would foster the expectation that vice would ultimately be punished and virtue rewarded. Repetition of desired associations of ideas conveniently made "traynes of thought" capable of being instilled by education. But, as philosophical critics recognized, custom and habit were subject to fashion, and different from culture to culture and period to period, rather than universal unchanging truths. This failed to place philosophical criticism in a position of authority above the fray of contending customs and opinions. It also made habitual associations as artificial and instrumental as those created by chronology and geography. Efforts were therefore made to circumvent these issues or to fudge them by counterfactual arguments.

Kames, for instance, asserted that "we are framed by nature to relish order and connection" and to admire works which are "conformable to the natural course of our ideas." In the natural course of our ideas, "not a single thing appears solitary and altogether devoid of connection"; consequently, a work is most pleasing to us when, "like an organic system, its parts be orderly arranged and mutually connected, bearing each of them a relation to the whole." Of course, most people did not seem know this, much less to experience texts this way; but that was only because "a constant train of trifling amusements may form such a habit in the mind, as that it cannot be easy a moment" without "variety in the objects" which amuse it. This bad "generic habit" could be corrected, and replaced by a superior and more refined taste for unity, regularity and uniformity through education, exercise and above all, habit: "those things which at first are but moderately agreeable, are the aptest to become habitual"; "the original agreeableness or disagreeableness of an object, is, by the influence of custom, often converted into its opposite quality."[108] In other words, people would eventually like what they now found disagreeable reading, if only they were made to read it enough. This was an uncertain way forward at best. Telling readers that it was "natural" for them to like what men of taste admired, and insisting that narratives and discourses must have unity, connections and a beginning-middle-and-end which most people seemed quite happy without, did more to obscure discontinuous, miscellarian manners of reading from twentieth-century critics, than to cure the public of its abiding preference for fragments, miscellanies, sound bites and tweets.

Another way forward was to domesticate novelty, variety and wonder while suggesting that unified, belletristic texts offered addicts of discontinuous, miscellarian reading analogical pleasures, but in 'higher,' more refined, and therefore more delicate, enlightened, "polite" and distinguished, forms.

Variety was tamed and subordinated to unity, uniformity and proportion, by substituting mild and tastefully modulated variation for its wild, unpredictable, miscellarian other. Readers of "correct and improved taste" could have their variety, but only in the controlled form of enlivening variations on uniformly developed moral themes. Granting that too much uniformity and regularity were tedious and that "most men" therefore liked to vary their studies, their business and their recreations, Gerard insisted in his prize-winning *Essay on Taste* (1759) that good taste demanded that "so much [uniformity] must be retained as to keep the variety from degenerating into perplexity and confusion," because where "the variety [is] boundless," the mind becomes "displeased and disgusted" at its inability to obtain "one entire conception of the object."[109] Limiting variety facilitated readers' conception of an object as it was presented to them, and made it easier to see it whole. Contained and controlled by a single unifying conception, and tamed into pleasing variation, variety easily slid back into a version of traditional neo-classical aesthetics.

The silent, but crucial, critical move here consisted of speaking of texts or books as the sole source and locus of that "one entire conception of the object" which formed in the reader's mind. Locke and miscellanists expected conceptions of objects to emerge in every *reader's mind* as his/ her understanding compared and connected ideas derived from the various, disconnected, experiences, conversations, scenes, passages, fragments, texts and books to which a person was exposed. But philosophical critics displaced higher-order reasoning, connection and reflection from the reader to the book. Books and writings were legally actionable, and capable of being monitored, controlled and restrained; readers' thoughts were not. However, this was not an entirely satisfactory solution to the problem either, for even if every text or book presented one entire conception of a physical, moral, social or political object, it was almost impossible to ensure that *every* text or book would present the same conception of it. The more the "boundless variety" of ideas and texts was banished from between the covers of miscellarian volumes, the more obviously it recurred between and among individual books. Moreover, far from eliminating controversy, presenting one entire conception of an object gave polemics a clarity and force they lacked while polemicists still attacked their adversaries by painstakingly working their rambling way through a miscellany of minor, obscure and unrelated points. One might therefore say that the publication of Gerard's own *Essay on Taste* (in the singular) symbolized philosophical criticism's failure to limit and control the variety of conceptions and tastes in the marketplace of ideas: for Gerard's essay was itself repeatedly published as part of a miscellany. Juxtaposed with essays by Voltaire and D'Alembert and a fragment from Montesquieu, Gerard's essay was intellectually described and materially positioned by its printer at the margin of a variety of other, more influential works.

Novelty presented a different problem, and not only because the public's abiding taste for new stories and for novel miscellarian genres marginalized and devalued the classics that men of liberal education alone brought to the table. Novelty itself became increasingly suspect as the century wore on. In political, legal and religious matters, where innovations were carefully couched as a return to ancient custom, to the ancient constitution or to the primitive Church, novelty increasingly became associated with dangerous or unwelcome change. Novelty was felt to be unsafe, creating a sense, as churchman William Reeves put it, that: "if Novelty is to be avoided, Antiquity is to be retained."[110] Conservative literary critics such as Hurd, Burke and Johnson implicitly followed this line: Johnson, for instance, ended his anatomy of the "dangerous prevalence of the imagination" in *Rasselas*, with his characters' return to the safe but boring Happy Valley of their ancestors, the wiser for having been taught by experience that imagination had only deceived them into thinking that something new could make them happier than they had been before. At least one physician warned his readers that "when indulged without moderation or restraint," the quest for novelty led to "misconduct, anxiety and distress," or indeed, to madness.[111] Novelty certainly caused the political establishment anxiety and distress. Yet given its indubitable appeal for readers, novelty could not just be dismissed as maddening or delusional.

Philosophical critics argued instead that there was good novelty and bad, while separating novelty from curiosity, and demoting both from their preeminent position in reading. Philosophical critics granted Addison that curiosity and the pleasure of encountering new ideas drove their own scholarly reading.[112] But like Kames, they distinguished between the curiosity of scholars in quest of knowledge and the curiosity of "persons of mean taste":

> Curiosity is a natural principle directed upon new and singular objects, in the contemplation of which its gratification consists, without leading to any end other than knowledge; and accordingly no man is ashamed to acknowledge that he loves to contemplate new and singular objects. But the man who prefers anything merely because it is new, hath not this principle for its justification; nor indeed any good principle: vanity is at the bottom, which easily prevails on those who have no taste, to prefer things odd, rare, or singular, in order to distinguish themselves from others. And in fact, this appetite...reigns chiefly among persons of mean taste, who are ignorant of refined and elegant pleasures.[113]

The novelty of as yet unknown objects of knowledge that scholars pursued was commendable; the novelty of those wondrous strange phenomena, and rare or uncommon events which supposedly appealed only to the vulgar and ignorant, was not. It made people singular; and singularity was an eighteenth-century dirty word. The intellectual elite could be curious; the multitude not.

Granting Hobbes' and Locke's point that "novelty in any object, or action or quality is a cause of wonder," Kames went on to distinguish between the legitimate wonder felt by men of taste for whatever was sublime in nature or art, and vulgar wonder at fairies, witches, monsters, ghosts and enchantments – "our judgment revolts against improbable incident; and if we once begin to doubt its reality, farewell relish and concern."[114] Burke helpfully developed Kames' distinction between vulgar wonder and the sublime, in order to redirect – and confine – readers' pleasure in wonders to higher and more refined things. In context, his much anthologized and decontextualized observation that "some degree of novelty must be one of the materials in every instrument which works upon the mind; and curiosity blends itself more or less with all our passions,"[115] meant that readers' "lust for novelty" and love of wonders could be satisfied in another, more legitimate way. Recent scholars of the Fantastic have argued that fantasy subsumes the sublime, the marvelous and the supernatural; they treat all these literary phenomena as akin on the assumption that the important "schism" in literature is between the fantastic and the mimetic.[116] But for eighteenth-century belletrists, it was important to distinguish between the legitimate aesthetic pleasures of Newton's heirs – who perceived sublime glimpses of divinity in seemingly boundless natural horizons or in terrible events productive of strong and painful emotions – from the superstitious wonder of the vulgar at providential deliverances, or at marvelous tales of fairies, monsters, goblins, specters and ghosts. This made for distinctions among readers and among times: admiring the marvelous in the poetry of ancient bards distinguished the superstitious past from the enlightened present, which dismissed such beliefs as untruths. Admiring the sublime not the marvelous distinguished the refined taste of enlightened men of taste from the vulgar. There was a good and bad, a right and wrong, in wonder too.

Perhaps due to "the great resemblance which false taste bears to true, which hasty and inaccurate observers will find it…difficult to distinguish," philosophical critics thought it best not to trust too much to fine distinctions. It was safer to discredit novelty and curiosity. Blair devoted only a single paragraph to them in Lecture 5. While noting that the pleasure of novelty had been "mentioned by Mr. Addison," he gave only the dismissive view: "An object which has no merit to recommend it, except its being uncommon or new, by means of this quality alone, produces in the mind a vivid and an agreeable emotion. Hence that passion of curiosity, which prevails so generally among mankind…Hence, in a great measure, the entertainment afforded us by fiction and romance." But "the emotion raised by Novelty" is "much shorter in its continuance" than other emotions, and "the shining gloss thrown upon [objects]" by Novelty "soon wears off." Indeed, "novelty soon degenerates into familiarity"; it is the most "superficial" and least universal of all affections because it "changes its object perpetually" and "because "those things which engage us by their novelty cannot attach us for any length of time."[117] Philosophical critics repeatedly dismissed pleasure in novelty as infantile, something belonging most properly to childhood and youth when all the world was new, or argued, as Reid did, that "the pleasure derived from new objects in many cases is not owing solely or chiefly to their being new, but to some other circumstance that gives them value."[118] Novelty was not a real or enduring pleasure of the imagination, and curiosity was not an important, much less universal, motive for reading.

Philosophical criticism allowed readers their novelty, as it allowed them their variety – co-opted, moderated and restrained. The ploy that eventually stuck was to associate the new with the original, which had heretofore only meant the primitive inception or ancient source of something. This enabled critics to attach novelty to antiquity, where it could be enjoyed once safely past. The innovations of a Homer or Virgil, or even of a Spenser or Milton if properly understood, were dangerous to no one now. This association of novelty with the old also enabled critics to claim that early "fathers" of English literature such as Chaucer, Spenser, Shakespeare and Milton – who had borrowed their plots and stories from others, imitated Roman, French and Italian characters, ideas and genres, and even "taken their most striking passages from other poets" – were original (new) nevertheless. "A vulgar mind can copy, a superior mind in copying, always becomes original." Originality meant that novelty was not *really* that "popular kind of novelty" which satisfies "the incessant demand of the tasteless public" and "is gratified by the irregular sallies of the imagination"; it was, instead, "that Novelty which now seduces and captivates in the productions of art."[119] The mischievous eighteenth-century author of these lines prudently left the verbs "seduces" and "captivates" without a direct object – we are not told who exactly in the real world was being captivated or seduced by ancient originals, the productions of true art. Not the tasteless public, evidently.

Oliver Goldsmith protested that true critics would praise nothing that was new: "Scarce a day passes in which we do not hear compliments paid to Dryden, Pope, and other Writers of the last age, while not a month comes forward that is not loaded with invective against the writers of this."[120] Henry Mackenzie suggested that the real problem for learned critics, and the reason they condemned the genre, was that the familiar novel made them superfluous since it was "of all [genres] the most open to the judgment of the people; because it represents domestic scenes and situation in private life, in the execution of which any man may detect errors."[121] True critics demonstrated their taste by attacking novels in contradictory fashion: for creating characters who were "above nature" and "below nature"; and for their immorality. They also sought to deflect novel readers to "original" texts, by trying to interest them in the characters delineated by ancient writers. Kevin Pask has demonstrated, for instance, that Chaucer, who had been valued for centuries as a "rhetor" who had created a literary

"*Hochsprache*" in the vernacular, was now praised for "his superior characterization, which encompasses the 'various manners and humours…of the whole English nation, in his age.' "[122] Homer and Shakespeare were touted in similar terms, for their inimitable representations of "human nature." One might say that true critics sought to attract readers to what they were calling "classics" by telling them that they would find in these what they appeared to enjoy most in contemporary novels: characters they could recognize, whose conduct they could talk about and judge.

Perhaps the major problem for philosophical critics was the one they did not mention or manage to overcome: the fact that the publications that men of learning and true critics used to educate the public themselves took discontinuous, miscellaneous forms. As we saw, schoolbooks were compilations of miscellaneous fragments. Spellers and copybooks presented discrete lists of spelling words serving a variety of purposes, that were separated by gaps and interrupted by diverse reading exercises. Grammars offered staccato catechismical Q & As, or lists of discontinuous grammatical rules in brief note form, and a variety of long discursive footnotes. "Study" produced such discontinuous, miscellaneous genres as digests, dictionaries and encyclopedias, where miscellaneous knowledge was presented in fragments. Even the belletrism of philosophical critics was imbricated in miscellarian forms, and dependent upon them for its dissemination – anthologies of verse, collections of the "best" authors, volumes of "beauties," scholarly editions, and collections of lectures.

John Clarke blamed readers' "rambling" and discontinuous reading habits on this kind of education: "Youth, having been used to vast Variety and Confusion, contract so good a liking to them, that…they commonly persist in that Misconduct all the Days of their Lives."[123] Men of Learning who taught were accustoming readers to miscellarian, discontinuous manners of reading which contradicted their theory. If the leisured gentlemen, men in trade or in the "genteel professions," and ladies of fortune whom Clarke was addressing preferred miscellarian genres and discontinuous reading, it was, he thought, as much because their education had made these familiar and comfortable, as because, as everyone agreed, "Variety is naturally more agreeable and entertaining to the Mind, than its contrary; and dwelling long upon the same subject is apt to become tedious," or because the "The Mind is indeed naturally fond of Novelty, and apt to be tired and jaded with frequent reviews of the same subject."

Perhaps this was why discontinuous manners of reading and writing continued to prevail both in Britain and America at the turn of the nineteenth century. Though taking continually changing forms (as one might expect from a miscellarian aesthetic), miscellaneous and fragmented genres, and discontinuous manners of reading continued to be favored by common readers. It should not therefore surprise us to find textual "fragments" produced by the canonical Romantic poets, in the "table talk" and miscellarian essays of early nineteenth-century critics, and by almost anyone who hoped to be read by the broader public.

NOTES

1 Philip Skelton, *The Candid Reader* (London, 1744): 2, 3, 5, 8, 9.
2 John Hawkesworth, *The Adventurer*, #XVII, Tuesday, January 2, 1753 (London, 1793): 1: 116.
3 Oliver Goldsmith, *Enquiry into the Present State of Polite Learning*, 1754 (London, 1774): 110, 116.
4 John Aikin, *Letters from a Father to his Son* (London, 1793): 63, 64.
5 Isaac Disraeli, *Miscellanies* (London, 1796): 5, 3.
6 Samuel Johnson, *The Rambler*, 8 vols. (Edinburgh, 1751): #22 Saturday, June 2, 1750: 1: 174, 177, 179.
7 Shields, "Eighteenth-Century Literary Culture," in Amory and Hall, *Colonial Book*: 434–45.
8 Hawkesworth, *Adventurer*, # CXXXIX, Tuesday, March 5, 1754, 4: 238.
9 Brewer, *Pleasures of the Imagination*; Domingo, "Unbending the Mind."
10 [Anon] *Constantia* (Dublin, 1751): iv, xiii, xvi.
11 Shaftesbury, *Characteristics of Men, Manners, Opinions, Times*, edited by Lawrence Klein (Cambridge University Press, 1999): 339, 340, 350, 349, 341, 342, 460.
12 Klein describes *Characteristics* as an "anthology" and "composite" containing "a wide range of subject matters and...different genres and styles." (Introduction, *Characteristics*: x). This anthology or miscellany is also "random" in Shaftesbury's sense: we could change the order of components, and in many cases move chapters around within each, without incoherence.
13 Stallybrass, "Books and Scrolls": 40, 43, 46.
14 Abbé Trublet, *Essays upon Several Subjects...Particularly upon the Manner of Writing in Single Thoughts* (London, 1744): 5, 6, 9.
15 Disraeli, *Miscellanies*: 20.
16 Vicesimus Knox, *Winter Evenings: Lucubrations on Life and Letters*, 3 vols. (London, 1788): 15, 20, 21.
17 Knox, *Winter Evenings*: 78.
18 Dr. Barrow, as quoted in Frances Brokesby, *Of Education with Respect to Grammar Schools and the Universities* (London, 1701): 179–80.
19 *Plutarch's Morals: Translated from the Greek by Several Hands* (4th edn., London, 1704): 1: Preface, 65.
20 Disraeli, *Miscellanies*, 21, 18, 19, 20.
21 Henry Felton, *A Dissertation on Reading the Classics and Forming a Just Style. Written in the Year 1709* (London, 1713): 24–5.

22 Henry Fielding, Preface to Sarah Fielding, *The Adventures of David Simple* (2nd edn., London, 1744): ix–x.

23 *Adventurer*, No. LXXX, Saturday, August 11, 1753, 3: 74; No. LXXXV, Tuesday, July 24, 1753, 3: 30.

24 Fuchs, *Romance*; R. Greene, *Unrequited Conquests*; Quint, *Epic and Empire*; Doody, *True History of the Novel*.

25 Hugh Blair, *Lectures on Rhetoric and Belles Lettres*, 2 vols. (London, 1783): 14.

26 Disraeli, *Miscellanies*: 11.

27 [Anon] *A Help to Elocution and Eloquence* (London, 1770): iv.

28 William Dover, *Useful Miscellanies* (Philadelphia, 1753): Preface, n.p.

29 John Constable, *Reflections upon Accuracy of Style* (London, 1734): 53; lines by Denham, quoted in Edward Bysshe, *The Art of English Poetry* (London, 1724): 89; Joseph Priestley, *A Course of Lectures on Oratory and Criticism* (London, 1777): 148.

30 Reprinted in *The Annual Register for the Year 1786* (London, 1787): 148.

31 Orr, "Genre Labels."

32 Joseph Addison and Richard Steele, *The Spectator*, 8 vols. (London, 1712–15): #454, 6: 320.

33 *Spectator*, #412, 6: 90.

34 *Spectator*, # 452, 6: 311, 310.

35 *The Moral and Political Writings of Thomas Hobbes of Malmesbury* (London, 1750): 21–2.

36 Ibid.: 119, 22, 667.

37 John Locke, *Some Thoughts on Education* (London, 1705): 215, 221, 218, 217. Also John, "Physiology of Reading": 149 ff.

38 Quoted in P. G. Walsh, "Rights and Wrongs of Curiosity": 78.

39 *Spectator*, #156, 2: 277.

40 Kenny, *Uses of Curiosity*: 19; Benedict, *Curiosity*. Examples in British titles include: Louis Moreri, *The Great, Historical, Geographical, Genealogical and Poetical Dictionary; being a Curious Miscellany of Sacred and Prophane History* (London, 1701); [Anon] *A Collection of Books. Consisting of a Curious Collection of the Most Eminent English Authors for Divinity, History, Travels, Miscellanies and Lives* (London, 1706); [Anon] *The Harleian Miscellany, or a Collection of Rare, Curious and Entertaining Pamphlets and Tracts* (London, 1744); Isaac Disraeli, *Curiosities of Literature*; and Rev. John Adams, *Curious Thoughts on the History of Man* (London, 1789).

41 *Spectator*, #210: 3: 235.

42 Merlin, "Curiosité et espace": 124. For development of the modern time-line, Chandler, *England in 1819*.

43 *The Bee* (1790 ff.): title page.

44 Paulson, *Beautiful, Novel and Strange*: 54.

45 *Spectator*, #131: 2: 58–9.

46 *Spectator*: 6: 320.

47 *Idler* #1; *Rambler* #144: VI: 109.

48 *Rambler* #145: VI: 108, 109.

49 *Rambler* #184: VIII: 2; #1: I: 7, 8.

50 *Rambler* #125: V: 159.

51 McGill, *Culture of Reprinting*: 3.

52 Martha Milcah Moore, *Miscellanies Moral and Instructive in Prose and Verse* (Philadelphia, 1787): iv.

53 John, "Miscellaneous Methods": 159, 163.

54 Bullard, "Digital Editing": 68. Also Bannet, *Empire of Letters*.

55 Kamrath, "Eyes Wide Shut": 498; also Kamrath and Harris, *Periodical Literature*; Gardner, *Early American Magazine Culture*.

56 Vicesimus Knox, *Essays Moral and Literary. A New Edition*, 2 vols. (London, 1782): 2: 8, 9, 3, 11.

57 Knox, *Winter Evenings*: 1: 74–5; 2: 106, 108.

58 Knox, *Essays:* 11.

59 Knox, *Winter Evenings*, I: 68, 70.

60 *Spectator* #412, 413, 419, 626; in *Papers of Joseph Addison*: 247, 251, 280, 328.

61 Henry Kames, *Elements of Criticism*, 2 vols. (3rd edn., Edinburgh, 1765): 300–1; Philip Freneau, "The Power of Novelty," in *Miscellaneous Works* (Philadelphia, 1788): 192; Aikin, *Letters*: 67, 66; Johnson, *Rambler* #LXXX, Saturday, December 22, 1750; [Anon] *London Unmasked* (London, 1784): 135; "The Pleasures arising from Novelty," in Walker, *The Academic Speaker* (Dublin, 1796): 83.

62 Gally, "Curiosité et fictions medievales": 262–82.

63 St. Clair, *Reading Nation*; David Hall in Amory and Hall, *The Colonial Book*: 392.

64 Jane Barker, Preface to *Exilius* (London, 1715): 2; Eliza Haywood, *The Female Spectator*, 4 vols. (London, 1745–6): 1: 6.

65 Ironically, Hawkesworth used *Adventurer* #4 to apply to novels arguments that Johnson had made for biography, and used against history, in *Rambler* #60.

66 Samuel Richardson, "Preface by the Editor," *Pamela* (London, 1741): A3.

67 Richard Cumberland (1795), in Nixon, *Anthology*: 121.

68 *Adventurer*, #4, Saturday, November 18, 1752, 19, 20.

69 Delarivier Manley, "To the Reader," in *The Secret History of Queen Zarah and the Zaranians* (London, 1711): n.p.; Mary Davys, Preface to *The Works of Mrs. Davys* (London, 1725): iv.

70 Jane Collier and Sarah Fielding, *The Cry* (London, 1754): 17.

71 Manley, "To the Reader," *Queen Zarah*, n.p.

72 In Nixon, *Anthology of Commentary*: 171.

73 Eliza Haywood, *Female Spectator*: 1: 4, 6.

74 Eliza Haywood, *The Invisible Spy*, 4 vols. (London, 1755): 1: 3, 22. Also Bannet, "The Narrator as Invisible Spy."

75 The difference was that secret histories displayed the secret intrigues at court in disguised, fictional forms, while amatory fictions displayed the hidden motives and dynamics in private families and domestic life.

76 London, *Cambridge Introduction to the Eighteenth-Century Novel.*

77 Peter Walmsley argues that the theory of Gothic was already fleshed out in *Spectator* #419. See "The Melancholy Briton."

78 *Adventurer*, #4, 10 and 11.

79 Penelope Aubin, *A Collection of Entertaining Histories and Novels* (London, 1739): title page and preface; Arthur Murphy on *Tom Jones*, in Nixon, *Anthology of Commentary*: 192.

80 From *The Morning Chronicle*, in *The Spirit of the Public Journals for 1798*: 200.

81 Price, *Anthology and the Rise of the Novel*: 24.

82 For other novelistic uses of chapter titles, Birke, "Direction and Diversion."

83 Barker, *Exilius*: Preface.

84 Fergus, *Provincial Readers*, calls such readers "desultory."

85 David Brewer, *Afterlife of Character*.

86 Tadmor, "In the Even My Wife Read to Me": 168, 166.

87 Woolf, *Reading History*: 119, Chap. 2.

88 *The Universal Spectator*, 2 vols. (London, 1736): Advertisement.

89 Elizabeth Griffith, *The History of Lady Barton* (London, 1771): v–vi; 1: 240.

90 Kames, *Elements of Criticism*: 1: 85.

91 Disraeli, *Miscellanies*: 191, 192.

92 Knox, *Winter Evenings*: 1: 26.

93 Disraeli, *Miscellanies*: 1: 193.

94 *Adventurer*, CXXXVII, Tuesday, February 26, 1754, 4: 351.

95 Disraeli, *Miscellanies*: 1: 193, 196, 194.

96 John Theobald, *Every Man his own Physician* (London, 1764).

97 Coleridge, *Biographia Literaria*, edited by James Engell and W. Jackson Bate, 2 vols. (Princeton University Press, 1983): 2: 14.

98 Knox, *Winter Evenings*: 1: 15; Disraeli, *Miscellanies*: 199.

99 Knox, *Essays* (2nd edn., 1779): 167.

100 *Adventurer*, # XLIX, Tuesday, April 24, 1753: 126, 128.

101 Disraeli, *Miscellanies*: 199.

102 Skelton, *Candid Reader*: 9.

103 Kallich, *Association of Ideas*: 99.

104 Adam Smith, "Of Wonder, or the Effects of Novelty," in *Essays on Philosophical Subjects by the Late Adam Smith* (Dublin, 1795): 22, 23.

105 Ibid.: 106.

106 Kallich, *Association of Ideas*: Chap. 1.

107 Tavor, *Scepticism, Society and the Eighteenth-Century Novel*.

108 Kames, *Elements of Criticism*: 1: 394, 386, 405.

109 Alexander Gerard, *An Essay on Taste, with three Dissertations on the same Subject by M. de Voltaire, Mr. D'Alembert and M. de Montesquieu* (London, 1759): note u, 34, 58, 35.

110 William Reeves, *The Apologies of Justin Martyr, Tertullian and Minutius Felix in Defence of the Christian Religion* (London, 1709): 356.

111 Thomas Arnold MD, *Observations on the Nature, Kind, Causes and Prevention of Insanity, Lunacy or Madness*, 2 vols. (Leicester, 1782–6): 1: 338.

112 Gerard, for instance, gave an almost phenomenological description of how pleasurably novelty exercised the bored or "languid" mind of scholars and

antiquaries and drove them to master difficult texts and persist in painful labor in their researches.

113 Kames, *Elements*: 255.
114 Ibid.: 245, 113, 293, 95; Burke, *Enquiry*: 35, 36; *The World*, #68, in *The Moral Miscellany* (1758): 282.
115 Edmund Burke, *A Philosophical Enquiry into our Ideas of the Sublime and the Beautiful*. 2nd edn. (London, 1759): 37.
116 Sandner, *Critical Discourses of the Fantastic, 1712–1831*; James and Mendlesohn (eds.) *Cambridge Companion to Fantasy Literature*.
117 Hugh Blair, *Lectures on Rhetoric and Belles Lettres*, 2 vols. (London, 1783): 1: 50–1.
118 Thomas Reid, *Essays on the Intellectual and Active Powers of Men*, 3 vols. (Dublin, 1790): 2: 434.
119 Disraeli, *Miscellanies*: 329, 335.
120 Oliver Goldsmith, *The Bee*, #4, November 3, 1759.
121 Henry Mackenzie, *The Lounger*, #20, June 18, 1785.
122 Pask, *Emergence of the English Author*: 49.
123 Clarke, *Essay on Study*: 79.

CHAPTER 5

Reading Secret Writing

Secret writing – and censorship, its principal cause – cast a long shadow which disturbed, destabilized, and sometimes derailed, most of the manners of reading considered so far. Following Quintilian's advice to "speak as openly as you like...against tyrants, as long as you can be understood differently"[1] gave all texts containing secret writing qualities of complexity, ambiguity and indirection that flouted establishment academic and clerical demands for a politely perspicuous, easy and decorous style conveying a single, conventional impression. Indeed, the more its ubiquity makes secret writing seem the default position, the more those calls for simplicity, transparency and universal truths sound like battle cries – and perhaps like calls for readers to ignore what was so frequently hidden in plain sight, in favor of safe, politically uncontroversial, surface "beauties."

Secret writing insinuated a disguised sub-text which communicated "seditious" attitudes and ideas, questioned political, moral or religious orthodoxies, conveyed the scandalous truth about what transpired behind closed doors, and/or publicized *arcana imperii* (state secrets) or *scandalum magnatum* (libels upon the great). It had a long history in Britain, which we are only beginning to systematically explore. During the long seventeenth century, its generic complex included politico-historical drama, poetry on affairs of state, historiography, heroic romance, pastoral, allegory, satire, fable, ballads and songs. Technologically, there was also underground printing, cryptography, and shorthand "both for dispatch in what men write for their own memory, and concealment of what they would not have lie open to every eye."[2] The long eighteenth century added memoirs, *romans a clef*, Procopian *anecdota* or secret histories, novels, almanacs, and the politico-philosophical, politico-theological and popularizing writings of free-thinkers, Masons, Schismaticks, the heterodox, Jacobites, Jacobins, self-taught "Radicals" and populist parliamentary reformers – to say nothing of the harlequin procession across the public prints of masquerading eidolons, masked personae, and mysteriously anonymous voices. Romanticists too are increasingly arguing not only that "reading an ambiguous surface for meaning was a commonplace activity in Jacobin culture," but that "those who pursued a political or religious vision different from that required by the state" between 1640 and 1830 were all "replicating" and renewing the same methods of "occult, underground textual... transmission."[3]

"Functionally ambiguous," double-voiced texts were not, as we once supposed, just "elitist obscurantism" intended to be "fully and easily comprehensible only to a select few."[4] Considering the "camouflage satires"[5] and parodies, allusive jests and satirical news ballads, sarcastic broadsides and clandestine newsbooks that had been circulating among the populace since the 1630s, recent scholars of censorship have shown that even "humble" early seventeenth-century singers, rumor-mongers, listeners and readers were capable of "deconstructing a political text in order to learn its true meaning."[6] People could be acute and active decipherers of double meanings who were unable or unwilling to write. Censorship changed its forms after lapse of the Licensing Act in 1695; but it remained virulent and dangerous, and impacted the common people as well as the elite. For censorship bore on speech and writing as well as on print, and in some periods punished possessors of unlicensed books or pamphlets, and those who failed to report "seditious" remarks heard in taverns or in casual conversation, as well as their writers, speakers and printers. This may be why the English were such a "laconic" people, as Mr. Spectator dryly observed: the restraint and polite reserve that safeguarded the urbane was fully matched by plebeian suspicion of strangers and wariness of spies.

Government censorship during our period was usually more concerned about what ideas and criticism of the great reached the common people than about what was said or written among gentlemen in a language and style supposedly inaccessible to the multitude. In *Sensus Communis* (1709), Shaftesbury mocked those who thus restricted freedom of "dialogue and free debate" (35) to "select companies," by observing that it was a breach of politeness, as well as of "respect" for "societies of men," to "affect a superiority over the vulgar and to despise the multitude" by "treat[ing] of matters in a dialect which many who are present have perhaps never been used to." This was mockery not merely because the "multitude" had long had their own forms of political "raillery and humour," but also because printed texts of all kinds were familiarizing the "vulgar" with the "dialect" of their betters. As Shaftesbury made every reader "with ears to hear" what he was saying about secret writing the friend whom he was addressing in *Sensus Communis*, his published "letter to a friend," so other authors used a variety of genres to initiate the public into that "Club" of "gentlemen and friends" who understood the "dialects" of secret writing. When we replace our modern term "secret writing" with the terms that eighteenth-century writers used, it also becomes apparent that popular grammars and rhetorics throughout the century not only alerted the generality of readers to the likelihood that texts meant something other than they said, but supplied them with the tools to read past texts' exoteric surfaces to their concealed or esoteric "under-meanings" (*hyponoia*).

One might add that to identify "free-thinkers," as we do, with deists, atheists, infidels and libertines, is to uncritically accept their characterization by antagonists who sought to demean and discredit them to protect the established Church and State. As Skelton, for one, admitted, free-thinkers held very various political and religious views; and there were many moral, religious, even ascetic men among them. What free-thinkers shared was the conviction that everyone must be free to think for themselves and use their own reason. They expected that once permitted to do so, people would soon realize that the ideas and belief-systems transmitted and imposed "by authority" of Church and State were designed to preserve the power, and serve the private interests, of ministers and priests, and that these ideas and belief-systems were therefore not, as the latter pretended, necessarily and incontrovertibly true. Ironically, therefore, the story of secret writing in this period is also the story of government and Church efforts to censor and suppress that freedom to employ one's reason and think for oneself, which, in Kant's wake, we consider the essence of Enlightenment.

Reading for "Irony" and "Banter"

Shaftesbury first published *Sensus Communis*, his guide to secret writing, in 1709, separately from *Characteristics* (1711) and anonymously as to author, printer and place of publication, as was usual with dangerous or subversive texts. For this was a guide designed not only to justify and situate secret writing in the socio-political matrix, but also to demonstrate through its own practice how "sober raillery" worked.[7] As he explained, "if men are forbid to speak seriously on certain subjects,"

> they will do it ironically. If they are forbid to speak at all upon such subjects, or if they find it really dangerous to do so, they will then redouble their disguise, involve themselves in mysteriousness and talk so as hardly to be understood, or at least not plainly interpreted, by those who are disposed to do them mischief. And thus raillery is brought more in fashion and runs into an extreme. It is the persecuting spirit has raised the bantering one. (34)

"Irony," "banter" and "raillery" are terms that Shaftesbury was using here to signify secret writing. During the seventeenth and much of the eighteenth century, irony and banter were the erudite and cant signifiers, respectively, for words or texts that say one thing and mean another. Applying equally to prose and verse, to satire and fiction, and to serious and humorous writings, both terms were also strongly identified with dissimulation, bamboozling and disguise.[8] This followed from irony's stock devices. In oratory and expository writing, these included blaming by appearing to praise, praising by appearing to blame and, Shaftesbury's favorite, assuming a mask of gravity in order to "mock with a straight face."[9] "Raillery" most often meant good-humored ridicule, but masking one's true meaning for purposes of mockery or derision also made raillery, ridicule, satire, burlesque and irony "loose and interchangeable terms" – as they are in this text.[10] By association with Socrates, who disguised his wisdom by assuming the character of a diffident and unknowing man, and with Aesop who hid his political commentary in animal fables, irony's other stock devices took the form of "mimicry" (34) – assuming or personating characters and "mystifying" one's meaning in a fable or fiction. Norman Knox found that during this period "Banter as deception was most often used to denote a verbal fiction of a sort offered with enough ostensible conviction to bamboozle an audience, temporarily at least."[11] And Shaftesbury took pains to include bamboozling fictions among the "ironical" disguises to which he said writers were driven by "the persecuting spirit": "It may be necessary, as well now as heretofore, for wise men to speak in parables, and with a double meaning, that the enemy may be amused and they only 'who have ears to hear' may hear." (31) Or as Delarivier Manly put it: "The Intrigues and Miscarriages of War and Peace are better many Times laid open and Satyriz'd in a *Romance*," for "such disguis'd Discourses as these, promiscuously personating every Man and no Man, take their full Liberty to speak the Truth."[12]

Shaftesbury blamed the fact that "the natural free spirits of ingenious men" resorted to "burlesque, mimicry or buffoonery" (34) and that "the most celebrated authors [had become] the greatest masters of burlesque" (30) on the ways writers were "imprisoned" and "controlled" by "the strictness of the laws" and by "the prevailing pedantry and bigotry of those who reign in them and assume themselves to be dictators in these provinces" (31). The principal persecutors of writers were the laws and agents of state censorship. Censorship was repeatedly presented as occasioning secret writing in guides and prefaces to instances of it. The preface to *Aesop at the Bell-Tavern* (1711), for instance, informed readers that Aesopian fables were designed to "direct us to a Sense of Affairs which the Dread of Authority would deter some Persons from enquiring into…" *The Doctrine of Innuendo's Discuss'd* (1731) declared that "Punishments that Law could inflict" "forced" writers "to have recourse to Allegories and History, that they may escape the Designs of their Enemies." Anthony Collins observed in 1739 that "a great Part of the Irony complain'd of, has its rise from the *want of Liberty to examine into the Truth of Things.*" Philip Skelton's free-thinking character declares that "nobody would care to risque his own safety with a set of persecuting antagonists, who are ready, on all occasions, to argue with us from Acts of Parliament, and to call us to an uncouth sort of disputations before courts of judicature, where bigotry often presides on the bench, and always reigns in both the boxes." The argument of Peter Pindar's *Ode to Irony* (1793) was likewise that "greybeards'" insistence that "No more in Britain must [Irony] dare be seen…/To take vile liberties with lofty men," made irony the mark of that "Liberty divinely strong" which "crowned" the "Poet of the People." As an anonymous pamphleteer put in 1788, "Irony, Banter, Sarcasm, Drollery, Lampoonery, Buffoonery, Taunting, Jesting, Scoffing, Burlesque etc" were "Instruments of War."[13] More than just explanation, the constant linking of censorship and irony ensured that, by a "natural association of ideas," every new instance of government censorship (verbal or written reports of trials or prosecutions, the sight of books burned before an author in the stocks) would prompt the public to look out for "irony" in what they read or heard.

Contemporary allusions to the impact of censorship make better sense to us now that we no longer assume that censorship disappeared in 1695 with lapse of the Licensing Act. We now acknowledge that after 1695, *pre-publication* censorship through licensing was replaced (except in the theatre) by forms of *post-publication* censorship, which included savage laws punishing transgressors with "fetters and halters": successive laws of seditious libel, treason, blasphemy and obscene libel and, during the repressive 1790s, gagging laws, and Traitorous Correspondence Acts, or in America, Alien and Sedition Acts. The persistence from Burghley to Pitt and John Adams of potentially lethal exercises of state censorship helps to explain the persistence of secret writing.[14] But modern scholars differ in their assessments of how censorship worked, with some arguing that there was collusion between writers and censors, together with "conventions that both sides accepted as to how far writers could go in explicit address to the contentious issue of the day,"[15] and others arguing on the contrary, that writers subverted the system by taking advantage of its "gaps and loopholes."[16]

Shaftesbury indicated that the operation of censorship was more complex, unstable and self-contradictory than this modern either/or allows. For
on the one hand, "whichever [party] chanced to have the power failed not
of putting all means in execution to make their private sense the public
one" (38); but on the other, "that which was according to the sense of one
part of mankind was against the sense of another" and "would change as
often as men changed" (37). In other words, the fact that government and
religion underwent such frequent, rapid and dramatic changes between
the Renaissance and 1800 not only meant that most religious and political
groups were obliged to resort to secret writing at one time or another; it
also meant that the authorities failed to present a united front either during
licensing or thereafter. What was agreeable to one censor, to the purists of
one political or religious party, or to one republican or monarchical ministry,
was treated as dangerous or seditious by another, with the result that writers
might fall victim to the "sense" of "one part of mankind" as often as the 'men
who chanced to have the power changed.' The careers of Prynne, Milton
and Dryden are notorious cases in point. This did not prevent prosecutions
deriving from changes in the political or religious landscape from being
entwined with collusion. But collusion – in the form of active encouragement, tacit toleration, or useful help from some of those who had the power
to censure and censor publications – only made publishing under censorship
like playing Russian roulette. Defoe, Steele, and George Ridpath offer one
example, as Paul Hyland showed.[17] They were all prosecuted by the Tory
ministry for authoring secret writings – texts "encased in cryptics" – about
the Hanoverian succession in 1713, the year before Queen Anne's death.
This was a moment when the Whig Opposition was already allied with
the future George I, and when Tories were divided between a pro-Hanover
group who made common cause with the Whigs, and Tories in the Ministry
and Parliament who were negotiating with James Stuart in France. A pro-
Hanoverian Lord Chief Justice, Thomas Parker, helped George Ridpath to
escape punishment for insinuating that Queen Anne sought to put her half-
brother, James, on the throne; but Defoe – in the pay of Tory Prime Minister
Harley, who now favored another Stuart restoration – was arrested by Parker
for "what were recognized as ironical productions" against the Hanover succession. Meanwhile, Harley-led parliamentary Tories voted Steele guilty of
seditious libel and expelled him from the Commons for his Whig-supported
publications in favor of Hanover. Because the authorities did not all speak
with one voice, collusion with one group which "put all means in execution
to make their private sense the public one," could get writers in trouble with
another group – and sometimes, out of trouble again.

Not all argument, satire and fiction contained secret writing; but secret writing always involved irony in Shaftesbury's sense. This is also where the "persecutors" of literature sought it. Under Queen Anne, Lord Chief Justice Holt declared punishable "an Information [that] will lie by speaking ironically"; at Jacobin Daniel Isaac Eaton's trial in 1793, the judge was still telling the jury that "a man may use such language, as in the plain terms of it at first may appear to be no libel," but that they might "perfectly understand," that "he uses language that is ironicall" and "means exactly the reverse of what he says."[18] Daniel Defoe, Delarivier Manly, the printer and authors of *The Craftsman*, John Thelwall, Eaton, and countless other writers and printers were arrested, charged or convicted in courts of law and at the Bar of the House of Commons because their accusers claimed that their written or printed texts meant something other than what they said. *The British Journal* complained in 1722 that this involved "strain[ing] their genuine signification to make [words or texts] intend Sedition"; and *The Craftsman* protested in 1730 that "if we don't explain meanings in what the most 'literal and common Acceptation' of them must import to every unprejudiced Understanding...no writer can be safe in Writings of any kind; since the Wit of man has not yet been able to invent Words, that can possibly carry but *One Interpretation*."[19] But this was disingenuous. For as Shaftesbury observed, ironical discourses and fictions sought to dissemble "in such a manner as to occasion no scandal or disturbance," by "respect[ing] and honour[ing] conventions and societies of men" and trying not to "offend the public ear" (36). And there was already a long history of that. As Perez Zagorin has shown, what Bacon called "the enigmatical method" of veiling unorthodox beliefs and esoteric meanings in exoterically conformist texts had been widely practiced in England since the Reformation by imitating precedents familiar from the Ancients and the Church Fathers.[20]

Ensuring that their texts outwardly conformed to received opinions and familiar genres was a practice that gave secret writers the putative protection of deniability, while placing the burden of interpretation squarely on readers or accusers – as rhetoricians bred on Quintilian explained:

> The way of distinguishing an *Irony* from the real sentiments of the speaker or writer, are by the accent, the air, the extravagance of the praise, the character of the person, the nature of the thing or the vein of the discourse: for if in any of these respects there is any disagreement from the *common sense* of the words, it plainly appears that one thing is spoken, and another is designed.[21]

It was up to readers to detect disagreements from the *sensus communis* – the "common sense" of words, persons or things – by "distinguishing an irony." Irony or ridicule was first and foremost a test of truth in communication for readers considering a text's common sense to determine whether the speaker or writer meant what they were saying in its "literal and common Acceptation," or whether their "real sentiments" and true "design" differed from that "ironically." Testing for "ironical" double meanings was a means for readers to discover whether secret writing was present in a text.

This is also why irony and banter appeared so dangerous to what Shaftesbury called "dogmatists," "zealots," "tyrants" and "enthusiasts." As he said, the problem was not so much, as they pretended, that religion, the State and morality were under threat from writers who ridiculed them. It was that irony was a method of "questioning received opinion and exposing the ridicule of things" (39) that readers could apply to any text. Readers, who did not necessarily know *a priori* which texts were designed to be "ironical," but did know – as John Toland put it – that "when a man maintains what is commonly believ'd, or professes what is publicly injoin'd, it is not always a sure rule that he speaks what he thinks,"[22] might find that even dogmatical texts could "carry more than *One Interpretation*." Readers applying this manner of reading to the common sense (opinion, judgment, p.37) of such texts might discover that "certain modern zealots in their own controversial writings" were ridiculous – "an executioner and a Merry Andrew acting their part on the same stage" (32) – or that "nonsense" was "the common sense of a great party among ourselves" (38), or that some parties were endeavoring "to make their private sense the public one" (38), where "public" meant "common" to "the generality" of mankind (37). Readers might find that the common sense (received opinions and judgments) promoted by interested parties, and the commonly accepted sense of their words or texts, ran counter to "the common good." *Sensus Communis*, the common sense of words and sentences, was the site where "disagreements" between "ironicall" secret writers and their "persecutors" occurred.

The fact that finding hidden meanings was more a function of *how* one read than *what* one read, was precisely what Philip Skelton complained about: readers "look upon themselves as sharing with the Author in his Honour when they find out his recluse and hidden meaning. The Sentiments seem to be generated between them; nay, the Reader seems to invent the Sentiments of the Author and ought, on many occasions, to have the whole Credit to himself, inasmuch as he frequently draws out a shining Sentiment from a Passage by which the Author either meant quite another Matter, or nothing at all."[23] Reading for recluse and hidden meanings disrupted "candid" reading of all texts – where "candid" meant open,

straightforward, innocent and free from malice (OED). An author's denial
that particular persons or topical issues were meant did not prevent readers
from reading for hidden meanings. On the contrary. The rhetorical figure
of *recusatio*, denying to affirm, was widely used in prefaces and prologues
to protect the writer from prosecution by denying that any specific person
or situation was intended while alerting readers to the hidden presence of
politically dangerous allusions or ideas. Thus when Eliza Haywood denied
all referentiality in *The Invisible Spy* (1755) – "Let no man pretend to point
at his companion and cry: "this is the man" – *The Monthly Review* went
looking. It then smugly informed the public that Mr. Invisible "penetrates
into the family secrets of all kinds of persons" and that these secrets "are
supposed to be founded on fact, but disguis'd to prevent consequences."[24]
Recusatio was a shining example of the double-voiced discourse it denied.

Even popular genres designed for "the multitude" could be "ironicall"
because one did not have to be highly educated to read for irony, or to
know that this was not necessarily signaled by overt satire, humor or jest.
Irony was, as we saw in Chapter I, a figure that readers learned from their
grammars, as well as from *Arts of Reading* and *Arts of Rhetoric Made Easy*.
Considered one of the four "chief tropes," irony was explained whenever
tropes were mentioned, and in much the same terms throughout the century: "the irony says one thing and means another"; it occurs when "a man
speaks contrary to his thoughts"; the word signifies "dissimulation." Often
included was Quintilian's observation that an irony might be known by
the manner of pronunciation, or by the nature of the persons or things,
when this contradicts the words. Many grammars, rhetorics and digests to
the end of the century also cited Blackwall's observation that:

> 'tis plain that there is a general Analogy and Relation between all Tropes; and
> that in all of them a Man uses a foreign or strange Word, instead of a proper
> one, and therefore says one thing, and means something different. When
> he says one thing, and means another, almost the same, 'tis a *Synechdoche*
> or Comprehension; when he says one thing, and means another mutually
> depending, 'tis a *Metonymy;* when he says one thing, and says another oppo-
> site or contrary, 'tis an *Irony;* when he says one thing, and means another
> like it, it is a *Metaphor;* a *Metaphor* continued and often repeated becomes
> an *Allegory.*[25]

All tropes said one thing and meant something different; and the phenomenon could extend to whole segments or texts. Readers were taught to
anticipate that writing and speech often meant what the words did not say.

Instructional books generally used instances from Scripture or the
Ancients to demonstrate how readers could discover and articulate irony's

"under-meaning" – Elijah's mocking speech to the priests of Baal was a favorite example. But readers could equally learn this from the models of ironical reading ubiquitously proffered by ephemeral polemical pamphlets in the perennial pamphlet wars – even at mid-century when we assume that "secret writing" had disappeared. For instance, the author of an obscure election pamphlet, *A letter to the Author of a Letter to Mr Buxton, in which it is proved that the design of that Letter has been entirely misunderstood and that the Author of it is the real Friend of Sir Edward Astly and Mr Coke* (1756), argued that the author of the letter to Mr. Buxton was only *pretending* to support Astly and Coke's rivals. To prove that readers were "misled" in supposing the Letter "rather serious than ludicrous," he used close reading of sentences from the offending text to show that its author had "artfully chosen the pleasing mask of irony, by means of which [he had] with utmost happiness commended with censure, and satirized with praise" in order to "burlesque and satirize" the candidate he pretended to support (6). The author of *Observations on a pamphlet entitled 'Christianity not founded on Argument'* (1765) demonstrated that "the piece in question is a continued irony throughout" and that "this mask being removed, the writer's arguments are…against real, primitive, gospel Christianity" in the same way – by showing that each of his sentences meant something other than what they said.[26] Periodicals and reviews frequently performed this office too. For instance, *The Briton* attacked *The True Briton* in 1724 by explaining that "Irony seems to be the Darling of our Author." He unmasked "the Artifice [*The True Briton*] perpetually makes use of to evade the Charge of Treason and Sedition" by articulating what was meant by its "palpable Innuendo"[27] – innuendo being the legal term for the libelous or seditious meaning/s obliquely hinted by words, texts or blanked out names. *The Monthly Review* outed Dobson's *Chronological Annals of the War* (1763) by likewise observing that Dobson's "remarks on the Liberty of the Press, specious as their appearance may be at first sight, are big with the most pernicious insinuations," and by extracting insinuations of Jacobite principles of passive obedience and non-resistance from Dobson's prose.[28] Fearing that unorthodox ideas would insinuate themselves into the minds of unwary, candid readers, defenders of the establishment made every effort to unmask and refute the ironical meanings of ironical writers. Ironically, however, in the process, these "dogmatists" not only cited, articulated, highlighted and exaggerated ideas that readers might otherwise have dismissed, taken with a grain of salt or entirely overlooked; they also repeatedly explained how irony works, and demonstrated how to read it. By the 1750s, this manner of reading for irony and banter was familiar enough for *The World* to mock those who assumed that in all writing "we speak contrary to what we think," and to whom "the most innocent Irony may appear Irreligion or Wickedness," by reading a letter bitterly blaming libertines for ruining young women to mean that "the nicest decorum and most exemplary chastity are the distinguishing characteristics of our young men."[29]

Tracts by defenders of secret writing such as Antoine Varillas, Anthony Collins or John Toland and tracts by attackers such as Philip Skelton or John Brown, also often showed readers how to recognize irony, satire and seditious wit for themselves. For Skelton, for instance, "obscurity" was the signal that something nefarious was being concealed – writers who embraced officially sanctioned ideas and values wrote "candidly" and perspicuously, openly stating the political or religious positions they espoused. John Toland explained and gave copious examples of the "double manner of teaching" by simultaneously exoteric and esoteric or "enigmatical" messages that had been used since ancient times. "Hinting that the External and Internal Doctrine, are as much in use as ever," he indicated that such texts could be recognized by "shiftings, ambiguities, equivocations and hypocrisy in all its shapes," as well as by "hints" in the text, since the "key" to hidden meanings was "for the most part, to be borrowed by the skilful from the writers themselves."[30]

Since secret writing characteristically masked itself in conventional arguments or literary forms in order to create texts capable of being read at least two ways, it was and remains easy to ignore contemporary warnings and take the exoteric mask for the text's entire meaning. For instance, we have ignored Philip Skelton's warning in 1749, that Shaftesbury "asserts so skeptically or rather hypothetically, that neither his disciple, nor his adversary, knows well what to lay hold of"[31] in order to make Shaftesbury a founder of the "moral sense" school of philosophy and the prime source of *The Spectator*'s urbane politeness. But if, rather than assuming like the New Critics that irony, banter and satire necessarily affirm shared or universal values, the reader follows Toland's advice by applying the protocols for reading irony under censorship that *Sensus Communis* describes to *Sensus Communis* itself, s/he will, like Skelton, recognize Shaftesbury's "assertions" to be "hypothetical" and wonder what he leaves readers to "lay hold of." Shaftesbury described *Sensus Communis* both as an essay and as a Letter to a Friend. Read exoterically as an essay, *Sensus Communis* presents itself as a latter-day *Areopagiticus*: it argues for "a liberty of decent language to question everything, and an allowance for unraveling or refuting any argument without offence" in "the way of dialogue and free debate" (33). Read

esoterically as a letter to a friend, its "sober raillery" of philosophers and
dogmatists "unraveled" their arguments "without offence" by putting ideas
into "dialogue and free debate" – but in the Pyrhonnic manner that leaves
conflicting or mutually refuting positions suspended and unresolved. For
instance, the idea that "according to common speech as well as common
sense, 'honesty is the best policy' "(61), is canceled out by "the common saying that 'interest governs the world' " (53) and by the "counterfeit viziers"
of the courtly and polite. Or again: humans' "natural" propensity to herd
deconstructs Hobbes' and Locke's opposition between the state of nature
and society and with it, the new contractual basis of the polity; but it is in
turn deconstructed by the coda, that the virtues and benefits of herding
are nowhere "so strongly felt or vigorously exerted as in actual conspiracy
or war," and therefore that "the most generous spirits are the most combining," conspiratorial, and seditious to the State (52, 53). This set ideas
in "dialogue and free debate" without committing the author to anything
beyond the joke, that the same admirable natural propensity to herd for
self-preservation, mutual welfare and support which establishes the State,
also destroys it. One might say, rewording Skelton, that Shaftesbury (who
repeatedly condemned "confessional" writing) wrote like Sidney's maker
or poet, who "nothing affirms, and therefore never lieth."[32] Understood in
this way, Shaftesbury was himself infiltrating the *sensus communis* to banter
a society governed by censorious men who sought stability in conformity
and unity in uniformity, by demonstrating the freedom with which unwelcome doctrines in esoteric sub-texts could circulate under their noses. He
was also showing readers how courtiers, ministers, Machiavels, and conspirators, as well as heretics, recusants, visionaries, and political or religious
dissidents had always used language under punitive regimes of censorship
to throw up a defensive cloak around what they thus secured: the freedom to think, soliloquize and self-converse in the "secret cabinet" of head
and heart.

Conversely, judged by the test of censorship, "secret history" appears
less secret and more officially sanctioned than it pretended – what other
form of secret writing dared openly declare itself such on its title page? The
vast majority of self-proclaimed "secret histories" that flourished between
the Glorious Revolution and the 1720s, were "Procopian" exposes of the
concealed sexual scandals, secret treaties, and corrupt political intrigues
at English or European, Catholic or Papal, absolutist courts. Given censorship, it is hard to see how so much thinly veiled *scandalum magnatum* and *arcana imperii* could have been published across three different
reigns and multiple changes of Whig and Tory ministries, without the

encouragement, or at least tacit approval, of the authorities. But if, as Rebecca Bullard has argued, its "primary political function" was "opposing arbitrary government,"[33] secret history was useful to a wide spectrum of the political elite. By publicizing the evils of court-centered personal rule by monarchs and their chosen ministers in widely accessible narrative forms, and circulating "keys" for those unable to recognize the personal allusions, scandalous secret histories of court intrigues served the interests of the majority of the political elite who were committed to mixed government and to the Protestant succession, and wished to see Parliament strengthened over against the Throne. This did not preclude individual writers from being charged with libel if they went too far. But it did mean that self-proclaimed secret historians found, as Shaftesbury said the "Roman satirists" had before them, that "it was no such deep satire to question whether ["humanity or sense of public good"] was properly the spirit of a Court" (48, 49). It is instructive to compare this to what generally happened, during these decades, to expressions of Jacobite sentiment, which the same broad political elite – committed for their own safety to ensuring that the Stuarts did not return – ruthlessly suppressed. As Toni Bowers discovered,[34] Jacobite writers concealed in Romances the dilemmas of passive obedience, conspiracy, complicity and consent facing subjects loyal to the Stuarts under William, Anne and George – using seduction plots, scattered, multiplied or incomplete parallels, and even scandalous "secret history" itself, to "redouble their disguise, involve themselves in mysteriousness, and talk so as hardly to be understood…by those who [were] disposed to do them mischief" (34).

Reading "Mimicry," History and Fable

Like irony and its cognates, fable, allegory, apologue, parable, myth and sometimes epic, were treated as "loose and interchangeable terms": they were used to explain one another, deployed as synonyms, or all subsumed under allegory. As Robert Lowth explained, this was because allegory, defined as "a continued metaphor" or as "a figure which, under the literal sense of the words, conceals a foreign or distant meaning," was called apologue by the Greeks, *fabulae* by the Romans, and parable by the Christians; and because there was a long tradition of reading Homeric epic and ancient myths and legends allegorically.[35] Since fable meant (and *was*) a story or narrative designed "allegorically" to convey a moral or political lesson beyond the literal sense of words and events, it overlapped with "history," which also meant "story" or narrative, and was also said to exemplify useful moral and political lessons for the present. Fable connoted a fictitious narrative, but "true histories" and "fictional histories" (romances, novels) were narratives that could be "allegorical" too. Contemporaries *also* applied these terms in narrower senses to distinguish particular genres; but the broader, fluid usage persisted because it captured the conviction that all narrative (and indeed dramatic) genres belong to a genus in which stories mean something more or other than immediately or literally appears. Secret writers and their establishment academic or belletrist antagonists agreed on this. They differed in the kinds of "foreign meanings" they taught readers to look for, and in whether their published writings showed readers how to uncover these for themselves.

As representative of academic-belletrist-formalists, we might take James Beattie's "On Fable and Romance," which was "first composed" as "part of a Course of Prelections" in "Moral Science" that he gave university students at Aberdeen.[36] Beattie divided fables into two major categories, each subdivided again. The first category, "Allegorical Prose Fable," included Aesop, Xenophon's *Cyropedia* and *The Arabian Nights* as well as "Fabulous Historical Allegory," which "exhibits real history disguised by feigned names, and embellished with fictional adventures," to convey political, moral and/or religious doctrines in serious, comic or satirical mode. The latter was exemplified in modern times by John Arbuthnot's *The History of John Bull* (1712), John Bunyan's *Pilgrim's Progress* (1678) and Jonathan Swift's *Gulliver's Travels* (1726) and *A Tale of a Tub* (1704). The second category, "Poetical Prose Fables," which Beattie equated with "Romance," included the old chivalric romances, seventeenth-century French romances and "modern romances" which we call novels, such as Samuel Richardson's *Clarissa* (1748), Henry Fielding's *Tom Jones* (1749) and Tobias Smollett's *Roderick Random* (1748) (2: 241, 250). The principal difference between the two categories lay in the manner in which they were read: "In reading Allegorical Prose Fable, we attend not only to the fictitious events that occur in the narrative, but also to those real events that are typified in the Allegory; whereas in Poetical Prose Fable we attend only to the events that are before us"(2: 249). But "Poetical Prose Fable" or "Romance" was in reality also "connected with many topics of importance, which would throw (if fully illustrated) great light upon the history and politics, the manners and the literature, of these latter ages" (2: 250). For, from "little tales" like Aesop's to the "higher sorts of fable" in modern novels or romance, stories were designed for the "rude multitude [who] cannot readily comprehend a moral or political doctrine," to "illustrate that doctrine by a fable, in order to make them attend, and understand it" (2: 234). Romances too meant something beyond "the events that are before us." As his division between allegorical and poetical fables showed, Beattie assumed that his students knew to read some kinds of texts "allegorically" for the "moral or political doctrine" they concealed, and that he need only demonstrate that "romances," which they read only for the story, contained "doctrines" too. Beattie therefore gave a lengthy explanation of the moral and political doctrines embedded in chivalric romance, which he related politically to feudalism and the crusades, and morally to concepts of social justice and cultural attitudes to women. But when he came to modern romance, he was careful *not* to "fully illustrate." It was Beattie's job, after all, to avoid "matters of doubtful disputation" and "guard [young minds] against the influence of bad principles" (1: ix). Here Beattie spoke only of moral doctrine, and that in purely individual and fictional terms – was Lovelace in Richardson's *Clarissa* represented as evil enough, or Grandison in *Sir Charles Grandison* represented as likeable enough, to inspire readers to choose virtue over vice? Were Smollett's novels indecent or obscene? All mention of the contemporary political system, of contemporary political doctrines, and contemporary concepts of social justice was avoided, to confine moral doctrine to questions of personal conduct. The message was no less political for that: forget about politics and the State; let each person look to their own morals, and cultivate their own garden. Or as Blake would put it with bitter irony, "Let all do their duty, and none need fear harm."

By contrast, in a cheap pamphlet of fewer than twenty pages designed for the popular market and for "Persons of the meanest Capacity," *The Art of Railing at Great Men* (1723) gave detailed "Rules" for reading and writing three kinds of "political raillery." Its anonymous author explained that these were rules to which writers had resorted since antiquity whenever "a Man…cannot talk or write Treason without incurring the Penalty of the Laws," and that they would be welcome to his "brethren" now that "Suspension of Habeas Corpus" made it particularly "unsafe" for them to express "unpopular" views.[37] The first and "most ancient" kind of political railing was "the fabulous or allegorical Mode," which had often been used against courts and court favorites because "the Ambiguity or double Entendre of a Fable raises the Curiosity of every Reader, to discover the secret Sting which it contains" (12). The allusion here was apparently to Horace and to contemporary secret histories. The fabulous or allegorical mode also inhabited other genres: animal fables like Aesop's, which used "merry stories" about animals "to reflect upon the Great Men of his Country" (for example, a minister of state was easily metamorphosed into a sly fox, set over an honest flock of sheep to guard them from dogs, but intent on their destruction); and fables in which "Virtues, Vices and Passions" are transformed into "Imaginary Persons" who "talk and act in such a Manner as the Great Ones whom they would expose, are said to do" (13). Manley's *Atlantis* (1709), Butler's *Hudibras* (1674–8) and Arbuthnot's *John Bull* (1712) were the modern examples here.

The second mode of railing was the "Ironical or Mock Panegyrick." Here one gave "ludicrous Approbation" to what others complained of or "banter[ed] on a Publick Proceeding which [was] generally applauded" by "giv[ing] it another turn." For instance, if money or provisions were scarce, one thanked God and the Ministry for the plenty the country enjoyed; if a war was accepted as unavoidable, one praised the "Knight Errantry" of a ministry willing "to free *Foreign* Nations [from Tyranny], without any *selfish* Regard to Domestick Considerations" (16). What a speaker or writer praised or affirmed most vehemently or with the most apparent "sincerity" was thus to be read with the greatest suspicion, and something diametrically opposite understood. This covered texts which, as *The Speculator* put it, "disguised" their unorthodox or impious meaning "in the specious mask of worth and piety" to "defy or secretly evade the powerful arm of Justice."[38]

Finally, there was the "Historical" mode of political railing that was "at present very much in vogue," which consisted of "drawing Parallels" between past political figures and events and present ones (16). The existence of parallels could be signaled in different ways: an author might adapt his description of public crimes, weak princes and corrupt statesmen in a past period to "modern Incidents," and thus "insinuate against the Great Men of his time and place." Or an author might use *recusatio* – "positively affirm that our present Ministers are guilty of none of the Crimes before mentioned" or "close with a declaration that what has been said bears only on former Reigns and other Countries" (17, 18) – to induce readers to compare past and present and discover parallels or similarities for themselves. This pamphleteer supplied a *recusatio* of his own: "the last but most useful mode [of political railing] is the fictitious mode which alarms with imaginary Dangers and designs of the writer's own Invention" (18). John Barrell has discussed the use of this *topos*, "alarms at imaginary dangers," by Jacobins and anti-Jacobins during the 1790s.[39] But here it directed readers to the pamphlet's own ambiguous language and design, to prompt reflection and judgment: What was imaginary here? Was political railing "*Treason*?" Who thought so? Did political railers resemble Lucifer "stirring up rebellion" against "God and his angelic ministers" by "pretending their beatific Liberties were in Danger?" (5). Did this historical parallel with its Miltonic overtones – which made King George, God, and his minister, Walpole (currently presiding over the South Sea Bubble as well as suspension of *Habeas Corpus*), an angel – really hold? Who thought so? *Was* the danger to men's beatific liberties more "imaginary" or "invented" than the "alarms" that obliged writers to conceal their political meanings in fables and history?

Neither Beattie's nor this anonymous pamphleteer's taxonomies hold up well upon examination. For instance, parallel history was deployed by fictional as well as true histories, and in dramatic as well as narrative fables. This could be wickedly effective because, as *The Doctrine of Insinuation* observed of Walpole's recognition of himself in the character of Macheath in *The Beggar's Opera*: "No Person in the Universe ever did or ever will understand any Person to be meant under a *Parallel* that has not the least Resemblance, Similitude or Affinity to his character" (14). The great man who publicly took offense stood publicly self-confessed as being like the offending character. The use of parallel history in dramatic fables to convey criticisms or political messages unwelcome to the Great also had a long history – one has only to think of Queen Elizabeth's recognition of herself as Richard II in Shakespeare's play when it was performed on the eve of the Essex rebellion. Here, as in secret history, "Parallel History" became almost indistinguishable from "the Fabulous or Allegorical Mode" long used against courts and court favorites.

But whether or not their categories hold up, Beattie and this pamphleteer were using print to guide readers in two characteristically different directions. Like the academic belletrists discussed in Chapter 3, Beattie was describing the formal features of different kinds of writing in general terms, while placing some within a generalized moral and political historical context, and delivering his judgment of the quality and morality of others. The pamphleteer, by contrast, was informing "Persons of the meanest Capacity" which genres were currently being used most frequently to convey "unpopular" ideas, how to recognize them, and which elementary reading strategies to deploy to decode their political messages: "read allegorically, dear reader, read for irony, read for historical parallels or similitudes – oh, and look out for 'hints' (as in *recusatio*)."

These were reading strategies that readers imbibed from their grammars. As we saw in Chapter 1, grammars were heavily weighted towards analogical substitution: one learned to look for similitudes or parallels between signs, syllables or words that were otherwise different. One learned that signs, syllables or words that were connected by similitude could be substituted for one other in that regard. Beginning readers substituted one analogical letter for another to learn new alphabets, and different words with similar functions or declensions for one another in "Analogy" or parts of speech. Substituting one word, sign or phrase for another – a known for an unknown, an unknown for a known, what was understood for what was expressed or what was stated for what was elided – was key to the act of comprehension. In parsing, for instance, one translated what was expressed in obscure complex sentences into simpler and more easily understood words and structures, by substituting analogical words and structures for those on the page. And as *The Monthly Review* pointed out, "irony is but another species of substitution."[40] As we saw too, spellers and grammars not only privileged fables for reading exercises; they taught beginning readers that in all tropes "one thing is expressed, and another understood"; and that fables, like allegories and parables, worked this way too, expressing one thing that another might be understood. "Keys" to secret histories might have to be circulated for provincial or non-elite readers, who did not hear enough court or town gossip to spot the similitudes; but even "unlearned" readers could be expected to know how to use those "keys" to substitute real names and events for the fictional ones on the page. Secret writing in fables, secret histories, romances, satirical narratives, or parallel histories, did not, *as such*, require higher order reading and interpretation skills than could be acquired from a grammar book for their fundamental mechanisms to be understood and deployed.

Consequently, fables were used throughout the century as vehicles for communicating abstract "Truth" and "doctrine" to readers of all sorts. "Aesopian" fables, with their speaking animals or animated things, and their characteristic "brevity," "simplicity," and everyday scenes, were particularly useful because they were familiar from schoolbooks and miscellanies designed for beginning readers, and because their characteristically "familiar language" made them relatively easy to understand. Aesopian fables were therefore deployed by writers for the popular market as well as by schoolmasters; by now canonical authors, such as Dryden, Mandeville, Swift, Gay and Henry Fielding, as well as by anonymous "hacks"; and by seditious opponents as well as supporters of monarchy, ministries and the established Church, from the Jacobites at the turn of the eighteenth century to the Jacobins and popularizing reformers at the turn of the nineteenth.[41] However, what Beattie said about "poetic fables" like *Clarissa* also held for "allegorical fables" like the *Arabian Nights*, *Gulliver's Travels* or Aesop's fables: these could be read just for the story too. The practice therefore developed of affixing a "detached or explicit moral" at the beginning or end of Aesopian fables in the knowledge that "a leading Thought…puts the reader in a proper track; he knows the game he pursues." Once told what it was, the reader would seek and find the moral indicated to him/her, "interwoven with [the] Fables."[42] This taught readers how to read beyond "what is expressed" to "what is understood"; but it also enabled masters and preceptors to keep them in "the proper track" of "universal truths" that bore on moral conduct: the fable of "The Dog and his Shadow" demonstrated "the disappointment that frequently attends an excessive desire for accumulation," "The Frog and Ox," the ruinous nature of ambition. In America, where British collections of Aesopian fables had been reissued since 1777, printers appropriated this technique for their paratexts to reprinted British novels. During the repressive 1790s, printers resorted to adding or changing subtitles, descriptions of contents on the title page, advertisements or other prefatory material in reprinted British texts to introduce "leading Thoughts" about how they might be understood differently, as interventions in controversial contemporary American political debates.[43] American printers thus put their readers on the track of reading carefully selected British stories as fables, or allegories for American events.

Following Sir Roger L'Estrange's *Fables of Aesop and other Eminent Mythologists*, which was reprinted twelve times between 1694 and 1738, all collections in English translation of fables by Aesop and other "Aeseopian" writers such as Phaedrus or Pilpey also included "morals and reflections" that were "adapted to all capacities," including "the meanest." But these commercial collections for the popular market used their prefaces, or sometimes an inserted "Essay on Fable," to denaturalize "detached or explicit morals" bearing on individual conduct, by making it clear both that the moral in Aesopian fables was political and squarely directed at men in power, and that the same fables were capable of different interpretations. Robert Dodsley's *Select Fables of Esop and Other Fabulists*, which was reprinted at least 27 times between 1761 and 1800, six of them in Philadelphia, observed that the morals one found in books under his name were not Aesop's: "Esop universally rejected any separate Moral." These "morals" were factitious later additions, and mutually contradictory besides: "Those we now find at the close of his Fables, were placed there by other Hands" and "different Expositors have given quite opposite interpretations." Rather than constituting an aid to understanding what Aesop really meant, the "morals" affixed to his fables – including those bearing on their conduct that readers had learned in their schoolbooks – were foreign incrustations, neither consistent with one another nor authoritative in themselves.[44]

Samuel Croxall's *Fables of Aesop and Others*, which was reprinted at least 43 times between 1722 and 1800, three of them in Philadelphia, made the same point by attacking L'Estrange's "morals and reflections" for their "pernicious Principles, promoting Popery and arbitrary Power," and by arguing instead that Aesop "takes all Occasions to recommend a Love of Liberty, and an Abhorrence of Tyranny and all arbitrary Proceedings." Liberty for Aesop meant "Liberty in a Political Sense," but L'Estrange's "morals and reflections" had twisted Aesop's "insinuations" to suit his Filmerian party-political affiliations. Believing that "children in Britain should be taught to cherish, love and vindicate Liberty," Croxall was taking Aesop back – and demonstrating in the process that "morals" couched in the language of universal truth disguised party and politics. Other Aesopian volumes achieved a similar result by indicating on their title pages or in their Prefaces that their editor-translators had new-minted the morals and reflections: "we have corrected both the Fable and the Moral Part"; *Aesop's Fables with Instructive Morals and Reflections. Designed to promote Religion and Universal Benevolence, to which are added Suitable Reflections to each Fable in Verse*.[45] *Fables Moral and Political,* supposedly translated from the Dutch of Pieter de la Court and appearing without a publisher's name, not only stated that de la Court had "explained them after [a] new manner," but that readers ought to do the same: "From all times, many Wise and Learned Men have drawn many and very different Lessons from them... Nevertheless many new Instructions that naturally flow from the same Fables, may daily be discover'd; and we know besides that every Man is at Liberty to do as we have done; and to interpret them in the manner he pleases, and draw such Inferences from them as he shall think fit."[46] By century's end, Vicesimus Knox and others were drily observing that the interpretative tasks that Aesop's Fables demanded were beyond the ability of children; Aesop's fables "are fitter for men than for children" and were indeed "originally addressed to men."[47]

Because Aesop's commercial translator-editors created their own "morals and reflections," made "new" interpretative translations to accord with these, sometimes significantly altered the original texts to suit this "moral," and often included fables of their own making among the ancient ones, they also included themselves among what they called "the fabulists." As Allan Ramsay put it in 1722, "good Judgments will allow such Imitations to be Originals formed upon the *Idea* of another."[48] This practice also figured in fabulists' use of parallel history in their prefaces and essays, to explain the properly subversive and/or corrective political functions of Aesopian fables.

Several fabulists presented the life of Aesop that was usually affixed to commercial collections of his fables as parallel history. La Motte, for instance, openly stated that Aesop's life was to be read as a fable that had modern parallels. As a slave Aesop dared not speak truth to his master without taking the precaution of presenting "his Philosophy in Disguise." Modern "Fabulists" (like La Motte himself who had dedicated his volume to the King of France) were likewise in the position of "slaves, who are willing to instruct [their reader/s] without making them angry." Another slave, the Roman fabulist Phaedrus "was not afraid with his Fables to interweave a History of his time" because presented in "a Fable [which] did not consist absolutely in Fiction…the History itself becomes an Allegory." Pilpay, a slave even as Chief Minister to the mighty Emperor of Indostan, likewise "lock'd up all his Politicks" in his fables, thereby showing that "we always see Slavery confirmed in the Honour of begetting a Fable."[49] Fables, which conveyed political doctrines and criticisms unwelcome to men in power in disguised, entertaining forms, were in all times and places the mark and method of the unfree; paradoxically, this was also how they "breathed Liberty in a Political Sense." De la Court made similar points through the parallel history of fabulists in "Eastern Nations" who "liv'd for the most part under Tyrants and Usurpers, whom they fear'd to irritate and offend, that they might not subject themselves to the lash of their Fury" (n.p.). Secured by clandestine publication and a foreign attribution, this republican-leaning fabulist made the modern political analogue explicit: "Not to speak of past Ages, we may observe that Monarchical Government has, in the Age in which we live, made such Progress both in Church and State, to the Oppression of many free Republicks, that if the Tyrants continue to tread the same Paths but for one Age longer, all the liberal Arts and Sciences, all Virtue, and the Liberties and Properties of Men, will throughout all Europe dwindle away." His pseudonym, "of the Court," intimated that he spoke of all courts, including the British one, not just of "Europe." In *Aesop: Truth in Fiction or Morality in Masquerade*, "Edmund Arwarker" (Awaker) used historical parallels from the Bible to demonstrate how "the wise" told truth to power: because "the "depraved…cannot endure a light that shows them their own deformity," the prophet Nathan did not openly reprove King David for the murder of Uriah, but told him the parable of a poor man deprived of his ewe lamb by his rich neighbor, bringing David to sentence the criminal before realizing that he himself was the man. Joab used a parable to tell the usurper, Absalom, "what he durst not mention in plain terms." Jotham too conveyed God's unwillingness for the Israelites to appoint an earthly king through the parable of trees who desired a king: finding that all the fruitful trees declined the office because they were more fruitful in their present stations, they promoted a useless and worthless Thorn to the throne instead. Aesop used his fables like this, as did "all Fables [that] have since come under the Shelter of his name."[50] It is worth noting that British schoolmasters' books of rhetoric presented Jotham's shockingly anti-monarchical tree parable as an example of allegory with surprising frequency, whether to hint at fables' political uses or at these educators' true political leanings, it is hard to say.

Aesopian fabulists repeatedly insisted that "it is the very business of Fable to beget Truth in the *Mind* of those who hear it," and that explicit statements of the moral were antithetical to the genre because they made "the precept direct and obvious, contrary to the nature and end of Allegory" which is "to give it birth in the Mind of the person for whom it is intended." Fables, they said, give precepts "birth" in the mind of the "discerning reader," rather than on the page, by leaving him/her to find out what the fable "insinuates" for him/herself. Fables "leave the reader to collect the moral" by "mak[ing] the Comparison" between the "common circumstances" that the fable recounts and "his own Affairs or those of Others." Fables were a "polite manner of instructing" because they taught readers as if they taught them not: rather than assuming an insulting "superiority of wisdom," they "gratified" the reader's "self-love" by giving him the pleasurable feeling of superiority that comes from "discover[ing] more than is shown him."[51] This served fabulists well, as William Pittis pointed out: "If anything in this Performance reminds the World of some unjustifiable Proceedings and Occurrences, it is the Fault of the Times, and not of the Author."[52] By displacing the meaning of occurrences from the text describing past or fictitious events to "the Times" in which it was read, fabulists shifted seditious judgments of present ministries and policies from the author to the mind of readers who "found out" parallels or similitudes between the text and the times. It was again all about how the text was read.

However, following Quintilian, the learned had made a distinction between "pure" and "mixed" allegories, that was now adapted and applied to readers of different abilities. In pure allegories, no mention is made of the text's real referent; in mixed allegories, words (such as real place names or other hints) are introduced to add "perspicuity," and clue readers in to what is meant. The meaning of pure allegories was hard to discern and easily overlooked, it often had to be transmitted by word of mouth, or by exegists like Quintilian himself. Consequently, those addressing the multitude were advised to "mix" their allegories "with words that make it clear and intelligible."⁵³ Considering readers "of all capacities" in the popular market, Aesopian fabulists agreed that "every story is not capable of telling its own moral." It was necessary to "show enough for the less acute" or even to ensure that the moral is somewhere "expressly introduced."⁵⁴ "Mixed" allegories, which showed enough for the less acute and those with the meanest capacities to discover what was meant, extended the fable's potential readership beyond the better educated, more informed, or better prepared. Mixing in hints of the presence of under-meanings and/or indications of their substance, permitted the fable's hidden or seditious political messages to spread.

Seditious fabulists did make efforts to show the public how to use allegory and modern parallels to reinterpret ancient texts other than Aesop's in terms of modern events. Quintilian, whose example of "pure allegory" was Horace's Ode 14, which described a ship tossed by storms at sea after leaving port, had explained that "by a ship [Horace] means the Commonwealth; by the agitations of the stormy seas, civil wars; by a harbor, peace and concord."⁵⁵ In 1715, in the wake of George I's ascension to the throne and of another Jacobite uprising, an anonymous author published *Horace's Allegorical Advice to the People of Rome. Being an Essay on the 14th Ode of the First Book of Horace with the Allegory explained.* The contents of this sixteen page pamphlet which sold for 3d began with Horace's Latin text, followed by a literal verse translation which began: "O Ship new Billows which surround thee roar/Will drive to the Ocean from the Shore; O what art thou doing?" (9). So far, it could be taken for a crib for schoolboys. The literal translation was followed by a verse translation of the allegorical meaning, beginning, "O Commonwealth, these new Intestine Jars/Will bring about your former Civil Wars/Why do not these unnatural factions Cease?" (13). This very free translation of the literal meaning explained the heading, "To the People of Rome, That are going the ready Way to enter upon a fresh CIVIL WAR." The allegorical translation was in turn followed by a modern letter about a lost battle at sea, that was prefaced by the following "hint": "Horace, in the foregoing Ode, having compared the Government of Kingdoms and Commonwealths to that of a Ship, it was thought not improper to subjoin the following letter sent to a Friend…the work of one not unacquainted with Horace's Allegorical Way of Writing" (17). The letter too was to be read allegorically, on the model provided by the author's allegorical reading of Horace and in the context of that reading. Read in this way, the modern letter about ships lost and sunk during an inept admiral's recent defeat in battle might be understood to mean that the poorly captained ship of state was sinking under strife and civil wars, or that, directed by inept leaders, the Jacobites' leaky and unseaworthy vessels (forces) were now sunk or floundering on the "rocks of despair," their civil war betrayed and lost.

Writers were still using and teaching readers to understand seditious historical parallelism at the turn of the nineteenth century. Michael Scrivener has shown that "popularizing texts was an important British Jacobin tactic in the 1790s to give artisans and others access to ideas and writings...outside their social experience." His example is John Thelwall's republication of Walter Moyle's *An Essay upon the Constitution of the Roman Republic*. Thelwall re-titled this *Democracy Vindicated*, and supplied a Preface and explanatory notes which functioned as "running commentary guiding the reading" to the text's modern political applications. To avoid prosecution, Moyle had himself used the Roman Republic as a parallel for England; this enabled Thelwall to use "double distancing" in his "parallel reference points": Republican Rome, Republican England, Moyle's post 1688 England and Thelwall's revolutionary present.[56] According to Tilottama Rajan, the canonical British Romantic poets likewise deployed allegory and parallel history extensively. Magnifying irony into an ontology and "hermeneutics of reversal," they doubled their disguise by burying all in discontinuous texts which "derealized" the author's full meaning and left that to the reader to psyche out.[57]

As these examples show, all "mixed" fabulists were not equally clear; they masked their meanings and preserved the protective obscurity of their texts to different extents. One might hypothesize that those secret writers who were most anxious to reach the most unlearned segments of the populace were also those who put themselves most at risk of apprehension by government censors, by making what they were doing or saying most easily intelligible. But there was another imperative at work here too. Seditious fabulists needed "mixed allegories" to alert readers to their unorthodox political or religious positions because they were inhabiting the same genre, and indeed the same texts, as their pro-establishment antagonists. The danger that mixed allegorizing sought to avert was that secret writers who disguised themselves as their "other" might also be mistaken for their other and thus help to underpin the very political or religious regimes they hoped to undermine. This was a problem for secret writers in all genres. Murray Pittock showed that Hanoverian and secret Jacobite writers inhabited and contested the meaning of the same songs (God save the King), the same symbols (the oak), and the same classical texts (Virgil's *Aeneid*).[58] And we not only acknowledge that "Jacobin" and "anti-Jacobin" novelists used the same literary *topoi* and devices in the same generic space, but have discovered that "Jacobin" novels can be read as "anti-Jacobin," and vice versa.[59]

As with irony, readers could learn to recognize and read fabulous political allegory and parallel history from pamphlet polemics. Here too their seditious hidden meanings were unmasked and articulated by indignant antagonists in ways that also explained how they worked. A pamphlet hostile to *The Craftsman* complained, for instance, that in that periodical, "All *History*, ancient and modern, was ransacked for the Names of disgraced Statesmen; whose Stories were severally tortur'd and forced into *Parallels*, and the Ministry from time to time pull'd down or executed in pretended Effigy, in a hundred different Tales, either Historical or Allegorical… *Examples* are produced of *Ministers* disgraced, of *Princes* dethroned, and Parliaments themselves oppos'd, by direct Arms, and popular Insurrections; interspersed here and there with the most pathetic *Lamentations* over the sinking State, as they represent it, of our whole *Constitution*, and strong *Innuendo's* that *like Circumstances* require *like Remedies*."[60] *The Doctrine of Innuendo's Discuss'd*, which defended *The Craftsman*, was almost as helpful. It used denials that any historical parallels were intended, to specify exactly where the modern parallels lay. But having pointed to the threats, fines and ministerial prosecutions that had "forced Caleb and his Assistants to have recourse to Allegories and History," this pamphleteer added a parallel history of his own: "Almost every schoolboy knows that the *Phillipicks* of Demosthenes were wrote to warn his Countrymen of the Danger they were in from the Attempts openly made upon their Liberties by Philip of Macedon, which differ from those of *The Craftsman* only in that his writings are not leveled against a Sovereign Prince, but a rapacious Minister."[61] He was willing to admit seditious libel (against a minister), but not treason (against the sovereign) in order to make the familiar point that "Allegories and History" were the last resort of the persecuted and unfree, thus themselves evidence of the Attempts made upon the people's liberties that they warned the people about.

Aesopian fabulists quite often indicated that what they wrote about fable held not only for apologues, parables and histories, but for romances too. While agreeing in *Sensus Communis* that "the chief theme and subject" of "the fabulous author" was "manners and the moral part" (63), Shaftesbury, in his brilliant way, gave this idea what would prove another, equally productive turn. He "unraveled" the Platonic equivalence of morality and aesthetics, the idea that "all beauty is truth" (65), by relegating this exclusively to "the fabulist" who does not paint any *"particular…*object of nature" (67) – there were no beautiful truths for those considering the particulars of nature or society. Society in particular had been perverted by the pervasiveness of informers and domestic spies (48, 58), and by a "standard of politeness and good sense" which, together, ensured that men were held "accountable" not only for "their actions and behavior" but for "their opinions too" (39). As "agreement" spread from the Court to the Town, and from courtiers to gentry, professionals and the middling sort "that there was only one certain and true dress, one single peculiar air, to which it was necessary all people should conform" (39–40), "counterfeit vizards" were everywhere put upon "the face of truth" (40). Polite society began to resemble "a Carnival" where "every creature wore a mask," and only the naively barefaced looked ridiculous (39). In the political realm, the secrecy with which rulers conducted their business was mirrored by the secrecy of conspirators. But in the social realm, secrecy pervaded the culture and the everyday through manners and prudential good sense. Jon Snyder showed that in the courtly and diplomatic culture of sixteenth- and seventeenth-century elites, where "a common metaphor for dissimulation…was the mask" and "the art of good manners amount[ed] to nothing other than the skilful practice of dissimilation," courtiers concealed self-interest and ambition, as well as their real thoughts, desires and designs, under "a pleasing and sincere countenance." They practiced "sprezzatura," the art of concealing art under an appearance of natural ease, in the knowledge that any sign of "affectation" (simulation) would give them away.[62] When the courtesy of courts was translated into the politeness of assemblies, coffee houses, and tea-tables, this feature carried over, to the point where, as Jenny Davidson showed, hypocritical dissimulation came to be regarded as an essential component of good manners; it was telling the truth to a person's face that became uncivil.[63]

Consequently, looking at the society around him at mid-century, Henry Fielding, could only echo Shaftesbury: "while the crafty and designing part of mankind, consulting only their own separate advantage, endeavour to maintain one constant imposition on others, the whole world becomes a vast masquerade, where the greatest part appear disguised under false visors and habits," and the "very few only showing their own faces become, by doing so, the astonishment and ridicule of all the rest."[64] Irony and "mimicry" – saying one thing and meaning another, impersonating the words and opinions of a character acceptable to society – were only sardonic twists on the manners of the polite, who said what was agreeable to others while concealing what they really thought, and controlled the betraying motions of their bodies to conform to "one single particular air." As Fielding's principal novels demonstrated, in a masquerading world such as this, it was those who gave themselves away by "affectation" and "those who showed their own faces" who made themselves ridiculous. Similarly, when Eliza Haywood turned her attention from the court to the town, she called her amatory fiction "secret history" because she was doing for the town what she and others had done for the court: display the vicious intrigues and scandalous sexual conduct masked by outward proprieties, and reveal the passions, cunning and self-interest dissembled by the language of compliment and courtship, in order to "prepare" the barefaced, credulous and unwary for what Shaftesbury called "a right practice of the world or a just knowledge of men and things" (57). As some modern critics have argued (but in Shaftesbury's words), she "led" women readers "through the labyrinth of the affections" and "render[ed] this music of the passions more powerful and enchanting" (63) to show them that "the only poison to reason is passion" and that "false reasoning is soon redressed where passion is removed" (43).

As we saw in Chapter 4, the scandalous, sensational secret was central to the familiar novel in all its forms. The explicit generic promise of "secret histories" and "histories of private life" to discover what others kept private – in the contemporary sense of "secret" and "removed from public view" (OED) – attracted curiosity about what could not be "conveniently told"; and by arousing curiosity, drew readers in. But like other fables, romances and novels might also create "under-meanings" and rely on what Shaftesbury called "the spirit of curiosity which would force a discovery of more truth than can conveniently be told" (30) to discover the presence of a political and/or social agenda that differed from, or contradicted, the work's expressed "moral." Novels which told what Samuel Jackson Pratt called *Family Secrets* also frequently used family secrets as what Shaftesbury called a "kind of defensive raillery" (30) – a screen to conceal the fact that they were arguing something more or other than the secret that immediately appeared, and relying on the reader's "spirit of curiosity" to "force a discovery of more truth than can conveniently be told." Thanks to the long-standing analogy between the family and the State, reflections on the hidden evils or corruptions of the family could be construed as insinuations about the State. Stories about contemporary Britain could be masked as "historical" or relocated to a European country. Fantastically improbable causalities could be devised to discredit the conventional distribution of poetic justice and decorously happy endings. Carefully scattered observations and contradictory scenes could be introduced to profile the overtly exemplary narrative as "maintain[ing] what is commonly believ'd, or profess[ing] what is publicly injoin'd," rather than what the author "really thinks." The novel's "general plan" of analogical characters and/or scenes could contain hints, and lead to reflections, more radical or reformist than its moralizing suggested. The didactic, sentimental and Gothic novel's standard practice of representing "the beauties of a [virtuous] human soul" against "proper foils and contrarieties" (63) could be used to transmit a subtext that contradicted the narrative's apparent reaffirmation of the *sensus communis* about the proper lady's conduct, place and roles.

Here again there were at least two main ways to play this, and many in between. Godwin shows us one. During the 1790s, when "Terror was the order of the day, and it was feared that even the humble novelist might be shown to be constructively a traitor," Godwin used novels himself to disguise "a general view of the modes of domestic and unrecorded despotism by which man becomes the destroyer of man."[65] He made a key distinction between the "moral" and the "tendency" of stories as part of an apparently innocent argument against parental (or state) censorship. Godwin defined "the moral of any work" as "that ethical sentence to the illustration of which the work may most aptly be applied," observing that, like "the formal and regular moral frequently annexed to Esop's fables of animals," this was often "one of the last inferences that occur to you" when you examine the story for yourself. "Tendency" was a word borrowed from those who attacked novels for their vicious, leveling, or anarchic "tendency." Godwin redefined "Tendency" as "the actual effect [the work] is calculated to produce upon the reader,"[66] and emphasized that this could be entirely different from the "moral." Indeed, he made the (rallying) argument that "Experiment" showed not only that a work's tendency might differ from "the moral contemplated by the Author," but that a book with a good moral might have a bad "tendency," and vice versa. For instance, Homer's moral design in the *Iliad* was to give "an example of the fatal consequences of discord among political elites"; but the epic's most "conspicuous" tendency had been to "enhance the false luster of military achievements and perpetuate the noxious race of heroes in the world." Good moral, bad tendency. Conversely, the moral deduced from the tragedy, *The Fair Penitent*, by one set of readers concerned the mischievous effects of unlawful love, and women's duty to obey their fathers' and husbands' will in all things; but there were readers who understood the tendency of this play as "a powerful satire" on the social institutions and modes of thinking currently afflicting the female sex. Works with a bad moral might have a very positive tendency if read "ironically," against the grain of their overt moral, for the "tendency" they concealed.

Consequently "Liberty" in reading and learning meant enabling people, even in early childhood, to read what they chose and judge its tendency for themselves. It meant leaving their "various reading to lead [them] into new trains of thinking," without a "censor" or preceptor to do "violence to the volition and individual judgment of the persons" involved.[67] Godwin thus used the word "tendency" – now meaning both "the effect," different from its overt moral, that a work "was *calculated* to produce on a reader," and the effect it had on readers who read it "ironically" against the grain – to describe and further open the space of liberty that remained to writers and readers under censorship. Liberty meant that the tendency of a work would be "various according to the various tempers and habits of the persons by whom the work is considered" – some readers would certainly read stories in traditional, orthodox and dogmatic ways. But other seditious or unorthodox possibilities nevertheless remained, which readers could learn to adduce, for here again, "Everything depends on the spirit in which [works] are read."[68]

In devising his "key to open scripture metaphors," Reverend Benjamin Keach took the opposite line. Addressing metaphor, irony and allegory as rhetorical issues at the beginning of his *Tropologia*, he showed that one could never be quite sure what any of these figures really meant, even or perhaps especially in Scripture. Keach defined allegory, conventionally, as an extended metaphor or continued irony, which partook of the difficulties each involved. His taxonomy showed that, considered rhetorically, the problem with irony was that this was not only a matter of saying things that are "manifestly false and spoken with an [obvious] Intention to deceive" – that would be fairly straightforward. Instead, in irony, "some things are spoken feignedly" but "uttered by Way of Trial"; "Some things are dissemblingly and hypocritically spoken which are true in themselves, but not conformable to the Mind of the Speaker"; and "there are some things where there seems to be an Irony, but when the thing is more exactly considered, there is none." There was no single "key" at any level of the ironic text that one could rely upon to determine which pertained. Similarly "one Metaphor may be brought to signify many things." For instance, Christ was called a Lion because he was "noble, heroic and unconquerable"; but the Devil was called a Lion too, because both were "roaring, rapacious and devouring" and so were Tyrants because they are "fierce...and cruel to other Men, as the Lion is to weaker Creatures." There was no "key" that would always open any metaphor. It therefore came down to how metaphors were read: "There must be great *Care* and *Accuracy* used to find out the *Reason* of the Similitude, and the *Scope* or *Intention* of the Comparison,

lest there may be an *Aberration* from the proper Coherence of the Text, or
from the *Analogy* of Faith."[69] This could not be left to the common reader,
or even to most clerics, for "metaphors" could be "falsely used" and people
reading Scriptures "without Grace" could "prove a dangerous Enemy to
the Christian Religion." What was required was an authoritative reader
like Keach – who, as several divines testified, could be relied upon to "steer
clear of the horrid Scylla of Antinomian Doctrines on the one Hand, as of
the gloomy Charybdis of Armenian Tenets on the other" – to "explain and
find out the true Sense of Meaning of the Holy Scriptures" and read them
in other Protestants' and other clerics' place.[70]

NOTES

1 Quoted in Patterson, *Censorship and Interpretation*: 14.
2 John Locke, *Some Thoughts Concerning Education* (5th edn., London, 1705).
3 Scrivener, *Seditious Allegories*: 11; Morton and Smith, *Radicalism*: 2, 26, 49.
4 Rabb, *Satire and Secrecy*: 34.
5 Ashley Marshall's felicitous term in *The Practice of Satire*.
6 Knights, *Representation and Misrepresentation in Later Stuart Britain*; Potter, *Secret Rites and Secret Writing*; Fox, "Rumour, News and Popular Opinion in Elizabethan and Early Stuart England"; Freist, *Governed by Opinion*; Hackel, *Reading Material in Early Modern England*.
7 Shaftesbury, *Sensus Communis* (London, 1709): 59. Other references to this volume will be in the text.
8 I rely in this paragraph on Norman Knox, *The Word Irony and its Context, 1500–1755*, and on the OED.
9 Shaftesbury described this elsewhere as "a Gravity not abhorrent from the use of…Mirth," and himself as assuming a "Middle Character" who combined "Jest" and "Ernest." In Klein, *Shaftesbury and the Culture of Politeness*: 96.
10 Knox, *Word Irony*: 181 and 193 ff.
11 Knox, *Word Irony*: 211.
12 Quoted in Backscheider, *Spectacular Politics*: 113.
13 William Pittis, *Aesop at the Bell-Tavern in Westminster* (London, 1711): Ar; [Anon] *The Doctrine of Innuendo Discuss'd* (London, 1731): 6; Anthony Collins, *A Discourse Concerning Ridicule and Irony* (London, 1729): 24; Skelton, *Ophiomaches* (London, 1749): 42; Peter Pindar, *Odes of Importance. To the Shoemakers. To Mr. Burke. To Irony. To the King…*(London, 1793); M. W. *The Sacred Outcry* (London, 1788): 175.
14 See, in addition to works cited below, Myers and Kerns (eds.), *Censorship and the Control of Print*; Ellenzweig, *Fringes of Belief*; Evans, *Debating the Revolution*; Patterson, *Reading Between the Lines*; Worrall, *Theatric Revolution*; Laerke, *Use of Censorship in the Enlightenment*.
15 Patterson, *Censorship*: 63, 11.
16 Robertson, *Censorship and Conflict*: 198, 1.

17 Hyland, "Richard Steele: Scandal and Sedition," in Hyland and Sammells (eds.), *Writing and Censorship in Britain*: 60 ff. For other examples, Smith (ed.), *Literature and Censorship*; McElligott, *Royalism, Print and Censorship*.

18 Quoted in Hamburger, "The Development of the Law of Seditious Libel and the Control of the Press": 731; and Scrivener, "John Thelwall and Popular Jacobin Allegory": 962.

19 *The British Journal*, # 6, October 27, 1722; *The Craftsman*, #228, November 14, 1730.

20 Zagorin, *Ways of Lying*: 11.

21 Thomas Gibbons, *Rhetoric: Or a View of its Principal Tropes and Figures* (London, 1767): 77–8. See also, John Ward, *A System of Oratory*, 2 vols. (London, 1754).

22 John Toland, *Clidophorus* (London, 1720): 94.

23 Henry Skelton, *The Candid Reader* (London, 1744): 17–18.

24 Eliza Haywood, *The Invisible Spy*, 4 vols. (London, 1755): I: 16; *Monthly Review*, December 1754, Article LXI: 498. Also Backscheider, "Shadow of an Author"; and Bannet, "The Narrator as Invisible Spy."

25 Anthony Blackwall, *Introduction to the Classics, Containing...Directions how to Study Them to Advantage* (London, 1737): 181.

26 [Anon] *Observations on a pamphlet entitled 'Christianity not founded on Argument'* (London, 1765): 46, 47.

27 *The Briton* (1724): 11.

28 *The Monthly Review*, # xxviii (1763): 25.

29 *The World*, # 80, July 11, 1754; and # 104, December 26, 1754 in Vol. III (1755–7): 101, 299–300.

30 Toland, *Clidophines*: 73, 69, 76.

31 Henry Skelton, *Ophiomaches* (London, 1749): 11, 326.

32 Sir Philip Sidney, "An Apology for Poetry," in *The Norton Anthology of Theory and Criticism*. Ed. Vincent Leitch. New York: Norton, 2001: 348.

33 Bullard, *Politics of Disclosure*: 6; also Bannet, "Secret History."

34 Bowers, *Force or Fraud*.

35 Robert Lowth, *Lectures on the Sacred Poetry of the Hebrews* (London, 1787): 214.

36 James Beattie, "Of Fable and Romance," in *Dissertations, Moral and Critical* (London, 1783): I: viii;. Subsequent page numbers will be in the text.

37 [Anon] *The Art of Railing at Great Men* (London, 1723): 18, 3. Other page numbers are in the text.

38 *The Speculator*, No. xxv, Saturday, June 19, 1790: 339.

39 Barrell, *Imagining the King's Death*: 4 ff. Also Essay VII (1766) in John Bethune, *Essays and Dissertations on Various Subjects*, 2 vols. (London, 1771): I: 42 ff.

40 *The Monthly Review*, February 1763, Vol XXVIII: 84.

41 For the "double tradition" in Aesopian fable, Loveridge, *History of Aesopian Fable*: Chap. 3; Lewis, *English Fable*; Noel, *Theories of Fable in the Eighteenth-Century*. For the subversive tradition, Patterson, *Fables of Power*; Marcus Wood, *Radical Satire*; Scrivener, *Seditious Allegories*.

42 [Dodsley's] *Select Fables of Esop and Other Fabulists. In Three Books* (London, 1761): xlviii, xlix.

43 Bannet, *Transatlantic Stories*, chaps. 2, 3, 4, 8.

44 [Dodsley] *Select Fables*: xlviii, xlix.

45 [Anon] *A New Translation of Aesop's Fables* (London, 1708): viii; [Joseph Jackson] *Aesop's Fables with Instructive Morals and Reflections* (London, 1775): Title page.

46 [Pieter de la Court] *Fables Moral and Political, with large Explications. Translated from the Dutch*, 2 vols. (London, 1703): n.p., images 23, 24.

47 Vicesimus Knox, *Winter Evenings: Lucubrations on Life and Letters*, 3 vols. (London 1788): 1: 175.

48 Allan Ramsay, *Fables and Tales* (Edinburgh, 1722): Advertisement.

49 [Antoine de La Motte] *A Hundred New Court Fables Written for the Instruction of Princes and True Knowledge of the World* (London, 1721): 16, 18, 64, 66.

50 [Edmund Arwaker, possibly John Churchill] *Aesop, Truth in Fiction; or Morality in Masquerade* (London, 1708): iii, v, vi.

51 [de La Motte] *A Hundred New Court Fables* (London, 1721): 22; [Dodsley] *Select Fables*, xlvii; [de la Court] *Fables Moral and Political*: n.p.

52 William Pittis, *Aesop at the Bell-Tavern* (London, 1711): Preface.

53 Quintilian, *Quintilian's Institutes of the Orator*, 2 vols. (London, 1774): 11, book 8, Chap. 6: 95, 97.

54 [Dodsley] *Select Fables*: xlix.

55 Quintilian, *Institutes*: 11: 95.

56 Scrivener, "John Thelwall and the Revolution of 1649": 128, 129.

57 Rajan, *Supplement of Reading*.

58 Pittock, *Poetry and Jacobite Politics*.

59 Grenby, *Anti-Jacobin Novel*; Wallace, *Revolutionary Subjects*.

60 [Anon] *An Address to the People of Great Britain; Occasioned by the Republication of the Craftsman* (London, 1731): 11, 15.

61 [Anon] *The Doctrine of Innuendo's Discuss'd; or the Liberty of the Press Maintain'd: being some Thoughts upon the Present Treatment of the Printer and Publishers of* The Craftsman (London, 1731): 5–6, 22.

62 Snyder, *Dissimulation and the Culture of Secrecy*: 6, quotations at 30, 99.

63 Davidson, *Hypocrisy and the Politics of Politeness*. For the transition from court to town, Bryson, *From Courtesy to Civility*.

64 Cited in Novak, *English Literature in the Age of Disguise*: 7, 1; Castle, *Masquerade and Civilization*.

65 Quoted in Miriam Wallace, *Revolutionary Subjects*: 43, 44.

66 *The Enquirer* (Edinburgh, 1823): Essay xv: 118, 121.

67 *Enquirer*: 130, 68.

68 *Enquirer*: 118, 122, 126.

69 Benjamin Keach, *Tropologia; a Key to Open Scripture Metaphors* (1682) (London, 1779): 192, 33, 34, 37.

70 Keach, *Tropologia*: ii, iii, 1, vi.

Afterword

Many a truth is spoken in jest. So it is with the elaborate jest, and *applicatio*, of manners of reading, in Fielding's two puppet-show chapters in *Tom Jones* that I conclude.

On one level, these chapters play with and on readers.

The situation is this: near a small rural inn where Tom is staying, the Puppet Master has performed a version of *The Provok'd Husband*, which had already "given great Satisfaction to all the Quality in every Town in England." This version of the play (which may have originated in Punch's theater at Covent Garden, once a favorite diversion of London's high society) eliminated all the "low Wit or Humour, or Jests" in the original drama, along with all the "low "characters and scenes (i.e. the servants), to preserve only upper-class characters and "the fine and serious Part." During the conversation about the play at the inn, which occupies the first chapter, the Puppet Master trots out all the mid-century belletristic commonplaces about the salutary impact and proper methods of didactic drama and fiction. He claims that this "serious" version of *The Provok'd Husband* supplies "rational Entertainment" which is "calculated to improve the Morals of young People"; that it conveys "good and instructive Lessons" through figures who "represent the Life in every particular"; and that it utilizes "the great Force of Example" to ensure that "the inferior Part of Mankind would be deterred from Vice, by observing how odious it was in their Superiors." As John Kerrigan has shown, awareness of reader diversity in taste, judgment and interpretation had been widespread in print culture at least since the Renaissance, when writers and editors subdivided their readerships into groups (courteous readers and captious readers, pretenders and understanders, gentlemen, ladies and merchants etc.) and sought to manage each group by including or addressing them in some way.[1] Fielding likewise includes the different reactions of different categories of hearers and readers. A "grave Matron" approves the adaptation, and plans to bring her daughters to see it in the belief that it is calculated to improve the morals of young people. An attorney's clerk, who saw the original play in London, approves the adaptation because his London acquaintances "are resolved to drive everything which is low from the stage." He and an exciseman both praise the characters of Lord and Lady Townley for being "highly in nature" to impress their interlocutors with their familiarity with the upper ranks as well as with their knowledge of the critical idiom. Only Tom disagrees: he thinks that the Puppet Master has spoiled his puppet-show by eliminating the traditional "low" characters of Punch and Judy (or Joan as she was then) and their traditional humorous plot.

In the second juxtaposed chapter, Grace – the maid at the inn whose mistress has called her a whore after catching her *in flagrante delicto* with Merry Andrew – understands the play quite differently from the matron, the Puppet Master, the excise man and the attorney's clerk: "If I am a Whore…my Betters are so as well as I. What was the fine Lady in the Puppet-show just now? I suppose she did not lie all Night out from her Husband for nothing." The landlady concludes from Grace's reaction that taking about "a Parcel of Puppets drest up like Lords and Ladies" only "turn[s] the Heads of poor Country Wenches," and that it would be better to go back to the days when puppet-shows consisted of "good Scripture stories." In these two scenes, therefore, the puppet-show is represented at once from the point of view of its production and from the point of view of its consumption, through the eyes of its immediate producer and through what a later period would call the *Weltanschauung* of a variety of types of consumer; the two are interlinked.

Fielding used mischievous stylistic cues to encourage extra-diegetic readers of these scenes, who are reading for the story, to side with the Puppet Master, the attorney's clerk and the exciseman in their "contempt" for Tom and for the wayward opinions of such ignorant countrywomen as Grace and the landlady. The scene in which the Puppet Master holds forth is itself presented as a "rational entertainment' rendered in "serious" mode, where arguments for the methods and impact of didactic literature are quite fully laid out, while the subsequent scene in which Grace and the landlady express their opinions is rendered in comic mode with little exposition. And where the Puppet Master's argument is identified with such authorities as the Quality and fashionable London, both of which lesser people and provincials were inclined to imitate, our hero, Tom, recognizes that he "can never maintain my Opinion against so many" and backs down. For a reader reading the text by these cues, the laughter is directed at Grace and the landlady for not knowing any better; and it produces that pleasant feeling of superiority over others which Hobbes said was invariably produced by humor and ridicule.

However, cued by Fielding's chapter title, "From which it may be inferred, that the best Things are liable to be misunderstood and misinterpreted," the classically educated reader could recognize in these scenes a modern exemplification of much repeated commonplaces from Horace and Seneca. Along with the notion that "our censures are as various as our Palats" so that what one person commends another condemns, these include the idea that "the venomous spider will sucke poison out of the most holesome herbe, and the industrious bee gather hony out of the most stinking weed."[2] Fielding was illustrating this last *sententia* by subjecting the Puppet Master's literary theory to experiment in the new scientific manner. In the second scene, he tests the didactic theory empirically, against the reaction of precisely the sort of person whose morals the Puppet Master boasted that his play was "calculated" to "improve": a "young person" belonging to "the inferior part of mankind." As Fielding's chapter title underscores, this empirical test demonstrated that Grace had sucked only poison (the discovery that ladies too were whores) from the supposedly wholesome herb of the adapted play, and that viewing the puppet show had not altered her sexual conduct at all. This redirects laughter from the women to the Puppet Master, who foolishly imagined that, like his marionettes, readers and audiences were incapable of dancing except as he dictated by calculated pulls to their strings. Fielding thus provided pleasure and a laugh not only for the common reader who followed along, but also for the learned reader, who read with one eye on the classical tradition, and enjoyed the superiority he felt at his ability to recognize allusions and imitations that others missed.

A more judicious reader would have known, however, that a well-wrought text always left the reader "somewhat to studie and gesse upon." Reflection and supplementation were required, whether on one's own or in conversation with others – as indeed, Fielding reminds his readers throughout the novel. Reasoning by considering what Locke called "the agreement and congruity or disagreement and connection of ideas" was, as we saw, the most fundamental form of reflection to be applied to reading (Chapter 1), and this has to be applied here to the two merely juxtaposed scenes to make sense of the connection between them. A judicious reader's reflections might therefore begin by taking the step omitted by the learned reader: reflecting on what "hony" could be gathered from the "stinking weed" of comedy and from the sort of low scene which Tom alone seemed to prize (here, that in which the landlady beats Grace, as Punch beats

Judy, and scolds at everyone else), and comparing this to what the Puppet Master taught. If, as the Puppet Master suggested, one criterion of good reading was to recognize where figures in a play "represent the Life in every Particular," then Grace has been graced with the ability to read better than anyone present. For not content with pointing out that the adaptation has shown her that there are whores among her betters, she has also noticed the incongruity it indicated in contemporary society between the treatment of maidservants who slept around – "if you don't like my Doings, you may turn me away" – and that of fine ladies who did the same, but who were neither beaten nor turned away without a character for it. This incongruity made nonsense of the Puppet Master's conviction that there was no need for such low characters as servants in a play or story because the example of lords and ladies sufficed to deter their inferiors from vice. The land-lady said as much when she complained that "bring[ing] about a Parcel of Puppets drest up like Lords and Ladies" only "teaches our Servants idle-ness and Nonsense" and argued that old plays based on Scripture, which showed "wicked People [being] carried away by the Devil," were far more effective deterrents to lower-class vice. But here the laugh is ultimately on the judicious reader. For without entertaining Grace's insight that ladies may be whores far more seriously than he is likely to do, it is impossible for the judicious reader to guess that Squire Allworthy's unmarried sister was whore enough to be the mother of the foundling, Tom Jones. When the judicious reader later realizes that this "ignorant" maidservant, Grace, has offered the closest thing in the novel to a clue to the secret of the plot, a rueful laugh is likely to be forced from him. That laugh, which denudes him of the pretension to superior judgment which he has affected, returns him to the humility that the Scriptures teach.

On another level, these chapters constitute a holograph of, and satire upon, diverse contemporary manners of reading which the novel both invites and re-presents.

These chapters take the form of a "conversation-piece" in which an orally enacted text is discussed by a group of adults under the implicit direction of an instructive guide (the Puppet Master), who conveys infor-mation about how the text is supposed to be read or heard. As we saw in Chapter 2, instructional conversation-pieces showed readers how to "make Application" of texts to their lives by reflecting or conversing with others; but in practice, they often led discussants to the "Truth" about the genre or text expounded by the guide, by marking his/her position as authorita-tive and portraying everyone agreeing with it. These puppet-show scenes mock this convention: here only the mother hoping to teach her daughters through the medium of the text deferentially accepts the Puppet Master's doctrine and demonstrates that the outcome of instructive conversation must be agreement. The rest of the conversation fractures both the Puppet Master's instruction and his text into a multiplicity of different views and reflections, according to the diverse dispositions, interests, ambitions, passions, beliefs and tastes of diverse hearers and speakers. Moreover, as we saw, this scene of conversations itself invites diverse extra-diegetic readers with diverse interests, abilities and tastes (the common, learned, and judicious) to read them in different ways, without providing any single "right reading."

Considered as a holograph of the novel, Fielding's "conversation-piece" in these chapters also illustrates how he recuperated the character-centered, conversational manner of reading we considered in Chapter 2 without closing reflection and interpretation down. From the novel's first sentence, the narrator is introduced as an "Author" who will accompany the reader through the book, and characterized as a host who will be attentive to the diverse interests and tastes of the company he proposes to entertain. He also advises readers that he will mark chapters with summary-titles, so that they can skip whatever chapter/s they wish, while famously addressing different kinds of reader as he goes and speculating about how each might respond to the characters and situations he describes. The narration thus conformed to the expectation of readers who thought of writing as transpiring between an "I" and a "You" about a he she or it, or as being addressed by an "I" to a "You" and anticipating a response. Far from depriving readers of their freedom to converse with the author, adducing the putative responses of imagined readers invites them to join an intra-diegetic conversation which can be continued outside the book. Indeed, reflection and conversation have to be continued outside the book, inasmuch as the novel leaves a great deal "to studie and gesse upon" and, as we saw above, invites different, even contradictory, readings of the same fragments of text. The narration thus formally re-presents the principle: "as we freely live, so let us freely read."

Fielding overlaid the conversation-piece in these puppet-show chapters with philosophical critics' ideal of uniting all ranks in the same "rational entertainments" and "refined pleasures." The Puppet Master has brought the village an adaptation of *The Provok'd Husband*, which, by eliminating the comic sub-plot and preserving only "the fine and serious part," has given the play something approaching Illiadic unity of action. The adaptation has therefore been approved by "the best judges." The Puppet Master markets his belletrized product like the "true" or "philosophical critics" we saw in Chapter 3, both by describing its moral benefits in abstract universal terms (virtue, vice, moral improvement, good instructive lessons) and by appealing to readers' and auditors' snobbery and social ambition: the play has already "given great Satisfaction to all the Quality in every Town in England." As Fielding uses Grace and the landlady in the second scene to ridicule the Puppet Master's moral claims for his belletrized play, so he uses the attorney's clerk and exciseman in the first scene to satirize this identification of belletrism with upper-class taste and with this, the idea that all society would be united through the same "refined" pleasures. The exciseman and the attorney's clerk make themselves ridiculous by turning up their noses at "everything which is low" (low wit, low humor, low characters, low scenes) while relying on their London acquaintances – who are footmen encountered in the upmost gallery of a theatre – to put themselves on a par with lords, ladies, and belletristic critics, and constitute themselves as judges of whether Lord and Lady Townley are "highly in nature" or not. The affectation of these characters also suggests that belletrism and its critical idiom appeal principally to lower-middle-class people such as these, who are blinded by their social aspirations to the absurdity of dressing up vulgar Punch and Judy puppet bodies as lords and ladies to enact the "refined" and "serious" part of a play. Indeed, dressing up demotic minds and bodies as refined gentlemen is precisely what they are doing to themselves. If Tom represents "the Quality" in this scene, the narrator makes it clear that "the Quality" does not share philosophical critics' belletristic prejudices; where "Quality" is defined by birth and natural superiority, it has no need to make a show of distancing itself from the "low." The landlady, who is their social inferior and lacks their social affectations, passes sterner judgment on her "betters": she enters the room to "scold" and "silence these philosophers" and banish them from her house.

More tolerant than the landlady in her inn, the author-narrator of *Tom Jones* did not entirely banish belletrism and philosophical criticism from his tavern's bill of fare. As several grave, belletristic New Critics proved, Illiadic unity of action can be discerned in the story-line of *Tom Jones* by following the example of the adapter of *The Provok'd Husband*, and eliminating the comic scenes and digressions and preserving only "the fine and serious part." For those inclined to philosophical criticism, there are also critical essays at the beginning of each book. But these are conjectural in the same way the Puppet Master's critical pronouncements are conjectural: they do not necessarily correspond to anything in the narrative as, without this holographic scene, we might expect they would. The novel was hospitable to men of learning, who could find in it what they loved: imitations of classical *topoi*, parodies of classical scenes, echoes of their classical reading. But Fielding's play with readers also demonstrated that readers are not necessarily united by "rational entertainments" and "refined pleasures" as philosophical critics imagined they must be. They are united only formally, by the words of the plays they see and texts they read; what they make of these remains diverse. As the chapter break between the two puppet-show conversations underlines, even when everyone did see the same play or read the same literature, England remained a hierarchical society with well-demarcated social divisions. The chapter break divides the physical and social space occupied by the landlady's conversation with her serv-ant from that occupied by the conversation among her lower-middle-class guests. And the perspectives are different in each case.

Fielding also used the graphic signal of this chapter break to separate those who seek to emulate "the Quality" from those who do not, thus opening a space below stairs for cautious expressions of populist criticism and resistance. The landlady rejects emulation of the vices of "idle" lords and ladies after measuring her social superiors against Scripture stories and finding them wanting. Grace indicates that lords and ladies are not fit objects for imitation by making a specific and practical "Application" of the play's morals to her own character and life: "If I am a Whore…my Betters are so as well as I. What was the fine Lady in the Puppet-show just now?" Grace's "application" borders comically on a libel against the Great. Consequently, she is duly beaten for it by the landlady, in a scene which marries the beatings and brutality of demotic Punch and Judy shows to the beatings and brutality awaiting those who transgressed the Libel or Sedition Acts.

One might expect that the judicious reader, familiar with the codes of secret writing, would recognize this as a hint that the narrative is struc-tured like other fables which concealed a hidden, occluded or unstated "under-meaning" or political "Truth" in a conventional literary form (Chapter 5). One might also expect such a reader to start looking for other "hints borrowed…from the writer" to discover what that truth might be. There are many such hints. For instance, almost each time a character tells his or her "history" to another character, we learn from the narrator that the character-narrator has omitted or withheld some important fact or piece of information from his/her narrative. The novel's first chapter heading warns us that the author will be doing this himself: "Containing as much of the Birth of the Foundling as is necessary or proper to acquaint the Reader with in the Beginning of this History" (1: 1). Running through the novel like a leitmotif alongside each narrated history, is the reason why listeners do not notice that something has been omitted, occluded or withheld: "I have no Impertinent Curiosity about me" (2, 196); "I enquire no further, Sir. Perhaps my Curiosity hath led me too far already" (2: 236); "though Sophia had great Curiosity to know why the other Lady...yet Fear, or Modesty, or some other Consideration, restrained her from asking the Question" (3: 67); "the Reader will perhaps be curious to know... but we cannot satisfy his Curiosity" (3: 121); "I have no Curiosity, Madam, to know any Thing" (4: 224); "You must suspend your Curiosity till our next Meeting" (4: 254). One might say that the reader's *failure* to recognize the hints and "shiftings, ambiguities, equivocations and hypocrisy in all its shapes," which present themselves in *Tom Jones* both between intra-diegetic narrators and their addressees, and between the author-narrator and his readers, is essential to drive home Fielding's satirical point about secret writing. Secret writing stands or falls by what Shaftesbury called "the spirit of curiosity which would force a discovery of more truth than can conveniently be told." It stands or falls by readers' readiness to recognize signals of a concealed secret, and depends on their possession of the curiosity to read for irony, historical parallels, and equivocations, and to ask the pertinent question: has something been secreted in this text? If notwithstanding all the instruction in, and dissemination of, manners of reading secret writing; if despite all the hints and occasions they are given to look beyond the words to what they meant but did not say; readers lack the curiosity or "impertinence" to ask the question; if readers "suspend all Curiosity" about what a text might be occluding; secret writing could only hope to communicate its concealed truth to the public by emerging from the shadows and revealing itself – as in *Tom Jones* it ultimately does.

Tom Jones was available to all these manners of reading without being reducible to any of them, and hospitable to all manner of readers, because it was one of popular print culture's most brilliantly crafted discontinuous and miscellaneous texts (Chapter 4). A man of learning who spent some years as a commercial writer, and an author who needed to appeal to as wide a reading public as possible, Fielding designed the novel as a "Feast" made up of "many kinds of Food." The novel promises and delivers a "prodigious Variety" of characters, subjects, genres and contrivances, all held together by the "packthread" of his authorial voice (1:2, 1, 4). Modeled on the *Odyssey*, which Fielding described as "a Fable consist[ing] of a Series of Separate Adventures detached from and independent of each other," the novel consists of modular parts, any of which could be skipped if they were not to a reader's liking, as Fielding takes pains to point out in his first chapter. He is also careful to explain that the novel includes "gaps" for readers to fill in any manner they wish; frequent stops, changes of direction and promises of further diversion; many new adventures, and strange and surprising turns of events. The bill of fare has been "Cooked" by following the miscellarian recipe for exciting the reader's curiosity and keeping it alive, so that "our Reader may be rendered desirous to read on forever" (1: 4). But Fielding also owed a great deal to a long-standing practice among British women novelists – that which consisted of asking readers to pause, stand back and reflect upon what they were doing and/or ought to be doing when reading the text. We are fortunate therefore. By satirizing many manners of reading included in this study, Fielding allows us to end by beginning to think about the strengths and weaknesses of each.

NOTES

1 Kerrigan, "The Editor as Reader": 110 ff.
2 Ibid.: 113, 110.

Bibliography

PRIMARY

[Anon] *A Collection of Books. Consisting of a Curious Collection of the Most Eminent English Authors for Divinity, History, Travels, Miscellanies and Lives.* London, 1706.

[Anon] *A Help to Elocution and Eloquence.* London, 1770.

[Anon] *A Needful Attempt to Make Language and Divinity Plain and Easy.* London, 1711.

[Anon] *A New Translation of Aesop's Fables, adorned with Cuts.* London, 1708.

[Anon] *An Address to the People of Great Britain; Occasioned by the Republication of The Craftsman.* London, 1731.

[Anon] *The Doctrine of Innuendo's Discuss'd; or the Liberty of the Press Maintain'd: being some Thoughts upon the Present Treatment of the Printer and Publishers of The Craftsman.* London, 1731.

[Anon] *Boeoticorum Liber: or a New Art of Poetry, Containing the Best Reciepts for Making All Sorts of Poems According to Modern Taste.* London, 1732.

[Anon] *Constantia; or a true Picture of human Life, represented in fifteen Evening Conversations,* 2 vols. Dublin, 1751.

[Anon] *Dr. Johnson's Table-Talk.* London, 1785.

[Anon] *Education for Children and Young Students in all its Branches, with a Short Catalogue of the best books in Polite Learning.* 2nd edn. London, 1752.

[Anon] *Horace's Allegorical Advice to the People of Rome. Being an Essay on the 14th Ode of the First Book of Horace with the Allegory Explained.* London, 1715.

[Anon] *London Unmasked.* London, 1784.

[Anon] *Observations on a Pamphlet Entitled 'Christianity not founded on Argument'.* London, 1765.

[Anon] *Several Letters Written by a Noble Lord to a Young Man at the University.* London, 1716.

[Anon/Society of Gentlemen] *A Supplement to Dr. Harris's Dictionary of the Arts and Sciences.* London, 1744.

[Anon] *The Art of Railing at Great Men, Being a Discourse upon Political Railers, Ancient and Modern.* London, 1723.

[Anon] *The Harleian Miscellany, or a Collection of Rare, Curious and Entertaining Pamphlets and Tracts.* London, 1744.

[Anon] *The Hive: or a collection of thoughts on civil, moral, sentimental and religious subjects, selected from the writings of near one hundred of the best and most approved authors*... London, 1791.

[Anon] *The Moral Miscellany*. London, 1758.

[Anon] *The Polite Student*. London, 1748.

Adams, John. *Curious Thoughts on the History of Man*. London, 1789.

Addison, Joseph. *The Papers of Joseph Addison*. Edinburgh, 1790.

and Richard Steele. *The Spectator*, 8 vols. London, 1712–15.

Aikin, John. *Letters from a Father to his Son*. London, 1793.

Allwood, Philip. *Remarks on Some Observations edited in* The British Critic *relative to a Work lately published under the Title of Literary Antiquities*. London, 1800.

Arnold, Thomas. MD. *Observations on the Nature, Kind, Causes and Prevention of Insanity, Lunacy or Madness*, 2 vols. Leicester, 1782–6.

Arwaker, Edmund [John Churchill]. *Aesop, Truth in Fiction; or Morality in Masquerade*. London, 1708.

Ash, John. *Grammatical Institutes; or An Easy Introduction to Dr. Lowth's English Grammar*. London, 1763.

Astle, Thomas. *The Origin and Progress of Writing*. London, 1784.

Aubin, Penelope. *A Collection of Entertaining Histories and Novels*. London, 1739.

Bacon, Francis. *Essays Moral, Economical and Political*, 1625. London, 1798.

Bailey, Nathaniel. *An Universal English Dictionary*. London, 1721.

An Universal Etymological English Dictionary. London, 1727.

Baillie, John. *An Essay on the Sublime*. London, 1747.

Baker, Thomas. *Reflections upon Learning* (1708). 8th edn. London, 1756.

Banson, Wiliam. *The Merchant's Penman*. London, 1702.

Barker, Jane. *Exilius*. London, 1715.

Beattie, James. *Dissertations Moral and Critical*. London, 1783.

Behn, Aphra. *Oronooko*. London, 1688.

Belknap, Jeremy. *Memoirs of the Life, Character and Writings of Dr. Isaac Watts*. Boston, 1793.

Bellamy, Mrs. *The Young Ladies' Miscellany...To which is Prefixed a short Essay on the Art of Pronunciation*. London, 1726.

Benezet, Anthony. *The Pennsylvania Spelling Book; or Youth's Friendly Instructor and Monitor*. 3rd edn. Providence, RI, 1782.

Bennett, John. *Letters to a Young Lady*, 2 vols. Warrington, 1789.

Bethune, John. *Essays and Dissertations on Various Subjects*, 2 vols. London, 1771.

Bickham, George. *The Universal Penman; Or, the Art of Writing*. London, 1741.

Blackwall, Anthony. *An Introduction to the Classics: Containing...directions how to study them to Advantage*. London, 1737.

Blair, Hugh. *The Importance of Religious Knowledge to the Happiness of Mankind*. Edinburgh, 1750.

Lectures on Rhetoric and Belles Lettres, 2 vols. London, 1783.

Blount, Thomas. *Glossographia* (1656). London, 1707.

Bolingbroke, Henry St. John. *Letters on the Study and Use of History*. London, 1752.

Boswell, John. *A Method of Study; or a Useful Library*, 2 vols. London, 1737.

Brightland, John. *Reasons for an English Education, by teaching the Youth of both Sexes the Arts of Grammar, Rhetoric, Poetry and Logic in their own Mother-Tongue.* London, 1711.

A Grammar of the English Tongue, with notes. (1712). 2nd edn. London, 1714.

Brokesby, Francis. *Of Education with Respect to Grammar Schools and the Universities.* London, 1701.

Buchanan, James. *The British Grammar.* London, 1762.

A Regular English Syntax, wherein is Exhibited the Whole Variety of English Construction. London, 1767.

A Plan of an English Grammar School Education. London, 1770.

Burgh, James. *The Dignity of Human Nature.* London, 1754.

The Art of Speaking. 2nd edn. London, 1768.

Burke, Edmund. *A Philosophical Enquiry into our Ideas of the Sublime and the Beautiful.* 2nd edn. London, 1759.

Bysshe, Edward. *The Art of English Poetry.* London, 1724.

Carter, Elizabeth. *A Series of Letters between Mrs. Elizabeth Carter and Miss Catherine Talbot from the Year 1741 to 1770,* 4 vols. London, 1809.

Chamberlayne, Edward. *Angli Notitia; or the Present State of England.* London, 1702.

Chambers, Ephraim. *Cyclopedia: or an Universal Dictionary of the Arts and Sciences,* 2 vols. London, 1728.

Champion, Joseph. *The Young Penman's Daily Practice.* London, 1760.

Penmanship or the Art of Fair Writing: A New Essay. London, 1770.

Chapone, Hester. *Letters on the Improvement of the Mind.* London, 1773.

Chesterfield, Philip Dormer Stanhope, Earl of. *Letters to his Son,* 4 vols. London, 1776.

Clarke, John. *An Essay Upon Study.* London, 1731.

Cobbett, William. *Parliamentary History of England.* London, 1806–20.

Coleridge, Samuel Taylor. *Biographia Literaria.* Ed. James Engell and W. Jackson Bate, 2 vols. Princeton University Press, 1983.

Collier, Jane and Sarah Fielding. *The Cry.* London, 1754.

Collins, Anthony. *A Discourse Concerning Ridicule and Irony.* London, 1729.

Constable, John. *Reflections upon Accuracy of Style.* London, 1734.

Cowper, Ashley. Commonplace Book of Ashley Cowper, begun in 1735. *British Literary Manuscripts Online.*

Croxall, Samuel. *Fables of Aesop and Others.* London, 1722.

Cumberland, Richard. *Memoirs of Richard Cumberland.* Boston, 1806.

D'Ancourt, Abbé. *The Lady's Preceptor; or a Letter to a Young Lady of Distinction upon Politeness.* 2nd edn. London, 1743.

Davys, Mary. *The Works of Mrs. Davys.* London, 1725.

Dawes, Sir William. *The Excellency of the Charity of Charity Schools.* London, 1713.

De Crousaz, Jean-Pierre. *A New Treatise of the Art of Thinking; or a Compleat System of Reflections concerning the Conduct and Improvement of the mind.* London, 1724.

Defoe, Daniel. *An Essay Upon Literature.* New York: AMS Press, 1999.

De la Court, Pieter. *Fables Moral and Political with large Explications. Translated from the Dutch,* 2 vols. London, 1703.

[De La Motte, Antoine, Sieur]. *A Hundred New Court Fables Written for the Instruction of Princes and True Knowledge of the World.* London, 1721.

Devis, Ellin. *The Accidence; or First Rudiments of English Grammar Designed for the Use of Young Ladies.* 8th edn. London, 1795.

Dilworth, Thomas. *A New Guide to the English Tongue.* 13th edn. London, 1751.

Disraeli, Isaac. *Curiosities of Literature.* London, 1791.

Miscellanies. London, 1796.

[Dodsley, Robert]. *The Preceptor: Containing a General Course of Education. Wherein the First Principles of Polite Learning are Laid Down* (1748), 2 vols. London, 1754.

Select Fables of Esop and Other Fabulists. In Three Books. London, 1761.

Dover, William. *Useful Miscellanies or Serious Reflections Respecting Men's Duty to God and Man.* Philephia, 1753.

Encyclopaedia Britannica; or a Dictionary of Arts, Sciences and Miscellaneous Literature. Dublin, 1790; Philadelphia, 1798.

Enfield, William. *The Speaker.* London, 1774.

Felton, Henry. *A Dissertation on Reading the Classics and Forming a Just Style. Written in the Year 1709.* London, 1713.

Fenning, Daniel. *The Universal Spelling Book; Or a New and Easy Guide to the English Language.* London, 1756.

A New Grammar of the English Language. London, 1771.

Fielding, Henry. Preface to Sarah Fielding. *The Adventures of David Simple.* 2nd edn. London, 1744.

"An Essay on the Knowledge and Characters of Men." In *Miscellanies.* Ed. Henry Fielding, 3 vols. (2nd edn., London, 1743), 1: 218–65.

The History of Tom Jones, a Foundling. London, 1749.

Fielding, Sarah. *The Governess.* London: Pandora, 1987.

Fisher, Anne. *A Practical New Grammar.* 8th edn. London, 1763.

Foster, Hannah Webster. *The Coquette and The Boarding School.* New York: Norton, 2013.

Freneau, Philip. "The Power of Novelty." In *The Miscellaneous Works of Philip Freneau.* Philadelphia, 1788.

Fuller, Thomas. *Introductio ad Sapientiem; or the Art of Right Thinking,* 2 vols. London, 1731.

Gerard, Alexander. *An Essay on Taste, with three Dissertations on the same Subject by M. de Voltaire, Mr. D'Alembert and M. de Montesquieu.* London, 1759.

Gibbon, Edward Jun. *An Essay on the Study of Literature.* London, 1764.

Gibbons, Thomas. *Rhetoric: Or a View of its Principal Tropes and Figures,* 2 vols. London, 1767.

Gildon, Charles, "The Art of Poetry." In Brightland, *Grammar of the English Tongue.* London, 1714. (p. 131 ff.).

"The Art of Rhetoric." In Brightland, *Grammar of the English Tongue.* London, 1714 (p. 186 ff.).

The Complete Art of Poetry in Six Parts, 2 vols. London, 1718.

Giles, Jacob. *Every Man his own Lawyer.* London, 1736.

Goldsmith, Oliver. *An Enquiry into the Present State of Polite Learning in Europe.* (1759). 2nd edn. revised. London, 1774.

Gough, James. *A Practical Grammar of the English Tongue.* 2nd edn. Dublin, 1760.

Greenwood, James. *An Essay towards a Practical English Grammar.* London, 1711.

Griffith, Elizabeth. *The History of Lady Barton.* London, 1771.

Harland, S. *The English Spelling Book Revis'd.* 3rd edn. London, 1719.

Harwood, Edward. *A View of the Various Editions of the Greek and Roman Classics, with Remarks.* London, 1775.

Hawkesworth, John. *The Adventurer: A New Edition.* (1752–4), 4 vols. London, 1793

Haywood, Eliza. *The Tea-Table.* London, 1725.
    The Female Spectator, 4 vols. London, 1745–6.
    The Invisible Spy, 4 vols. London, 1755.

Hearne, Thomas, *Ductor Historicus: or a Short System of Universal History, and an Introduction to the Study of It.* 2nd edn. London, 1704.

Hitchcock, Enos. *Memoirs of the Bloomsgrove Family.* Boston, 1790.

Hobbes, Thomas. *The Moral and Political Writings of Thomas Hobbes of Malmesbury.* London, 1750.

Holmes, John. *The Art of Rhetoric Made Easy; or the Elements of Oratory briefly stated.* London, 1739.

Honoria. *The Female Mentor: or Select Conversations,* 3 vols. London, 1793.

Hoole, Charles. *A New Discovery of the old Art of Teaching Schoole.* London, 1661.

Hume, David. *Essays, Moral and Philosophical.* Edinburgh, 1741.
    Essays Moral and Political. 2nd edn. corrected. Edinburgh, 1742.

[Jackson, Joseph]. *Aesop's Fables with Instructive Morals and Reflections. A New Edition.* London, 1775.

Jarman, John. *System of the Court Hands...with all the Abbreviations Explained and Applied.* London, 1723.

Jaudon, Daniel. *A Short System of Polite Learning: being a Concise Introduction to the Arts and Sciences and Other Branches of Useful Knowledge, Adapted for Schools.* London, 1789.

Johnson, Mary. *The Young Woman's Companion, or the Serving Maid's Assistant.* London, 1753.

Johnson, R. *An Introduction to the Study of History: Wherein is considered the proper Method of Reading Historical Works...* London, 1772.

Johnson, Samuel. *The Rambler,* 8 vols. Edinburgh, 1751.
    A Grammar of the English Tongue. In Dictionary of the English Language. London, 1755.
    Rasselas, 2 vols. London, 1759.
    The Idler, 2 vols. London, 1761.
    The Lives of the Most Eminent English Poets, 4 vols. London, 1783.

Kames, Home, Henry, Lord. *Elements of Criticism,* 2 vols. 3rd edn. Edinburgh, 1765.

Keach, Benjamin. *Tropologia: a Key to Open Scripture Metaphors* (1682). London, 1779.

Knox, Vicesimus. *Essays Moral and Literary. A New Edition,* 2 vols. London, 1782.
   Elegant Extracts: or Useful and Entertaining Passages in Prose, Selected for the Improvement of Scholars at Classical and Other Schools in the Art of Speaking. London, 1784.
   Winter Evenings: Lucubrations on Life and Letters, 3 vols. London, 1788.
   Elegant Extracts; or Useful and Entertaining Pieces of Poetry. London, 1789.
Lackington, James. *Memoirs of the first forty-five years of the life of James Lackington... Bookseller... Written by himself.* London, 1791.
Lane, A. *A Key to the Art of Letters; or English a Learned Language.* 2nd edn. London, 1706.
Lennox, Charlotte. *Charlotte Lennox: Correspondence and Miscellaneous Documents.* Ed. Norbert Schürer. Lewisburgh: Bucknell, 2012.
L'Estrange, Sir Roger. *Fables of Aesop and Other Eminent Mythologists with Morals and Reflexions.* London, 1694.
Locke, John. *Some Thoughts on Education.* 5th edn. London, 1705.
   "Of the Conduct of the Understanding." In *Posthumous Works of Mr. John Locke.* London, 1706.
   Essay Concerning Human Understanding. In Four Books. 5th edn. London, 1706.
Lovechild, Mrs. *The Child's Grammar.* Dublin, 1790.
   The Mother's Grammar, being a Continuation of the Child's Grammar. London, 1798.
Lowth, Robert. *A Short Introduction to English Grammar with Critical Notes.* 2nd edn. corrected. London, 1763.
   Lectures on the Sacred Poetry of the Hebrews. London, 1787.
Maidwell, Lewis. *An Essay upon the Necessity and Excellence of Education.* London, 1705.
Makin, Bathsua. *An Essay to revive the Antient Education of Gentlewomen in Religion, Manners, Arts and Tongues.* London, 1673.
Manley, Delarivier. *The Secret History of Queen Zarah and the Zarazians.* London, 1711.
Mason, John. *Self-Knowledge.* London, 1745.
   An Essay on Elocution or Pronunciation, intended chiefly for the assistance of those who instruct others in the Art of Reading and those who are often called to speak in Public. 2nd edn. London, 1748.
Massey, William. *The Origin and Progress of Letters.* London, 1763.
Milns, William. *The Well-Bred Scholar, or Practical Essays on the best method of improving the Taste and assisting the exertions of Youth in their Literary Pursuits.* London, 1794.
Montesquieu. *The Spirit of Laws.* London, 1750.
Moore, Martha Milcah. *Miscellanies, Moral and Instructive in Prose and Verse.* Philadelphia, 1787.
Moreri, Louis. *The Great, Historical, Geographical, Genealogical and Poetical Dictionary; being a Curious Miscellany of Sacred and Prophane History.* London, 1701.
Murray, Ann. *Mentoria, or the Young Ladies Instructor, in familiar Conversations on Moral and Entertaining Subjects.* Dublin, 1779.

Murray, Lindley. *English Grammar Adapted to the Different Classes of Learners.* York, 1795.

M.W. *The Sacred Outcry. Upon a View of the Principal Errors and Vices of Christendom in the Eighteenth Century.* London, 1788.

Newbery, John. *An Easy Introduction to the English Language, or a Compendious Grammar.* London, 1745.

    Poetry Made Easy to Young Gentlemen and Ladies. 2nd edn. London, 1748.

    Rhetoric Made Familiar and Easy to Young Gentlemen and Ladies. Being the Third Volume of the Circle of the Sciences. 3rd London edn. London, 1769.

Nichols, John. *Anecdotes Biographical and Literary of the Late William Bowyer, Printer.* London, 1778.

Nicholson, Edward. *A Method of Charity-Schools Recommended.* Dublin, 1712.

Ollyffe, Thomas. *Practical Penman.* London, 1713.

Palmer, Samuel. *Abridgement of Johnson's Lives of the English Poets.* London, 1787.

    Vindication of the Modern Dissenters against the Aspersions of the Revd. William Hawkins, M.A. London, 1790.

Pindar, Peter, *Odes of Importance. To the Shoemakers. To Mr. Burke. To Irony. To the King...* London, 1793.

Pittis, William. *Aesop at the Bell-Tavern in Westminster.* London, 1711.

Plutarch. *Plutarch's Morals: Translated from the Greek by Several Hands.* 4th edn. London, 1704.

Pointer, John. *Miscellanea in usum juventis academicae.* Oxford, 1717.

Pope, Alexander. *Essay on Criticism.* London, 1711.

    The Rape of the Lock. London, 1718.

Postlethwayt, Malachi. *Universal Dictionary of Trade and Commerce.* London, 1755.

Priestley, Joseph. *A Course of Lectures on Oratory and Criticism.* London, 1777.

Quintilian. *Quintilianus his Institutes of Eloquence.* Tr. William Guthrie, 2 vols. London, 1756.

    Quintilian's Institutes of the Orator, 2 vols. London, 1774.

Ralph, James. *The Case of Authors by Profession or Trade Stated.* London, 1758.

Ramsay, Allan. *Fables and Tales.* Edinburgh, 1722.

Reeve, Clara. *The Progress of Romance.* London, 1785.

Reeves, William. *The Apologies of Justin Martyr, Tertullian and Minutius Felix in Defence of the Christian Religion.* London, 1709.

Reid, Thomas. *Essays on the Intellectual and Active Powers of Men,* 3 vols. Dublin, 1790.

Rice, John. *An Introduction to the Art of Reading with Energy and Propriety.* London, 1765.

Richardson, Samuel. *Pamela.* London, 1741.

Rollin, Charles. *The Method of Teaching and Studying the Belles Lettres,* 4 vols. London, 1734.

Saunders, Erasmus. *A Domestick Charge; or the Duty of Household Governours.* Oxford, 1701.

Scott, Sarah. *A Journey through Every Stage of Life.* London, 1754.

Searle, Ambrose. *A Treatise on the Art of Writing.* London, 1782.

Scott, William. *Lessons in Elocution, or Miscellaneous Pieces in Prose and Verse selected from the Best Authors*. Edinburgh, 1779

Shaftesbury, Anthony Ashley Cooper. *Sensus Communis*. London, 1709.

Characteristics of Men, Manners, Opinions, Times. Ed. Lawrence Klein. Cambridge University Press, 1999.

Sheridan, Thomas. *A Course of Lectures on Elocution; together with two Dissertations on Language*. 2nd edn. Dublin, 1764.

Sidney, Sir Philip. "An Apology for Poetry." In *The Norton Anthology of Theory and Criticism*. Ed. Vincent Leitch. New York: Norton, 2001.

Skelton, Philip. *The Candid Reader*. London, 1744.

Ophiomaches. London, 1749.

Smith, Adam. *Essays on Philosophical Subjects by the Late Adam Smith*. Dublin, 1795.

Smith, Charlotte. *Minor Morals, interspersed with Sketches of Natural History, Historical Anecdotes and Original Stories*, 2 vols. 2nd edn. London, 1799.

Smith, William. *The Student's Vade Mecum Containing 1. An Account of Knowledge and its General Divisions*. London, 1770.

Snell, Charles. *The Art of Writing in its Theory and Practice*. London, 1712.

Smollett, Tobias, *The Expedition of Humphrey Clinker*. Ed. Angus Ross. Harmondsworth: Penguin, 1975.

Spence, Joseph. *An Essay on Pope's Odyssey*. London, 1726–7.

Stonecastle, Henry. *The Universal Spectator*, 2 vols. London, 1736.

Swift, Jonathan. "An Essay on Education." In *Miscellanies in Prose and Verse*. Dublin, 1733.

Temple, Sir William. *Introduction to the History of England* (1695). London, 1708.

Theobald, John. *Every Man his own Physician*. London, 1764.

Tiffin, William. *A New Help and Improvement of the Art of Swiftly Writing*. London, 1751.

The Annual Register for the Year 1786. London, 1787.

The Bee [Oliver Goldsmith]

The British Journal

The Briton

The Connoisseur

The Craftsman

The Critical Review

The Enquirer (1823)

The Free Thinker, 1718–19. [Ambrose Philips]

The Guardian, 2 vols. London, 1794.

The Lounger. [Henry Mackenzie]

The Monthly Review

The Speculator

The Spirit of the Public Journals for 1798…with explanatory notes. London, 1799. [Henry Stonecastle]

The Westminster Magazine

The World

Walker's Hibernian Magazine

Talbot, Catherine. *Essays on Various Subjects in Prose and Verse,* 2 vols. Dublin, 1773.

Toland, John. *Clidophorus.* London, 1720.

Trenchard, John. *Cato's Letters,* 4 vols. London, 1723.

Trublet, Nicholas-Charles-Joseph (Abbé). *Essays upon Several Subjects of Literature and Morality.* London, 1744.

Tuite, Thomas. *The Oxford Spelling Book.* London, 1726.

Turner, R. *An Easy Introduction to the Arts and Sciences, being a short but comprehensive system of Polite Learning.* London, 1783.

Tryon, Thomas. *The Merchant, Citizen and Country-man's Instructor.* London, 1701.

Ussher, James. *Clio; or a Discourse on Taste, addressed to a Young Lady.* Dublin, 1778.

Wakefield, Priscilla. *Mental Improvement, or the Beauties and Wonders of Nature and Art, conveyed in a Series of Instructive Conversations.* London, 1794.

Walker, John. *Exercises for Improvement of Elocution, being Extracts from the Best Authors for the Use of those who study the Art of Reading and Speaking.* London, 1777.

The Academic Speaker. Dublin, 1796.

Wallace, James. *Every Man his own Letter-Writer.* London, 1782.

Ward, John. *A System of Oratory,* 2 vols. London, 1754.

Watts, Isaac. *Logick: or the Right Use of Reason in the Enquiry after Truth.* 2nd edn. London, 1725.

The Improvement of the Mind; or a Supplement to the Art of Logick. (1741). 2nd edn. London, 1743.

The Art of Reading and Writing English. 2nd edn. London, 1722.

Watts, Thomas. *An Essay on the Proper Method of Forming a Man of Business.* London, 1716.

Webster, Noah. *A Grammatical Institute of the English Language.* Hartford, 1784.

An American Selection of Lessons in Reading and Speaking. Philadelphia, 1787.

The American Spelling Book. 2nd edn. Boston, 1790.

Wesley, John. *The Complete English Dictionary.* London, 1753.

Wollstonecraft, Mary. *Original Stories from Real Life.* London, 1788.

SECONDARY

Allan, David. *A Nation of Readers: The Lending Library in Georgian England.* London: British Library, 2008.

Commonplace Books and Reading in Georgian England. Cambridge University Press, 2010.

Alston, R. C. *A Bibliography of the English Language to the Year 1800.* Ilkeley: Janus Press, 1974.

Amory, Hugh and David Hall. Eds. *The Colonial Book in the Atlantic World.* Cambridge University Press, 2000.

Ashfield, Andrew and Peter de Bolla. Eds. "Introduction." In *The Sublime: A Reader in Eighteenth-Century Aesthetic Theory.* Cambridge University Press, 1996.

Axtell, James. *The School upon a Hill.* New Haven: Yale University Press, 1974.

Backscheider, Paula. *Spectacular Politics: Theatrical Power and Mass Culture in Early Modern England.* Baltimore: Johns Hopkins University Press, 1993.

  "The Shadow of an Author: Eliza Haywood." *Eighteenth-Century Fiction* 11:1 (October 1998): 79–102.

Bailey, Richard. "Variation and Change in Eighteenth-Century English." In Hickey. *Eighteenth-Century English.*

Bannet, Eve Tavor. "Analogy as Translation: Derrida, Wittgenstein and the Law of Language." *New Literary History* 28:4 (Autumn 1997): 655–72.

  The Domestic Revolution: Enlightenment Feminisms and the Novel. Baltimore: Johns Hopkins University Press, 2000.

  Empire of Letters: Letter Manuals and Transatlantic Correspondence, 1680–1820. Cambridge University Press, 2005.

  "Secret History: Talebearing Inside and Outside the Secretorie." *Huntington Library Quarterly* 68:1–2 (March 2005): 375–96.

  Transatlantic Stories and the History of Reading 1720–1810: Migrant Fictions. Cambridge University Press, 2011.

  "The History of Reading: the Long Eighteenth Century." *The Literary Compass* 10:2 (February 2013): 122–33.

  "The Narrator as Invisible Spy: Eliza Haywood, Secret History and the Novel." *Journal for Early Modern Cultural Studies* 14:4 (Fall 2014): 143–62.

  "Discontinuous Reading and Miscellaneous Instruction for the Fair Sex." In *Women's Periodicals and Print Culture in Britain: 1690–1820s.* Ed. Manushag Powell and Jennie Batchelor. Edinburgh University Press, forthcoming.

Bantock, G. H. *Studies in the History of Educational Theory. Vol. 1: 1350–1765.* London: Allen & Unwin, 1980.

Barker, Nicolas. "The Morphology of the Page." In Suarez and Turner, *Cambridge History of the Book.*

Barrell, John. "The Language Properly So Called: The Authority of Common Usage." In Barrell. *English Literature in History 1730–1780.* New York: St. Martin's Press, 1983.

  Imagining the King's Death, 1793–1796. Oxford University Press, 2000.

Barry, John. "Literacy and Literature in Popular Culture: Reading and Writing in Historical Perspective." In *Popular Culture in England 1500–1800.* Ed. Tim Harris. New York: St. Martin's Press, 1995.

Bartine, David. *Early English Reading Theory.* Columbia: University of South Carolina Press, 1989.

Batchelor, Jenny. *Women's Work: Labour, Gender and Authorship, 1750–1830.* Manchester University Press, 2010.

Benedict, Barbara. *Making the Modern Reader.* Princeton University Press, 1996.

  Curiosity: A Cultural History of Early Modern Enquiry. University of Chicago Press, 2001.

Birke, Dorothee. "Direction and Diversion: Chapter Titles in Three Mid-Century Novels by Sarah Fielding, Henry Fielding and Charlotte Lennox." *Studies in Eighteenth-Century Culture* 41 (2012): 211–32.

Blair, Ann. "Reading Strategies for Coping with Information Overload ca.1550– 1700." *Journal of the History of Ideas* 64:1 (2003): 11–28.

Bowers, Toni. *Force or Fraud: British Seduction Stories and the Problem of Resistance, 1660–1760.* Oxford University Press, 2011.

Brant, Claire. *Eighteenth-Century Letters and British Culture.* Houndmills: Palgrave Macmillan, 2006.

Brewer, David. *The Afterlife of Character.* Philadelphia: University of Pennsylvania Press, 2005.

Brewer, John. *The Pleasures of the Imagination: English Culture in the Eighteenth Century.* New York: Farrar Straus Giroux, 1997.

"Reconstructing the Reader: Prescriptions, Texts and Strategies in Anne Larpant's Reading." In Raven et al., *Practice and Representation of Reading.*

Briggs, Julia, Dennis Butts and M. O. Grenby. Eds. *Popular Children's Literature in Britain.* Aldershot: Ashgate, 2008.

Brown, Matthew. *The Pilgrim and the Bee.* Philadelphia: University of Pennsylvania Press, 2007.

Bruckner, Martin. *The Geographic Revolution in Early America.* Chapel Hill: University of North Carolina Press, 2006.

Bryson, Anna. *From Courtesy to Civility.* Oxford: Clarendon, 1998.

Budor, Dominique and Walter Geertz. Eds. *Le Texte Hybride.* Paris: Presses Sorbonne Novelle, 2004.

Bullard, Paddy. "Digital Editing and the Eighteenth-Century Text: Works, Archives, Miscellanies." *Eighteenth Century Life* 36:3 (Fall 2012): 57–80.

Bullard, Rebecca. *The Politics of Disclosure 1674–1725.* London: Pickering & Chatto, 2009.

Bushman, Richard. *The Refinement of America.* New York: Knopf, 1992.

Bushnell, Rebecca. *A Culture of Teaching: Early Modern Humanism in Theory and Practice.* Ithaca: Cornell University Press, 1996.

Castle, Terry. *Masquerade and Civilization.* Stanford University Press, 1986.

Chandler, James. *England in 1819.* University of Chicago Press, 1998.

Chaquin, Nicole and Sophie Houdard. Eds. *Curiosite et Libido Sciendi de la Renaissance aux Lumieres.* Fontenay/St. Cloud: ENS edns., 1998.

Chard, Leslie. "Bookseller to Publisher: Joseph Johnson and the English Book Trade, 1760–1810." *The Library* 2:2 (1977): 138–54.

Chartier, Roger. "Text, Printing, Readings." In *The New Cultural History.* Ed. Lynn Hunt. Berkeley: University of California Press, 1989.

The Order of Books. Oxford: Polity Press, 1994.

Cohen, Michel. "Familiar Conversation: the Role of the Familiar Format in Education in Nineteenth-Century England." In Hilton and Shefrin, *Educating the Child.*

"A Little Learning: The Curriculum and Construction of Gender Difference in the Long Eighteenth Century." *Journal of Eighteenth-Century Studies* 29:3 (September 2006): 321–35.

Cohen, Murray. *Sensible Words: Linguistic Practice in England 1640–1785.* Baltimore: Johns Hopkins University Press, 1977.

Cohen, Ralph. "History and Genre." *New Literary History* 17:2 (January 1986): 203–18.

Colclough, Stephen. "Procuring Books and Consuming Texts: the Reading Experience of a Sheffield Apprentice, 1798." *Book History* 3 (2000): 21–44.

Consuming Texts: Readers and Reading Communities, 1695–1870. Houndmills: Palgrave Macmillan, 2007.

Colie, Rosalie. *The Resources of Kind: Genre Theory in the Renaissance.* Berkeley: University of California Press, 1973.

Colley, Linda. *Britons: Forging the Nation, 1707–1837.* New Haven: Yale University Press, 2009.

Cope, Kevin Lee. *In and After the Beginning: Inaugural Moments and Literary Institutions in the Long Eighteenth-Century.* New York: AMS Press, 2007.

Copeland, Edward. *Women Writing about Money, 1790–1832.* Cambridge University Press, 1995.

Court, Franklin. *Institutionalizing English Literature.* Stanford University Press, 1992.

Crain, Patricia. *The Story of A.* Stanford University Press, 2000.

Crane, Mary Thomas. *Framing Authority: Sayings, Self and Society in Eighteenth-Century England.* Princeton University Press, 1993.

Crawford, Robert. *The Scottish Invention of English Literature.* Cambridge University Press, 1998.

Devolving English Literature. 2nd edn. Edinburgh University Press, 2000.

Cummings, Brian. *The Literary Culture of the Reformation: Grammar and Grace.* Oxford University Press. 2007.

Crystal, David. *Prosodic Systems and Intonation in England.* Cambridge University Press, 1969.

Culpepper, Jonathan and Merja Kyto. *Early Modern English Dialogues.* Cambridge University Press, 2010.

Dacome, Lucia. "Noting the Mind." *Journal of the History of Ideas.* 65:4 (2004): 603–25.

Davidson, Jenny. *Hypocrisy and the Politics of Politeness.* Cambridge University Press, 2004.

Davis, Arthur Paul. *Isaac Watts, his Life and Works.* New York: Dryden Press, 1943.

Dawson, Hannah. *Locke, Language and Early Modern Philosophy.* Cambridge University Press, 2007.

Dierks, Konstantin. *In my Power: Letter-Writing and Communication in Early America.* Philadelphia: University of Pennsylvania Press, 2009.

Dille, Catherine. "The Dictionary in Abstract: Johnson's Abridgments of The Dictionary of the English Language for 'the Common Reader'." In Lynch and McDermott. *Anniversary Essays.*

Dolven, Jeff. *Scenes of Instruction in Renaissance Romance.* University of Chicago Press, 2007.

Domingo, Daryll. "Unbending the Mind; or Commercialized Leisure and the Rhetoric of Eighteenth-Century Diversion," *Eighteenth-Century Studies* 45:2 (Winter 2012): 207–36.

Doody, Margaret. *The True History of the Novel*. New Brunswick: Rutgers University Press, 1996.

Duff, David. *Romanticism and the Use of Genre*. Oxford University Press, 2009.

Durey, Michael. *Transatlantic Radicals and the Early American Republic*. Lawrence: University of Kansas Press, 1997.

Eden, Kathy. *Hermeneutics and the Rhetorical Tradition*. New Haven: Yale University Press, 1997.

Elfenbein, Andrew. *Romanticism and the Rise of English*. Stanford University Press, 2009.

Ellenzsweig, Sarah. *The Fringes of Belief*. Stanford University Press, 2008.

Elsky, Martin. *Authorizing Words: Speech, Writing and Printing in the English Renaissance*. Ithaca: Cornell University Press, 1989.

Evans, Chris. *Debating the Revolution: Britain in the 1790s*. London: Tauris, 2006.

Ezell, Margaret. "The Gentleman's Journal and the Communication of Restoration Coterie Practices." *Modern Philology* 89:3 (March 2000): 323–41.

Feather, John. *The Provincial Book Trade in Eighteenth-Century England*. Cambridge University Press, 1985.

Fergus, Jan. *Provincial Readers in Eighteenth-Century England*. Oxford University Press, 2006.

Ferreira-Buckely, Linda and Michael Halloran. Eds. *Lectures in Rhetoric and Belles Lettres by Hugh Blair*. Carbondale: Southern Illinois University Press, 2005.

Ferris, Ina and Paul Keen. Eds. *Bookish Histories*. Houndmills: Palgrave Macmillan, 2009.

Fliegelman, Jay. *Declaring Independence*. Stanford University Press, 1993.

Fowler, Alasdair. *Kinds of Literature*. Cambridge, MA: Harvard University Press, 1982.

Fox, Adam. "Rumour, News and Popular Opinion in Elizabethan and Early Stuart England." *The Historical Journal* 40:3 (1997): 597–620.

Oral and Literate Culture in England 1500–1700. Oxford: Clarendon, 2000.

Freist, Dagmar. *Governed by Opinion: Politics, Religion and the Dynamics of Communication in Stuart London*. London: Tauris, 1997.

Froide, Amy. *Never Married: Single Women in Early Modern England*. Oxford University Press, 2005.

Fuchs, Barbara. *Romance*. New York: Routledge, 2004.

Galisyer, Natasha and Sara Pennell. Eds. *Didactic Literature in England 1500–1800*. Aldershot: Ashgate, 2003.

Gally, Michelle. "Curiosite et fictions medievales: le Questionement sur L'Autre." In Chaquin and Houdard, *Curiosite et Libido Sciendi de la Renaissance aux Lumieres*: 262–82.

Gardiner, Ellen. *Regulating Readers: Gender and Literary Criticism in the Eighteenth-Century Novel*. Newark: University of Delaware Press, 1999.

Gardner, Jared. *Early American Magazine Culture.* Urbana: University of Illinois Press, 2012.

Garrett, Matthew. *Episodic Poetics: Politics and Literary Form after the Constitution.* New York: Oxford University Press, 2014.

Genette, Gerard. *Paratexts.* Cambridge University Press, 1997.

Golden, James and Doughlas Ehninger. "The Extrinsic Sources of Blair's Popularity." *Southern Speech Journal* 22 (1956): 16–32.

Goldie, Mark. "Civil Religion and the English Enlightenment. In Schochet, *Politics, Politeness and Patriotism.*

Grafton, Antony and Lisa Jardine. *From Humanism to Humanities.* Cambridge University Press, 1986.

Grantley, Darryll. *Wit's Pilgrimage: Drama and the Social Impact of Education in Early Modern England.* Aldershot: Ashgate, 2000.

Grasso, Christopher. *A Speaking Aristocracy.* Chapel Hill: University of North Carolina Press, 1999.

Green, Ian. *The Christian's ABC.* Oxford: Clarendon, 1996.

 Print and Protestantism in Early Modern England. Oxford University Press, 2000.

 Humanism and Protestantism in Early Modern English Education. Aldershot: Ashgate, 2009.

Greene, Jack P. *Creating the British Atlantic.* Charlottesville: University of Virginia Press, 2013.

Greene, Roland. *Unrequited Conquests.* University of Chicago Press, 1999.

Grenby, M. O. *The Anti-Jacobin Novel.* Cambridge University Press, 2001.

 The Child Reader, 1700–1840. Cambridge University Press, 2011.

Griffin, Dustin. *Authorship in the Long Eighteenth Century.* Newark: University of Delaware Press, 2014.

 "The Rise of the Professional Author." In Suarez and Turner, *Cambridge History of the Book.*

Griffiths, Paul. *Religious Reading.* Oxford University Press, 1999.

Gross, Robert and Mary Kelley. Eds. *An Extensive Republic.* Chapel Hill: University of North Carolina Press, 2010.

Grundy, Isobel. "Women and Print: Readers, Writers and the Market." In Suarez and Turner, *Cambridge History of the Book.*

Guillory, John. "The English Commonplace: Lineages of a Topological Genre." *Critical Quarterly* 33 (1991): 3–27.

Gustafson, Sandra. *Eloquence is Power.* Chapel Hill: University of North Carolina Press, 2000.

Hackel, Heidi Brayman. *Reading Material in Early Modern England: Print, Gender and Literacy.* Cambridge University Press, 2005.

Hamburger, Philip. "The Development of the Law of Seditious Libel and the Control of the Press." *Stanford Law Review* 37:3 (February 1985):661–765.

Hammond, Brean. *Professional Imaginative Writing in England 1670–1740: Hackney for Bread.* Oxford: Clarendon, 1997.

Harries, Elizabeth Wanning. *The Unfinished Manner.* Charlottesville: University Press of Virginia, 1994.

Heal, Ambrose. *The English Writing Masters and their Copy Books 1570–1800*. Hildesheim: Georg Olms Verlagsbuchandlung, 1962.

Heath, M. *Unity in Greek Poetics*. Oxford: Clarendon, 1989.

Hector, L. C. *The Handwriting of English Documents*. London: Edward Arnold, 1966.

Hickey, Raymond. Ed. *Eighteenth-Century English: Ideology and Change*. Cambridge University Press, 2010.

Hilton, Mary and Jill Shifrin. Eds. *Educating the Child in Enlightenment Britain*. Farnham: Ashgate, 2009.

Hilton, Mary, Morag Styles and Victor Watson. Eds. *Opening the Nursery Door: Reading, Writing and Childhood, 1600–1900*. London: Routledge, 1997.

Howell, Wilbur Samuel. *Eighteenth-Century British Logic and Rhetoric*. Princeton University Press, 1971.

Hoyles, John. *The Waning of the Renaissance 1640–1740: Studies in the Thought and Poetry of Henry More, John Norris and Isaac Watts*. The Hague: Nijhoff, 1971.

Hume, Robert D. "Construction and Legitimation in Literary History." *Review of English Studies* 226 (2005): 632–61.

Hyland, Paul and Neil Sammels. Eds. *Writing and Censorship in Britain*. London: Routledge, 1992.

Jackson, H. J. *Marginalia: Readers Writing in Books*. New Haven: Yale University Press, 2001.

  Romantic Readers: The Evidence of Marginalia. New Haven: Yale University Press, 2005.

Jager, Eric. *The Book of the Heart*. University of Chicago Press, 2000.

James, Edward and Farah Mendlesohn. Eds. *The Cambridge Companion to Fantasy Literature*. Cambridge University Press, 2012.

Janowitz, Anne. "Amiable and Radical Sociability: Anna Barbauld's 'Free and Familiar Conversation.'" In *Romantic Sociability 1770–1840*. Ed. Gillian Russell and Clara Tuite. Cambridge University Press, 2002.

John, Adrian. *The Nature of the Book*. University of Chicago Press, 1998.

  "The Physiology of Reading in Restoration England." In Raven et al., *Practice and Representation of Reading*.

  "Miscellaneous Methods: Authors, Societies and Journals in Early Modern England." *The British Journal of the History of Science* 33:2 (June 2000): 159–86.

Jones, Charles, *English Pronunciation in the Eighteenth and Nineteenth Centuries*. Houndmills: Palgrave Macmillan, 2006.

  "Nationality and Standardisation in Eighteenth-Century Scotland." In Hickey, *Eighteenth-Century English*.

Jung, Sandro. *The Fragmentary Poetic*. Bethlehem: Lehigh University Press, 2009.

  Ed. *Experiments in Genre in Eighteenth-Century Literature*. Guent: Academica Press, 2011.

Justice, George, *The Manufacturers of Literature*. Newark: University of Delaware Press, 2002.

Kallich, Martin. *The Association of Ideas and Critical Theory in Eighteenth-Century England*. The Hague: Mouton, 1970.

Kamrath, Mark. "Eyes Wide Shut and the Cultural Poetics of Eighteenth-Century Periodical Literature." *EAL* 37–3 (December 2002): 497–537.

and Sharon Harris. Eds. *Periodical Literature in Eighteenth-Century America*. Knoxville: University of Tennessee Press, 2005.

Kelley, Mary. *Learning to Stand and Speak*. Chapel Hill: University of North Carolina Press, 2006.

Kenny, Niel. *The Uses of Curiosity in Early Modern France and Germany*. Oxford University Press, 2004.

Kenshur, Oscar. *Open Form and the Shape of Ideas*. Lewisburg: Bucknell, 1986.

Kenyon, Jane. *The History Men: The Historical Profession in England since the Renaissance*. University of Pittsburgh Press, 1984.

Kerrigan, John. "The Editor as Reader." In Raven et al., *Practice and Representation of Reading*.

Klancher, Jon. *Transfiguring the Arts and Sciences: Knowledge and Cultural Institutions in the Romantic Age*. Cambridge University Press, 2013.

Klein, Lawrence. "The Political Significance of Politeness in early Eighteenth-Century Britain." In Schochet, *Politics, Politeness*.

Shaftesbury and the Culture of Politeness. Cambridge University Press, 1994.

Knights, Mark. *Representation and Misrepresentation in Later Stuart Britain*. Oxford University Press, 2005.

Knott, Sarah. *Sensibility and the American Revolution*. Chapel Hill: University of North Carolina Press, 2012.

Knox, Norman. *The Word Irony and its Context, 1500–1755*. Durham, NC: Duke University Press, 1961.

Kroll, Richard. *The Material Word: Literate Culture in the Restoration and Eighteenth Century*. Baltimore: Johns Hopkins University Press, 1991.

Laerke, Mogens. Ed. *The Use of Censorship in the Enlightenment*. Leiden: Brill, 2009.

Langford, Paul. "The Uses of Eighteenth-Century Politeness." *Transactions of the Royal Historical Society* 12 (2002): 311–31.

Lauzon, Matthew. *Signs of Light: French and British Theories of Linguistic Communication 1648–1789*. Ithaca: Cornell University Press, 2010.

Law, Alexander. *Education in Edinburgh in the Eighteenth Century*. University of London Press, 1965.

Levinson, Marjorie. *The Romantic Fragment Poem*. Chapel Hill: University of North Carolina Press, 1986.

Lewalski, Barbara Kiefer. Ed. *Renaissance Genres*. Cambridge, MA: Harvard University Press, 1986.

Lewis, Jane Elizabeth. *The English Fable: Aesop and Literary Culture 1651–1740*. Cambridge University Press, 1996.

London, April. *Literary History Writing 1770–1820*. Houndmills: Palgrave Macmillan, 2010.

The Cambridge Introduction to the Eighteenth-Century Novel. Cambridge University Press, 2012.

Loughran, Trish. *The Republic in Print 1770–1870*. New York: Columbia University Press, 2007.

Loveridge, Mark. *A History of Aesopian Fable*. Cambridge University Press, 1998.

Lynch, Deirdre. *The Economy of Character*. University of Chicago Press, 1998.

Lynch, Jack and Anne McDermott. Eds. *Anniversary Essays on Johnson's Dictionary*. Cambridge University Press, 2005.

Mandelbrote, Scott. "The English Bible and Its Readers in the Eighteenth Century." In Rivers, *Books and Their Readers*.

Mangel, Alberto. *A History of Reading*. New York: Viking, 1996.

Manning, Susan. *The Poetics of Character*. Cambridge University Press, 2013.

Marshall, Ashley. *The Practice of Satire in England 1658–1770*. Baltimore: Johns Hopkins University Press, 2013.

Martin, Timothy and Nigel Smith. Eds. *Radicalism in British Literary Culture, 1650–1830*. Cambridge University Press, 2002.

McDowell, Paula. *The Women of Grub Street, 1678–1730*. Oxford: Clarendon, 1998.

McElligott, Jason. *Royalism, Print and Censorship in Revolutionary England*. Woodbridge: Boydell Press, 2007.

McGill, Meredith. *American Literature and the Culture of Reprinting, 1834–1853*. Philadelphia: University of Pennsylvania Press, 2003.

McMahon, Lucia. *Mere Equals: The Paradox of Educated Women in the Early Republic*. Ithaca: Cornell University Press, 2012.

Mee, John. *Conversable Worlds, 1762–1730*. Oxford University Press, 2011.

Meikle, Henry. "The Chair of Rhetoric and Belles Lettres at the University of Edinburgh." *The University of Edinburgh Journal* 13 (1945).

Merlin, Helene. "Curiosite et espace particulier au XVIIeme Siecle." In Chaquin and Houdard, *Curiosite et Libido Sciendi*.

Michael, Ian. *English Grammatical Categories and the Tradition to 1800*. Cambridge University Press, 1970.

  The Teaching of English. Cambridge University Press, 1987.

  Early Textbooks of English: A Guide. Reading: Colloquium on Textbooks, Schools and Society, 1993.

Milroy, Jim. "Historical Description and the Ideology of Standard English." In Wright, *Development of Standard English*.

Mingay, G. E. *English Landed Society in the Eighteenth Century*. London: Routledge & Kegan Paul, 1963.

Mitchell, Linda. *Grammar Wars*. Aldershot: Ashgate, 2001.

Monaghan, E. Jennifer. *Learning to Read and Write in Colonial America*. Amherst: University of Massachusetts Press, 2005.

Moncrieff, Kathryn and Kathy McPherson. Eds. *Performing Pedagogy in Early Modern England: Gender, Instruction and Performance*. Farnham: Ashgate, 2011.

Money, John. "Teaching in the Marketplace." In *Consumption and the World of Goods*. Ed. John Brewer and Ray Porter. London: Routledge, 1993.

Morison, Stanley. *Politics and Script*. Oxford: Clarendon, 1972.

  "The Development of Handwriting." In Heal, *The English Writing Masters*.

Morrissey, Lee, *The Constitution of Literature: Literacy, Democracy and Early English Literary Criticism*. Stanford University Press, 2008.

Morton, Timothy and Nigel Smith. Eds. *Radicalism in British Literary Culture 1650–1830: From Revolution to Revolution*. Cambridge University Press, 2009.

Moss, Ann. *Printed Commonplace Books and the Structure of Renaissance Thought*. Oxford: Clarendon Press, 1996.

Mugglestone, Lynda. "Registering the Language: Dictionaries, Diction and the Art of Elocution." In Hickey, *Eighteenth-Century English*.

Myers, Robin and Michael Kerns. Ed. *Censorship and the Control of Print in England and France 1600–1910*. Winchester: St Paul's Bibliographies, 1992.

Nevalain, Tertu. "Early Modern English Lexis and Semantics." In *The Cambridge History of the English Language. Vol. 3: 1476–776*. Ed. Roger Lass. Cambridge University Press, 2000.

Nixon, Cheryl. Ed. *An Anthology of Commentary on the Novel, 1688–1815*. Toronto: Broadview Press, 2009.

Noel, Thomas. *Theories of Fable in the Eighteenth Century*. New York: Columbia University Press, 1975.

Noggle, James. *The Temporality of Taste*. Oxford University Press, 2012.

Novak, Maximillian. Ed. *Literature in the Age of Disguise*. Berkeley: University of California Press, 1977.

O'Brien, Karen. "The History Market." In Rivers, *Books and Their Readers*.

Okie, Laird. *Augustan Historical Writing*. Lanham: University Press of America, 1991.

Orr, Leah. "Genre Labels on the Title Pages of English Fiction, 1600–1800." *Philological Quarterly* 90:1 (Winter 2011): 67–95.

Osselton, N. E. "Informal Spelling Systems in Early Modern English: 1500–1800." In *English Historical Linguistics*. Ed. N. F. Blake and Charles Jones. University of Sheffield, 1984.

Pask, Kevin. *The Emergence of the English Author*. Cambridge University Press, 1996.

Pasley, Jeffrey. *The Tyranny of Printers*. Charlottesville: University Press of Virginia, 2001.

Patterson, Annabel. *Censorship and Interpretation*. Madison: University of Wisconsin Press, 1984.

 Fables of Power: Aesopian Writing and Political History. Durham, NC: Duke University Press, 1991.

 Reading Between the Lines. Madison: University of Wisconsin Press, 1993.

Paulson, Ronald. *Breaking and Remaking: Aesthetic Practice in England 1700–1820*. New Brunswick: Rutgers University Press, 1987.

 The Beautiful, Novel and Strange: Aesthetics and Heterodoxy. Baltimore: Johns Hopkins University Press, 1996.

Pearson, Jacqueline. *Women's Reading in Britain 1750–1835*. Cambridge University Press, 1999.

Percy, Carol. "Learning and Virtue: English Grammar and the Eighteenth-Century Girls' School." In Hilton and Shifrin, *Educating the Child in Enlightenment Britain*.

Piper, Andrew. "The Art of Sharing: Reading the Romantic Miscellany." In Ferris and Keen, *Bookish Histories*.

Pittock, Murray. *Poetry and Jacobite Politics in Eighteenth-Century Britain and Ireland*. Cambridge University Press, 1994.

Potter, Lois. *Secret Rites and Secret Writing*. Cambridge University Press, 1989.

Powell, Manushag. *Performing Authorship in Eighteenth-Century English Periodicals*. Lewisburg: Bucknell University Press, 2012.

Prescott, Sarah. *Women, Authorship and Literary Culture, 1690–1740*. Houndmills: Palgrave Macmillan, 2003.

Price, Leah. *The Anthology and the Rise of the Novel*. Cambridge University Press, 2000.

Prince, Michael. *Philosophical Dialogue in the British Enlightenment*. Cambridge University Press, 1996.

Quint, David. *Epic and Empire*. Princeton University Press, 1993.

Rabb, Melinda Aliker. *Satire and Secrecy in English Literature from 1650–1750*. Houndmills: Palgrave Macmillan, 2007.

Rajan, Tilottama. *The Supplement of Reading*. Ithaca: Cornell University Press, 1990.

Raven, James. *Judging New Wealth*. Oxford: Clarendon, 1992.

The Business of Books, 1450–1850. New Haven: Yale University Press, 2007.

"The Book Trades." In Rivers, *Books and Their Readers*.

Raven, James, Helen Small and Naomi Tadmor. Eds. *The Practice and Representation of Reading*. Cambridge University Press, 1996.

Rawes, Alan. Ed. *Romanticism and Form*. Houndmills: Palgrave Macmillan. 2007.

Regier, Alexander, *Fracture and Fragmentation in British Romanticism*. Cambridge University Press, 2010.

Remer, Rosalind. *Printers and Men of Capital: Philadelphia Book Publishers in the New Republic*. Philadelphia: University of Pennsylvania Press, 1996.

Richardson, Alan. *Literature, Education and Romanticism*. Cambridge University Press, 1994.

Rivers, Isabel. Ed. *Books and Their Readers in Eighteenth-Century England: New Essays*. London: Leicester University Press, 2001.

Robertson, Rand. *Censorship and Conflict in Eighteenth-Century England*. University Park: Pennstate University Press, 2009.

Rogers, Pat. *Grub Street: Studies in a Sub-Culture*. London: Methuen, 1972.

Rose, Jonathan. *The Intellectual Life of the British Working Classes*. New Haven: Yale University Press, 2001.

Ross, Trevor. *The Making of the English Literary Canon from the Middle Ages to the Late Eighteenth Century*. Montreal: McGill-Queen's University Press, 1998.

Round, Philip. *Removable Type: Histories of the Book in Indian Country 1553–1880*. Chapel Hill: University of North Carolina Press, 2010.

Russell, Gillian and Clara Tuite. Eds. *Romantic Sociability: Social Networks and Literary Culture in Britain 1770–1840*. Cambridge University Press, 2002.

Salmon, Vivian. "Orthography and Punctuation." In *The Cambridge History of the English Language. Vol. 3: 1476–776*. Ed. Roger Lass. Cambridge University Press, 1999.

Sanderson, Elizabeth. *Women and Work in Eighteenth-Century Edinburgh*. Houndmills: Macmillan, 1996.

Sandner, David. *Critical Discourses of the Fantastic, 1712–1831*. Farnham: Ashgate, 2011.

Scaglione, Aldo. *The Classical Theory of Composition from its Origins to the Present*. Chapel Hill: University of North Carolina Press, 1972.

Schellenberg, Betty. *The Professionalization of Women Writers in Eighteenth-Century Britain*. Cambridge University Press, 2005.

"The Society of Agreeable and Worthy Companions: Bookishness and Manuscript Culture after 1750." In Ferris and Keen, *Bookish Histories*.

Schmitz, Robert. *Hugh Blair*. New York: King's Crown Press, 1948.

Schochet, Gordon. Ed. *Politics, Politeness and Patriotism*. Washington, DC: Folger Institute, 1993.

Schoenfelds, Michael. "Reading Bodies." In Sharpe and Zwicker, *Reading, Society and Politics*.

Schürer, Norbert. Ed. *Charlotte Lennox: Correspondence and Miscellaneous Documents*. Lewisburg: Bucknell University Press, 2012.

Scragg, D. G. *A History of English Spelling*. Manchester University Press, 1974.

Scrivener, Michael. "John Thelwall and Popular Jacobin Allegory." *English Literary History* 67:4 (Winter 2000): 951–71.

Seditious Allegories: John Thelwall and Jacobin Writing. University Park: PennState University Press, 2001.

"John Thelwall and the Revolution of 1649." In Martin and Smith, *Radicalism*.

Sharpe, Kevin. *Reading Revolutions: The Politics of Reading in Early Modern England*. New Haven: Yale University Press, 2000.

Sharpe, Kevin and Steven Zwicker. Eds. *Reading, Society and Politics in Early Modern England*. Cambridge University Press, 1994.

Sher, Richard. *Church and University in the Scottish Enlightenment*. Princeton University Press, 1985.

The Enlightenment and the Book. University of Chicago Press, 2006.

Shields, David. *Civil Tongues and Polite Letters in British America*. Chapel Hill: University of North Carolina Press, 1997.

"Eighteenth-Century Literary Culture." In Amory and Hall, *The Colonial Book in the Atlantic World*: 434–76.

Simonton, Deborah. "Schooling the Poor: Gender and Class in Eighteenth-Century England," *Journal of Eighteenth-Century Studies* 23:2 (September 2000): 183–202.

Smith, Nigel. Ed. *Literature and Censorship*. Cambridge: Brewer, 1993.

Snyder, Jon. *Dissimulation and the Culture of Secrecy in Early Modern Europe*. Berkeley: University of California Press, 2009.

Spufford, Margaret. "Women Teaching Reading to Poor Children in the Sixteenth and Seventeeth Centuries." In Hilton et al., *Opening the Nursery Door*.

Stallybrass, Peter. "Books and Scrolls: Navigating the Bible." In *Books and Readers in Early Modern England.* Ed. Jennifer Andersen and Elizabeth Sauer. Philadelphia: University of Pennsylvania Press. 2007.

Starnes, De Witt and Gertrude Noyes. *The English Dictionary from Cawdray to Johnson.* Chapel Hill: University of North Carolina Press, 1946.

St. Clair, William. *The Reading Nation in the Romantic Period.* Cambridge University Press, 2004.

Street, Brian. *Literacy in Theory and Practice.* Cambridge University Press, 1989.

Styles, Morag and Evelyn Arizpe, *Acts of Reading: Teachers, Texts and Childhood.* Stoke-on-Trent: Trentham, 2009.

Suarez, Michael and Michael Turner. Eds. *The Cambridge History of the Book in Britain. Vol. 5: 1695–1830.* Cambridge University Press, 2009.

Sullivan, Robert. "The Transformation of Anglican Political Theology." In Schochet, *Politics, Politeness.*

Sundby, Bertil et al. Eds. *A Dictionary of English Normative Grammar, 1700–1800.* Amsterdam: John Benjamins Publishing Co., 1991.

Tadmor, Naomi. "In the Even My Wife Read to Me." In Raven et al., *Practice and Representation of Reading.*

Tavor, Eve. *Scepticism, Society and the Eighteenth-Century Novel.* London: Macmillan, 1987.

Tennenhouse, Leonard. *The Importance of Feeling English, 1750–1850.* Princeton University Press, 2007.

Tieken-Boon van Ostade, Ingrid. Ed. *Grammar, Grammarians and Grammar Writing in Eighteenth-Century England.* Berlin: Mouton de Gruyter, 2008.

"Lowth as an Icon of Prescriptivism." In Hickey, *Eighteenth-Century English.*

Thomas, Keith, "The Meaning of Literacy in Early Modern England." In *The Written Word: Literacy in Transition.* Ed. Gerd Bauman. Oxford: Clarendon Press, 1986.

Thornton, Tamara Plakins. *Handwriting in America.* New Haven: Yale University Press, 1996.

Towsey, Mark. *Reading the Scottish Enlightenment.* Leiden: Brill, 2010.

Tribble, Evelyn. *Margins and Marginality.* Charlottesville: University Press of Virginia, 1993.

Trolander, Paul and Zenep Tenger. *Sociable Criticism in England 1625–1725.* Newark: University of Delaware Press, 2007.

Tuer, Andrew. *History of the Horn Book.* New York: Arno Press,1979.

Turner, Cheryl. *Living by the Pen: Women Writers in Eighteenth-Century England.* London: Routledge, 1992.

Valenza, Robin. *Literature, Language and the Rise of the Intellectual Disciplines in Britain 1680–1820.* Cambridge University Press, 2011.

Walker, William. *Locke, Literary Criticism and Philosophy.* Cambridge University Press, 1994.

Wallace, Miriam. *Revolutionary Subjects in the English 'Jacobin' Novel, 1790–1805.* Lewisburg: Bucknell University Press, 2009.

Walmsley, Peter. "The Melancholy Briton: Enlightenment Sources of the Gothic. In *Enlightening Romanticism, Romancing the Enlightenment*. Ed. Miriam Wallace. Farnham: Ashgate, 2009.

Walsh, Marcus. "Literary Scholarship and the Life of Editing." In Rivers, *Books and their Readers*.

Walsh, P.G. "The Rights and Wrongs of Curiosity: Plutarch to Augustine." *Greece and Rome*. 2nd ser. 35:1 (April 1988): 73–85.

Watson, Victor. "Illuminating Shadows: Jane Johnston's Commonplace Book." In Styles and Arizpe, *Acts of Reading*.

Wellek, René. *A History of Modern Criticism*, 4 vols. London: Jonathan Cape, 1970.

Wendorf, Richard. "Abandoning the Capital." In Sharpe and Zwicker, *Reading, Society and Politics*.

Whyman, Susan E. *The Pen and the People*. Oxford University Press, 2009.

Wood, Marcus. *Radical Satire and Print Culture, 1790–1822*. Oxford: Clarendon, 1994.

Woolf, D. R. "A Feminine Past? Gender, Genre and Historical Knowledge in England 1500–1800," *American Historical Review* 102:3 (June 1997): 645–79.

Reading History in Early Modern England. Cambridge University Press, 2000.

The Social Circulation of the Past: English Historical Culture 1500–1730. Oxford University Press, 2003.

Worrall, David. *Theatric Revolution: Drama, Censorship and Romantic Period Subcultures, 1773–1832*. Oxford University Press, 2002.

Wright, Laura. Ed. *The Development of Standard English 1300–1800*. Cambridge University Press, 2000.

Wulf, Karin. *Not All Wives: Women in Colonial Philadelphia*. Ithaca: Cornell University Press, 2000.

Wyss, Hilary. *English Letters and Indian Literacies, 1750–1830*. Philadelphia: University of Pennsylvania Press, 2012.

Yates, Frances. *The Art of Memory*. University of Chicago Press, 1966.

Yeandle, Laetitia. "The Evolution of Handwriting in the English-speaking Colonies of America." *The American Archivist* 43:2 (Summer 1980): 294–311.

Yeo, Richard. "Ephraim Chambers' Cyclopaedia and the Tradition of Commonplaces." *Journal of the History of Ideas* 57:1 (1996): 157–75.

"A Solution to the Multitude of Books." *Journal of the History of Ideas* 64:1 (2003): 61–72.

Zagorin, Perez. *Ways of Lying: Dissimulation, Persecution and Conformity in Early Modern Europe*. Cambridge, MA: Harvard University Press, 1990.

Zwicker, Steven. "Poltics and Literary Practice in the Reformation." In Lewalski, *Renaissance Genres*.

Index

abridgment
  by American printers of British novels, 206
  chapbooks, 194
  Isaac Watts on abridgment, 141
  of non-fictional material, 15, 72, 74–75,
    129, 144
  of novels, 203, 206
  by the reader, 143
  work of abridgers, 175
Addison, Joseph, 178–79, 180–81, 189, 191, 201
Aesop's fables
  as allegorical prose fable, 238
  animals as mimicry, 228, 239–40
  broad readership of, 238
  for communicating abstract truth and
    doctrine to readers, 242–45
  the explicit moral in, 243–44, 246
  in grammars, 69, 228
  as secret writing, 228–29
Aikin, John, 172, 198
Allan, David, 3, 137, 142
allegory, *see also* fables
  allegorical modes in secret writing, 237–38,
    239–40, 241
  allegorical prose fable, 238, 239
  figures and tropes, 69, 110–12
  mixed allegory, 246–47, 248
  pure allegory, 246–47
  readings of the Bible as, 69
  writers of, 248–49
Allwood, Philip, 43
alphabets
  alphabet tables, 53
  in copybooks, 53
  juxtaposed, 52–55
  script alphabets, 39–41, 52–55
America
  abridgment of British novels by American
    printers, 206
  Aesopian fables, 243
  American novelists, 204, 206

belletrism in, 166–67
booksellers/book trade, 29–30
contemporary America in
  conversation-pieces, 115
cultural importance of British taste, 166–67
hand scripts, 48
literacy through mission schools, 47
miscellarian genres, 171
miscellarian texts, 171, 188–89
national unity through cultural unity, 164
New England, 29, 47, 48, 52, 76, 93, 106, 115
novels as discontinuous texts, 204
novels in, 206
political doctrines in fables, 245–46
pronunciation instruction for women and
  girls, 106
pronouncing-anthologies, 94, 104–05
public oration, 93
regional print markets, 30
reprints of British books, 188–89, 243
scripts, 48, 51
secret history novels, 200
Sedition Acts, 19, 30
speech in relation to pronunciation,
  41–42, 73–74
tradition of imported British books, 29
analogy, *see also* mental operations
  agreement and disagreement, 39
  analogical reasoning, 78–79
  analogical substitution, 53–55, 241–42
  analogical substitution in grammars,
    66–67
  in applications, 39–41, 111–12
  in novels, 113–14
  regulated analogical substitution, 79–80
anthologies
  American pronouncing-anthologies,
    94, 104–05
  of *Clarissa* (Richardson), 205
  manual anthologies, 102–03
  as miscellarian texts, 206, 209

288

For EU product safety concerns, contact us at Calle de José Abascal, 56–1°,
28003 Madrid, Spain or eugpsr@cambridge.org.

www.ingramcontent.com/pod-product-compliance
Ingram Content Group UK Ltd.
Pitfield, Milton Keynes, MK11 3LW, UK
UKHW020357140625
459647UK00020B/2530